Practical Radicalism
and the Great Migration

Parochial Education
and the Great Big Clock

SERIES EDITORS

Sarah E. Gardner, Mercer University

Jonathan Daniel Wells, University of Michigan

Print Culture in the South addresses the region's literary and historical past from the colonial era to the near present. Rooted in archival research, series monographs embrace a wide range of analyses that, at their core, address engagement and interaction with print. Topics center on format/genre—novels, pamphlets, periodicals, broadsides, and illustrations; institutions such as libraries, literary societies, small presses, and the book industry; and/or habits and practices of readership and writing.

Practical Radicalism and the Great Migration

The Cultural Geography of the Scott Newspaper Syndicate

Thomas Aiello

The University of Georgia Press
Athens

© 2023 by the University of Georgia Press
Athens, Georgia 30602
www.ugapress.org
All rights reserved

Set in 10.4/13.5 URW Century Old Style

Most University of Georgia Press titles are
available from popular e-book vendors.

Printed digitally

Library of Congress Cataloging-in-Publication Data

Names: Aiello, Thomas, 1977– author.
Title: Practical radicalism and the Great Migration : the cultural geography
   of the Scott Newspaper Syndicate / Thomas Aiello.
Description: Athens : The University of Georgia Press, [2023] | Series:
   Print culture in the South | Includes bibliographical references and
   index.
Identifiers: LCCN 2022022430 | ISBN 9780820362861 (hardback) |
   ISBN 9780820362854 (paperback) | ISBN 9780820362878 (ebook)
Subjects: LCSH: Scott Newspaper Syndicate—History—20th century. |
   African American newspapers—Southern States—History—20th century.
   | African American newspapers—History—20th century. | Syndicates
   (Journalism)—Southern States—History—20th century. | Syndicates
   (Journalism)—United States—History—20th century. | Radicalism and
   the press—Southern States—History—20th century. | Radicalism and
   the press—United States—History—20th century. | Great Migration, ca.
   1914–ca. 1970.
Classification: LCC PN4882.5 .A443 2023 | DDC 071/.308996073—dc23/
   eng/20220705
LC record available at https://lccn.loc.gov/2022022430

Though I was a mere child during the preparation for the Civil War and during the war itself, I now recall the many late-at-night whispered discussions that I heard my mother and the other slaves on the plantation indulge in. These discussions showed that they understood the situation, and that they kept themselves informed of events by what was termed the "grape-vine" telegraph.

—BOOKER T. WASHINGTON, 1901

Contents

Introduction	The Migration of the Scott Syndicate	1
Chapter 1	Georgia	20
Chapter 2	Florida	36
Chapter 3	The Carolinas	56
Chapter 4	Alabama	82
Chapter 5	Tennessee	130
Chapter 6	Mississippi and Louisiana	164
Chapter 7	The Syndicate Moves West	186
Chapter 8	From the Upper South to the Midwest	205
Chapter 9	The North	225
Conclusion	The Twilight of the Scott Syndicate	247

Appendix A. Maps of the Geographic Growth of the Syndicate 253

Appendix B. Newspapers and Their Time with the Syndicate 266

Notes 275

Bibliography 327

Index 355

**Practical Radicalism
and the Great Migration**

Introduction

The Migration of the Scott Syndicate

The beginnings of the Scott newspaper empire were humble. William Alexander Scott, a well-traveled entrepreneur from Mississippi, settled in Atlanta after college and dreamed of a newspaper in the city that would challenge the established *Atlanta Independent*. He began in 1928 with a small four-page weekly, the *Atlanta World*. In the next year, the paper's page count grew, and the year after that it became a semiweekly. In 1931, the *World* became a triweekly, and Scott began other *World* newspapers in Memphis, Birmingham, and Columbus. In 1932, he created the Southern Newspaper Syndicate to manage his growing empire, and the year after that, with some of his newspapers stretching beyond the bounds of the South, he changed its name to the Scott Newspaper Syndicate (SNS).

In the generation that followed, the Syndicate helped formalize knowledge among the African American population in the South. Black southern newspaper reporting and the subsequent interpretation of that news were largely the same. "The Negro Press," as sociologist Lincoln Blakeney explains, was "the foundation of the Negro citizen's social thinking."[1] And social thinking was largely facilitated by the systematic dissemination of information through the region: that dissemination was principally the project of the SNS. From the period March 1931–March 1955, there were at least 241 newspapers associated with the Syndicate. Because so many of its newspapers were small, didn't last long, weren't saved, or didn't leave behind business records, the Scott Newspaper Syndicate has often been given short shrift in discussions of the Black press. The syndicates associated with the *Pittsburgh Courier*, *Baltimore Afro-American*, and others hold sway.

Stories abound of Pullman porters toting copies of the *Chicago Defender* down south to provide Black southerners with information they otherwise wouldn't have. Porters actually did that, and the northern and eastern syndicates were incredibly influential. But Black newspapers native to the South flourished during that same period, many of them facilitated by a distribution network that didn't require brave and surreptitious activity from train porters. This book is a description of that network, its geography, and its relationship to the Black South in the generation before the civil rights movement, tracing its development through the region and the nation.[2]

It was a network with a long legacy. Kinship networks were palpable influences on Black radicalism, argues Steven Hahn, as enslaved people developed communication systems across multiple plantations in the antebellum era. These kinship networks acted as cultural unifiers, and they also facilitated the spread of news, rumors, and religion. These connections didn't free enslaved people in any way—the power of slavery always trumped kinship—but those relationships formed the bedrock of Black action once slavery was no longer in place. During the Civil War, enslaved people drew on the information traveling along those networks to flee their plantations and, often, the South itself. Hahn describes this as dually an "individual and collective intelligence." The South (particularly the lower South) during the war conscripted Black workers who did not leave into forced labor on abandoned lands. Others stayed on plantations in slavery. But both groups had a new leverage in the war-torn South, based largely on those kinship networks. Black southerners demonstrated a new organization and discipline. Because of the wartime needs of white enslavers, they were able "to redefine the rules and rights of wartime labor."[3]

In his discussion of Reconstruction, Hahn emphasizes the rural masses rather than the urban middle classes, arguing that the most meaningful political changes for the Black population happened in the countryside. It was in rural areas that power was gained through personal confrontation and rumor (much like the kinship networks). Chief among Black expectations and demands was land reform or, perhaps, land distribution. While white leaders used these demands as reasons for racial crackdowns, freedpeople used land reform and white fear to attempt to gain an upper hand in bargaining for concessions. It was Black rural mobilization, Hahn argues, that ultimately made presidential Reconstruction untenable. The push for landownership became the cornerstone of Black political consciousness into the twentieth century.

The Black southern press in the post–World War I period became the modern version of those kinship networks. They looked much the same and served similar ends. Syndicate newspapers dominated in small towns of the southern countryside. Calls for land reform were replaced with calls for voting rights, but the authors in the press network had learned from earlier racial crackdowns. In a pragmatic effort to avoid confrontations developing from white fear, newspaper editors developed a practical radicalism that argued on the fringes of racial hegemony, picking their spots, urging local compromises, and saving their loudest vitriol for tyranny that wasn't local and thus left no stake in the game for would-be white saboteurs. "To be black and Southern in those perilous times, and to stake out a position at variance with the canons of segregation and white supremacy," explains historian John Egerton, "required a mixture of conservatism and tactful independence that few non-Southerners could understand or appreciate. Patience and diplomacy and flank-covering caution were essential to survival."[4] The effort to push against racial abuses while managing race relations, using the ingrained assumptions of white supremacy to facilitate a publication strategy, was effective at both countering such assumptions and turning a profit for the business.[5]

"Negroes," the *Atlanta Daily World* reminded its readers, "are different in Dixie." The Scotts were adamant on the point. "Northern Negroes (including those who packed their handbags down in Dixie and got that way) may pass up the Northern Negro papers because white dailies print Negro news, or because they feel a certain guilt in reading [the] Negro medium. But the Southern Negro pores over Southern Newspaper Syndicate presentations," explained one advertisement. "While his northern brother is busily engaged in 'getting white' and ruining racial consciousness, the Southerner has become more closely knit. The SNS goes into thousands of homes and carries unaltered facts with it. In view of this fact the SNS is forever expanding, pioneering, and improving these presentations which suddenly have aroused race consciousness."[6]

Despite such rhetoric, many Syndicate papers were outside the South. In July 1932, less than a year and a half after its March 1931 founding, the Southern Newspaper Syndicate added the *St. Louis Argus*. It wouldn't stretch the imagination, of course, to classify St. Louis as a southern city, but the following month the Syndicate added the *Indianapolis Recorder*, the *Gary American*, the *Newark Herald*, the *Columbus Voice* (Ohio), and the *Detroit Independent*. That month the SNS consisted of twenty-six newspapers, including the *Atlanta Daily World*, by far its most prolific month to date (the previous high was eight), and either five or six of them, depending on your definition of the relationship of St. Louis to the South, were in the Northeast and Midwest. That the spread of the SNS would mirror the spread of the Black population during the Great Migration is not surprising. Instead, one interesting fact about the spread is that a company that originally sold itself as uniquely and fundamentally southern to compete with more radical northern competitors like the *Chicago Defender*, which sent editions down south, would in relatively short order move outside those bounds to compete with the established northern syndicates emanating from Chicago, Pittsburgh, Baltimore, and New York. Though the Scott Syndicate receives far less historical treatment than its larger, more activist neighbors to the north, it spent much of its time and resources in the generation before the civil rights movement in areas outside its traditionally understood bounds.

As the *Norfolk Journal and Guide* noted, "Up to 1928 the Negro electorate in Norfolk and throughout Virginia was 100 per cent Republican. In that year the *Journal and Guide* declared for the national Democratic candidates and in subsequent years has supported also the state and local Democratic administrations. At first there were thunderous repercussions of disapproval from its own group, but the newspaper persisted." Ten years later, "75 per cent of the Negro vote cast in Virginia [was] Democratic." Similar analysis came from the *Baltimore Afro-American*: "We were the first of the larger weekly newspapers to advocate a division of the ballot among all the parties and used our editorial columns to urge the election of such men as [Al] Smith and [Franklin] Roosevelt. Locally we have been able to persuade 30,000 out of the 50,000 registered colored voters to support local Democratic candidates."[7]

T. Ella Strother's study of the *Chicago Defender* has demonstrated that despite the paper's use of sensationalism, scandal, and crime on the front page, the overall Black image the *Defender* propagated was one of middle-class values, seeking integration and race rights through the political process, an analysis backed by more recent works by authors such as Ethan Michaeli.[8] Sensationalism sold papers, but was generally limited to the front page, giving way to more balanced accounts in the other pages and editorials that could, for example, turn a voting bloc to a new political party. Strother also found that more than a third of the *Defender*'s coverage was devoted to sports and fine arts, similar to that of its southern counterparts, often in service to local interests, to building a positive Black image that compensated for sensationalism on the front page. That sort of coverage may have slightly lessened the page space devoted to active advocacy, as did the crime coverage on page 1, but it did not keep it from happening and might even have exacerbated its reach by bringing in audiences otherwise unconcerned. "Why not," asked sociologist Frederick Detweiler in 1938, referencing the emphasis of Black newspapers on social news, sensational crime, sports, and theater, "since we all desire to see ourselves in the eyes of a larger audience and the Negro has no other paper that will print him?" He argued that "many are the comings and goings of colored people that are never noted in the white man's press. Why should they not have the normal satisfactions of publicity?" But there were counterarguments from sociologists like E. Franklin Frazier, who criticized the press for emphasizing society over the class issues that dramatically affected Black America. Although the press "claims to be published primarily in the interest of the 'race,' it represents primarily the interests of the black bourgeoisie and promulgates the bourgeois values of the make-believe world of the black bourgeoisie." Southern and northern papers were in lockstep in their coverage ratio and front-page strategy, only really veering at the editorial messages in between those dominant elements of the publications.[9]

Syndication contributed to shaping those messages. Whereas the syndicates associated with the *Chicago Defender*, *Pittsburgh Courier*, and *Baltimore Afro-American* centralized the process of content production, hired editors to produce local editions, and supplemented the bulk of their papers' editorial content, the Scotts and their *Atlanta Daily World* did not "own, publish, manage or control" the vast majority of the papers under their banner.[10] Instead, in most cases, would-be newspaper publishers wrote articles and editorials about the local news in a given region, generated advertisements from local businesses, and then sent that collected material to Atlanta, where SNS staff organized a layout using the material and added national news from the *World* and other syndicate papers. The SNS then printed the finished product and sent it back to the local publisher, making the Syndicate's contact with local content limited to proofreading and the occasional addition of a headline.

"We have certain standard non-controversial non-partisan matter that we give these various papers we print," C. A. Scott explained. "Then, they supply the local stuff for the editorial page, social page and sports, and we supply four pages of standard material that is non-controversial, non-partisan that is circulated, to these various cities." He noted that the Syndicate was different from the Associated Negro Press (ANP), which provided content for any paper that paid for the service, but the SNS did provide syndicated material written or rewritten in Atlanta for use in member papers.[11] "We charge them so much for each column of newspaper composition we set up," said Scott, "so much per inch for the advertising, so much for making up the page, and so much per hundred copies for the paper, and we print those papers, in most cases, if they haven't paid us in advance, c.o.d." The cost for a larger paper that averaged between one and two thousand copies generally totaled roughly fifty dollars per week. The Syndicate set a paper's local material, then inserted material from the *Atlanta Daily World*, the ANP, or other member newspapers. The local publisher could choose which material they wanted included, or they could allow those choices to be made in Atlanta.[12] It was, unlike other syndication efforts, a democratization of news, putting editorial choices into the hands of locals who with a little money and experience could become an arbiter of Black knowledge in a given town or region.

The Associated Negro Press provided syndicated news coverage for its subscriber newspapers to fill coverage gaps for editors who could not afford to send reporters across the country and world to cover major events. Formed in 1919 with eighty member papers, the ANP was the original twentieth-century attempt at a new grapevine that would bind the new Black diaspora. It was the *Chicago Defender*, Lawrence Hogan has explained, "along with the possibilities of a national black press it exemplified, that came to serve as the catalyst for the establishment of the Associated Negro Press." Emanating from Chicago under the leadership of its founder, Claude Barnett, the ANP made possible the growth of the Black press through World War II. At the same time, that kind of service priced out smaller papers, which could never afford such luxuries. Scott essentially tried to fill that gap by using one ANP subscription for all of the papers he eventually printed, bringing him into regular conflict with Barnett.[13] Conflict or not, the SNS was fundamentally different from its rival syndicates and from sole content providers like the ANP.

Black newspaper ventures continued despite the constant racial attacks of a white South opposed to their existence. Others were the result of a Black population that escaped such violence by way of the Great Migration. The mass movement of disaffected Black citizens out of the South had started slowly in the late nineteenth century. At that time, most Black southerners were far more likely to migrate to Africa, to the American West, or to urban hubs within the South, and by the beginning of the 1910s, 90 percent of Black Americans still lived in the South. The larger Great Migration to northern urban industrial hubs didn't really begin until the middle of the decade. Of course, not everyone was happy about this. In 1879, Frederick Douglass insisted that the South was the place for Black Americans to be: "Not only is the South the best locality for the Negro on the ground of his political powers and possibilities, but it is best for him as a field of labor. He is there, as he is nowhere else, an absolute necessity."[14] Douglass, however, was pushing back against a rising tide.

Between 1910 and 1940, 1.75 million African Americans left the South, doubling the Black population outside the region. People escaped because of agricultural problems, Jim Crow, disfranchisement, and racial violence. Most went to urban centers in the North like Washington, Philadelphia, New York, Pittsburgh, Cleveland, or Detroit. A much smaller number went west. The residential segregation they found upon their arrival led to the creation of strong, all-Black neighborhoods: Harlem in New York, the South Side of Chicago, Paradise Valley in Detroit, the Hill District of Pittsburgh. And the grapevine followed.[15] The Syndicate, for example, supported newspapers from Arizona, Connecticut, Illinois, Indiana, Iowa, Kansas, Minnesota, Nebraska, New York, Pennsylvania, and Wisconsin. There were seven papers from New Jersey, fifteen from Ohio, and sixteen from Michigan, compared to only twelve from the Syndicate's home state of Georgia.

Of course, the Syndicate represented all of the southern states as well, for a total of thirty states, but there remained a significant northern presence for a newspaper group that had begun by reminding readers that "Negroes are different in Dixie." If the totals are controlled for states of the former Confederacy, a full third of the Syndicate newspapers fell outside those bounds. The South, however, is bigger than the eleven former Confederate states. When the totals are controlled for a broader vision of "the South," including all of the states (and, in the case of Oklahoma, territories) that still permitted slavery in 1860 and thus with large Black populations not the result of the Great Migration, the proportions do change, but the number of newspapers existing outside even that version of Dixie was significant.

Regardless of location, the Syndicate based its strength on its total number of newspapers, a figure that was small in its first year. The massive growth in the Syndicate's member newspapers began in mid-1932, when the total rose from eight in July to twenty-six the following month. That expansion came right before a break in the available data, but when the existing records begin again in February 1934, the SNS had grown to thirty-one papers. There were thirty-six in March, then a record forty-one in April, a monthly total that the SNS would repeat over the course of the 1930s. In fact, the largest expansion and most significant sustained success of the Syndicate occurred between 1934 and 1940, a period defined most immediately by the Great Depression, which decimated all of the country and the Black population in particular.

"The Negro was born in depression," said Clifford Burke, a community volunteer who described his Depression experience for Studs Terkel. "It only became official when it hit the white man."[16] African American urban unemployment rose to 50 percent by 1932, making the maintenance of Black businesses—newspaper or otherwise—a tenuous prospect at best. In the North, approximately half of all Black families were receiving some form of Depression relief. It was even worse in the South. In the Syndicate's home of Atlanta, for example, 65 percent of Black families needed aid. And that aid, despite the mandates of federal law, was not distributed equally. Monthly relief checks in Atlanta totaled $32.66 for whites and $19.29 for Blacks, with leaders arguing that the discrepancy simply reflected the typical lower standard of living to which Black Georgians were accustomed.[17]

Despite such realities, between February 1934 and November 1940, the Syndicate's monthly average number of papers was 32.45. Beginning in June 1941 and lasting until March 1955, the Syndicate averaged 14.39 newspapers per month. Before February 1934, the average was only 3.92. Over the full period discussed in this book, the monthly newspaper average was 19.63. The SNS worked to develop itself over its first year and a half in the midst of the worst economic crisis in U.S. history, then managed to build on those initial gains despite the hardships of the period. Though the Syndicate's number of newspapers declined during World War II and beyond, its newspapers became more stable.

While the average run of SNS newspapers was 22.81 months, the majority of newspapers within its period of greatest growth did not last more than 9 months. This indicates that though the Scotts' organization was stable, with a dedicated customer and advertising base in Atlanta, the vast majority of Black newspapers were far more susceptible to the whims of the economy. They relied on Atlanta for content and printing services, but were either unable to convince businesses to spend their limited advertising budgets selling products to an impoverished Black community in an increasingly impoverished country or unable to convince that community to buy the papers themselves. As the nation moved through Depression and war, the businesses that survived had proven themselves stable, but few were willing to take further risks.

The Syndicate's interest in those that took risks was based largely on how many people they were able to reach. To gauge the reach of the SNS, I examine three tiers of influence, using population totals for city, county, and state. News, in this view, is not a static entity that must be read to be consumed. Instead, news is something that spreads after being planted in an area. Like a rumor. Like a virus.[18] News and opinions about the news move in much the same way, spreading outward from those who personally have the information. From the 1930s to the 1950s, that personal holding came from reading the newspaper, but that type of spread had always been the case in the Black community from the earliest days of slavery, with information moving through the grapevines and kinship networks of viral news dissemination, the earliest and most complex American version of meme theory in action. The papers of the SNS became a new grapevine, spreading information and a distinctly Black southern version of activism throughout the South, then up and out of the region following the path of the Great Migration. A May 1938 evaluation of Black newspapers and periodicals by the Department of Commerce, for example, noted that the surveyed papers reported that 57.5 percent of their circulation was local: "However, it should not be concluded that Negro newspapers are not valued in other urban communities." More than 30 percent of the combined circulation "was reported as being in urban communities other than the cities of publication."[19]

That being the case, tracking the city, county, and state populations for the location of each newspaper is vital to understanding the tiers of a newspaper's influence. A paper had the most influence at the city tier, declining at the county and then the state tiers, radiating outward and getting weaker as the information spread. This research strategy is best employed for small Black southern newspapers in the age of Jim Crow because they were news entities without circulation figures (for the most part). Even with circulation numbers, understanding the dissemination of news as viral and tiered is beneficial, but Black newspapers in particular have less available information about their structure and reach. Therefore, in this book I describe newspapers' potential influence by using Census figures for the Black population in cities, counties, and states, acknowledging that such numbers only represent those with the potential to be influenced, not those who definitely had contact with a newspaper or its information. Additionally, because of this approach, I have not included literacy rates, because literacy is unnecessary for contact with information gleaned from newspapers, just as it was unnecessary for the earlier grapevines and kinship networks.[20]

Lauren Kessler's study of the dissident press explains that the circulation of the Black press during World War II was just over 1.5 million, but in actuality "the readership probably exceeded 5 million."[21] The Syndicate was no exception, and its most immediate influence came at the city level, where the Black residents in an area were in closest proximity to the information provided by the source.

By far the largest number of people within the Syndicate's immediate reach peaked in August 1934, when its tier 1 reach totaled 1,776,641. With the exception of the two months surrounding August, no other month in the entirety of this study came close to being within 300,000 of that number. The county/metro numbers are similar. August 1934 had the highest tier 2 population reach at 2,269,573, and again only its surrounding months came within 300,000 of that number. On the first two levels of the Syndicate's reach, the numbers demonstrate an unsurprising consistency, indicating a flourishing of activity beginning during the second data break and then slowly descending following 1934. This descent is also not surprising, as in January 1934 W. A. Scott was murdered, leading to a long and ultimately inconclusive investigation and the takeover of the business by his brother C. A.[22]

That is not to say that C. A. Scott was a poor manager. He served as the head of the Syndicate, after all, for a far longer time than its founder. C. A. is largely credited with steering the newspaper chain through a particularly tumultuous time and maintaining the Syndicate's success throughout the period. That can be demonstrated by the continued recruitment of newspapers, which held far more steady than the populations in which they resided, and by the longevity of later newspapers, demonstrating a far more stable, if consolidated, organization. His success can also be demonstrated by expanding the view of the population numbers, extending them to the state level.

As time moved on, the grapevine grew north and west, as did the Great Migration. The Syndicate's migration, however, did not happen in the same order as the larger diasporic push of Black southerners—which tended to see movement to the American West in the earlier stages of its development, followed by an emphasis on northern urban industrial hubs—but it did take similar routes. During its first two years, the Syndicate's center of influence remained in the heart of the traditionally understood South. No records survive for 1933, but 1934 demonstrates an explosion not only in the number of newspapers supported by the Syndicate, but also in its geographical reach. The SNS pushed aggressively into the Midwest, Texas, and the East Coast (see appendix A). By 1937, the Syndicate's relationship with Michigan had begun. It also reached as far west as Phoenix, Arizona. By 1939, the emphasis on Michigan was even greater, led by the Scotts' relationship with Leroy White, who created a series of Michigan papers and aligned all of them with the SNS. While the Syndicate also had a presence in New Jersey, and while there were other outliers at various points, it is clear that its core lay in the corridor running from the Gulf of Mexico to Michigan, with its presence heavier in regions closest to Georgia. As the number of papers associated with the SNS began to wane in the mid-1940s, the top of that corridor disappeared in favor of its stronger southern core. With the exception of Cincinnati, just on the border of traditionally southern Kentucky, SNS newspapers in the cities of the Midwest had disappeared. The paper numbers were dwindling, but the Syndicate's core remained stable.

Such was the nature of a grapevine. Kinship was the basic unit of Black political communities, Hahn explains, but it was not their only element. Church congregations, mutual aid societies, fraternal organizations, and even militia groups were also dominant modes of Black political power during Reconstruction and beyond. Black political participation during Radical Reconstruction, according to Hahn, was more significant in the countryside—at the level of tax assessors, registrars, sheriffs, county commissioners, and so on—rather than in more high-profile state positions.[23] The same could be said for the Black southern press in the first half of the twentieth century.

Hahn interprets emigrationist Black nationalism as developing from this political grapevine, but so too did integrationist activism. Particularly in Virginia, some frustrated African Americans joined biracial coalitions in an attempt to defeat Redeemer candidates for state offices. This was successful in giving some Black Republicans scattered offices and local pockets of power, but it really only created a thin layer of "black political bosses" who sought power over providing land reform to the rural masses. It created a new, compromising Black middle class that was conservative, Hahn argues. But rural whites were almost completely hostile to Black aspirations, and thus those in the countryside arguing for separatism necessarily had to take a different tack.[24] The same regional and urban-rural divide appeared again in twentieth-century Black syndicated journalism with the same significance for small communities and the same argumentative trajectory. The outgrowth of this struggle was ultimately the Great Migration, the culmination of a nationalist development from slavery to the early twentieth century, and the Black southern press, the new grapevine for a new Black South, followed that migration up and out of the region.

Historians like John Egerton and Glenda Gilmore have made the case for expanding the idea of the South to include those from there who migrated away. The region, according to Gilmore, was "a state of mind as well as an actual place." By that reckoning, the closed society of an isolated South was never actually isolated. Its separateness was a form of delusion, even propaganda, concerning a place that was always interacting with the larger world.[25]

The Great Migration was beneficial to those escaping poverty and Jim Crow, and it did provide many new opportunities for better jobs and higher wages. But it could be a daunting journey. There were glass ceilings, new kinds of race fights, housing and employment discrimination, and even, as one economic analysis has demonstrated, higher death rates.[26] There was also the loss of and separation from the communities and mores of the region those migrants left, making the connective tissue of information all the more important, the establishment of a new grapevine a necessity as the population was spread thin in new territories that were more welcoming in some ways and less welcoming in others.

Newspapers were one venue where, as literary historian C. K. Doreski has explained, "the discourses of what we conventionally label 'news,' 'history,' and 'literature' coalesce into an African-American narrative of history and nation." Newspapers helped mold a racial memory and thus "a racially charged national identity." While in this book I do not employ a comparative approach that finds affinities with the Black southern press's editorial politics and Black literature being produced about the region from the distance of the Great Migration, it is important to note that such could be done: regional identity combining with racial identity to create a very specific version of nationhood. "Narrative," as Doreski notes, "is the basis of individual and community conceptions of national identity."[27] And while Black southern readers had less access to many of the literatures of history and fiction—logistically, financially, educationally—they did have important dialogues with other literatures of the Great Migration, including the editorial positions of Black newspapers.

Those literatures trace the narrative of civil rights progress. In 1948, for example, the Supreme Court ruled in a case focusing on the University of Oklahoma law school. Ada Lois Sipuel, a Langston honors graduate, had been denied admission to the law school in 1946. As it had done ten years prior in its *Missouri ex rel. Gaines* decision, the Supreme Court reversed the state court's decision in 1948, arguing that the equal protection clause of the Fourteenth Amendment and the precedent of *Gaines* required she be admitted. But as Missouri had responded in 1938, Oklahoma attempted to evade the spirit of the law. The Oklahoma Supreme Court argued that the ruling in *Sipuel* would find compliance in the establishment of a Black Oklahoma law school. Of course, in the two years since Sipuel's unsuccessful application for admission, the state had done nothing to make provisions for such a school, and it seemed clear that such an interpretation of the ruling was blatantly wrong and self-serving.[28]

The Oklahoma Supreme Court's response appeared five days after the U.S. Supreme Court ruling, and the bulk of the Black weeklies did not appear until after both courts had their say. The *Chicago Defender* represented the cautious optimism of many, arguing that the U.S. Supreme Court's ruling was positive but was in no way "the death knell of Jim-Crow higher education in Dixie." The *St. Louis Argus* sought to capitalize on the decision by urging a suit for Black entry into the Missouri medical school or the Rolla School of Mines. Facilities at Missouri's Lincoln University, the paper argued, were inadequate, and a ruling for integration in neighboring Oklahoma could only be positive for Missouri. Still, as encouraging as *Sipuel* might have been, the reaction of the Oklahoma Supreme Court seemed frustratingly like more of the same. "Every time the enlightened people of America have reason to believe that the people of the South are gaining wisdom," declared the *Philadelphia Tribune*, "an incident of this kind happens to prove their continued stupidity." The *Michigan Chronicle* noted that "in one breath intolerant whites charge that Negroes are ignoramuses and in the next they denounce attempts to provide Negroes with adequate educational opportunities. They want to keep us ignorant and then hold us responsible for it."[29]

The *Atlanta Daily World* published the statement of George M. Johnson, the dean of Howard's School of Law, which was syndicated by the National Negro Publishers Association (NNPA): "it takes more than brick and mortar to provide separate but equal educational facilities." The bulk of the paper's *Sipuel* coverage was syndicated, but the *World*'s opinion pieces made it clear that the paper enthusiastically endorsed the decision. One editorial praised the "clear and ringing unanimous decision" requiring Oklahoma "to make immediate provisions for the equal educational opportunities for Negro applicants seeking to study law" and clearly stated that it "lays the foundations upon which Negroes in other states of separate and unequal status may seek relief." The newspaper explained the vast disparities in educational spending per pupil in southern states like Alabama, Mississippi, and Louisiana. Fitting the practical radicalism model, it didn't include its home state of Georgia in its screed, but made a clear call that "the time is at hand for all the southern states to meet these simple tests of fairness and justice to the Negro without a hint of force or compulsion from any source, save the hearts of those who administer the funds."[30] Key to the paper's vocal support was the provision in the ruling that segregated education was allowable as long as equal accommodations were made. This, too, fit the practical radicalism model, emphasizing positive change for the Black population within the existing system rather than challenging the fundamentals of the system itself.

That practical radicalism became the hallmark of many of the southern papers of the Syndicate, emanating from the dominant thinking of the Scotts and the *Atlanta Daily World*. It was a strategy similar to what Tomiko Brown-Nagin has called "pragmatic civil rights," and it was followed by most of the Syndicate papers. The *Alabama Tribune*, for example, included no editorial at all on the *Sipuel* decision. Its coverage, also syndicated from the NNPA, was above the paper's masthead: "Furnish Law Education, Oklahoma Ordered." Accompanying the article was another about Walter White and the NAACP encouraging people to vote in the 1948 elections. The following week, SNS coverage of Oklahoma's tentative plan to establish a separate law school also appeared above the masthead in the *Alabama Tribune*. With that kind of bold headlining, the paper didn't need an endorsing editorial. Instead, clearly understanding the mind of its readers, the paper editorialized on the need to become part of the NAACP: "More and more American Negroes are recognizing the power and far-reaching influence which the National Association for the Advancement of Colored People is exerting in behalf of full citizenship rights for minorities, irrespective of race or class."[31] The editorial did not mention the group's effort in Oklahoma, but it didn't have to.

The month after *Sipuel*, on February 25, 1948, the governors of Georgia, Tennessee, Maryland, Virginia, and Florida sent a proposal to Congress arguing that further NAACP suits could be circumvented through the pooling of funds from southern states to establish a Black graduate school at Meharry Medical College—a proposal that Congress ignored and the Black press categorically denounced. There was a general acknowledgment that the expansion of opportunities for Black southerners was a positive step, but as the *New York Amsterdam News* noted, the Meharry plan sought "to establish Jim Crow on a more solid and permanent foundation, [and] any such project, so far as it upholds the separation of the races, should be vigorously opposed." It was "a solution by the South to solve the problem in its own nefarious Jim Crow way before it is too late to keep the sunlight of democracy from coming over the horizon of the Southland." The *Chicago Defender, Pittsburgh Courier*, and *St. Louis Argus* all had similar reactions, interpreting the plan as a nefarious hustle to squash legitimate attempts at equal education.[32]

The Syndicate's *Tropical Dispatch* joined in the condemnation. "It is good to know that the National Association for the Advancement of Colored People is making plans to institute [a] suit to test the legality of the segregated regional college plan, approved recently by the southern governors and educators," the paper said. "Now is the time to stem the tide against these so-called regional colleges before they are permitted to have official sanction." The *Dispatch* excoriated the president of Meharry, M. Don Clawson, who had claimed that the college's students would "fail to make the grade" if they attended white medical schools. "By that statement, President Clawson is admitting that Meharry is carrying on an inferior quality of medical training, and is therefore, turning out Negro physicians and dentists manifestly and admittedly below the recognized American standard." The paper was outraged. "What a let down such an admission must be to the practicing doctors and dentists of Meharry in the hundreds of communities of America! . . . That is why we must once again, repeat our unqualified opposition to the establishment of Regional schools."[33]

Months after the Supreme Court issued its *Sipuel* decision, another Black student who had been denied admission to a University of Oklahoma graduate school successfully appealed for entrance. George McLaurin's early tenure, however, was marked by forced separation, a segregation within the newly integrated institution, as the library, cafeteria, and even the classrooms each had a Black section designed to force McLaurin to feel the weight of his difference. When he sued, a federal district court denied that the university was forcing a "badge of inferiority" upon him. On June 5, 1950, the U.S. Supreme Court disagreed, arguing that "such restrictions impair and inhibit the ability to study, to engage in discussions and exchange views with other students, and, in general, to learn his profession."[34]

June 5 was a big day. Along with *McLaurin*, the Court decided *Henderson v. U.S.*, striking down segregated diners associated with interstate travel. It also made another landmark education decision. Herman Marion Sweatt had undergone the same problems in Texas that Lloyd Gaines had experienced in Missouri in the 1930s. The University of Texas had denied his admission to its law school and then, at the demand of the district court, had created first a separate Black law school in Houston and then another in the basement of a building in Austin. That basement facility was three rooms, a very small library, and only a few instructors, all of whom were there just to lecture to Sweatt alone. The Supreme Court's decision in *Sweatt v. Painter* (1950) ruled that "the law school, the proving ground of legal learning and practice, cannot be effective in isolation from the individuals and institutions with which the law interacts."[35] The Court specifically stated that its decision did not merit a reexamination of *Plessy*, but there was a precedent being established. The NAACP's legal strategy had clearly demonstrated chinks in the legal armor of the separate-but-equal doctrine.

The reaction of the Black press was tempered by decades of disappointment. The *Michigan Chronicle* noted the small number of Black students who would actually see a benefit from the decision over the next decade. The *Afro-American* was far more frustrated with the Court's unwillingness to examine *Plessy* than it was pleased with the *McLaurin* and *Sweatt* decisions themselves. The Court had "pruned a noxious weed instead of pulling it out by the roots." The *Indianapolis Recorder* agreed, describing the action as "hand-washing in the face of dangers." The *Chicago Defender, Los Angeles Sentinel*, and *St. Louis Argus*, similarly frustrated, urged new cases that would build on the precedents and ultimately bring about a more comprehensive decision. Bill Weaver and Oscar Page have argued that the Black press was integral to the progress toward integrated graduate education by both lobbying for the actions and tempering the enthusiasm of readers over the true meaning of the Supreme Court's decisions. Black newspapers kept "a surprisingly united front regarding where blacks were, where they wanted to be, and what the difference was between the two."[36]

The Syndicate's coverage of the *Henderson, Sweatt*, and *McLaurin* decisions was celebratory while noting that the Court had "stopped short of saying whether segregation is unconstitutional." The SNS also emphasized the reactions of southerners. Georgia governor Herman Talmadge promised that "as long as I am governor, Negroes will not be admitted to white schools," a sentiment echoed by the bulk of Georgia's white politicians. The president of the Atlanta NAACP lauded "the most significant decisions since the rulings on the White Primary cases," but Benjamin Mays, president of Morehouse, warned that "we must not be fooled by these rulings." The *World*'s editorial position, however, differed from the view of Mays and its northern counterparts. "The court seemed to have made sterile this innocuous doctrine" of separate but equal "without striking it down in body. So far as interstate railroad travel is concerned only the corpse of this doctrine seems to stand." The decisions were "heartening" and "will pave the way for higher education for Negroes and other minorities all over the South." The Court "just about blots out dining car segregation and deals a heavy blow to racial discrimination in higher education." These were progressive steps that could only have positive benefits for the Black South. "Thus we rejoice in the decisions and hope that they will serve the good ends of progressive democracy," the *World* concluded. "Southern states would do well to effectuate these decisions and admit students into their schools of higher education on the basis of merit without regard for race or color."[37]

This was a decidedly different response than northern and eastern Black newspapers provided, replete with the optimism of possibility in the South rather than skepticism based on historical evidence. That kind of positive, hopeful message in the face of overwhelming difficulty, always with an eye to the white response to Black responses, came to distinguish the southern civil rights movement from its northern and eastern counterparts as well, undeniably conditioned, at least in part, by southern Black news coverage. Syndicate reporting in the *Chattanooga Observer*, for example, emphasized the Justice Department's amicus brief in both *Sweatt* and *McLaurin*, noting that the executive branch was urging the Supreme Court to repudiate the doctrine of separate but equal as fundamentally unconstitutional. The brief pointed out that the incidents in Texas and Oklahoma were not isolated exceptions, but instead were representations of "practices systematically engaged in by the States."[38] Fitting the practical radicalism of Syndicate papers, the *Observer* sought to justify its own opinion through authoritative surrogates like the federal government's executive branch.

The kinds of bigotries that papers like the *Chattanooga Observer* dealt with prior to *Brown v. Board of Education* also were afoot in Alabama, Arkansas, Georgia, Louisiana, and Mississippi well before such stories developed on international television in the early era of civil rights. Thus, Mississippi needed papers like the *Jackson Banner*, and Louisiana needed the *Bayou State Register*. And so the *Arkansas World*, *Alabama Tribune*, *Southwest Georgian*.

At the same time, those papers never presented a united position, each providing a distinct and individual worldview under the broader banner of opposition to Jim Crow in all of its myriad forms. Ted Poston illustrated the division in the Black press, for example, in a 1949 analysis using Walter White's marriage to white advertising executive Poppy Cannon: "Liberals, Negro and white, were considerably relieved at the calm acceptance of an interracial marriage on so high a level. But it turned out that their relief was premature." The Black press saw the marriage as a betrayal, and many called for White's resignation. Poston saw the incident less as a renunciation of mixed marriages and more as a reaction to White's outsized influence in both the Black and white worlds, while Black newspapers played only to a limited, segregated audience.[39]

Many small-town Black editors provided a vital service to their communities while simultaneously toiling in relative obscurity. Before the international media made southern race relations the cause célèbre of the late 1950s and 1960s, the Black southern press was, for better or worse, on the front lines of a battle for an expanded version of freedom. Their practical radicalism became more negotiable and more perilous the farther away a paper was from Atlanta. The nature of the Scotts' syndication model ensured that individual editors were able to buck the editorial policy of the *Atlanta Daily World* if they so chose and to present a message that was far more directly challenging to the local racial status quo. The Scotts did not censor any of the material sent to them for printing, creating within the broader ontology of the Syndicate a panoply of ideology and relative bravery that represented the whole of the Black population in various parts of the country in the generation prior to the civil rights movement.

Historian Fred Carroll has described a Black press during the world wars where "government pressure" in various forms "forced commercial black publishers . . . to modify their newspapers' political positions. Publishers who pushed too aggressively for reform risked losing their mailing privileges, quarreling over gratuitous censorship, or defending themselves against criminal charges of sedition. Publishers, though, rarely capitulated outright to ominous threats leveled by state authorities. They could not abandon the fight for racial justice without being forsaken by their readers." In between the two wars, however, the major northern Black presses became gradually more progressive, pushed by racial indignities, the Great Depression, and an "alternative black press" editorializing to their left.[40] The Scotts were largely free from content negotiations because their comparatively conservative position made them far less of a threat at the national level. Their status as racial threat was instead decidedly local. The increasing radicalism of the mainstream northern press provided a potential foil and point of differentiation for the SNS papers following the trajectory of the Great Migration, since the Syndicate was far more familiar with intrusive racial control.

"It now becomes more imperative than ever before that Negroes prepare themselves for this new freedom. As the bar falls down, Negroes have responsibilities and duties greater than ever before. Things which were excusable under Jim Crow laws and practices are no longer permitted," worried the *Philadelphia Tribune* in 1950. "The danger is that the change may catch Negroes unprepared. So many Negroes have suffered from persecution that they do not realize what is happening." Among those who did realize what was happening, many had lost faith in the principles of liberty and had come to a position of stasis, accepting the inferiority that had been thrust upon them by an unfair system. "The leadership which has fought so brilliantly for equality of opportunity must now engage in the herculean effort of getting Negroes prepared for its enjoyment," the paper declared.[41] In the Deep South states in the last phase of the Syndicate's run, the papers of the SNS did just that: engaged in the herculean effort of getting Black people prepared for the better days to come.

The number of individuals reached by the Syndicate totaled in the millions, despite the economic rigors of the Great Depression. Though it was southern, the scope of its influence for much of the generation prior to the civil rights movement included a significant presence in the Midwest, following the trajectory of the Great Migration. Newspapers in smaller communities had less stability than those in larger cities. Most of the papers I discuss in this book have left only the sparsest historical traces. But they existed, and the recorded information created by Scott syndication helped propagate knowledge in the regions and during the time of the most stifling Jim Crow segregation.

What follows is a geographical portrait of the Syndicate and some of its representative papers. My earlier volume, *The Grapevine of the Black South: The Scott Newspaper Syndicate in the Generation before the Civil Rights Movement*, emphasized the owners of the *Atlanta Daily World* and the operation of the Syndicate between 1931 and 1955. In that book I reexamined historical thinking about the Depression-era Black South, the information flow of the Great Migration, the place of southern newspapers in the historiography of Black journalism, and the ideological and philosophical underpinnings of the civil rights movement. This volume traces the development and trajectory of individual newspapers of the Syndicate, evaluating those with extant issues and presenting them in relation to their proximity to the Syndicate's Atlanta hub. This cultural geography of the SNS is a supplement to *The Grapevine of the Black South*, providing a fuller picture of the Black press in the 1930s, 1940s, and 1950s.

Chapter 1

Georgia

The Great Migration Black Population Changes (%)

City	1910–1940	1940–1970
Atlanta	16.7	1.1
Augusta	8.9	−3.7
Columbus	6.5	−4.4
Macon	−6.9	−0.4
Savannah	−0.2	−6.1

The listed cities are the ones large enough to be included in Census statistical materials. "The Great Migration, 1910 to 1970," U.S. Census Bureau, 13 September 2012, https://www.census.gov/dataviz/visualizations/020/508.php.

Georgia was depressed before the Depression. The effects of the boll weevil on agricultural production, beginning in 1915, combined with a drop in cotton prices and a series of irrigation problems to drive a rural economic decline in the state through the 1920s, when much of the country was experiencing the roar of the Roaring Twenties. Black sharecroppers, the vast majority of rural Black Georgians, were even more dramatically affected than whites since racism and a lack of landownership made them particularly susceptible to such economic pressures. The stock market collapse and its consequences were exacerbated in the state by a drought in 1930–1931. Then there was chain gang labor, segregation, disfranchisement, and systemic racial violence. The state seemed an inhospitable climate for African Americans.[1]

But Georgia was also the home of Atlanta's Auburn Avenue, a thriving urban Black population in the state capital and other hubs across the state, and entities like the *Atlanta Daily World* and its Scott Newspaper Syndicate. Several Black newspapers associated with the SNS developed in smaller state urban centers during the Depression, and several of them thrived, built on the model that the Scotts had built in Atlanta. For the most part, largely because of that proximity to the syndication hub, the papers in the state were steeped in the practical radicalism that redounded to them from Atlanta.

The *Columbus Advocate*, for example, began publishing in Georgia in June 1937 as a collaboration between Methodist pastor J. J. Lewis, who edited the paper, and local businessman A. T. Jackson, who published it. The *Advocate*'s editorials were understandably less radical than its Syndicate counterparts in larger cities outside the South, instead choosing to emphasize the proven practical elements of southern editorial positions that had come before them. Columbus's position on the western border of Alabama, in fact, put it within the orbit of the Tuskegee Institute and the conservative self-improvement model it evinced. A July 1937 editorial, for example, presented a rambling diatribe on the broad subject of truth: "Listen World! What is Truth? Why do you hate truth and crush truth to the earth? You may hate the truth and crush it to the earth but it shall rise again. The truth shall triumph." There followed several hundred words on truth, broadly conceived, being a good thing, without any correlation of the topic to the racial issues of the day, a turn that other papers in other climes would surely have taken. It was, to be certain, not the activism of others.[2]

When two Black men were unjustly convicted in Columbus for murdering a white man, C. A. Scott sent a telegram to Lewis asking about a new trial for one of the defendants. Lewis responded that "sentiment in Columbus is that the convicted men were not given fair trials."[3] Railing against the convictions in his paper was most likely impossible, but his telegram to Scott allowed him to get his message into the *World* and Syndicate papers. This was another version of practical radicalism, allowing others to print or amplify one's more racially charged local political opinions so as to push back against white supremacy while maintaining a functional plausible deniability. It was also an example of the evolution of the grapevine, the kinship networks that spread news of racial injustice without the awareness of local southern whites, who would have reacted violently to the dissemination.

More publicly, the *Advocate* approvingly covered the efforts of a local civic group to petition the city commission for a swimming pool for Black residents. There was, however, never mention in the paper's reporting about the possibility of integrating an existing pool. "There is even a greater need of a pool for colored people than for white people, because the white people have numerous private pools."[4] Such requests passed for activism in small towns in the Depression-era South. It was the closest proximity to radicalism that a press could maintain.

In nearby Albany, Georgia, the Syndicate founded another paper with a far different model. The *Southwest Georgian*'s original publisher was V. W. Hodges, former dean of Clark College in Atlanta. Hodges had graduated from Boston University before coming to Clark as a professor of contemporary civilization and director of the Division of Social Sciences. After serving at Clark for six years, he became dean of Georgia Normal College for three years before founding, editing, and publishing the *Southwest Georgian*. He was also the president of Albany's branch of the NAACP.[5]

The *Southwest Georgian* first appeared in November 1938, becoming the twenty-eighth paper in the Scott Syndicate, and it fittingly devoted many of its resources to covering Black education. In January 1939, the paper reported on the creation of Fort Valley Normal and Industrial College, which entailed the move of the State Teachers College for Negroes from Forsyth, and attempted to assure skeptical readers that the consolidation did not mean the death of quality public normal education for Black Georgians. It signaled, the paper hoped, a new devotion to Black public education. The paper cited a recent study that demonstrated that the majority of Black college graduates in Georgia went to private schools: "This must not be." The *Southwest Georgian* urged the state's Board of Regents to use the model of Florida, which was devoting far more money to Black public higher education, providing access for many more students. It hoped the move to the more centrally located Fort Valley would encourage more people to attend. It encouraged the eventual inclusion of graduate education at either Fort Valley or Atlanta University. And it called for a leader of the new school at Fort Valley to be chosen in conjunction with Black support: "For Negroes do not feel that leadership at their state supported institutions represented the most intelligent, unselfish, nor the very best the race had to offer." Still, the paper was broadly optimistic. "We congratulate the Regents," the article closed. "And we express the hope that this is only a beginning."[6]

Meanwhile, there were problems at Georgia Normal College in Albany. In 1941, Georgia governor Eugene Talmadge referenced a speech the college's president, J. W. Holley, had made six years prior, in which he lamented the lack of progress made by Black Americans and slurred American Jews as being part of the problem. Among other things, Holley had said, "The southern white man and the ancient Egyptians are the only people who ever got any real work out of the Negro and the Jew." The speech was originally made to the general council of the University of Georgia in 1935 and largely was forgotten until it was brought to the fore by a notorious racist. The *Southwest Georgian* pounced, denouncing Talmadge's address as "inflammatory and criminal," claiming that it was "calculated to work untold harm to the Negro people. It is difficult to understand how Mr. Holley could again appeal to his Jewish neighbors in Albany for further favors and help for his school." It was a bold attack on both the governor and Holley for the insensitive remarks and demonstrated the paper's willingness, in relation to specific behaviors, to craft direct and stinging responses. If Holley had been white, that attack might not have come, of course, but the paper was certainly willing to spar. It even took the liberty of writing a suggested script for Holley when he met with the regents, publishing a first-person address complete with an apology for his earlier remarks and a plan for a more equal allotment of resources corresponding with the Supreme Court's *Missouri ex rel. Gaines* decision. In early August 1941, John Wesley Dobbs, president of Atlanta's Civic and Political League, spoke in Albany in "a double-barreled attack upon the lethargy of Negro people towards intelligent citizenship and the attitude of educational appeasers towards the United States Supreme Court decision in the Lloyd Gaines case." He also, however, denounced Holley as "a traitor to his race."[7]

Gaines loomed large in much of the educational thinking of the Black southern press in the late 1930s and early 1940s. In the early days of the Depression, the NAACP Legal Defense Fund had decided to target graduate and professional education as a point of emphasis for an assault on segregation. There was a statistically small portion of the population that attended such schools, making the risk to whites minimal. Those who did attend were among the most educated of the southern populace and therefore the most likely to accept the argument of unconstitutionality. Even more important, southern states had no publicly funded institutions for Black students, leaving the door open to challenge segregation without directly challenging *Plessy v. Ferguson*. It was, if nothing else, a point of entry onto the battlefield.[8]

In response to the new strategy, several southern states passed laws providing compensation for out-of-state tuition so that would-be Black graduate students could attend school in another state. It was a vastly unequal compromise, and the law was soon challenged in Maryland. With the aid of the NAACP, Donald Murray successfully sued after being denied admission to the University of Maryland law school, the Maryland Court of Appeals validating his claim that separation could not foster equality. The St. Louis chapter of the NAACP sought to test the Maryland standard in Missouri and recruited Lloyd Lionel Gaines from a pool of several volunteers. Gaines had attended segregated primary and secondary schools in Missouri and was a graduate, with honors, from Missouri's Lincoln University. The NAACP's assumption was that any claim of inadequate preparation for entrance into the University of Missouri law school would both open up graduate education and also be a de facto admission that separate education in the state was fundamentally unequal.[9]

The University of Missouri predictably denied admission to Gaines in March 1936, citing state segregation laws and a provision that empowered Lincoln University to create graduate programs as the need arose. Along with the traditional Fourteenth Amendment claim, the NAACP argued to the Missouri Supreme Court that Lincoln's school creation appropriation was no remedy, because rights were a collective, rather than an individual, entity. Gaines, for example, should not have to wait for demand to rise to a level that would make such a creation viable. The waiting made any future admission to Lincoln fundamentally unequal. Of course, the Missouri Supreme Court was not convinced, but in December 1938, the U.S. Supreme Court was. In a 5–2 decision, the Court ordered Missouri to come up with a better approximation of equal opportunity. Unsurprisingly, the state's choice wasn't to allow Gaines admittance to the University of Missouri. Instead, state leaders slowly began establishing a St. Louis law school for Lincoln, far from its main campus in Jefferson City.[10]

The bulk of the northern Black press saw the *Gaines* decision as a qualified success. It was, reported the *Pittsburgh Courier*, "a practical though not idealistic victory." In other coverage, however, the *Courier* was more optimistic, referring to the ruling as "the greatest decision in that court since the grandfather clause was declared unconstitutional." Similar laudatory accounts appeared in the *New York Amsterdam News*, the *Indianapolis Recorder*, and the *Cleveland Gazette*. The *Chicago Defender* was less excited, describing the decision as "one of limited character and effect" and arguing that "there is no hope for the black man until through death, resignation and political pressure justices are appointed to the Supreme Court who will directly overrule the Jim Crow theory adhered to by the Court and interpret the 14th and 15th Amendments to the Constitution in a manner which will accomplish the intentions of the Congress and of the people at the time of their passage."[11] Of course, such caution came from doubt about Missouri's intentions of fulfilling the spirit of the Court's decision.

In the South, however, the interpretation of *Gaines* was far different. The *Atlanta Daily World*, hub of the SNS, argued that it was not "sensible to think that co-education of both groups could be immediately injected into our complex society." Instead, the *World* interpreted Missouri's original solution as being the best possible option: "Perhaps the scholarship arrangement is the best suggestion, after all."[12]

That perspective put the parent paper far to the right of its small-town counterpart in Albany, but the *World*'s interpretation was the one passed along the grapevine through syndication. Still, the papers maintained a symbiotic relationship, as the *World* did with all of its member papers that staked out different positions from its own. In February 1940, for example, a devastating tornado swept through Albany, hitting the Black section of town particularly hard. It killed eighteen people, seventeen of them Black. It injured five hundred and amassed more than $5 million in property damage. Almost one thousand homes were destroyed, along with two Black churches and two Black schools. In response to the massive, unprecedented devastation, the *Atlanta Daily World* worked in conjunction with the *Southwest Georgian* to raise money to help the community.[13] It was a gesture by C. A. Scott that went beyond the usual Syndicate relationship, but demonstrated the bonds that could form between the regions (or, more pragmatically, the tangible benefits that synergistic business relationships could have for customers).

In 1942, the *World* hired Hodges away from Albany for editorial and promotional work for the SNS. He was replaced as *Southwest Georgian* publisher by Albany State alum A. C. Searles, "whose story on the lynching by Newton County police officials attracted nationwide attention and resulted in a federal indictment of the county's sheriff."[14] That willingness to engage in bold action, that lack of trepidation shown by the Atlanta paper, pushed the paper ideologically further from the Syndicate, sometimes yielding problematic results.

In June 1943, Searles joined Hodges, Cliff MacKay, and C. A. Scott as the Georgia delegation to the National Negro Publishers Association annual meeting in Louisville. Founded three years prior to coordinate the efforts of Black publishers throughout the country, the association worked for the success of both the Black press and the Black race, holding annual meetings to coordinate its efforts. At the 1943 meeting, Searles watched appreciatively as the association appointed a special committee to investigate his recent draft notice. Searles believed that the order stemmed from his coverage of the lynching of Robert Hall in Newton, Georgia, in late January, "which resulted," his Atlanta counterpart reported, "in the indictment of three law-enforcement officials of Baker County in Federal Court." The *Southwest Georgian*'s report on the lynching explained that Hall was killed for allegedly stealing a tire from a truck. It was, the paper reported, "a story of white hot hatred, the misuse of police authority, the forging of a warrant, a midnight abduction and a fiction-like conspiracy to take the life of a human being, that is so often told in the South." When that misuse of police authority led to indictments, the local draft board responded by calling Searles's number. Searles appealed for an occupational deferment, which applied to managing editors of newspapers, but the local draft board rejected the appeal, as did the state's Selective Service headquarters. The *World* took up his case, arguing that his draft notice came in early February, "exactly two days after the appearance of the lynching story." It seemed, the paper argued, like retribution, and it wouldn't have happened if there were Black representatives on local southern draft boards: "We have contended in these columns several times previously that as a protection against the misuse of the draft power we must have representation on the boards." Scott even formally called upon James Keelin, Georgia's director of Selective Service, to investigate. He explained that the local draft board also sent the police to intimidate Searles's replacement and had threatened him with an FBI investigation after he published an article about the draft controversy, which forced the paper to suspend operations for two weeks.[15] It was a clear demonstration of the pressure Black southern editors faced and the consequences that could redound to them for exposing the racism that surrounded them every day.

The *Southwest Georgian*, however, continued to fight its battles with white supremacy. In February 1948, the paper reported the story of Rosa Lee Ingram. Ingram's sharecropper husband had died in 1947, and for months after his death she had been accosted by white cropper John Ed Stratford, who worked on a neighboring plot. One day, Stratford came with a rifle, complaining that Ingram's mules and hogs were on his parcel of land. She investigated the claim and found no hogs, but when she returned Stratford attacked, hitting her with the rifle. Two of her sons intervened, first asking him to stop, then in desperation using the butt of the rifle to hit him over the head. The blows ultimately killed Ingram's attacker. She and two of her twelve children were arrested, charged, and tried for murder in front of an all-white jury at Ellaville. Even though the sons were only seventeen and fourteen years old, all three were convicted and sentenced to death. The paper covered the event, the trial, and a prayer service held at the jail, which also served as a protest of the family's incarceration and pending execution. And it covered the lengthy appeal process as Ingram fought for a new trial. "No trial and conviction since the infamous Scottsboro Case has brought such tremendous emotional response from the public," the paper reported.[16] This was another example of the tenuous line walked by Black southerners attempting to maintain a base level of self-respect, and thus the need for progress in increments, and of the practical radicalism of the papers covering those steps.

The Ingram case was not the only scandal that consumed the paper in 1948. Later that year, the Dougherty County Board of Registrars began a "wholesale purging" of Black voters from the rolls. When Atlanta lawyers filed a motion with federal authorities, the registrars were ordered to show cause for the action. The paper exhaustively explained the arguments of the motion, translating the legalese for a popular audience and claiming that there was no reason for the purge except "to deprive the Negro voters of their vote rights."[17]

The educational effort associated with Black southern journalism wasn't localized to Albany. In nearby Macon, a paper formed in May 1939, the *Macon Broadcast*, edited by V. Trenton Tubbs, a Morehouse graduate and public school teacher who helped found the Delta Phi Delta journalistic society while in college. The racial situation in Macon that Tubbs and his paper dealt with was a mixed bag of success and resistance. The *Broadcast*, for example, reported in July 1939 on a speech of local white manufacturer W. D. Anderson, who excoriated President Franklin D. Roosevelt and argued that the only real handicap to the South's progress "is found in its large Negro population." Anderson also rehearsed common conservative rhetoric against the New Deal as antibusiness, claiming that the "South is going to save the nation," particularly if it could overcome the combined threat of the president and the Black population. Tubbs declined to denounce the speech in print, however, avoiding the potential for reprisal and letting Anderson's words speak for themselves.[18]

The paper was more effusive when reporting in depth on a September vote for a seat on the board of the Macon Water Commission. At least 250 Black voters participated, although their votes did not sway the election. Macon's civic and political league, known as the Quizz Club, was actually split over the choice of candidates, and thus Black citizens didn't vote as a bloc. But the fact that they voted, that they cared enough to appear, and that pollsters allowed them to cast ballots were all clearly victories in the eyes of the *Broadcast*.[19]

In October 1939, Tubbs was part of the press retinue at Georgia Baptist College in Macon, where it was announced that philanthropist James H. Porter was donating $10,000 to the school. Tubbs's account in the *Broadcast* noted that Porter "has been a constant and liberal benefactor of the local colored institution of higher learning." It was significant that Tubbs and "Mrs. Minnie D. Singleton of the colored section of the Macon Telegraph and Evening News" were invited to the event, part of an integrated press corps at an integrated fundraising event, a rare occurrence in small southern cities.[20] At the same time, this demonstrated the paper's inclination to only comment directly on local whites when that commentary was positive.

Such is not to say that the *Broadcast* wasn't willing to discuss more controversial local issues. In February 1940, the paper reported on the "seventh of a series of mysterious burning crosses," which had all appeared on the same Georgia Baptist College campus. It was not the work of a "prankster," as all seven of the crosses were "constructed of strong timber with layers of gasoline soaked burlap tightly wired to them." The *Broadcast* reported that many believed that the burnings represented "an effort to reawaken interest in the Ku Klux Klan locally." That same month, plans for a radio program broadcasting news of Black Macon were thwarted by the white editor of the local daily newspaper, who was "otherwise liberal and cooperative"; he published a page of Black news in his paper and argued that the program would be a potential competitor. Thus, "one more attempt of the southern Negro to assert himself as an asset rather than a liability to a community is characteristically 'gone with the wind.'" The *Broadcast* noted that there was an effort under way to convince the editor differently, and it solicited letters of opinion to the paper's offices.[21]

That kind of practical radicalism was mimicked in Georgia's nearby *Columbus World*. The *World* was in an interesting position, founded as the first link of the SNS newspaper chain in March 1931. That early incarnation, however, did not survive for long. Black businesses in Georgia communities were "pushed off on side streets and back alleys," reports Asa Gordon in a 1937 study of the state's Black residents: "In many smaller towns any sign of marked progress by a Negro business house is taken as a notice that that business should be crippled or destroyed." So the city had to wait ten years, until May 1941, for the *World* to reorganize in Columbus, replacing the earlier *Advocate*.[22]

William H. Spencer Jr. agreed to take the editorship of the *World* in March 1941. While he did have editorial experience, Spencer's primary vocation was being a dentist. His father had served as supervisor of the Colored Public Schools of Columbus for fifty years, and Columbus's Spencer High School was named for him. During World War II, the *World*, under Spencer Jr.'s editorship, provided valuable Syndicate reprints of news from nearby Fort Benning. While those dispatches tended to be incredibly positive, there were exceptions. In September 1942, for example, Columbus city commissioners rescinded a ban on two local liquor stores, which they had originally punished because Fort Benning officials had accused them of "harboring women for Negro soldiers stationed at the Army Post." While tensions between city and military leaders were common and inevitable, divisions on racial issues where southern municipal governments showed a greater degree of racial sensitivity were far more rare. Still, Fort Benning's worry wasn't necessarily racially motivated. There was a legitimate problem with venereal disease among the Black recruits, and the work to prevent it also spread through the Syndicate.[23]

Fort Benning was one of a handful of military staging grounds where the federal government, in "having the military police to aid in keeping order in town among the soldiers, set up a colored unit of the Military Police," the paper reported. This was taken by the *World* as a sign of progress, but after an incident in which a military police officer killed a civilian in an act of what he claimed was self-defense, the ensuing controversy led to rumors that some white local officials were lobbying to have the Black MPs removed. *World* editorials disseminated through the Syndicate lauded the "Colored Military Police" and argued that if anything the concept should spread to all bases: "Let us put our collective shoulders together, white and black, and fight Hitler—A REAL MENACE to America."[24]

World publisher and editor Percy Taylor wrote a syndicated column during the war, "Shifting Sands," where he raged against Hitler and the Japanese and urged unity in the war effort, but he also demonstrated the kind of pragmatic advocacy exemplified in his paper's defense of Black MPs. In 1942, for example, he used the vitriolic attack ads of Georgia's gubernatorial candidates to argue that "maybe some Negro votes would have a purifying effect upon Georgia's political situation." At the very least, "Negro votes certainly couldn't cause the political situation in this state to sink any lower than it has." It was a revision of women's suffrage arguments of the 1890s: even if you don't acknowledge our equality, our votes can be uniquely helpful to the state's politics. They can calm the political storm. Taylor also made Black rights a foreign policy issue, arguing that white discord over Black employment and the racial crises of 1943 were essentially giving aid to the enemy. "Hitler's Axis is catching hell over the seas from our boys," he explained, "but the 'home front' boys certainly are giving the enemy some joyful moments." Discrimination and racial prejudice were the bailiwick of the Nazis. "Anytime a person is forced off a defense job, or any time a person becomes a habitual absentee, the Axis scoundrels have joy and glee in their hearts."[25] Taylor stopped short of claiming that anything less than full racial equality was a form of treason, but he was clearly driving down that road. It was a tactic used time and time again during World War II (and later during the Cold War), but Taylor's use of such familiar tropes demonstrated an activist pragmatism that situated him on the correct side of the patriotic spectrum, thus allowing him to make the case for Black voting and workers' rights without running afoul of the white supremacist watchdogs hovering throughout Columbus, Georgia, and the wider territory covered by the Scott Syndicate.

After the war had come and gone, the *World* celebrated the fifth anniversary of its reconstitution in 1946. Editor and publisher Percy Taylor lauded the paper's relationship with Fort Benning, with the Scott Syndicate, and with Columbus, and he publicly hoped that all of those relationships would continue. In the late 1940s and early 1950s, the *World* covered high school football, officer elections for the state organization of beauticians, and even the birth of Taylor's seventh daughter.[26] The articles were filler, special interest pieces from one of the lesser known territories of the Syndicate, but they also demonstrated that the ravages of the racial home-front war, always so magnified near one of the nation's largest and most significant military training grounds, had dissipated. All was well in the home of Fort Benning, and the beauticians were electing officers.

And the news about Fort Benning continued. Visiting military dignitaries arrived, as did civilians like the NAACP's Walter White and Robert Weaver, a former member of Roosevelt's Black Cabinet. In neighboring Columbus, famous explorer Admiral Richard Byrd arrived to speak to Black mill workers, and the city in January 1952 hired four Black policemen, the first in its history, partly at the urging of the *Columbus World*. Coverage of the police hiring did not emphasize the significant rights implications of a middling Deep South city acknowledging the benefits of including Black officers to police its Black citizens almost three years before *Brown*, but instead celebrated the officers themselves, including a picture and describing their hard work and qualifications.[27] It was a decidedly Black southern response, in the pattern stitched together two generations prior by Tuskegee and its adherents. But it was at the same time a demonstration of pride at a real gain.

In circulating stories like this one, the Syndicate wasn't adding its own analysis of the implications of such milestones. It was cutting and pasting the stories from the local paper. In national journals of commentary and race advocacy, the response to the hiring of Black officers in Columbus would have been presented differently, but in Columbus itself, where the *World* writers actually knew the recruits, pride in each individual was the order of the day. That being the case, news of this nature spread in a manner that did not appear militant, that did not appear to be in the vein of advocacy. But it was. By January 1952, when the Black Columbus policemen were hired, the Syndicate no longer had a national presence, but it was distributed throughout the South, from Little Rock in the west to Cincinnati in the north and down into every major southern market. And in those markets, a story like the Black officers of Columbus mattered. Dissatisfaction with states of affairs crystallizes when viable alternatives are modeled publicly. Birmingham, for example, awash in racial violence, would have welcomed Black policemen with open arms. Such stories didn't give activists there the idea of pushing for Black officers. They had been doing that for years. Instead, these stories subtly shifted the emphasis from racial crime to the racists who supposedly policed it, a necessary inversion of traditional white assumptions. This was significant because it established goals for other municipalities that had a much better chance of success than, say, convincing Klan members to have a racial epiphany, and because it simultaneously maintained the Tuskegee ethic: "If given the opportunity, we can do this ourselves."

Meanwhile, on the other side of Georgia, the *Savannah Journal* had a longer pedigree, founded in 1918 as a vehicle for the city's Black Republicans. The weekly paper's one surviving edition from September 1934, more than half a decade before it affiliated with the Syndicate, was four pages whose lead editorial lamented a lack of "community consciousness" in Black Savannah. "Why should we complain of the white group's treatment of the Negro when the Negro seems satisfied with the way he is treated?" the paper asked. "He does not express through the public press nor through concerted action his disapproval of the treatment meted out to him until he has been driven to the wall." By developing a more activist bent, that "community consciousness," the population wouldn't be left reacting to atrocities and would make proactive gains in bad times and in good.[28]

In 1940, six years after that one surviving issue, the *Journal* underwent a sea change and joined the Scott Syndicate. Dr. Asa H. Gordon, the paper's new editor, was also the director of the Divisions of Social Sciences and Research Publication at Georgia State College, having come from South Carolina State A&M in Orangeburg. "Dr. Gordon is a man of culture and fine character and by study and contact possesses a very excellent education," said M. F. Whittaker, president of the college in Orangeburg. "I think of him as an able educator, a brilliant scholar, and a cultured gentleman." In August 1941, Gordon resigned from Georgia State after ten years to take the post of director of the Recreation Center for Colored Soldiers then developing in Savannah. At least, that was the story originally told by the *Journal*. In reality, Georgia State chancellor S. V. Sanford dismissed Gordon (against the recommendation of school president B. F. Hubert) over editorials he had published in the *Journal* about the salaries of Black and white professors.[29] It was the kind of trouble that an activist editorial policy could create in the Deep South. When editorial work was an avocation, bold stances could have consequences for an editor's vocation.

But bold stances characterized Gordon and the *Journal*. In January 1941, the paper covered the beginning of the second term of Ike Thomas, a Black deputy sheriff from Savannah and "the only member of his race in Georgia holding this office." That July, it reported on Attorney General Ellis Arnall's denunciation of those who "wave the bloody shirt of prejudice," which was believed to be directed at Governor Talmadge after he fired Walter Cocking from the University of Georgia for supporting racial integration. Speaking in Brunswick, Arnall "expressed the hope that the University of Georgia would never become another Louisiana State University, 'politically dominated by a second Huey Long.'"[30]

In August 1941, the paper received a letter from a white southern antilynching activist, Jessie Daniel Ames, requesting information about a lynching in Cordele. "We feel sure nothing untoward will happen to any Negro in Cordele as the result of your receiving this memorandum," she assured the *Journal*. Thus the paper printed her letter and the information it gathered in response to the lynching in Cordele. It told how Arthur Johnson, a Black man, owed "Mr. Booth," a white man, seven dollars. He was arrested, and the police summoned Booth "to come and beat up the Negro." Booth, however, was busy until six o'clock. When he finally arrived, he and the chief of police began beating Johnson, who tried to fight back. When Johnson reached for a Coca-Cola bottle lying nearby, the police chief drew his gun and shot him seven times. The white men "called a Negro undertaker to get the body of a man who had fallen out dead in jail," then told him to have Johnson buried by ten o'clock the next morning.[31] It was an egregious case, a horrifying murder, but of a type that was all too common in the region, making Ames's report and its syndication a representation of so many others that went unreported. The *Journal* felt comfortable printing the material because Cordele was in the southwestern part of the state, almost two hundred miles from Savannah, and thus the paper was not implicating any local whites.

That distance gave the paper a form of safe harbor, but at other times it was willing to approach, if not actually cross, the state's racial lines. Also in 1941, the paper printed a letter from the pastor of Savannah's First African Baptist Church to J. W. Holley, the president of Georgia Normal and Agricultural College in Albany. Holley had recently and controversially supported Eugene Talmadge after the governor blamed the dismissal of a group of white teachers on the growing requirement for Black teachers in the state.[32] The pastor's letter, which the *Journal* described as expressing "the true feeling of every right thinking citizen of the state," called Holley "the Benedict Arnold of this age," someone who was "willing to sell out the interests of your own people in the hope that by winning the favor of one of our enemies, you may become the dictator of State education where the Negro is involved." It was a caustic and denigrating screed against one of the state's Black leaders, but it was also, by default, against the "demagogue" governor whom he was supporting. And it was far more brazen than most of its southern counterparts were willing to be.[33]

In September 1942, a *Journal* editorial described the Black person's desire "to use his inherent ability and training to help his country do its part in winning this war," but there were "deliberate efforts being made" to keep that from happening. "Right here in Savannah—yes, the Southeastern Shipyard is an example—skilled and semi-skilled Negroes are being turned down and being made victims of a cruel system to keep the Negro from using his ability as a mechanic." Not only was hiring skilled Black workers the right thing to do, and not only would it benefit the Black community, but it would also alleviate Savannah's housing problem, because there would be no need to import white workers to places like the Southeastern Shipyard.[34] It was a comprehensive argument and also a direct attack on unequal treatment by a specific entity in the city, which cut against the more traditional practical radicalism of its peers. The *Journal* served the most cosmopolitan market—with the exception of Atlanta—of the SNS papers in the state, and it had the largest potential tiered reach.[35] The size and relative urbanity of a region often provided a form of cover that allowed Black newspapers to push further against the racial line than some of their rural counterparts could, particularly in fights over hiring and labor.

World War II was often a theater for such fights. In May 1942, the *Journal* published a piece demonstrating that "Negro farmers in Georgia and the South are showing their loyalty to their country by their increasing energy and activity on their farms." It wasn't idle patriotism that spurred the article, as "some people question whether or not the Negro farmer can still keep going when there is such a demand for labor in urban defense industries." The article described Black farmers as ultimately necessary to the war effort, and assured readers that they would not be disappearing, even through the last major wave of the Great Migration. When a commanding officer praised "Negro troops in a crack Engineer organization at Hunter Field Army Air Base" in Savannah for showing "a high level of intelligence and education," the paper followed with its own praise of the Black engineers.[36]

Such was the common strategy in the postwar southern press. An analysis of the northern and southern Black press by *Fortune* magazine in 1945 demonstrated that stories in southern papers were more likely to be "supporting or furthering friendly Negro-white relations" and far less likely to be "unfavorable to whites' conduct of Negro-white relations." Southern papers were more likely to include more social and church news but less crime and disaster news than their northern counterparts. They were more likely to report "favorably on the armed services" and less likely to protest "discrimination against Negroes in the armed services." The figures were significant. Only 23 percent of African American people lived outside the South. That population was wealthier and better educated than its southern counterpart, and it produced 52 percent of the country's Black newspapers. The *Pittsburgh Courier* and *Chicago Defender* sent large numbers of each of their editions to the South, where the bulk of the Black population lived. "The implication is that certain stories may be safely published north of the Mason Dixon Line," *Fortune* stated. "This may explain the lower proportion of racial controversy already noted in the southern Negro press."[37]

That isn't to say that newspapers like the *Journal* did not take political stands. In 1954, for example, the paper joined with SNS stalwarts the *Atlanta Daily World* and *Southwest Georgian* to endorse former acting governor Melvin Thompson in his gubernatorial contest against the archsegregationist and Herman Talmadge acolyte Marvin Griffin. Thompson was a Democrat and, to be sure, simply the lesser of two racisms, but the endorsement was emblematic of the kinds of choices that Black southern editors had to make. Pragmatism dictated that the *World* and the *Georgian* endorse a white supremacist, but by stumping for the candidate who would least harm the Black populace of Georgia, the compromise position was actually the most militant that the paper could take.[38]

Chapter 2

Florida

The Great Migration Black Population Changes (%)

City	1910-1940	1940-1970
Jacksonville	-13.4	-15.1
Miami	1.3	-19.9
Orlando	1.0	-7.9
Pensacola	0.2	-11.5
St. Petersburg	-4.9	-7.0
Tallahassee	-14.6	-24.6
Tampa	-1.8	-2.2

The listed cities are the ones large enough to be included in Census statistical materials. "The Great Migration, 1910 to 1970," U.S. Census Bureau, 13 September 2012, https://www.census.gov/dataviz/visualizations/020/508.php.

"Jacksonville, Florida, is the latest key city in the South to get a newspaper published by the Southern Newspaper Syndicate," announced the *Atlanta Daily World* in June 1932. "Today sees the birth of the *Jacksonville World*, which is to be published every Tuesday and Friday in Jacksonville." The Syndicate claimed that it was the fourth paper in the chain, though there had been several other short-lived attempts that hadn't demonstrated the staying power of enterprises like those in Birmingham or Memphis. Jacksonville, "with approximately 50,000 Negroes, is a splendid field for an SNS paper."[1]

Florida was more prosperous than its neighbor Georgia in the early 1920s, but the land boom went bust in 1926, coinciding with a devastating hurricane season. Two years later, as W. A. Scott was founding the *Atlanta World*, another hurricane ravaged Florida, leaving the economy in tatters when the stock market collapsed in 1929. Florida's experience with the boll weevil was less substantial than that of Georgia, but it faced instead the influx of a Mediterranean fruit fly, which hurt the citrus crop that helped drive the rural economy. That economic collapse added to an already precarious position for Black Floridians, who were suffering under

Jim Crow, voting restrictions, and racial violence. Slowly but surely there would, however, be progress. In 1937, the state repealed its poll tax. In 1944, the Supreme Court struck down the white primary. But such victories were cold comfort to those suffering under a mountain of racial and economic indignities in the state.[2]

Jacksonville had the largest Black population of any Florida city participating in the Syndicate, giving the SNS its longest reach in the state. The size of its tiered influence and its urban setting allowed the *Jacksonville World* to be more willing than some of the papers to its north in Georgia to insert itself into controversy. After two Black assailants were charged with shooting a white man, for example, the *World*, in its inaugural edition, managed to interview one of the suspects, who told a story that completely contradicted that of the white man who was injured. Richard Brown and Laura Hawkins had not attempted to rob Robert Whitley, according to the *World*. Brown, instead, was attempting to stop the sexual assault of his girlfriend, Hawkins. This coverage was a subtle radicalism, to be sure, but it was radicalism nonetheless. In the *World*'s debut issue, its first article syndicated by the SNS questioned the claims of a white shooting victim and, by extension, the local police.[3]

The Black press had dealt with such controversies before. When, in 1906, for example, a Black regiment in Brownsville, Texas, was harangued by the locals and eventually accused of a shooting spree in the town, President Teddy Roosevelt had discharged the soldiers, essentially punishing the men for the bad behavior of the white citizens of Brownsville. The Black press responded swiftly and angrily. Even Ben Davis's *Atlanta Independent* (the city's precursor to Scott's *Atlanta Daily World*),[4] rock-ribbed Republican as it was, denounced Roosevelt's action. "The hand of Ben Tillman nor [James] Vardaman never struck humanity as savagely as did the iron hand of Theodore Roosevelt," he claimed. As historian Lewis Wynne has explained, the vitriol over the Brownsville incident didn't turn the Black population from the Republicans en masse largely because the Atlanta riot followed soon on its heels later that year, dwarfing the smaller Texas body count and thus overshadowing it in media importance, but it was "a blot on Roosevelt's humanitarian record" nonetheless.[5] The Black southern press had demonstrated even in that early era that it was not afraid to castigate someone whom it had been pivotal in helping to elect.

In Florida, the Jacksonville paper also covered more pressing community issues. It described the plan by the Negro Grocers of Jacksonville, for example, to begin co-op buying to offset the rigors of the Depression. It reported on the new teacher standards in Duval County, which required Black teachers to take a qualifying exam for certification. The previous standard had been a third-grade education, and teachers were obviously worried not only about their qualifications and about transportation to and from the exam, but also about the fairness of an exam created by white superintendents of education. When the economic collapse affected the insurance industry, the *World* covered the layoffs at the Afro American Insurance Company, the "largest Negro business interest in the State of Florida."[6]

The *Jacksonville World* was also willing to be a loud voice on the racial disparities of the day, following the strategy of practical radicalism by emphasizing national stories far from Duval County. In October 1932, for example, a syndicated article from the *World* noted that "early this year the entire nation was appalled by the kidnapping and subsequent murder of the son of one of the country's foremost heroes," referring to the dramatic case of the Lindbergh baby. The article used the sensational event to compare the reality that "since the beginning of this year eight Negroes have been criminally murdered. They, too, were kidnapped, taken by force, usually from the so-called sanctuary(?) of the law." It went on to describe and denounce lynching in the United States. The comparison with the Lindbergh case was radical because it took on two of the media's sacred cows—white children and the police. It was, for its time, a bold statement.[7]

There were similar bold statements by the Syndicate's *Miami Times*, published by Henry E. Sigismund Reeves.[8] The *Times*, with a circulation hovering around five thousand in the 1930s and a potential population influence second only to that of Jacksonville newspapers, explained in its first issue that it was dedicated to the "betterment of the Negroes of the community." The paper was an ardent supporter of civil rights and remained willing to criticize the local racial situation in and around Miami. At the same time, it was pragmatic. Articles reported on the efforts of Black residents of Miami to find employment, for example. The Civil Works Administration was a boon to the area, the *Times* explained, as was the Colored Women's Work Committee of Miami, which helped develop a women's center in the city.[9] It was a positive message that belied the negative reality for so many in South Florida, a modification of the Washingtonian position that dominated in parts of Georgia and the broader South in the early twentieth century. And it was representative of the practically radical position that Syndicate papers developed in the volatile early years of the Depression in the South. That position, however, was not reflective of the country's economic volatility. As the white U.S. economy moderated throughout the decade, the southern Syndicate papers did not become appreciably more caustic in response.

Sanders Mason was in much the same position while publishing the *Tampa World*. Mason was a laborer who made far less money than a teacher, but in March 1935 he took over a paper established late in 1932 by C. W. Jennings, an Atlanta University graduate who had worked with friends W. A. Scott and Ric Roberts to put the Syndicate in the Tampa market, the state's third largest. By 1934, the paper's circulation had grown to three thousand copies. The success of Jennings and the *World* was such that in April 1934, the Syndicate began using his story as an advertising mechanism for other towns that might want to become part of the SNS. "All you need is a dash of determination and the will to win," the ad assured potential entrepreneurs. The Syndicate would print the newspaper. "You assemble your own news and mail it. We mail you a full fledged publication in return carrying COMICS, SPORTS, ROTOGRAVURE and your own Editorials and Society and Headlines." It was a journalism do-it-yourself kit, and it formalized the grapevine across the South.[10]

Mason, meanwhile, began as a newspaper delivery boy and then became a worker in the *Atlanta Daily World*'s print shop. He took over for Jennings early in 1935.[11] The paper he now published had fit the Syndicate mold from the beginning. It trumpeted business as the highest pinnacle of Black life, and it railed against Tampa's Board of Education when it raised pay for white teachers and failed to provide a proportionate increase for Black teachers. But the tale that defined the *World* was its coverage of local lynchings. In January 1934, for example, Robert Johnson was arrested in Tampa on suspicion of attacking a white woman, whereupon "a band of unmasked men," the paper explained, "took him from Deputy Constable T. M. Graves, and fired five shots into his body." The *World* covered both the event and the ensuing investigation, which was ordered by Florida governor David Sholtz after intense public pressure. In September 1935, "the body of an unidentified Negro appearing to be slightly over 40 years old, real dark complexioned and very stout, was dragged out of the Hillsborough River." The man had been cut and burned, and it was obvious that the stranger had been lynched. No one claimed the body. Another mob action in December led a local man to be tarred and feathered.[12] With the kind of racial violence that existed in Tampa, having a Black newspaper with syndication across the South and much of the nation was vital to publicizing such terroristic acts.

In the southern part of the state, the Miami *Tropical Dispatch* was another long-running SNS paper, but it demonstrated that editorial policies like those of Mason were by no means uniform. The *Tropical Dispatch* first appeared in 1929, replacing the *Florida East Coast Dispatch*, created in 1923. It was founded by James E. Scott, who had no direct relationship to the Atlanta Scotts but did ally with his Georgia counterparts in 1933 after the demise of the *Miami Times*. Scott was a community organizer, working as the manager of Douglas Community Center and as executive secretary of the Negro Welfare Federation while publishing his paper.[13]

"Are we Southern Negroes a motley group of shiftless, lazy, lousy, and blandly ignorant group of misfits who deserve no other place in the role of American affairs save the one of singing 'spirituals,' shouting, yelling 'hallelujah,' and servilely responding 'Yassah' to questions?" asked one of Scott's *Dispatch* editorials. Because that was, it assured readers, the opinion of those outside the South: "Most of my friends out here are entrapped in the notion that the Southern Negro doesn't want to do anything and doesn't do anything except eat, work when he has to, go to church, and otherwise wastefully spend his time dancing or gambling or employing some other type of activity that is at variance with sane ethics and sane behavior." Any Black southerner who didn't fit the stereotype was considered an exception to an otherwise hard-and-fast rule. Fixing that problem, noted the syndicated *Dispatch* column, was at least in part the responsibility of the Black press: "Our papers must relieve themselves of their smugness and often unfair tactics of 'presenting' news. The newspaper must more and more become the interpreter of the present scene rather than a callous chip chopping, hint dispensing hatred breeding critic." This was an inversion of the typical self-flagellation of the press and its acolytes. When syndicates like the Scotts' developed, they gave the Black South a mechanism with which to communicate with the rest of the country. Press vanity, over and against the mind-set of their less informed and less educated readers, the *Dispatch* argued, was functionally hurting the cause, providing an unfair caricature of the Black South that only reinforced the image already maintained by those beyond its borders. Since the Scott Syndicate had finally provided the Black press in the South with a link to national assumptions, at least part of its responsibility had to be an attempt to rehabilitate the Black southern image. "You have no idea," the editorial surmised, "how scrutinously a Negro from Dixie is watched by even his fellow brother of the West."[14]

Or by local whites. "Respectable Negro citizens are not voting tomorrow," said one Miami Klan sign. "Niggers stay away from the polls." The race fires were hot in Miami in May 1939, the night before the city was holding primary elections. At least fifty cars full of hooded members of the Ku Klux Klan drove through Black neighborhoods lighting crosses and dangling nooses in an effort to intimidate Black Miami away from the polls. But Black Miami wasn't intimidated. Led by Samuel B. Solomon, a local mortician and president of the city's Negro Citizens Service League, roughly 1,500 Black Miami residents went to the polls on May 2 to vote in the primary. The Black vote was high because two years prior the state's poll tax had been repealed, opening up voting to so many more in the city. Solomon had led the way, becoming the "Moses of Miami," and the city's Black population followed him to defy the Klan.[15]

The Florida state legislature was not happy about the increased presence of the Klan nor about the increased voting of Black Miami, and in response it passed a 1939 bill mandating "non-partisan white primaries" in the city. The NAACP vowed to challenge it if the governor signed it into law. The Negro Citizens Service League petitioned him to veto the bill, while white supremacist groups in Tallahassee lobbied for his signature. Covering those machinations and staking out a place on the front lines of what would become a national controversy was the *Tropical Dispatch*, which simultaneously reported on the new law and pointed out that the U.S. Supreme Court had already declared a similar Texas statute unconstitutional. The governor signed the legislation, and a resulting court fight led by Solomon and the NAACP ultimately overturned it in *U.S. v. Classic* (1941), while the *Dispatch*'s coverage and willingness to put itself in harm's way on the issue demonstrated its devotion to Black political rights. While Miami had many of the trappings of southern white supremacy, it also had a Black activist population ahead of its time, one that sometimes made South Florida look ideologically farther north than Georgia.[16]

Among the *Dispatch*'s editorial mastheads, the paper included:

> For the cause that lacks assistance,
> For the wrongs that need resistance;
> For the future in the distance,
> And the good that we can do.

James E. Scott, the paper's original editor, did not survive the decade, and Daniel R. Francis took over as editor and publisher.[17] Under his leadership, the *Dispatch* described itself as "an aggressive and progressive Negro weekly" and quoted Franklin Roosevelt that "the right to vote must be open to all our citizens irrespective of race, color, or creed—without tax or artificial restriction of any kind. The sooner we get to that basis of political equality, the better it will be for the country as a whole." When a group of Black voters in 1941 held a massive convention in Tampa, sponsored by Miami's Florida State Negro Civic Council, the *Dispatch* covered it. When the American Federation of Labor's Brotherhood of Maintenance of Way Employees began intimidating Black employees of the Florida East Coast Railway in order to establish a labor claim over the United Transport Service Employees of America, the *Dispatch* covered the work of the National Mediation Board to solve the impasse.[18]

The paper's coverage of racial issues was just as substantial when it reported on stories with more than one act, that evolved over time, often as a result of news coverage. When local attorney Lawson E. Thomas ran as a Republican for Miami justice of the peace, for example, the first Black candidate to ever make the attempt, the *Dispatch* not only covered the story but openly encouraged its readers to vote for him. The newspaper was a tireless proponent of the city's hiring of Black officers to police its Black citizens. It didn't hesitate to report early in 1943 that "police brutality is showing its head again in Washington Heights among its Negro population and presents the citizenry with only one alternative and that is to ACT and do wisely." When the demand for Black officers became a reality in 1944, the *Dispatch* celebrated the hiring while reminding readers that the victory was not a get-out-of-jail-free card: "They are your friends, but remember, they are policemen first and have a duty to perform. You cannot expect any half-way treatment or any favors."[19]

When children were found in deplorable living conditions in the city in 1946, the *Dispatch* began crusading for a "colored health officer" to protect vulnerable children. The report turned by the end into a desperate, all-caps call to action: "IF THE WHITE AGENCIES WON'T DO IT THEN A COLORED DEPARTMENT OR AGENCY SHOULD BE SET UP TO HANDLE SUCH CASES."[20] Such was the nature of the Black press in Miami and elsewhere. The news was not simply related neutrally. The stakes for the community that read the paper were too high, the people's situations too precarious not to propose solutions to the problems depicted in the paper's pages every week.

An April 1945 *Dispatch* front page featured stories about the successful performance of Black members of the Ninety-Second Division in combat, which were juxtaposed with an article about sixty officers arrested "for defying a ban on colored officers at the swanky and modern officers club" at Freeman Field in Seymour, Indiana. The paper covered challenges to the white city primary in Atlanta and other Jim Crow stories from outside the area, pragmatically choosing to criticize targets farther from home. Its only local coverage on the front page was an announcement that scholarships were available to attend Florida A&M and a report on the successful leadership of Black Miami's division of the Red Cross. A January 1946 editorial argued, "The colleges and universities of the country are turning away thousands of discharged war veterans, who are seeking admission, because of insufficient housing and facilities." The paper took up the cause with adamance, knowing that patriotism was a prerequisite of civil rights legitimacy and that housing was inadequate on Black college campuses.[21]

In another intersection of patriotism and civil rights activism, the Klan was common fare for the *Dispatch*. In June 1946 the paper reprinted an *East Tennessee News* editorial excoriating the KKK. "Aside from the fire hazard arising when disciples of the Ku Klux Klan engage in their nefarious practices," the editorial proclaimed, "and the curiosity that arises in the minds of decent and law abiding citizens as to what individuals are concealed behind the peak-topped white coveralls worn by the Klansmen," Black southerners were "not at all excited over the renewed depredations of the iniquitous order." The editorial went on to criticize the group from every conceivable vantage point, and the message was clear. We aren't afraid of you anymore.[22]

That lack of fear freed the paper to tackle subtler racisms. In a March 1946 edition, the *Dispatch* included on its front page a letter to the editor of the *Miami Herald* describing "the number of Negro subscribers to your paper, yet there is nothing written about him socially or culturally." It mentioned a recent visit of Channing H. Tobias, director of the Phelps Stokes Fund, who had come for a King of Clubs event in the city. It was "real news," and yet it was virtually ignored by the *Herald*. The letter writer was also frustrated with the use of a lowercase *n* in "negro." This was an actual letter to the editor, not written by a member of the *Dispatch* staff, but the paper printed it on the front page.[23]

The *Dispatch* claimed to be "non-political, sectarian, or propagandist in purpose, practice or character." Still, despite that statement, the front page of an August 1946 edition featured syndicated coverage of the lynching of two Black couples in Monroe, Georgia; Klan activity in Memphis; and the Council on Race Relations. Its local coverage featured a story on a Black war veteran killed by a local white police officer. The veteran had attacked the officer, but the article's place on the front page alongside stories of lynchings and Klan activity did its own work, and that work could easily be described as political. The next month, syndicated stories about Monroe and the Klan continued. A local Black clerk was beaten severely and almost killed by two sons of the white owner of the store for which he worked after the boys discovered that he had stolen some cigarettes. Black Miamians were protesting the construction of new bars and package stores in their neighborhoods, claiming there were "more than enough" already. Partly, the protest was a religious one, but it was also clearly political. The new construction was owned by whites, and the fact that white merchants were attempting to use vice to profit off lower-income Black people was itself a problem. The inherent critique was that Black drunkenness and the behavior that stemmed from it were the self-fulfilling prophecy of whites who brought such substances into the neighborhood in order to make money.[24]

Coverage in the *Dispatch* developed over the years into something more overtly radical than many of the paper's more practical southern counterparts, but its focus during the tumultuous wartime period from the late 1930s to the mid-1940s was representative. Papers reported on foreign policy as it related to Black soldiers or Black interests, and used the fight against the Nazis to make the case for rights back home. That formula, however, still left newspapers with a wide range of ideological and strategic interpretations based on pragmatic racial calculations for safety and survival.

Any deviation in news coverage from the mean did not last long. After the war, the *Tropical Dispatch* turned to the development of business infrastructure as the key to securing equality in the city. One above-the-fold headline promised a "Negro banking system in Miami," and the article noted that "attention is being directed toward organizing a community type Credit Union here in Miami to be wholly owned and operated by Negroes." There were more than 14 million Black citizens, which meant 14 million potential customers, comprising a "multi-billion dollar market." As part of its encouragement of development, the *Dispatch* began a "bulletin board" in the paper, where clubs, churches, welfare groups, schools, and other organizations could list meetings, programs, and functions free of charge to better meld the community together as one economic unit.[25] The vote was still crucial, but the *Dispatch*'s turn after the war demonstrated that equality also came with buying power. Economic infrastructure was vital.

In 1948, the paper began publishing "Parade of Progress" editions in an effort to "pictorially and graphically depict the progress of Negroes in Dade County in Religion, agriculture, education, the professions, the types of businesses owned and operated by the group, as well as the kinds of employment in which they are engaged for others." While this was sure to create a unity that could only bolster economic infrastructure, it was also clearly a "talented tenth" approach to demonstrating Black social and economic effectiveness to white Miami. (W. E. B. Du Bois had made the argument that the top of the intellectual and economic hierarchy, the "talented tenth," had a responsibility to carry along the race as it accrued new social opportunities.) The same edition that described the motives of the "Parade of Progress," for example, included a substantial front-page graphic telling readers, "Behave yourself. It is not necessary to talk so loud to be heard—everyone is not interested in your conversation."[26] Such statements also provided cover for the paper's syndicated material describing the federal antilynching law effort, the movement of the Klan in Georgia, and the fight for a permanent Fair Employment Practices Committee (FEPC).

"One of the most fantastic things about both of the World Wars has been the attitude of the American Legion toward Negro veterans," one *Dispatch* editorial stated. "In both wars the nation drafted Negroes for service, sent them to the front where they fought, suffered, were wounded, and died like all men in all wars have ever done. When the soldiers came home and began an organization of veterans of the war they drew up a constitution which allowed some states to refuse to recognize the Negro veteran." But it seemed like there was progress as of 1948: "The district division embracing North and South Carolina, Georgia and Alabama, has decided to lift the ban and allow the creation of Negro units affiliated with the district and state organizations."[27] It wasn't integration, but it was a step toward equality in separation, the same tack taken by Syndicate papers in relation to teachers' salaries and school facilities.[28]

When Dothan, Alabama, opened a new Black high school at a cost of $350,000, for example, the *Dispatch* celebrated without making a case against segregation. Quite to the contrary. Alabama was "going ahead with its own program of solving the Negro problem, rather than waiting until some so-called 'Northern agitator' proposes better treatment." It was refreshing, the paper thought, that the southern states "set about doing something more tangible than being against any vote of progress and advancement of the Negro." Black citizens didn't need white schools. They needed equal schools: "Let other cities and states in the South follow the lead by Governor [James] Folsom and the splendid example of the Dothan education Board."[29]

This strategy existed for a reason. In February 1949, the Ku Klux Klan burned crosses at the homes of two ministers, one white, one Black, because the white minister had asked his Black counterpart to preach at his church as a part of the city's Brotherhood Week. A defiant *Dispatch* went to the front page with its editorial. Miami had come a long way, the paper claimed. Long a racist bastion, "Miami has come of age and has put away quite a number of the foolish things it did as a child." But "Negroes, too, have come of age. The day has passed when the mere burning of a cross somewhere in their section or the parading of hooded cowards can wreak fear among them." Black soldiers had served overseas, had faced real terror against the Germans, and "the families of these gallant warriors served their country in no less a degree at home." They were patriotic Americans and would not be bullied in the country they had defended: "BURN YOUR CROSSES—MAKE YOUR RIDES—YOU MAY EVEN LYNCH—BUT THERE ARE 14 MILLION NEGROES AND MILLIONS OF SOUTHERN WHITES WHO KNOW THAT NEGROES ARE HUMAN TOO."[30] The *Dispatch*'s editors were not afraid; they wanted to demonstrate that the paper was not afraid; and they had a tested Black southern journalistic strategy to keep the burning crosses at bay.

In 1947, James B. LaFourche was the city editor of the *Tropical Dispatch*. He was originally the editor of the *New Orleans Broadcast*, an earlier Syndicate effort. As of July 1947, he and his coeditor, Dan Francis, had expanded their operation to other media, hosting a Saturday radio program called *News and Views* on Miami's WKAT.[31] LaFourche was also the race relations advisor for the Miami Negro Business Men's Association. When he realized that the American Legion was considering Miami as a possible site for its 1948 convention, he worked to convince the group not to come to his city, fearing that the Black delegates would be treated harshly.[32] This was an example of the paper making an active rights stand over and against a very specific local economic interest.

The campaign didn't work, and the National Convention of the American Legion came to Miami in October. The convention, however, had significant benefits for the *Dispatch*, as the paper's C. A. Irvin and Daniel Francis were given press credentials for President Harry Truman's visit to the event. Both attended the press luncheon, where they were the only Black reporters present. White waiters served them. Then they followed Truman with the press corps to his American Legion speech, before seeing him off at the airport. In addition, the Black legionnaires reported mostly good treatment at the convention. There were only roughly 150 Black delegates because of the history of racial exclusion in Miami and in the American Legion, but those who attended found that the only Jim Crow issues were at the convention dances.³³

The *Dispatch* was involved in its community in other ways as well, helping, for example, two local Miami students obtain scholarships to Alabama State in Montgomery. It also fought to end loan sharking in the area. The reputation of the paper earned the trust of Miamians, paving the way for interviews with local young men like "Ivan," who told the paper about the brutal treatment of Black workers by white officers at the Civilian Conservation Corps camp in Milton, Florida, in 1935. The Black men were beaten, threatened with death, and refused the discharges they requested. As many as forty fled, and the *Dispatch* was able to obtain an exclusive exposé.³⁴

When a Black woman shopping at Hemly's Furniture Store in 1947 was told, "Hemly's doesn't 'Mrs.' Negro women," the *Dispatch* sent a reporter, who was accosted by the manager for even questioning the policy. The paper reported on the event and rallied its readers to action, noting that Black people's "biggest weapon at this particular time is BUYING POWER and there are many stores as big and bigger than this one that will open up 'RESOURCES UNLIMITED' to their patronage. This is a NEW DAY for the Negro and he is waxing strong—intelligently. He is not willing to and WON'T stand for SECOND CLASS CITIZENSHIP where spending his hardearned money is concerned."³⁵ This was a radical message—not only an attempt to use the paper's pages for local activism, but an uncompromising stand against discrimination, which was syndicated across the region by the SNS. It was hardly the equivocating message that many southern Black papers would later make infamous.

The *Dispatch* was allied with both the Black press and the white press in the state. In July 1948, Daniel Francis became the chair of the newly created Florida State Newspaper League, an organization of the state's Black newspapers. The league was spearheaded by Francis and created in conjunction with Florida A&M's annual journalism seminar. At the same time, when the *Miami Herald* reported on the work of Ralph Bunche to mediate the dispute between Egypt and Israel in 1949, the *Dispatch* publicly commended its white counterpart and reprinted its coverage. There was in the synergy with state and local journalism another version of practical radicalism, creating alliances that would both help the paper's bottom line and support the advancement of the race.³⁶

But the re-reporting and syndicated coverage that became most crucial to Black Miami and the broader region came in the form of stories that moved within the Black press network throughout the South via the Scott Syndicate. In 1948, for example, the federal government indicted four Palm Beach County police officers and one Florida East Coast Railway agent for beating a Black man in response to their assumption that he had stolen cigarettes from a railroad boxcar. They held him for two days without booking or charging him, then tortured him until they had a confession. The *Dispatch* was unable to get local justice, but it reported on the incident and the federal indictment that stemmed from it. The Syndicate then took that report and broadcast it across the South and the nation.[37] In this role of the voice of the voiceless, the Black press did its most valuable work.

The *Dispatch* continued publishing until the mid-1960s, but its run with the SNS ended in the summer of 1950. It had been a vital part of the Syndicate, but it was also part of a nexus of Black newspapers in Florida, its longevity and stability a needed constant among a group that often changed. The *Jacksonville Progressive News*, for example, a venerable SNS stalwart of the World War II period, moved briefly to Miami for several months in 1946 after the war's conclusion. It continued to ally itself with the Syndicate even as it competed with the *Dispatch* before moving back to Jacksonville in October. When it returned to the northern part of the state, the paper did not bring its SNS affiliation with it, and it published into the mid-1950s as an independent press.[38]

Near to the *Dispatch* was the Syndicate's *Palm Beach Tribune*, published by O. T. Portier. Ted Samms, the *Tribune*'s editor, wrote an editorial encouraging everyone to "PAY YOUR POLL TAX." He told his readers, "The amount is a small one, make preparations NOW, for delay is destructive to our needs. We are a great people, if we will only consider ourselves such, and do the things necessary to gain recognition." It was an important message that Black Floridians needed to hear, but at the same time it came with statements like "Let's don't embarrass ourselves by asking for that which we have not made ourselves eligible to attain."[39] Samms was referring to making political demands without voting, but it sounded more like a Washingtonian insistence that Black Florida had yet to attain a status that precluded having to pay a poll tax to begin with. It was a subtle point, but however his audience took the critique, it was familiar to southern readers.[40]

North of Palm Beach was the *Orlando Sun*, published by Jasper Lawrence Bowden, the president of Orlando's Imperial Mutual Benefit Association. The *Sun* celebrated the city's leadership appointments at the annual

Christian Methodist Episcopal conference in Jacksonville. It proudly announced that the director for "Negro Health" of the Julius Rosenwald Fund was coming to visit "the new State Tuberculosis Sanatorium at Orlando." It published a "Back to the Bible" column.[41] The *Orlando Sun* was—in its civic and religious coverage, in its association with insurance, and in its give-and-take with the Syndicate—the quintessential Black southern newspaper.

That paper was one of the Syndicate's several attempts in the second half of the 1930s to acquire more territory in Florida, a similar effort to that of the *St. Petersburg World*, published by locals Robert H. Saunders and Gilbert Leggett from 1935 to 1936.[42] Others were the *Ft. Myers World*, *Panama City World*, Tallahassee's *Florida Crusade*, Ft. Lauderdale's *Florida Guardian*, and Gainesville's *Florida American*. There was also the *Tampa Journal*, probably edited by Evelio Grillo, an Afro-Cuban from Ybor City just outside Tampa. Class, language, and culture divided Black Americans and Black Cubans. "Black Cubans still built dependent relationships with black Americans," Grillo explained in a later memoir, "especially our black American teachers, [with] whom we formed deep, affectionate bonds. But we lived clearly on the margins of black American society, while we worked out our daily existence in the black Cuban ghetto in Ybor City. Yet, our identity as black Americans developed strongly."[43] Whether Grillo was the paper's editor or not, it is clear from his account that the *Journal*'s association with the Syndicate demonstrated the Afro-Cuban population's identification with the rest of the Black South. It was a different kind of diasporic contact, but it was diasporic contact nonetheless.

Broader international relationships or interest in the larger diaspora was never the norm in the Syndicate, which usually relied on the Associated Negro Press for its international coverage. Commentary on foreign policy was almost always in service to domestic racial equality arguments. As Gerald Horne has demonstrated, Claude Barnett developed a substantial anticolonialist, Pan-African position that influenced much of the content of the ANP, particularly during the civil rights movement in the 1950s and 1960s, and that emphasis was nascent in the 1930s and developing in the 1940s. The papers of the SNS never matched Barnett's enthusiasm or his perspective, but the influence of his service ensured that such a worldview made its presence felt in Syndicate papers, even when there wasn't a Caribbean influence in their editorial positions.[44]

In March 1938 another Florida paper, the *Pensacola Courier*, joined the Syndicate. Nathaniel N. Baker, a bellman for several different hotels in the city, who had only a high school education, founded the *Courier* in 1935 and edited it until the early 1950s, when his wife, Cora, took over.[45] Pensacola was far from Miami in the northwestern corner of the state, the more traditionally southern region of the Florida panhandle. The couple's paper was correspondingly more reticent to directly attack white supremacists than was its neighbor to the south. The Bakers were more interested in practicing the practical radicalism of the paper's traditionally southern neighbors.

One of the *Courier*'s most sustained fights was common to much of the Black South in the late 1930s and early 1940s: the equalization of teacher salaries. This issue was spearheaded by the NAACP, which, as Tomiko Brown-Nagin has explained, "perceived African-American educators as being at once a core constituency of, and a political threat to, the association's agenda." The fight for equalizing teacher pay was important because of the fundamental injustice to Black teachers and the ancillary demeaning of Black children's education, but it would also help the NAACP "shore up its support among educators," who comprised "a large segment of the NAACP's middle-class constituency." The fight would dominate much of the wartime period.[46]

In 1941, the *Courier* covered the case of Vernon McDaniel, a Black school principal who sued the state, alleging discrimination in pay against Black teachers in Escambia County. In July, the U.S. District Court denied Florida's motion to dismiss the suit, which was seen as a de facto victory for McDaniel. The principal's wage of $165 per month was less than white principals' $200 per month. The judge, Augustine V. Long, commented that McDaniel and his counterparts were "qualified school teachers and have the civil right as such to pursue their profession without being subjected to discriminatory legislation on account of race or color." The following March, he signed a declaratory judgment mandating that Escambia County's Board of Public Instruction equalize teacher salaries by September 1943. It was a monumental victory in Pensacola, but McDaniel ultimately paid the price. In April 1944, the school board fired him for a variety of supposed sins, from firing a teacher unjustly to negligence of leadership, which had resulted in two white vendors being robbed near the campus.[47]

Fitting the strategy of practical radicalism that had been established by other southern newspapers in the early 1930s, the *Courier* allowed its reporting to do the work of demonstrating inequality in the McDaniel case, but it was willing to do far more when the site of an event wasn't local. In a 1946 editorial, for example, the paper lamented a notorious lynching of two Black couples in Monroe, Georgia. "It represents a pattern for suppressing the rights and liberty of minority groups in this country," the paper explained. "The pattern is that of Hitler." The *Courier* reminded readers that segregating and murdering minority groups was precisely the tactic of the Nazis. It then closed by foreshadowing a later pronouncement by Martin Luther King Jr.: "The injustice done to them is an injustice done to us all. The human rights violated in their case is the violation of the rights of us all."[48]

When looking at issues closer to home, though, the editorial strategy was less radical. Another editorial that year, for example, encouraged readers to play individual roles in eliminating prejudice by being "a good neighbor," refusing "to spread lies and rumors about people of a different race or religion," keeping "your children's minds free of prejudice," and encouraging "employers and employees to avoid discrimination." It was a simplistic plan that put the onus on the Black community rather than on the white, a distinctively southern mode of advocacy.[49] This strategy argued by its very nature that an event's location was as important as its content in determining editorial policy.

In December 1941, the *Jacksonville Progressive News* reported on a delay in the new trial that was supposed to be given to the Black men originally convicted for the murder of Robert Darcy in Pompano Beach. Darcy was an elderly white man whose robbery and murder had enraged the community. In response, local officials arrested dozens of Black men without warrants and held them without charges. After days of harsh and intense interrogation, police were able to secure confessions from some of those being held, and the courts quickly convicted them for the murder. The convictions, however, were overturned by the U.S. Supreme Court in *Chambers v. Florida* (1940), which ruled that the confessions by the defendants had been coerced. Their lawyer, Samuel McGill, struggled with the state over a new trial: "Eight years is a long time to fight one case, says the attorney, but if it takes time to do justice, then let us take time." The paper rejoiced in March 1942 when McGill finally freed the "Pompano Boys." "It came after a toil of nine long and hard years," the paper crowed, "but that which is worth having is worth working for no matter how many years it takes."[50]

In May 1942, the paper reported on two attacks on Black women made in Setzer stores, a local grocery chain. One had been struck with a milk bottle after an argument with a white customer, "who demanded that he be served before she did, despite the fact her turn was ahead of his." Another woman at another Setzer store saw she was being cheated by an employee weighing her potatoes. When she complained, the employee threatened to cut her throat. The *News* contacted the vice president of Setzer, who told the paper that the company was paying the medical bills of the woman attacked with the bottle but was unaware of the other incident. He told the paper of the company's policy of fairness to "all customers regardless of color, and [he] promised that matters of this kind would be looked into more carefully in the future."[51] In reporting the incidents and contacting the company for comment, the *Progressive News* was using the financial needs of Setzer to pit its statement of equality against the racist actions of its customers. It was, again, a demonstration of practical radicalism, recruiting a white corporation to denounce racial violence. This was the easiest way to walk the line between "the advancement of the Negro race and the creation of inter-racial harmony."[52]

In May 1944, the paper explained that a popular local minister had been denied the ability to vote in the Democratic primary after threats and intimidation by two white men outside the polling place. The minister wrote a lengthy statement describing his experience, and the *Progressive News* published it in total. "If we fail now to fight for the cause that we know is right, it will be a sad state for our children," the article explained. "We must stand up and equip ourselves as men. When God is for us, who can be against us?"[53] These were the words of a frustrated victim, but they were also fighting words, a radicalism really only displayed in southern papers when discussing the effort for the franchise.

In February 1946, the *News* reported on "scores of Negroes" who were "finding their way to the county courthouse where they are registering as Democrats in qualification for voting purposes" in the May primaries. They did so "despite threats believed to be from members of the Ku Klux Klan," including a series of phone calls to Porcher Taylor, editor and publisher of the rival *Florida Tattler*, another Black weekly. Florida's Democratic Executive Committee had ruled in January that Black voters could participate in the primary as long as they did so in segregated polling booths.[54]

In May, Albert McKeever, editor of the *Progressive News*, reported that a special edition of "the race-baiting, race-hating, anti-Negro Crescent City Journal" featured a "photostatic reproduction" of an edition of the *Progressive News* "with harsh and vulgar criticism directed at this publication relative to an unsolicited open letter furnished [to] this newspaper by Dr. Mary McLeod Bethune in which she urged a total registration of the Negro citizenry of the state." The paper covered the attacks in detail, along with attacks on Congressman Adam Clayton Powell and the *Pittsburgh Courier*, and noted that at least four copies of the hate-filled paper had been sent to the offices of the *News* with threatening letters attached. In addition four more letters arrived without copies of the paper. All of them "were poorly written, were nasty in content and too vulgar to reprint here." The unintimidated McKeever announced that he was turning all of the material over to the FBI.[55] Crescent City was almost ninety miles south of Jacksonville, and its paper and readership were not something that McKeever and Black citizens had to deal with every day, but the editor's response was still a bold public reaction to the threats.

And that reaction was needed. While copies of Black newspapers from outside the region were available, they were far from ubiquitous. Writing to Carl Murphy, publisher of the *Baltimore Afro-American*, in January 1940, publisher Davis Lee made it clear: "The *Afro* cannot be found in the majority of these cities in South Georgia," highlighting both that he didn't see larger northern papers as competition and that smaller southern papers were important.[56] From Miami to Pensacola to Jacksonville and throughout the rest of the South, local southern papers on the front lines of wartime fights for equality sought to advance Black people and create interracial harmony at the same time. The bulk of northern Black newspapers were good at the first, but southern Black newspapers realized that success at both required a subtlety that recognized that for local whites, Black advances and interracial harmony were contradictory aims.

Advancement also required a more quotidian presence in regions with substantial Black readerships. In February 1947, the Syndicate was back in the South Florida market when Cullen E. McCoy helped found the *Florida Record Dispatch* in West Palm Beach. McCoy was born in Georgia but had moved with his family south instead of north in a reverse of the Great Migration trend, ultimately graduating high school and working in the thriving hotel business in West Palm Beach. Like many others, however, he saw a need for a press that would cover the issues of his community and so founded the *Record Dispatch* with the aid of the Syndicate. With a circulation of roughly two thousand, it was not a massive paper, but it reached an underserved community.[57]

When those with the largest stake in a paper's outcome worked jobs that left them susceptible to the whims of the market economy, it usually left the small southern newspapers as casualties. The *Florida Record Dispatch* solved that problem, as did many of its contemporaries, by simply moving with its founder. At the onset of the 1950s, McCoy took a job as the "affable, efficient and congenial manager of the Paradise Hotel" in Tallahassee, and his paper followed him north, lasting until the summer of 1952.[58]

Such were the economic realities of publishing Black southern newspapers in the generation before the civil rights movement, even after the economic devastation of the Great Depression and the existential uncertainty of World War II had run their course.

Other editors and publishers responded to the new world in a familiar fashion, creating short-lived small-town papers facilitated by Scott syndication and printing. One was the *Marion County Citizen* from Ocala, Florida, first published in December 1952. One of its reports explained that local Black physicians, "without any outside help performed a major abdominal operation," the first time that any Black doctor in Marion County had performed a major operation without calling in white help. It was a precedent-setting event, not because the county's Black doctors were incapable, but because they were denied access to surgical facilities, and the *Citizen* sought to take advantage of the moment. "Perhaps the authorities at our hospital will eventually let the bars down," it commented in the classic form of southern practical radicalism, "when they see that our physicians will not let the fact that they cannot use the facilities there, stop them from doing the major operating for which they are prepared to do."[59]

Of course, the other classic southern strategy was for established Black papers to join the Syndicate to alleviate cost concerns. That is precisely what Ft. Lauderdale's *Florida Spur*, published since 1947, did in January 1954. Dr. Von D. Mizell, the paper's editor and publisher, was in a far more stable position than, say, the *Record Dispatch*'s Cullen McCoy. He was the chief of surgical services and medical director of Provident Hospital in Ft. Lauderdale. Mizell was from Dania, Florida, but he went to Atlanta to go to Morehouse. From there he went to Meharry Medical College and interned at Kansas City General Hospital Number 2 and J. A. Andrews Hospital in Tuskegee before ultimately returning to Ft. Lauderdale. Through the 1940s, Mizell developed close relationships with some of the medical faculty at Emory, and he traveled to Atlanta in the summers to work with them, the "first negro physician to be accepted for postgraduate work" at Grady Municipal Hospital. He was also the "first negro to run for office on the Democratic ticket in Florida." An article in the *Atlanta Daily World* described his 1948 run for the Broward County school board, and that relationship with Atlanta ultimately became a formal relationship with the Syndicate.[60]

Describing the variety of vocations of Black southern publishers, Melvin Tolson, a columnist for the *Washington Tribune*, wrote, "My contacts with editors and publishers, white and black, are very extensive. I know what they preach... and what they practice.... My pals are aristocrats and scrubwomen, scholars and dumbbells, millionaires and tramps." It was, C. K. Doreski explains, a "superficial class-leveling rhetoric," but it was also an instructive commentary on precisely what the Scott Syndicate had demonstrated in its collection of publishers from a variety of towns and cities.[61] Wealthy magnates and hotel bellmen created newspapers, and experienced journalists and novices contributed to the information traveling on the grapevine. A surgeon was in charge of the *Spur*.

Commenting on the *Brown* decision in May 1954, a *Spur* editorial described the building of a new elementary school in Broward County. It would be a sight, the paper predicted, that would be replicated all over the South in the future. The editorial noted a tendency among school boards "to build all elementary schools as far to the west of the Negro community as possible with the general idea in mind that for years to come, Negro children will be required to attend the schools in their district rather than migrate to distant white schools." It was a prescient statement about the insidious nature of zoning restrictions and their effects on integration. The paper praised the NAACP for its work in Florida and for school desegregation nationally. It suggested that the county's new elementary school be named for Harry T. Moore, an educator and founder of the first NAACP chapter in the state, who had been ruthlessly killed in a bombing of his house on Christmas 1951, the first NAACP member murdered for civil rights activism and a martyr to the cause of integrated education.[62]

Moore had founded Brevard County's NAACP branch in 1934 and eventually became the organization's Florida executive director. His most ardent and dangerous activism came in the infamous Groveland case, where four Black men were falsely accused of raping a white woman in July 1949. The mob action that ensued, the behavior of the local sheriff, and the show trial that ultimately convicted the three surviving suspects drew national and international attention, and Moore led the way among the state's Black activists to argue for the defendants' release. When the Supreme Court agreed in November 1951 that the two plaintiffs sentenced to death needed a new trial, the local sheriff simply shot them, claiming that they had attacked him. Six weeks later, Moore and his wife were killed when their house was bombed.[63] The murder of the Moores served as a dire warning not only to NAACP organizers in the region, but also to the journalists who covered them and became their southern mouthpieces. Journalistic caution was understandably a necessary response, since such pressure could quiet an editor or shutter a paper.

Chapter 3

The Carolinas

The Great Migration Black Population Changes (%)

City	1910–1940	1940–1970
Charleston, S.C.	0.6	−8.2
Charlotte, N.C.	−0.9	−3.4
Columbia, S.C.	−5.6	−8.3
Durham, N.C.	0.0	1.1
Greensboro, N.C.	0.7	−8.4
Greenville, S.C.	−9.0	0.1
Wilmington, N.C.	−6.1	−6.8
Winston-Salem, N.C.	−10.9	5.1

The listed cities are the ones large enough to be included in Census statistical materials. "The Great Migration, 1910 to 1970," U.S. Census Bureau, 13 September 2012, https://www.census.gov/dataviz/visualizations/020/508.php.

South Carolina

Daniel Jenkins, publisher of the *Charleston Messenger*, attached his paper to an orphanage that he managed, which allowed him to fund the paper through charitable donations, Charleston City Council contributions, and other methods. Jenkins was a Washingtonian who was praised by many white South Carolinians, and he even raised funds from whites for his orphanage. Historian Theodore Hemmingway has argued that Jenkins "proved more conservative than Booker T. Washington on relations between the races." It was a problematic position, but one that may have been necessary for simple survival. There had been a previous *Charleston Messenger*, for example, published by Francis P. Crum. It was one of eleven Black newspapers operating in 1895 in South Carolina. By 1899, there were only six in the state, and the original *Messenger* wasn't one of them. It was obviously a harsh climate for Black publishing and entrepreneurship.[1]

It was a harsh climate all the way around. Like the rest of the South, the Carolinas were already suffering prior to the onset of the Great Depression, and the economic downturn only exacerbated the effects of rural poverty and of Jim Crow. Poverty and violence necessarily ballooned the orphan population during the 1930s and simultaneously made that population more vulnerable. The second version of the *Messenger* billed itself as the "Big People's Weekly." Because the paper had a clear mission and one particular "sponsor," all of the advertisements were pushed to the final two pages. Most of them were local, but there were also advertisements for hair straighteners and patent medicines. The paper reported on local crime, local clubs, and local churches. But news from local orphanages was still the *Messenger*'s raison d'être.[2]

Another South Carolina paper associated with the Syndicate was Robert Baker's *Pee Dee Weekly* in Florence. Baker, a schoolteacher, produced the newspaper as an avocation, a model followed by so many others in the region. In 1940, for example, Baker made the relatively paltry annual salary of $360 as a South Carolina teacher, and papers like the *Weekly* rarely turned a profit. It was more likely that the news outlet was a drain rather than a supplement to Baker's meager finances, a situation emblematic of small-town Black journalists throughout the South. Still, the newspaper at times held the distinction of being "the largest Negro weekly in the state," its circulation hovering between 400 and 650 in the troubling Depression years between 1934 and 1936.[3]

The *Weekly*'s syndicated coverage revolved almost uniformly around stereotypical church and crime news.[4] There were, however, more substantive efforts by the paper. The *Weekly* called for social reforms, then worked to enact them. It wanted, for example, a public park and playground for Black people and established a committee to lobby the city council. The council agreed, probably motivated by the desire to stave off attempts at integrating white parks rather than by any sense of fairness, and the Black citizens of Florence received a new park. The paper also secured "better accommodations for colored people at the New Carolina Theater" through the work of another committee established for the purpose.[5] This was the practical radicalism that was available to Black editors. The *Weekly*'s various committees sought support from the white government and white businesses for additional facilities and improved accommodations, rather than pushing for integration of the facilities and accommodations that already existed, assuming quite rightly that the latter was not possible in the early 1930s.

In Greenville, South Carolina, the Syndicate created the short-lived *Carolina World* in 1934. After several months, the SNS built a new paper in the city on the ashes of that effort, founding the *Greenville World* in October.[6] Greenville was facing a series of race and class issues unique to the state. In a powerful June 1934 editorial, for example, the *World* had complained that stores in the Black wards of Greenville were owned principally by "members of foreign races." They were "neighborhood parasites" that "suck the very life blood" from "Negro customers and give nothing in return for their trade and support." They didn't advertise in Black newspapers nor employ Black "clerks or delivery boys." They made their money off the Black population and sent it back to "Greece or Sicily." The *World* encouraged readers to pressure the store owners and managers to invest in the local Black community by boycotting those establishments. "The pathway to racial progress and independence is not strewn with roses and sweet scented flowers," it explained. "The American Negro has been emancipated from human bondage," but "he is still an economic slave, industrial serf and social ward," and nothing would change without economic action. "Lets stop fattening frogs for snakes and enriching other people to use their wealth and power in crushing and pauperizing our race."[7] It was a radical message that would find echoes throughout the twentieth century in urban areas in the North and West. Still, in November 1934, when "six white men, indicted as members of a Ku Klux band," committed a Greenville lynching and were found not guilty, the Syndicate used Associated Negro Press coverage because the local paper feared reprisals for such a report.[8] Local immigrants were fair game, but attacking the behavior of local whites required the cover brought by syndication.

In 1934, the *Charleston Telegram*, published by S. E. Anderson, joined the Syndicate. It was a relatively saccharine effort compared to its state counterparts when it came to racial issues, but there were glimpses of an approximate radicalism.[9] In an otherwise soft editorial about the need for better teachers in Black schools, for example, the *Telegram* included "those who do not believe in and patronize Negro enterprises" as one of the categories for which "teachers should be discharged." The bulk of the editorial then preached about expertise in subjects and people of good character, but it closed on a different note: "We need more teachers with Race pride and sense of dignity, racial respect and worth. A person cannot advance higher than his race and the race cannot advance without the aid of members of the race." The best way to support the race was to "patronize racial institutions" because creating an economic infrastructure was the only way for the race to succeed. This argument clearly benefited from Washingtonian thought, but it made connections that Tuskegee's leader might not have chosen to make. "I have noticed a number of Negro school teachers passing a Negro grocery store to patronize a white grocer," the editorial closed. "I do not call this a qualified teacher."[10] This was an interesting bar for qualification, but it demonstrated that there was a latent radicalism in the "cast down your bucket where you are" philosophy.

Such was not the exception in small-town coverage. It was often the rule. The *Anderson Messenger*, founded by former janitor Lewis Linden Branch in northwestern South Carolina, was similar in style and scope.[11] Founded in 1939 by Davis Lee and edited by John Henry McCray, the *Carolina Lighthouse* did much the same on a larger scale. The one surviving issue of the *Lighthouse* modeled the practical radicalism of southern papers. Its front page blared a headline announcing that a local man had shot his wife, then reported on the desire of Black Missouri to see the *Missouri ex rel. Gaines* (1938) decision enforced and on the work of Northwestern University students to battle Jim Crow in Evanston, Illinois. Such was the model. Sensational crime on the front page was followed by calls for racial change in places far from the site of the publication. The edition's lead editorial lamented, "Seldom does one find advertisements of Negro-owned companies in Negro newspapers." That wasn't altogether true, but the writer continued: "The tacit fact is that most colored companies do not believe newspaper advertising is a paying proposition. Yet white companies choose it. They must get results."[12] As so many before it, the *Lighthouse* used white decision-making as the measuring stick of legitimacy in attempting to convince its readers of proper conduct.

Lee soon moved on to other endeavors, McCray took over the operation, and the paper began its long relationship with the Syndicate. The original *Lighthouse* was published in Charleston, but in July 1940, McCray combined it with the rival *People's Informer*, headquartered in Columbia, and the resulting *Lighthouse and Informer* became South Carolina's most influential newspaper in the generation before *Brown*.[13]

McCray was born on August 25, 1910, near Youngstown, Florida, and grew up in Lincolnville and Charleston, South Carolina, before attending Talladega College. There, he got his start in journalism, working for the Talladega College monthly, the *Mule's Ear*, where he tackled everything from world peace to the beauty of sunrises and sunsets at the college. After his education, he took a job as the city editor of the *Charleston Messenger*. Feeling restricted, McCray decided to start his own paper, the *Lighthouse*, along with Lee, and from there go it alone in the summer of 1940. McCray's editorship of the *Lighthouse and Informer* lasted until 1954, when he joined the staff of the *Baltimore Afro-American*.[14]

Like so many others, McCray went into journalism because he was frustrated at the amount and type of representation Black southerners were getting in the mainstream white press. In 1940, he began a column called "The Need for Changing," which highlighted civil rights issues like poor academic facilities, white men preying on Black women, lynchings, and equal pay for Black teachers. "What has the South ever done for the Negro?" he asked. "Nothing they didn't have to do. Everything that has been done has been done by the Negro, or by the threat of Federal court action." His activism also led him to create the Progressive Democratic Party in 1944. His associate editor, Osceola McKaine, also played a role in creating the party. A World War I veteran, a merchant seaman, and a Belgian cabaret owner in previous decades, McKaine had returned home to South Carolina to fight for civil rights. The party didn't win any elections, but it did increase the Black role in South Carolina's electoral politics, and its conduit to the Black population of the state was the *Lighthouse and Informer*.[15]

Journalism historian Sid Bedingfield has argued that McCray and his paper worked to "spur black political engagement by framing the civil rights struggle to emphasize African-American agency and self-assertion during a time when strategies of accommodation and negotiation remained dominant in the deep South." In so doing, McCray "redefined the meaning of full citizenship for black Carolinians and linked it directly to political confrontation." Such stands made his *Lighthouse and Informer*, along with the state's other major Black weekly, the *Palmetto Leader*, the dominant activist voices for civil rights in postwar South Carolina.[16]

McCray advocated for equal teacher pay and school facilities. He criticized the governor, James Byrnes, for not appointing Black representatives to a committee to plan for postwar life in South Carolina. In January 1950, McCray was indicted for libel for reporting that a Black man accused of raping a prominent white Greenwood woman had claimed to have consensual sex with her. He never named the woman, but under South Carolina law he could still be prosecuted for libel, and he was. Willie Tolbert was executed for the supposed crime, and McCray pled guilty to the libel charge despite standing by his reporting. In response to the guilty plea, a Greenwood judge gave McCray a year in prison and a $5,000 fine, but reduced the jail time to sixty days and cut $2,000 from the fine, leaving him with a $3,000 bill. The following year, however, a judge ruled that two out-of-state speeches had violated McCray's probation and ordered him to serve his sixty days on a chain gang. His supporters were outraged, but McCray saw the sentence as proof that he was doing something right. "Somewhere along the way I was bound to catch it," he wrote. "I accept it as nothing more than another step in our battle to obtain respect, and our rights as Americans." Following his sentence, he returned to his work without regret, claiming, "I'd do it again." He was "proud" of his indictment, "and I shall always be," he said. "I had nothing about which to be ashamed."[17] It was the sort of trouble that a Black southern editor advocating for equal rights and criticizing the governor had to expect as part of the job.

In May 1942, the paper had commented on the possibility of South Carolina eliminating or modifying its white primary. The state's "1876 rule" excluded Black citizens from the Democratic Party "who did not vote for Wade Hampton in 1876." Hampton was the state's Redeemer governor, a Confederate veteran whose election effectively ended Reconstruction in the state and ushered in the long period of white retrenchment that had yet to end as of World War II. His election had been facilitated by violence and intimidation designed to keep Black voters from the polls. Therefore, those who had voted in that election were white, angry, and racially motivated. If there were any Black Democrats in the state who had voted for Hampton, they were few and, as of 1942, probably dead. The rule was, according to McCray, "a state-wide malady" that needed to be eliminated.[18]

By 1943, McCray had made himself an institution in the state. Churches were asking him to give speeches on special occasions. He was in correspondence with the governor, Olin Johnston, and when the paper ran a special editorial on the role of Black soldiers fighting in World War II, Johnston sent McCray a statement for the paper declaring his pleasure "with the way the negroes of our state are doing their part in the war effort" both in the military and in support roles back home. "The people of South Carolina are glad to know that there is full cooperation between the colored and white people in the matter of winning this war," he wrote. "We are not unmindful of what your race is doing in an orderly and cooperative way to bring a glorious victory to the allied nations."[19] It was pandering and paternalistic, but it was closer to sincerity than many southern governors approached, and it was written directly to McCray himself.

"I hope you will continue your work," one correspondent said. "You are writing some fine editorials, and do not be afraid to say and do what is best for all concerned." Another commented, "You are in a position of tremendous power for good in moulding the thought and attitude of your readers—

for alas most people today read the newspapers *first*." Companies had much the same reaction. North Carolina Mutual Life Insurance, for example, was very conscious of the content of the papers in which it advertised. When paying for an ad in the *Lighthouse and Informer* in 1943, the company complimented the paper on its coverage of a Carolina prison farm, which had resulted in the promise of a state investigation, and on its call for Black representatives on local draft boards. Meanwhile, a local minister fawned that "never before has the State of South Carolina had a newspaper whose editor had GUTS enough and the proper approach therewith to sponsor the interests of a RACE so deeply in need of help." The paper was "perhaps the greatest thing which has come to Columbia, in its history, for colored people."[20]

McCray's position put him in the role of confessor to many. One correspondent, for example, wrote to him about his pain upon hearing a white man speaking to a Black woman with disrespect; the man had defended white people and blamed Black people in a discussion of the Detroit race riot of 1943. "I got sick from the portion of the conversation that I heard," the correspondent told McCray, describing racial epithets and paternalistic whitesplaining that preyed on the woman's sense of inferiority. "At that point I was forced to leave."[21] The letter wasn't written to the editor seeking publication, but rather was written to a known sympathetic ear. Such was the stature of the Black editor during Jim Crow.

That prominence could prompt equal and opposite reactions from local whites. In August 1943, Columbia's police court reporter declared that the *Lighthouse and Informer* "has done more than any 1,000 other things I can think of to agitate conditions" in the city. Columbia authorities threatened to launch a grand jury investigation against McCray and his paper as revenge against his activist stances. McCray told C. A. Scott about the potential trouble at home, and Scott replied that "at times and under certain circumstances it is best to avoid provocative statements." It was this sense of practicality that many saw as subverting any broader radicalism. "I think our best strategy as a minority group," Scott told McCray, "is to take more of a positive attitude rather than a challenging attitude which defies a lot of things that some of the intolerant prejudiced white people say."[22] By emphasizing the Black talented tenth, he seemed to be saying, we give lie to the myth of white supremacy. Radicalism simply makes us its victims.

This was advice that McCray was disinclined to take. In January 1944, the paper explained that there were two primary forces that Black South Carolinians were struggling against: "those white people yet unconvinced as to 'rights and justice' and those traitors within the race." The vast majority of the effort was focused on those "unyielding white people," but more focus was needed in "weeding out the traitors within." That April, however, it was the unyielding whites who posed the largest threat. In response to an announcement "that colored citizens through their Democratic organization, planned to have their own complete ticket in the general election," white lawmakers, who were in the process of changing primary laws in response to the Supreme Court, decided that a way to thwart Black electoral efforts was to deny their voter registrations and convince more white people to participate in general elections.[23]

To aid in the endeavor to get Black people to the polls and in response to frustration with their exclusion from the Democratic Party's white primary, the *Lighthouse and Informer* published a plan to create a new state organization, the Colored Democratic Party. The party would sever democratic advocacy from the racist white Democrats and provide Black voters an "escape from the mediocre and neglected Republican party which has forsaken them." It would also serve as a voter registration vehicle and an opportunity to run candidates so that Black voters need not compromise their values. When officials from North Carolina Mutual read about the plan, A. J. Clement wrote McCray to "express the hope that you will follow through on this," reminding the publisher that "I endeavored to sell you the idea that this forming of our own party would give our group the stature and power that we wanted." At the same time, the move prompted significant protest from the Republican Party, which had always counted on Black votes as the backbone of its southern strategy. The party's white state chair self-servingly wrote to McCray in an attempt to convince him that steering Black voters away from the Republicans was counterproductive.[24]

The paper advocated for other civil rights legislation as well. The long list of the *Lighthouse and Informer*'s 1944 policies and programs included fighting for a new president of Morris College, working for a more progressive leadership group for the Palmetto State Teachers Association, and a statewide speaking tour urging educational and voting equalities. McCray kept tabulations on instances of Black policemen in forty-one different southern cities and shared that information with the Southern Regional Council for wider circulation. His paper demanded the integration of public services, Black employment opportunities in public works jobs, and a "firm denunciation of those race members 'hostile' to progressive programs."[25]

In March 1945, the southern and western regions of the National Negro Publishers Association (NNPA), with C. A. Scott serving as vice president for the southern region, called for a special meeting at Mississippi's Jackson College "to work out strategy for fighting for equal education in the Southern States," particularly in response to the Supreme Court's *Missouri ex rel. Gaines* decision. At that meeting, Scott praised McCray, declaring that because of "his leadership in the Progressive Democratic Party, there are more Negroes registered and qualified to vote in South Carolina than at any time previously since the Reconstruction Period."[26]

McCray's circulation analysis for 1945 showed 950 papers going to Charleston, with another 28 going to North Charleston. There were 532 copies going to Rock Hill, 555 to Remini, 297 to Sumter, 234 to Welterboro, 177 to Spartanburg, 162 to Graniteville, and 152 to Dillon. Meanwhile, there were 150 distributed in the paper's hometown of Columbia and various quantities in all of the other towns and hamlets of the state, for a total circulation of 10,373 in South Carolina. This is an example of the spread of tiered influence to the boundaries of a state, an evidentiary breakdown not available in the historical record for smaller Black southern newspapers. But the *Lighthouse and Informer* even went beyond those tiers. There were also 511 papers going to neighboring North Carolina. There were 9 papers going to Alabama, 5 to Florida, and 22 to Georgia. People in Connecticut, California, New York, and Wisconsin all received papers. There was even one subscriber in Squirrel Island, Maine. All told, McCray's circulation analysis for 1945 counted 11,044 copies of the paper reaching all parts of the country, though 94 percent of them stayed in South Carolina.[27]

Since McCray's effort was a comparatively small operation, the publisher also served as reporter, editorialist, accountant, subscription manager, and even bill collector, writing to those with delinquent accounts and urging payment: "you know how the Lighthouse operates, how urgently necessary it is to obtain collections on time and avoid all losses." Explaining to one submitter why his material went unpublished, McCray demurred, "We are very much pressed for space. We must carry a certain percentage of serviced news, that is news we pay various news agencies to send us through their reporters that The Lighthouse might have good national news." That could be a large proposition. "When our news copy is too heavy, then we must condense the whole batch of news matters so as to include some from all parties. When conditions improve we hope to add a few more pages to our paper."[28]

That didn't happen, but McCray's star was still on the rise. In late 1945, for example, the city of Columbia declared January 11, 1946, to be Joe Louis Day, demonstrating the fighter's near-universal appeal outside his native Detroit. The Columbia recognition was, Louis wrote to McCray, "one of the greatest honors ever accorded to me. I will remember this day for the rest of my life." He noted that he had long admired the work of the *Lighthouse and Informer* and asked McCray if he could visit while in Columbia "so that I can have the added thrill of personally meeting you."[29] The *Lighthouse and Informer*'s crusading activism during World War II led to more of the same after the war's end, often putting McCray in harm's way for his trouble.

Charles F. Behling has argued that the *Lighthouse and Informer* had a strong editorial voice on racial issues "with fair, although not adequate, news coverage. Local news seems especially weak." The paper lasted until 1954, and McCray claimed that "the labor problem" ultimately did in the enterprise. The *Lighthouse and Informer* would train workers, but those workers would move on to other employers for higher salaries. "Then too," he explained, "by 1954 we had achieved our goals. Throughout the paper's history we were dedicated to winning the right to vote and to breaking up the most gross educational discrimination. By 1954 we had won these fights, at least in law." Though the paper had reached a circulation of around 14,000 during World War II, it dipped to roughly 6,400 by 1952 and remained at that level for its remaining years.[30]

Its work, however, remained vital. Andrew Secrest has noted that Black citizens were "just as thoroughly segregated in the pages of South Carolina newspapers" as they were in public schools.[31] Coverage of those citizens was largely limited to civil rights groups and crime. As Sid Bedingfield has explained, the postwar *Lighthouse and Informer* attempted to frame "the civil rights struggle to emphasize African-American agency and self-assertion during a time when strategies of accommodation and negotiation remained dominant in the deep South." Bedingfield gives the paper and its editor, McCray, credit for "redefin[ing] the meaning of full citizenship for black Carolinians and link[ing] it directly to political confrontation."[32] The paper that was so important for the Syndicate during World War II stayed with the group until 1949, remaining perhaps its most radical representative.

In October 1945, for example, following the war's end, the *Lighthouse and Informer* produced a scathing editorial against white liberal groups that, "in the South, are more mythical than real." The paper did not denigrate "temporary alliances" with white liberals and admitted that "the salvation of the south is wrapped up in a final union among colored and white southerners." But the white liberal program, the paper argued, "calls for the stamping out of every purely Negro organization and the handcuffing of all Negroes into a new body where they would fit into the party's machinery." The remedy for the problem was simple: "Let us southern Negroes build our organizations," and "let us have more of them."[33]

A November editorial commented on the police killing of a local Black veteran. A coroner's jury had absolved the officer of fault, claiming that the shooting was "in the discharge of duty." The paper was predictably displeased: "It seems established that all police officers kill Negroes 'in discharge of duty,' that they ofttimes beat them brutally 'in discharge of duty.'" A furious *Lighthouse* suggested that if white South Carolina "will not move to destroy this inhuman practice, the colored people ought to move to erase it. They would then be acting 'in discharge of duty.'"[34]

In January 1946, the paper cited a report from the Palmetto State Teachers Association's Committee on Transportation that explained that in 1944 the state had spent $687,642 on busing for white high school students and $2,045 for busing Black students: "In other words, the state spent three-tenths of one percent of funds for high school transportation on Negroes." For comparison, the paper explained that "forty-four percent of the state's population is colored and fifty-six percent white." When this disparity was combined with discrepancies in facilities and other forms of funding, a depressed *Lighthouse* concluded that "all the talk made in some circles about postwar opportunities and development of more trained people is no more than theory."[35]

Another syndicated editorial that month criticized Black crime, particularly from returning soldiers who "seem to feel that they are immune to law and order." This lawbreaking was a hindrance to the paper's attempts at racial justice because "every Negro," the editorial explained, "who encourages friction and exemplifies poor breeding and integrity hurts the entire race." It was a well-worn argument, but coming from a paper with the credentials of the *Lighthouse* the jeremiad had a legitimacy that made it sound less southern and self-hating than similar declension narratives published by its peers.[36]

In January 1947, McCray stumped in the pages of his paper for a broader approach to rights advocacy by the NAACP. He noted an NAACP committee formed in North Carolina that had been tasked with liaising with the state legislature "in the interest of having introduced and passed this year bills which would reduce conditions not desirable and correct educational inequalities," and he hoped that South Carolina and other southern branches of the group would adopt such a strategy. There was certainly no guarantee that it would work, but McCray was frustrated that the NAACP's approach "has been restricted to court suits, which may or may not be the easiest way out." So often, the southern Black press was criticized for emphasizing the sins of its own community over those of white state governments, but this was different. McCray's criticism was in aid of adopting better strategies specifically to better deal with those governments.[37]

When, for example, Thurgood Marshall and the NAACP planned a voting lawsuit in South Carolina to challenge the state's white primary, the *Lighthouse and Informer* enthusiastically endorsed the strategy. South Carolina had repealed all of its laws relating to primary elections in 1944 in response to *Smith v. Allwright*, leaving primaries completely free of any government oversight and thus allowing political parties to conduct business as they saw fit—as private entities without any government involvement. It was a strategy that was successful in allowing southern Democrats to keep Black voters from the primaries, and other southern states were beginning to adopt it. The paper, however, was hopeful that "after two years of waiting and study, we may soon see a test of the move."[38]

When Greenville resident Willie Earle was lynched, the *Lighthouse and Informer* demonstrated that it was not intimidated and covered the case. Earle was killed by a mob of taxi drivers in Pickens County after a local cab driver was found murdered by his vehicle. Locals assumed Earle to be the driver's last passenger, and thus he was arrested and held in the Pickens County jail, only to be pulled out by a group of the victim's white colleagues and lynched. McCray's paper reported the incident and also reported that federal oversight and interest in the case led to the capture and indictment of the perpetrators. The paper was "comforted and much encouraged by the excellent work and finesse with which our law enforcement officers, those of the FBI and of Governor J. Strom Thurmond attacked the case until its apparent solution." But it also reported that even though more than two dozen men had admitted to participating in the mob, and there was substantial evidence that the defendants were also present, an all-white jury acquitted all of them. To drive home the injustice, the *Lighthouse* even published a picture of Earle's mutilated body on the front page.[39]

The incident dovetailed with the introduction of a new federal antilynching bill in Congress, and the *Lighthouse* channeled its indignation over the acquittal of Earle's murderers into advocacy for the new law, making the case that the jury's decisions were all the evidence the federal government needed to demonstrate the vital necessity of the bill. In response to the acquittal, the National Negro Publishers Association met in an emergency session in Atlanta, producing telegrams for the president, attorney general, and members of Congress making that very case. The body, hosted by Scott at Syndicate headquarters, noted in its telegram to Truman that the acquittals represented "the most contemptuous disregard for moral consciousness and basic social laws in the recent history of our nation" and urged his support for the bill. In a vicious editorial in the *Lighthouse*, McCray argued that the whole indictment process was simply an excuse for white southerners to claim that there was progress enough in places like South Carolina to make federal antilynching legislation unnecessary, to give them a better argument against federal overreach. The acquittal, he argued, proved the point, demonstrating that lynching was a function of collusion among all whites in power, even those who were not at the site of the lynching itself. "Lynching, the sport of illiterates, and semi-illiterates as was the case at Greenville, is a collusive affair," McCray wrote. "It is an incorporation, doing business on the strength of the support it gets from tributaries." Even if the federal law did not pass, South Carolina could take its own step in the right direction by including Black members on juries, providing an accurate representation of the community. "Lynchers would be less inclined to lynch were they assured beforehand that their penalty would be partially fixed by the people they wronged."[40]

When the Southern Regional Council met in April 1947 in Columbia, the *Lighthouse and Informer* covered the meeting assiduously, emphasizing in particular the speech of clergyman Dr. Charles L. Hill, who argued that African Americans "ask no special privilege." They just wanted the same basic rights as any human deserved, "and [they] will sink or swim by [their] own wit." It was a message that the paper had offered time and again. Opponents of rights for Black people claimed that Black activists wanted an end to racial distinctions (amalgamation), which, they assumed, would "usher in an era of general decadence and danger to white people." Nothing, the *Lighthouse* argued, could be further from the truth. The Black population was just as proud of its culture as white people were of theirs and also saw amalgamation, or race mixing, as a problem. They just wanted what every human deserved.[41]

The principal demonstration of that argument in the summer of 1947 was Jackie Robinson. Robinson was an army veteran and a former four-sport star at UCLA. He was also a proponent of integration. He had been court-martialed (and acquitted) for challenging an illegally segregated army bus at Fort Hood in Texas. Robinson was playing baseball with the Kansas City Monarchs when he was approached by Branch Rickey, the general manager of the Brooklyn Dodgers. Rickey was no racist, but he was also no civil rights activist. He was a baseball man who wanted to win and wanted to bring more people to the ballpark. Black sportswriters had been calling for integration for years, but Rickey was the one who finally listened. He knew that Negro Leagues games filled stadiums and that the talent was very good. He decided to take advantage of it. Robinson agreed to be the test case and promised Rickey that he wouldn't respond to the inevitable racist provocations he would receive. He played the 1946 season with the Dodgers' AAA team in Montreal before joining the Dodgers in 1947.[42]

The *Lighthouse* covered his every move that summer, as did all of its contemporaries. Jackie Robinson was the most important story in the country, but particularly for the Black press. The sports pages of the *Lighthouse* and other Black newspapers covered Robinson's games, his interviews, and his life on the road. That coverage often sat beside stories of Negro Leagues teams and games that would soon be made obsolete by the effort that Robinson was making.[43]

William Simons has made the case that the Black press "tended to view itself as the prime force behind the signing of Robinson," claiming in column after column that a particular writer had been stumping for the change for years. That attitude was dominant in northern papers but was largely absent in the South, a region that didn't have major league teams. There, papers like the *Lighthouse and Informer* were just happy that Robinson was signed and succeeding.[44]

The papers were celebrating all the while knowing that integration was killing the autonomous Black business model that also sustained the Black press. As Brian Carroll has demonstrated, Black newspapers began reporting almost exclusively on Robinson's baseball exploits with the Dodgers, and "little room or resource[s] remained to spend on Negro league teams." If that were not bad enough, "the stance of the black papers towards the [Negro] leagues became paternalistic and highly critical." There were consequences, however, that would be prophetic for the Black press. The Negro Leagues' autonomy allowed Black control of the endeavor. In the white-controlled majors, however, "black ball players had to play by someone else's rules and always as a minority."[45]

Robinson was Rookie of the Year in 1947, taking the place of Joe Louis, who would retire (for the first time) two years later, as the ultimate sports figure in the Black community. Black spectators flocked to major league ballparks. Robinson was such a sensation that other teams began seeing the benefits of Black players not only for team success, but for box office draw. Five National League clubs set new season attendance records in 1947, thanks largely to Robinson. And so others decided to follow Brooklyn's lead. Larry Doby integrated the American League when the Cleveland Indians signed him that July. But when the Black population was spending its money at white parks, they weren't spending it at Black parks. The success of the integration of baseball also meant the doom of the Negro Leagues. In 1948, Satchel Paige and other major players from Black baseball were brought to the majors, thus taking the star power from their Black counterparts. In 1948, the Negro National League folded. The Negro American League stuck around until 1960 but was never the same. It was an object lesson for the Black press, a vital Black industry that was essentially dependent on segregation not only for its survival, but for its unique relevance.[46]

The *Lighthouse and Informer* was different than many of its southern contemporaries, but it was clearly a southern paper. In May 1947, McCray explained that "two men and a woman, all colored, have been put to death so far this year for the murder of other colored people," with another man waiting on death row. It was unquestionably a positive development, he argued, because it demonstrated that South Carolina courts were taking Black victims of crime seriously, and it augured well for the possibility of diminished violence within the Black community. He took those to task who denigrated the executions just because those executed were Black. Such was actually a show of respect. He cited a variety of cases where white lawyers had referred to such cases as "just a darky affair," and courts had provided relatively light sentences for violent crimes against Black victims. "It doesn't make any sense to squeal and howl about lynchings," McCray argued, "and at the same time, and in the same brutal, ugly fashion, [be] snuffing the lives of hundreds of times as many of their own number." It was a strong case—not the typical southern jeremiad against bad Black behavior—but the editorial never mentioned, for example, that all of those convicted were tried by white juries.[47]

One year later, the paper encouraged readers to "pay no attention to the handful of southern officials conducting what they call a 'revolt' against civil rights." That revolt was being discussed after white southern Democrats felt disaffected over Truman's Committee on Civil Rights and his order to end segregation in the military. The *Lighthouse* believed that the talk was just talk, "and so long as they refuse and fear to break away from it in toto, there's no need for concern." White southern Democrats would, of course, do just that, giving birth to the Dixiecrats and ultimately dashing the paper's hope "for building a greater unity between the races in the South."[48]

In March 1949, the *Lighthouse* blasted the state legislature for applauding the grand dragon of the Ku Klux Klan, who had spoken in Columbia. McCray had attended the meeting, writing about the ignorant and nonsensical philosophy of the group. At its conclusion, he had "a feeling of emptiness and that the time had been wasted on seeing and hearing nothing which makes sense." McCray's coverage was important because it humanized the group and made it less frightening. He knew that many "are really scared to death of the Ku Klux Klan," and he used his simple and straightforward reporting to show the ridiculous and ignorant message that the grand dragon espoused.[49] It was an effort at demystification that pulled the veneer of invincibility from the otherwise mysterious terrorist group.

McCray felt the effects of his activism soon after his paper's time with the SNS ended, in particular with his 1950 libel trial. But he remained proud of his crusading journalism, which represented the more radical side of southern practical radicalism.[50]

North Carolina

North Carolina was more urban than its southern counterpart, creating a larger potential influence for papers at each tier of state reception. This raised the stakes, and the opportunities, for those attempting to take advantage of SNS services to produce a contribution to the broader Black information network. Henry Houston's *Charlotte Post*, for example, used the SNS for syndication and printing. "I have never had but one job outside of the newspaper business. That was when I worked as an insurance agent for several years," said Houston. He began work as an office boy for a newspaper, then worked for Charlotte's Southern Newspaper Union for eighteen years. Houston had been born in Mecklenburg County and lived in Charlotte all his life. "I attended the city schools and have never been to nobody's college. I went to school at night for a short time but, for the most part, my education was limited to the grades." As an adult, Houston fought tirelessly for educational opportunities for Black children and sent his son to college. He also helped found the local Negro Citizens League, which fought for voting rights.[51]

Houston ran his newspaper out of his house, and at the time of his Works Progress Administration (WPA) interview, he had a small print shop behind the building. He and his son operated the paper and the press. "We do job printing in connection with the other work. We belong to the Associated Negro Press as well as other news agencies. The paper is edited weekly and is sent all over North and South Carolina. The present weekly circulation is about forty two thousand copies."[52]

The *Afro-American* described Houston as a "moderate crusader"—someone who worked for several civic and religious causes, but was broadly moderate in his political views. Charlotte, for example, like many urban areas, was a hub for the "numbers racket," and when a turf war developed between two rival factions, the *Post* was positioned perfectly to cover a series of bombings that rocked the city and simultaneously to lament the moral failings that led to such actions. Such was the equivocation involved in moderate crusading.[53]

In 1935, Black Charlotte was inflamed by a case of prisoner abuse, when five prison officials were arrested after two short-term convicts lost their feet to frostbite after being placed in unheated solitary confinement cells. The chains around their legs had cut off circulation, adding to the effect of the cold. After the amputations, an investigation led to the arrest of the five men for torture, but after a week of hearings in July, two guards were freed by superior court judge William Warlick, who felt that the state had not provided enough evidence for the jury to consider the case. Warlick then reduced the charges of the prison doctor and one additional guard to "neglect of duty," a simple misdemeanor. Finally, after all the reductions, an all-white jury acquitted the three remaining prison officials anyway.[54] The *Post*'s coverage, and thus that of the Syndicate, was straightforward and objective, but such stories didn't need commentary about an inherent lack of fairness to drive home the point. Syndication took a story that would have been at best a state-level phenomenon, at worst a report only in the local Black press, and spread it around the South and much of the Midwest.

Houston's *Post* was emblematic of the familial nature of local Black journalism. His son helped with the project, sometimes serving as its editor. Family journalism and moderate crusading were common in North Carolina, like the work of Robert Smith Jervay and his *Cape Fear Journal*, a Syndicate paper from Wilmington.

Jervay's father, William, had been enslaved in South Carolina and escaped during the Civil War to fight for the Union army. He then returned to South Carolina during Reconstruction and served in the state constitutional convention, followed by stints in the House and Senate. So when Robert was born in 1873 in Summerville, he had a clear model for activism. Robert attended Avery Institute in Charleston, then Claflin University in Orangeburg. Meanwhile, his father retired from politics and became a Methodist minister. After Robert Jervay's education, he got his start in journalism by printing his father's church newspaper, the *Christian Star*.[55]

In 1892, Jervay moved to Columbus County, North Carolina, and worked as a bookkeeper for a local lumber company. He still printed church programs and newspapers when possible, and in 1901, he founded the R. S. Jervay Printing Company. It was a family operation, with Jervay's wife and children helping to manually typeset and feed the press. In 1911, he moved the company and the family to Wilmington. The big city was no salve against the racial turmoil of the early century, so one of Jervay's children, Henry, encouraged him to create a Black newspaper for the Wilmington area. In 1927, he did. The *Cape Fear Journal* began as a four-page weekly, selling for five cents. The following year, Jervay acquired a linotype machine and a flatbed press, standardizing the operation and even earning the respect of the white *Wilmington Star*, which proclaimed in 1929 that the *Journal* was "one of the most constructive Negro papers in the South."[56]

Another of Robert's sons, Paul Reginald Jervay, worked during the 1930s for both the *Norfolk Journal and Guide* and the *Chicago Defender* and taught printing at his alma mater, Hampton Institute, before returning in 1938 to North Carolina to work for H. E. Fontillo-Nanton, who owned Raleigh's *Carolina Tribune* (Jervay was also associated with Durham's *Carolina Times*, a Scott Syndicate paper).[57] Another son, Thomas Clarence Jervay, returned to Wilmington in 1937 to work with his father after finishing a degree in business administration at Virginia State. When Robert died in 1941, Thomas took over the business, renaming the paper the *Wilmington Journal* in 1945. Under his leadership, the *Journal* championed civil rights, argued for the hiring of Black policemen, encouraged Black voting and political candidates, and fought for affordable housing for Black Wilmington residents. Such efforts continued after the formal beginning of the first wave of the civil rights movement, as the Jervays used their journalism and their fortune to help promote Black equality.[58]

But when, for example, a "colored Guest House and Service Club" opened for Black soldiers at Camp Davis in Wilmington in December 1941, the *Journal* greeted it warmly. It was "one of the first colored Service Clubs and Guest Houses in the country." Nowhere in the *Journal* or Syndicate coverage was criticism of the segregated nature of the camps, less because of a willingness to be segregated and more because of the celebratory nature of the grand opening of the club and the close temporal proximity of

Pearl Harbor and the U.S. declaration of war. There were three Black regiments at Camp Davis, constituting almost a third of the force there in the early days of the war. The masthead on the paper's editorial page exemplified the kind of dueling goals evident in the Camp Davis coverage and in much of the southern Black press: "This Newspaper Is Dedicated to the Advancement of the Negro Race and to the Creation of Inter-Racial Harmony."[59] Those goals were sometimes in harmony and at other times completely contradictory, and thus it became a line almost impossible to walk.

Louis E. Austin, who founded the *Carolina Times* in Durham by buying the *Standard Advertiser* with a loan of $250 from the president of Mechanics and Farmers Bank, was engaged in much the same project, with fewer compromises or contradictions. Austin was fearless in arguing for Black education, voting rights, and civil equality. He condemned the Ku Klux Klan. He criticized the Commission on Interracial Cooperation—a southern organization founded in 1919 to advocate for "legal and economic justice" and "better educational and living conditions" for Black southerners without upending segregation—for its ineffectiveness. He attempted to convince Thomas R. Hocutt, a graduate of North Carolina College for Negroes, to integrate the graduate school of the all-white University of North Carolina. Austin's radicalism brought him under criticism from Durham's and North Carolina's influential Black citizens, among them C. C. Spaulding, president of North Carolina Mutual Life Insurance Company and a significant Syndicate and *Atlanta Daily World* advertiser. Austin criticized Black leaders for working in tandem with whites to maintain the status quo. "Each knows the other is lying," he argued, "about educational opportunities, but neither will admit it."[60]

In November 1932, the *Times* went after the Alabama Klan, which had been distributing handbills encouraging Black Alabamans to avoid communists and their influence. "Alabama is a good place for good Negroes to live in," said the flyers, "but it is a bad place for Negroes who believe in SOCIAL EQUALITY. The Ku Klux Klan is watching you. Take heed." The paper took issue with equating the desire for social equality with communism. "The members of Alabama's Ku Klux Klan ought to look about them at the thousands of Negroes whose skins bespeak the undeniable truth that 'social equality' in America is an ancient reality," the *Times* railed. "There is no place in America for the Ku Klux Klan, or any other organization that does not have the moral courage to show the faces of its members."[61] The editorial's radicalism was aided by its focus on Alabama, but the Klan in North Carolina could read it too. By criticizing the principles and actions of the terrorist group, but emphasizing a branch other than the one in its immediate proximity, the *Times*, like its counterparts, displayed the practical radicalism required of southern rights activists.

After the *Times*'s run with the SNS, the Syndicate created the *Durham Dispatch*, which existed throughout much of 1934 and followed a similar model. "The Negro lawyer should be the watchdog of Negro interest," the *Dispatch* explained in one editorial. He should "object to the term 'nigger' used so frequently in the court room." Black lawyers should be in politics. Most important, there should be more of them. The *Dispatch* understood Black defendants' desire to use white lawyers and the resulting hesitation of Black students to enter the field. But the paper was confident: "If Negroes think you KNOW, and will not sell them, they will employ Negro lawyers."[62]

The other benefit of Black lawyers was that it eliminated the need for controversial white interlopers like International Labor Defense (ILD), the legal arm of the Communist Party USA. When the ILD approached the local ministerial alliance about allowing its representatives to speak in local churches, for example, and take a collection to donate to the defense fund for local sharecropper Emanuel Biddings, the ministers refused, with the approval of the *Dispatch*. Biddings's landlord, T. M. Clayton, had refused him his share of the tobacco crop, arguing that "his work had not been satisfactory." When Biddings tried to take it anyway, Clayton attacked his child, threatened to shoot him, and then moved for his gun. Biddings grabbed his own gun in turn and shot in self-defense, killing Clayton and earning the sharecropper a seat on death row. "The struggle to free Biddings is a struggle against the whole system of oppression of the share croppers and the Negro people in the South," the ILD noted with familiar hyperbole. But the local ministers decided against allying with the communists. They wanted to help Biddings and agreed to take a collection for him, but they didn't want it going to the ILD. The rejection pleased the *Dispatch* as well as the Syndicate, which titled the Durham copy with hyperbole of its own: "Durham Pastors Flay Communism."[63]

The biggest benefit of having an affiliate newspaper in Durham was that it put the Syndicate in the home city of one of the largest and most important Black businesses in the nation, the North Carolina Mutual Life Insurance Company. Charles Clinton Spaulding had led the group since 1923 and used his success and that of his company to play a leading role in Democratic politics, particularly in the hard years of the Depression, when he recommended nominees for Roosevelt's famed Black Cabinet. He testified in front of the all-white North Carolina legislature often, and never let his larger national and state concerns interfere with his work for race rights in Durham.[64]

North Carolina Mutual occupied a nebulous space in the world of the Black southern press and in the world of the Syndicate in particular. The company was a large and important advertiser, but because of that influence, its doings were also legitimate news. When C. C. Spaulding forecasted in October 1932 that the Depression was sure to end soon, for example, the statement was worthy of coverage. Given the economic and educational state of Black southerners, when North Carolina Mutual began offering an "educational endowments" policy, that too was news. At the same time, positive statements from the company's president buoyed the company's image, and news articles covering new policy offerings buoyed its bottom line. When the Syndicate included pictures of the company's Durham cashier's office in its rotogravure section, that synergy (or that conflict of interest) became even more apparent. The company's advertising even admitted that it planned "to use the Rotogravure Section of the Southern Newspaper Syndicate of Atlanta to run photographs of members of the club from time to time." The club to which it referred was a "Thrift Club," a marketing gimmick designed to convince people to save money. "We think of you as we do the petal of a beautiful rose, blushing because of having been kissed by the dew drop from God," one advertisement explained to its unthrifty customers. "All of us carrying on the business of North Carolina Mutual Life Insurance Company, the largest Company of our race in the World, have been once just where you are now, innocent and irresponsible."[65]

That was one of many paid advertisements that North Carolina Mutual ran in Syndicate newspapers in the early 1930s, advertisements that often ran concurrently with four-column front-page articles headlined, for example, "C. C. Spaulding Praises Negro's Business Achievements: Historians Listen to Spaulding." Taken in conjunction with the Syndicate's stated rotogravure strategy and its paid advertisements, the lines between reporting and shilling were blurred. And they continued to be blurred. In March 1934, for example, a front-page article trumpeted, "1933 Best Health Year for NC Mutual Policyholders." The report was based on the company's filings with state insurance departments and noted that there was a record low morbidity rate among the insured, certainly information worthy of note in such a troubled time and "an indication that the American Negro has an unusually strong physical constitution to be able to withstand the ravages of both poverty and depression." The paid advertisements and news items that doubled as such continued through August 1934, the final month of the *Durham Dispatch*'s relationship with the Syndicate.[66]

The *Asheville World* appeared in Asheville, North Carolina, in late 1932, and its coverage of two self-defense cases in the first half of 1934 demonstrates the climb that Black southerners had to make. In February, Viola Samuels shot and killed Henry Johnson and wounded his partner when they attempted to drag her from her house. All three participants in the incident were Black, and Samuels was never charged with a crime, as police determined that her action was clearly in self-defense. Beatrice Glover also shot her attempted rapist. She didn't kill him, but because he was white and she was Black, Glover was sentenced to the state penitentiary in Raleigh. The North Carolina NAACP and a variety of citizens groups mobilized to petition the governor and the commissioner of pardons for her release, though they were ultimately unsuccessful.[67] There were constant reminders like these of the unfair justice system in southern states, the susceptibility of Black women to sexual violence, and the double standard in response to assaults on the bodies of white and Black women.

Perhaps the most successful of the mid-1930s *World* creations was the *New Bern World*, founded by Daniel F. Martinez in the small coastal town of New Bern, North Carolina. Martinez had been a professor at Roger Williams College in Memphis and North Carolina A&T in Greensboro. He was also a minister in the African Methodist Episcopal (AME) Zion church. It was a busy career, but he found time to publish the *New Bern World*.[68]

Early in 1934, Martinez listed in his paper a broad series of resolutions for the year. He argued that "the American Negro should come out of his lethargy in 1934 and burst forth into an era of self-independence and personal Emancipation. He should resolve to stop seeking empty sympathy, and with a resolute mind be a productive and law-abiding citizen; maintain in his conviction a Herculean Resolution for right and justice in the courts. He must continue his clamor for an equal opportunity to earn a livelihood, and as a true American citizen, contribute his full economic quota to America's growth and independence." This was a distillation of the approach of many of the southern papers in the Syndicate—an argument for rights coupled with a self-flagellating insistence that those rights come with a set of responsibilities required of Black readers. Those responsibilities extended beyond simple "law-abiding citizen[ship]" and included a charge to "stop seeking empty sympathy."[69] The first was paternalistic at worst, the second paternalistic at best. But significantly (and typically forgotten in generic summaries of the "conservative" southern Black press), the demand for rights was there. Martinez was a preacher, and his readers were certainly religious, steeped in the southern Protestantism of the hand-wringing jeremiad. Religious Black southerners believed that humanity had been damaged since Eden and could only be redeemed by the acceptance of certain responsibilities. Such language, while it reads like the "conservative" southern Black press, would not have been read that way by either *New Bern World* or Syndicate readers.

When local white protests began in response to "200 Negro CCC Boys being stationed at Camp Patterson," a local outpost of the Civilian Conservation Corps near Piney Grove, North Carolina, Martinez went after both the protesters and the white daily newspapers that seemed to support them. All involved were behaving in a "nonsensical, inhuman and unreasonable" way, and Martinez refused to flinch in his criticism. When Govan Ward was lynched in Franklin County, North Carolina, in late July 1935, Martinez was equally adamant: "Truly we must admit that maniacs and crazy individuals running amuck, killing and attempting to kill innocent people, whites or Negroes, are better off dead or incarcerated." This was radical talk, bolstering the activist credentials of Martinez and earning him a reputation as someone who was willing to fight for Black rights, even as, in many instances, he chastised his readers in the tradition of the southern Protestant declension narrative.[70]

Martinez was just as willing to celebrate successes as he was to castigate unjust treatment. In January 1937, Robert Glen Brown, a Black man charged with killing a white merchant, went on trial in front of a jury more closely resembling his peers. The presiding judge, E. H. Granmer, had ordered that Black citizens be part of the jury pool, and three made the final cut. The move was a response to the U.S. Supreme Court, which had remanded an Alabama case for not including Black jurors, but it was progress, the first integrated jury in North Carolina since the nineteenth century. For Martinez and the *World*, it was an example of "true democracy." The fact that the jury sentenced Brown to death was merely an afterthought. Integrated juries had come to New Bern, North Carolina.[71]

Meanwhile, in Greensboro, physician Joseph L. Alexander began publishing his own newspaper, the *Cuttings*, in July 1936. The month after its founding, the paper used the success of Jesse Owens in the 1936 Olympics to trumpet opportunities for local Black Greensboro citizens: "Right here in our midst we urge our colored men and women to a more spirited aggressiveness in fields that are yet virgin lying at their feet." It pointed out, for example, that though many Black Americans owned cars, "there has not been a known request of automobile dealers to give us a chance to sell these cars to our people." In Greensboro, "our investigation reveals that a colored man could gainfully be employed today by at least three automobile agencies," the paper said. "Why then has not someone sought this opportunity?" Like Jesse Owens, Black citizens should make bold efforts against long odds and hope to take the laurels that were possible for the effort.[72]

And Owens had laurels. A child of the Great Migration, Owens was an Alabama native whose parents had brought him to Ohio as a nine-year-old boy. There, he became a high school track and field star, which led him to Ohio State, where he continued his success. His crowning achievement came at the 1936 Berlin Olympics, where he won four gold medals and in the process became a symbol of the failed racist thinking of Adolf Hitler and the Nazis. At home, he also became a symbol of the failed racist thinking of the American South and the white supremacy of the country at large. He was a hero of Black newspaper readers across the nation.[73]

David Welky has written about the previous Olympics, explaining that Black stars like Eddie Tolan and Ralph Metcalfe, the gold and silver medalists, respectively, in the 100- and 200-meter dashes in 1932, stood as exemplars of success in the Black press, while being virtually ignored in the white press. Without the imperative of Nazism pressing on the minds of white readers, it wasn't necessary to laud Tolan and Metcalfe in the white press, which "worked to locate black athletes in a place that was acceptable to traditional white society."[74] Black newspapers celebrated Tolan and Metcalfe as the heroes that they were, both as ambassadors for the country and as ambassadors for the race. They did so again four years later with Jesse Owens.

Early in 1937, Alexander's *Cuttings* became the *Greensboro Tribune*, seemingly developing a new radicalism in the process. The *Tribune*'s editorials were far more intense than those of its progenitor. "Too often, have we watched with faltering disgust the drift of human lives and human sacrifices in some of our streets that lead to no where," claimed an early example. "Tragedies piling upon tragedies have grieved and disgraced us. Human lives and human sympathies have been wasted and trampled upon as if there were no God to account to, and yet our leaders and citizens of note rear back in supine blissfulness as if all is well in Greensboro." But all was not well in Greensboro: "We are in hell and in its abysmal chasm in our dark unlighted, unpoliced ghetto." And there was no help in sight. "Who cares? The church does not give a damn," the frustrated writer claimed. "Does anyone care? If so, speak up."[75]

There was similar strategic coverage coming from Kinston's *East Carolina News*, which joined the Syndicate in December 1938. While it heavily emphasized salacious crime stories, it was also clearly concerned with the racial news that affected the area. Early in 1939, federal legislators modified a wage and hour law that originally had allowed forty-four hours of work per week. That ruling had led to significant layoffs of North Carolina tobacco stemmers, who were almost uniformly Black. The revision, however, stated that "because tobacco is a perishable agricultural product, stemmers may work 56 hours weekly." There was no stipulation for overtime, but the extension of hours meant that the "reemployment of many local people['s] hands seems quite probable" and indicated "a bright outlook to Kinston industry." In another example, when white residents protested to Kinston's board of aldermen that the police commissioner had cleared an area near their homes for Black children to skate, even threatening to picket the street or attack the children, the *News* reported on the controversy. It did not include any malice toward the white protesters, but it did argue that children needed a safe place to skate and made suggestions for different possible locations.[76]

A March 1939 editorial by Oscar E. Holder, the paper's editor, described the efforts of North Carolina senator Robert Rice Reynolds to fight Nazism, fascism, and communism. Holder reminded his readers, however, that there were "some 'isms' which the Senator has overlooked in his program of extermination. We refer to the 'isms' peculiar to the South." This, too, was practical radicalism. Holder commended the senator for his stand and simply described other isms that needed addressing, without directing a lot of criticism toward Reynolds. Holder's column was syndicated through the SNS. In another edition, he complimented Wilmington's new community hospital for Black citizens and used the opportunity to push for further public works. "We need to erect some parks for colored people, playgrounds and swimming pools," he argued. "We need to DEDICATE OURSELVES to the proposition that the 'more abundant life' is no Utopian dream but a possibility and a challenge."[77]

The abundant life was difficult to find for many in the Carolinas, but the relative consistency of the Black press and its message in the 1930s and 1940s provided a connection to the possibilities of abundance and served as a lodestar for many Black people in the generation before the classical civil rights movement.

Chapter 4

Alabama

The Great Migration Black Population Changes (%)

City	1910-1940	1940-1970
Birmingham	1.3	1.3
Mobile	-1.5	-7.3
Montgomery	-10.8	-6.4

The listed cities are the ones large enough to be included in Census statistical materials. "The Great Migration, 1910 to 1970," U.S. Census Bureau, 13 September 2012, https://www.census.gov/dataviz/visualizations/020/508.php.

In 1886, a frustrated Mansfield Edward Bryant, editor of Selma's *Southern Independent*, stated to whites, "You have had your revolutionary and civil wars and we here predict that at no very distant day we will have our race war, and we hope, as God intends, that we will be strong enough to wipe you out of existence and hardly leave enough of you to tell the story." Selma's Black newspaper in the early 1930s was a Syndicate paper, the *Selma Post*, and it was decidedly less radical than Bryant's Redeemer-era effort. But such is not to say that it wasn't radical at all. For example, when a local white businessman, unhappy with the National Recovery Administration's wage scale for Black workers, proposed what he called a "Basic Code for Subnormal Labor," which would lower pay for Black workers, the *Post* reported the attempt, as well as the attempt of the National Urban League to counter him. The paper's coverage was extensive, even reprinting the questionnaire that was sent to white southern businessmen. It didn't include editorial denunciations, but it didn't need to. This was such a blatantly racist proposal that the facts were their own form of indictment. Such a presentation was, to be sure, a far cry from the work of the 1880s. But if the 1930s Black press in Selma was less radical than that of the 1880s, it still bore witness to prejudice in its midst.[1]

Alabama's experience in the 1930s was encapsulated best by the work of James Agee and Walker Evans in *Let Us Now Praise Famous Men*, which painted a searing portrait of the desperation of the rural state. Cotton prices hit Reconstruction levels; unemployment hit 25 percent; personal income fell by more than 60 percent. The Black population was even more dramatically affected than these averages indicate, and it shaped the contours of press reaction to racism in the decade.[2]

Another Alabama paper forced to react to racism in that decade was the *Mobile Sun*, founded in 1933, which remained independent until April 1936, when it was taken over by the local *Press Forum*, itself a merger between the *Mobile Press* and *Mobile Forum*. The *Sun* was concerned more than anything else with uplifting the race. Articles speculated about the "greatest Negro." Editorials thrilled to cite the work of Harvard philologist Leo Weiner, who controversially claimed that Africans had arrived in the Americas before the fifteenth century and that much of the journals of Columbus were outright lies. "It is becoming more and more obvious how idiotic most of the anthropologists have been," the paper quoted him as writing. "The effect of the Negroes on the American civilization has been nothing short of enormous." A controversial and largely discredited treatise, Weiner's three-volume *Africa and the Discovery of America* had been published more than a decade prior to the *Mobile Sun* editorial about his work, but the paper wanted to let readers know to demonstrate the past success (and thus the potential success) of the race.[3]

To ensure that success would continue, the *Sun* also included religious instruction to help guide its readers spiritually. At the same time, it castigated them for "Negro economic unpreparedness." It was the typical southern philosophical strategy. Government won't save you. Adhere to the dictates of religion and use them to save yourself.[4] This was where the Black southern experience was situated—there were efforts at reform, but they were bounded on each side by racism and religion.

The *Sun* also made the case for Black newspapers themselves, which the Syndicate gladly reprinted. L. D. Cunningham argued in 1935 that the Black press presented facts that Black readers simply couldn't get anywhere else. Black publishers used their editorial pages for "arguments and discussions, pro and con," and thus served as the most prominent public political forum for Black readers. Plus, "this service rendered by Negro newspapers is largely gratis and therefore becomes the wide-awake servant and friend of the people."[5] The notion that the papers were "largely gratis" seems a stretch, but the statement did speak to the shoestring budgets of the small newspapers that syndicates like Scott facilitated. Such business development centered around the reification of the information grapevine. It was a self-serving attempt to convince readers to buy more newspapers, but it was also a legitimate summation of the benefits of the Black press.

In 1936, the *Press Forum* merged with the *Sun*, creating the *Mobile Press Forum Sun* and bringing the paper under the umbrella of the SNS, which had long controlled the *Sun*, and making it one of the leading Black presses in the state. The paper was edited in its new form by William Sheppard, a mixed-race native of Mobile who had worked as a railroad employee and an insurance salesman before becoming an editor.[6] His paper featured, like its predecessor the *Sun*, a concern more than anything else with uplifting the race. A December 1936 editorial told the story of a man without children who never celebrated Christmas "because he did not believe in the story of the birth of Christ, nor very soundly in the existence of God." He was invited to a Christmas party, however, where he provided presents for an underprivileged boy. They maintained contact over the years, and the boy, now a man with a family, still wrote him letters. "These letters," he said, "are the greatest things in my life."[7] This story was certainly well intentioned, but it demonstrated that the paper wasn't particularly interested in tackling the broader racial issues that faced Black Mobile. The editorials were very much in the philosophical tradition of Booker T. Washington, encouraging self-help as a palliative for the systemic problems of the race.

It also demonstrated the influence the *Sun* had on the Black newspaper consolidation in Mobile. Surviving editions of the *Press Forum* published prior to the merger showed a more activist bent, reporting on the remaining vestiges of convict leasing and the use of the term "nigger" in a Washington, D.C., poetry textbook. It stumped for a free medical clinic to help those "who need medical attention but are unable to pay for it. Why let them suffer?" And it reported assiduously on the anguish of the Scottsboro Boys.[8] That the *Press Forum*'s greater activism fell to the *Sun*'s self-help ethic is not surprising, considering the needs for survival in the Deep South, but it was a voice surely missed in the leanest, most troubling years of the Depression.

In 1932, the Syndicate continued its move into Alabama by founding the *Montgomery World*, edited and published by the Reverend John D. Dowdell and his nephew James Bozeman, which lasted until the end of 1935. To replace the *World* after it faltered, the SNS made another, more successful attempt in Montgomery: the *Alabama Tribune*, founded in 1936 and lasting until 1964.[9] It was a substantial relationship that bound Atlanta and Montgomery for decades.

Those bonds took many forms. Eloise Keller, for example, a switchboard operator and "SNS home economist" who went to Atlanta after graduating from Tennessee State, was "the only demonstrator of her color to conduct cooking schools for newspapers." In July 1935, Keller spent a week in Montgomery, "where she conducted a highly successful Cooking School and Homemakers Institute for the Montgomery WORLD." The Syndicate also disseminated *Montgomery World* editorials on how youths really loved disciplinarian parents, on the need for greater civic participation in Negro History Week, and on the value of courageous preaching from local ministers. Because the paper was located in the Alabama state capital, the location of both the state government and Kilby Prison, home of the state's electric chair, there were also plenty of SNS stories emanating from the *Montgomery World* on crime, executions, and failed attempts by Black voters to participate in the political process.[10]

The *World* was upholding a long tradition of Black opposition papers in Montgomery, which began in the 1870s with the *Republican Sentinel* and the *Negro Watchman*, but was really exemplified in the following decade with the founding of Jesse Chisholm Duke's *Montgomery Herald* in 1886. Duke's was a staunchly Republican weekly that pushed back against the original conception of the "New South," which was made famous by the *Atlanta Constitution*'s Henry Grady, who argued that the New South was a place where whites "love the Negro and delight to protect him." Duke and the *Herald* were unable to stem the tide of Redeemer politics in Alabama and the broader South after Reconstruction, but they established a precedent for Black Alabama journalists in the generations to come. That precedent situated the *World* perfectly to report from the epicenter of the national and international symbol of the confluence of crime, executions, and Black exclusion from the political process: the Black boys and men from Scottsboro convicted of rape, sentenced to die, and held in Kilby Prison.[11]

In March 1931, after a fight between white and Black youths riding in an Alabama freight car, nine Black passengers were arrested when the train stopped in Paint Rock, Alabama. They were taken to a larger town nearby, Scottsboro. Two white women had been in the car as well, and Victoria Price and Ruby Bates accused the Black passengers of rape. Throughout 1931, the case garnered significant attention, which generally came in two forms. White Alabama wanted the boys executed. Lynch mobs formed around the jailhouse, ready to engage in the time-honored tradition of safeguarding southern white womanhood. Outside the state, the case prompted outrage of a different kind. The stories of the women were suspect, as were their characters. The trial that followed the arrests did not give the nation any new confidence. Observers questioned the competence of defense attorney Stephen Roddy. They questioned the all-white jury and the Alabama justice system when two weeks after the arrest, eight of the nine Black men and boys were sentenced to death.[12]

After the sentence, the most consistent news from Scottsboro concerned the jockeying for control of the appeal between the NAACP and the International Labor Defense (ILD). In March 1932, however, the Alabama Supreme Court upheld the convictions of seven of the eight men and boys, and their executions were scheduled for May. The verdicts were expected, and Scottsboro news throughout 1932 centered on the ILD's federal appeal. In November, that group helped to convince the U.S. Supreme Court to grant the Scottsboro Boys a new trial. The defendants' dispatches from Montgomery soon followed. "Sence the Supreme Court have granted we boys a new trial I thank it is my rite to express my thanks an appreciation to the whole ILD for their care of me and the wonderful and faithful struggle for my rights," wrote Olin Montgomery in a characteristic letter. The good news was short-lived, however. In June 1934, for the second time, the Alabama Supreme Court upheld a circuit court conviction of Haywood Patterson and Clarence Norris, two of the Scottsboro Boys, and set their execution for August.[13]

In October, however, Patterson and Norris were still alive, awaiting a rehearing on the death sentence handed down by the Alabama Supreme Court. In November, that court provided a sixty-day stay of execution, postponing the event until February so that the ILD could prepare its appeal to the U.S. Supreme Court. In April 1935, the Supreme Court ruled that the Scottsboro trials were invalid because Alabama had not included any Black jurors, and thus the defendants were not tried before a jury of their peers. The ruling didn't mean that they were free—there would be yet another interminable trial—but it did mean that if white Alabama wanted to convict them, jury duty was going to have to include all of the state's citizens. The Syndicate's report from Montgomery proudly reprinted the statement of Alabama governor Bibb Graves. The Scottsboro decision "means that we must put the names of Negroes in jury boxes in every county in the state." Graves was no egalitarian, and it was only his desire to execute Patterson and Norris that drove his command. Still, "Alabama is going to observe the supreme law of America." Soon after the decision, in June, Patterson and Norris were removed from death row at Kilby and returned to their original prison home in Birmingham, where they were reunited with their fellow Scottsboro Boys to await new trials.[14]

The state acted quickly, and by September, the *Montgomery World* reported for the Syndicate that Alabama lieutenant governor Thomas Knight, acting as "special state counsel" in the Scottsboro case, had announced that "he would ask for a special session of the Jackson County Grand Jury in about three weeks to re-indict the nine Scottsboro defendants." That time wasn't to be spent idly. "The new jury commission would require approximately three weeks in completing the refilling of the county's jury box" with "names of Negroes." Like many of the Scottsboro articles emanating from Montgomery, the paper's coverage was listed as "Special to SNS." While the story was a scoop, it didn't come with any of the satisfaction or disgust that often accompanied such political reporting. That was largely because stories such as Knight's announcement were hard to pin down as proper subjects of satisfaction or disgust. An indictment was probably inevitable, but at least it was a fresh start. The grand jury would reconvene, but this time with Black names in the pool. Before there was any certainty about the debits and credits of any racial situation, the Syndicate contented itself with scoops, with articles "Special to SNS." And so the *World* and the Syndicate waited along with everyone else, maintaining its privileged place in the Alabama state capital, and reported on Knight's plans for the grand jury, his investigation in Alabama and New York, and ultimately the November meeting of the new grand jury constituted from the reconvened interracial pool.[15]

The Scottsboro Boys, however, were not the only victims of the racialized Alabama criminal justice system at the time. There was also, for example, the case of Willie Peterson, a Black man who was scheduled to die in Kilby in January 1934 for the August 1931 murders of Augusta Williams and Jennie Wood and the wounding of Nell Williams. The white women had been attacked in Birmingham, and while riding through the city with a male friend some days after the attack, the surviving Williams saw Peterson at a distance and decided that he was the assailant. Her friend jumped out of the car, pulled a gun, and held the unsuspecting Peterson until the police arrived. The first trial against Peterson ended in a mistrial, the second in a conviction, and when Black men were convicted of killing white women in the South, death was the only penalty that the public would allow. The Syndicate reported, however, that a stay of the January execution was imminent, thanks to an unlikely appeal for clemency from Jefferson County sheriff James Hawkins and an announcement from Alabama governor B. M. Miller that the execution would be delayed. It was, until late March, but before then yet another hearing featured a member of the original grand jury, who testified that the group had felt that they had to indict Peterson because otherwise his accuser, Nell Williams, would appear to be lying. Time and again, white law enforcement officials publicly expressed doubts about Peterson's guilt. Williams, for example, originally had described her assailant as having gold inlays in his teeth, and the original police circulars described him that way. When it turned out that Peterson didn't have gold inlays, Williams decided that she had been mistaken about them. Peterson was definitely the guy, she said. Adding even more sensationalism to the case, Peterson wasn't at the clemency hearing because he was hospitalized for a gunshot wound to the abdomen after being attacked by Dent Williams, the brother of two of the victims, during a conference at the prison. Williams, a local lawyer, was quickly cleared of all potential charges against him. Thus when the governor commuted Peterson's sentence to life in prison, the Syndicate expressed both relief and frustration. "Willie Peterson will not die soon!" announced its exclusive report from Montgomery. "That is, Willie Peterson, the emaciated Negro who became so ill in connection with his services during the World War in the United States army that he will be an invalid for the rest of his life will not die in the electric chair at Kilby prison, March 30, this year, as scheduled, although he may die a natural death shortly."[16] This was the quintessential report of the Depression-era Black press in the South. It toed the line of objectivity, providing only demonstrable facts, but managed at the same time to convey the frustration with the violent racism and racial scapegoating during a time of economic hardship.

This sensationalistic case, overlapping the Scottsboro trials, was a cause célèbre for the NAACP, for the Black press, and for everyone who had been following the race trials in Alabama. The Syndicate was positioned to be the voice of the opposition since the *Montgomery World* was stationed in the heart of Dixie and had the local connections to Black leaders that allowed for exclusive coverage, which was disseminated through the newspapers of the SNS.

The Peterson case, however, served largely as an exclamation point on the damning sentence that was Scottsboro. The case of the Scottsboro Boys began to dominate Black news in the country as the *Atlanta World* was making its transition to a daily. The paper covered every nuance of the case as it made its way through the appellate courts and eventually landed in the Supreme Court. The *World* supported the defendants' release, but the case proved divisive regardless. The NAACP and the Communist Party battled over who would handle the appeals, and though the communists had rushed to the men's aid from the beginning, the *World* and many similar Black news outlets supported the role of the NAACP, fearing communist motives and wringing their hands about the possibility of being painted with a communist brush.[17]

The most important fruit on the Scottsboro grapevine was necessarily in Montgomery. The *Alabama Tribune* replaced the *Montgomery World* in the state capital in June 1936 and remained until the collapse of the Syndicate in 1955. Being in Montgomery again located the Syndicate in an advantageous position for covering significant news, just as it had during the run of the *Montgomery World*.[18] In May 1937, Alabama officials announced that the Scottsboro Boys would plead guilty to a lesser charge of "felonious assault," which would come with six-year sentences that would "retroactively satisfy the six years already spent in jails by the nine youths" and thus free them. Samuel Leibowitz, attorney for the defendants, vehemently denied the plea deal, arguing that they were innocent, had continued to maintain their innocence, and refused to admit any sort of guilt. He claimed that the costs of the trials and retrials were the reason for the county's attempt at a deal. Still, the Alabama Supreme Court unsurprisingly sustained Haywood Patterson's guilty verdict in June. It was, the paper and the Syndicate reported, the "Same Old Story," as the court ruled against "all points" of his appeal. Despite yet another setback, "it is understood that the case will be appealed to the United States supreme court."[19]

In March 1938, the paper reported on slashes to the face and chest of Charlie Weems, one of the Scottsboro Boys remaining in prison (others had been released over the years); the injuries had been caused by a Kilby Prison guard. Kilby's warden claimed publicly that Weems had crafted a shank to attack the prison's employees. The *Tribune* didn't comment on the warden's claims, instead using the incident to remind readers of the Scottsboro case and the seven-year ordeal it had become. In August 1938, that ordeal continued when Alabama's board of pardons denied parole to Haywood Patterson and Ozie Powell and dismissed out of hand the petitions of Charlie Weems, Andy Wright, and Clarence Norris for appearing prematurely. In response, the leader of the Scottsboro Defense Committee, headquartered in New York, publicly pledged to "rehabilitate" the defendants if the governor would pardon them despite the board's inaction. Those pardons hit yet another snag in October 1938 when former senator J. Thomas Heflin, who had railed against the Scottsboro Boys since their original arrests, claimed that authorities had found a knife on one of the defendants before they appeared before Governor Bibb Graves for their pardon plea.[20] While patently untrue, the report of Heflin, given in person to Graves, obviously carried weight as both were white supremacists who had a vested political interest in keeping the men and boys in jail.

The *Tribune*'s location also proved beneficial in covering cases with more local interest. In June 1937, for example, the Alabama Supreme Court dismissed charges against a Henry County sheriff stemming from an Abbeville lynching the previous year. The state had charged the sheriff with "negligence, grave fault, connivance and cowardice" for leaving open the cell of Wes Johnson, a Black man arrested for "attempting to attack a white woman," and allowing a white mob to enter, take the prisoner, and hang him from a tree. "Only 33 minutes were required" for the court to absolve the sheriff of all responsibility. A few hours after that decision, a local Black Montgomery "house girl" was "lodged in jail here for safekeeping" after yet another angry white mob threatened her. Boys had been throwing rocks at her and pelting the house. She threw one back "to scare the pelters away" and earned, in the minds of many, a death sentence.[21] When the state's highest court was willing to vindicate such behavior, the actions of impromptu white mobs became normalized.

Whether people chose to navigate the dictates of the system or escape them entirely, the Black press was both a road map and the tie that bound its readers together. Birmingham was an important point on the road map. Though the *Birmingham World* had been publishing since early in the Scott Syndicate's life, Emory O. Jackson took over editorial duties for the paper in 1941. He remained in that position until 1975, using the paper to fight for civil rights in one of the most notoriously racist cities in the South. He was often at odds with the Scott family, which was more conservative. "Emory Jackson was a man that really brought this paper to where it is," recalled reporter Joe Dickson. "He did the voting rights, he challenged Bull Connor all the way to the segregated law. He dealt with no black officers, no black firemen. Emory Jackson and this newspaper led the fight. In addition to what he did in the city of Birmingham, Emory would leave at night and go into the black belt areas and other areas of this state. He would train other blacks in the methods of getting blacks registered to vote."[22]

Emory Overton Jackson was born in Buena Vista, Georgia, in 1908, but he grew up in Birmingham's Enon Ridge, a Black middle-class neighborhood on the city's west side. He then moved to Atlanta to attend Morehouse, where he edited the school's *Maroon Tiger* newspaper. He graduated in 1932 and briefly taught high school English before joining the staff of the *Birmingham World* in 1934 as a sportswriter and book reviewer. Not only did he become the paper's editor in 1941, but he also led the Alabama conference of the NAACP and authored a column called "The Tip Off," which tirelessly advocated for voting rights.[23]

The paper covered the Scottsboro Boys and other instances of injustice extensively—and militantly. After Haywood Patterson's Scottsboro conviction, for example, the *World* included a statement on its first page for readers to sign, cut out, and send to Franklin Roosevelt. Less nationally sensationalized, the Dadeville riot occurred in Tallapoosa County, Alabama, in July 1931. Black communists had come into the area to organize a sharecroppers union, putting local white authorities on edge. Sheriff's deputies broke up meetings and confiscated materials. Then, on July 17, many Black locals held a meeting to protest the convictions of the Scottsboro Boys. The unjust convictions were gasoline on an already simmering fire, and the police raid on the meeting led to a shootout: a local sheriff's deputy was wounded, one Black man was killed, and several others were injured. Large posses of white men roamed the area rounding up suspected participants. Tensions ran incredibly high through the rest of the year and through 1932. In one incident, a leader of Black Tallapoosa who had been constantly hounded by white authorities was deeply in debt, and sheriff's deputies arrived to seize his mules and cows. The action led to another shootout, which wounded four white deputies and killed three Black men. That, in turn, led to a series of trials for the Black shooters. There were, of course, convictions of the Black participants.[24]

The *World*'s most vehement stands for rights were during and after World War II, which highlighted the country's problematic relationship with its Black population. In the early 1950s, the *World* started a voter registration drive to push the rights envelope. When *Brown* was decided, Jackson and the *World* optimistically believed that the case would end segregation and that there would be no "serious friction between the races as a result of this school decision." It was an unjustified optimism, to be sure, but the *World* dutifully followed every aspect of the movement to live up to the ideals of *Brown* that followed.[25] "He had been a warrior," Dickson said of Jackson, "writing the stories, going out and really moving the people to better themselves economically, educationally, and spiritually. He was a strong churchman. To be honest, Emory Jackson was the newspaper, and that probably happens in most places. We don't even profess to try to live up to any of the stuff that Mr. Jackson did by way of being able to."[26]

In October 1939, Jackson—serving as a reporter and columnist before becoming editor of the paper—had taken the state's political writers to task for celebrating the just-completed legislative session, which had featured work on reapportionment and "requiring that applicants for marriage licenses be free of syphilis." What the legislature didn't do was "move in the direction of making any provisions for graduate technical and professional training for Negroes" in the wake of the Supreme Court's *Missouri ex rel. Gaines* decision. North Carolina had worked toward compliance, however begrudgingly, and other states had provided scholarships for Black graduate students to attend schools out of the area. Not Alabama. Its failure to make even a token effort, Jackson believed, worked against the state. It "is passing up a chance to handle this delicate educational problem in her easiest way." It was easier to do something than be forced by the federal government since "the demand that Alabama provide university training for Negroes on [the] essentially identical level as given other students is coming."[27]

In January 1940, he criticized the state's rural grammar schools. "Off many of the main highways of rural Alabama are many unbelievable sights called school houses where black children are educated to live in a democracy," he explained. "These contrast awfully with those gracefully viewed for whites along the highways." There was a relatively consistent standard for white education throughout the state, and it was always better than Black education. But perhaps more insidious was the reality that education for Black Alabama children suffered even more in rural areas, where there was no bus transportation, little money for construction, and high labor costs, all of which put rural Black students at a massive disadvantage.[28]

Months later, in April 1940, Jackson celebrated when the state passed a tenure law for primary and secondary education teachers, which provided protection for teachers after three consecutive years of service. "Teachers cannot under the tenure law be fired for political or personal reasons," he reported. "In the case of Negro teachers, this is considered the greatest virtue of the law." It was a godsend for those who for years had suffered under fickle white school boards or administrators who often fired Black teachers for little or no reason. "Little recourse has been open to Negro teachers dominated by unfair principals who could at [their] word have teachers thrown out of employment for petty personal reasons."[29]

In March 1944, Jackson reported approvingly on a speech by Fisk professor St. Elmo Brady to the Alabama Science Association in Montgomery, which veered far afield from science. White leaders were mistaken, Brady argued, to "substitute benevolent paternalism for economic justice to the Negro people." This problem left Black people "to make [their] way in the polluted backwaters of discrimination." The conference report was absent editorial comment, but the message was inherent in what Jackson highlighted and whom he quoted. It was advocacy by proxy. Jackson did the same the following month while covering the Alabama State Teachers Association, which deplored "the increasing appeal to racial prejudice in some current national and state legislative discussions." A full report of the conference followed, all without editorial comment, but the association's statement against prejudice led the account.[30] Jackson knew that when the subjects of the story did the advocacy, the paper could simply allow them to speak.

In 1946, Jackson led an NAACP challenge to Birmingham zoning laws. Black residents were limited to neighborhoods formerly designated for commercial use. After a lawsuit, the U.S. District Court declared the zoning laws unconstitutional, opening the possibility for Black residents to live in poor white neighborhoods. The Ku Klux Klan responded with retributive bombings in those neighborhoods, which tended to be supported even by the whites who lived there. In the decade that followed the ruling, there were almost fifty unsolved bombings in the city, prompting Jackson to denounce police apathy (or collusion) and call for the hiring of Black police officers.[31]

That kind of advocacy yielded a devotion that spread beyond the bounds of Birmingham. When soldiers from the city were drafted and sent to military training sites throughout the country, they ordered mail subscriptions to the *World* to ensure that the grapevine would keep them close to home. Such was the primary function of the grapevine, shrinking and expanding the country at the same time: growing the area of the nation inhabited by Black residents while simultaneously keeping them in closer contact through the easy flow of information. Wartime subscriptions to the *World* went to California, New York, Nebraska, Colorado, Massachusetts, and Virginia. They went to Seattle, Washington, and Washington, D.C. They went to Camp Ellis, Illinois, and Fort Knox, Kentucky, not permanently expanding the grapevine into those areas, but instead using it to bind its members during their temporary absence, making of it the bread crumbs that would help them find their way home.[32]

Jackson was the guiding force behind much of the Syndicate's work in the state. In July 1945, he wrote to C. A. Scott at SNS headquarters in Atlanta about the "intensified racial tension in Alabama," particularly in relation to calls by white supremacist groups to restrict the sale of guns and ammunition to Black purchasers. Organizations like the United Sons of Dixie and the White Supremacy League stoked fears in the state about the potential for Black armed insurrection. As of the end of the month, however, Jackson had turned his frustration on the paper. "I wanted to see the WORLD grow, gather prestige and be placed on a basis that will reflect credit to the efforts I make in its behalf," he told Scott, but "our competitive paper has outstripped us in circulation and now has state coverage. It carries more advertising." Jackson, a lifelong bachelor, complained that he had given up other opportunities to stay at the paper, but was being run ragged, "doing the work of three, and seeing my own work suffer." He questioned whether he could continue editing the paper, which he saw falling behind, "for all this time the Birmingham WORLD, unlike the Memphis office, has not had a fair chance."[33]

Jackson stayed on, however, and the following year continued airing his frustration. Payment for Acme Engraving for columnar work had never arrived, and "these clerical shortcomings loom just as large as they do in the composing room." He was also still worried about competition, enclosing tear sheets from the *News*, the *Age-Herald*, and the *Post* in his correspondence. "The suggestion you should get," he told Scott, "is that right through here the largest effort must be made to give us plenty of local news matter and more papers because of the struggle for the Birmingham Negro market." There was "ruthless competition" in the city, and "if the public gets the opinion that the WORLD will not serve them, that it fails to publish their news, the WORLD suffers." Even more, there was a "failure to print enough papers for the subscription demand." Jackson suggested running an apology, against the wishes of the Syndicate, which "seems to be ashamed of the fact that it cannot produce as newsy a paper as its contemporaries."[34]

Jackson was an irascible colleague, to be sure, but his irritation was also channeled toward local race problems. When he discovered in 1946 that Black citizens in Russell County, Alabama, were being denied voter registrations, for example, the editor contacted the U.S. Department of Justice. When the teacher salary equalization issue raged in 1946 in Jefferson County, Jackson reported the case to Fisk's *Monthly Summary*. He also wrote to officials with the Republican Party asking them to help enact legislation to create a permanent Fair Employment Practices Committee.[35]

Through his *Birmingham World*, Jackson reported in 1946 on the replacement of Black ticket takers with whites at City Auditorium during an Erskine Hawkins dance. J. Earle Hensley, a local promoter, wrote to Emory Jackson in response to the piece. He hadn't handled that particular performance, but he had handled the Count Basie performance earlier in the year, where several ticket takers were fired for reselling tickets at a profit. The promoter told Jackson, "You can rest assured that I will at all times use Colored help as much as possible. Knowing that you will print the news as you see it I want to call this to your attention." When white businesspeople profited from Black customers, the leverage of a local Black newspaper that was willing to report on slights could have a dramatic impact. The coverage didn't play to whites' morality but instead to their economic bottom line, which proved powerful in many situations. The *World* was "standard household equipment in thousands of Negro homes in this area," said attorney Arthur Shores. The paper was, according to pastor H. B. Gibson, "one of our most firmly-established institutions" and was "respected as a tradition and a necessity in our everyday lives."[36]

The newspaper's place in the community and Jackson's role as managing editor made him the subject of data collection efforts by the city's FBI office. In August 1941, an informant reported to the bureau that Jackson's name "appeared on the roll of the Communist books." A later internal document, however, admitted that though Jackson had worked "in close cooperation with some known Communists and functionaries of Communist fronts" in the city, the bureau had no credible information that he was a member of the party as of 1946.[37]

Perhaps even more important than Birmingham during the war years was Montgomery, the state capital, where so many of Alabama's racial problems began. There, the Syndicate still relied on its *Alabama Tribune*. In 1940 the *Tribune*, like Jackson's paper, tried to work out how Alabama would provide for Black higher education in the wake of the Supreme Court's 1938 *Missouri ex rel. Gaines v. Canada* decision mandating that states provide equal educational facilities for Black students. "A Negro university, if it is to meet the requirements of the Supreme Court decision, should be substantially just as good as the white one," the *Tribune* explained. It acknowledged the cost of such an endeavor and that Alabama didn't have the money. Still, it assured white readers, "No Negro wants to go to the University of Alabama nor does one want to be inferiorly trained. This is the big problem." The paper explained that groups arguing for equal education "must not be interpreted by ill meaning and spiteful persons in the light of a crusade against Alabama or the South's social system. Negroes, both intelligent and unintelligent, plan no damage to white society, being as anxious as white people themselves, I believe, to preserve it." The article went on to advocate for Black education as a net benefit to both the Black population and the state. Black citizens needed doctors, dentists, nurses, lawyers, and electricians. By creating qualified service providers for Black customers, the state could help curb "crime, illiteracy, poverty," and other problems. There was no reason for whites to fear "general Negro progress in Alabama" because Black college graduates would only be helping their own and removing a burden from white people.[38] This was a call distinctly southern, arguing for equal educational facilities, but doing so with hat in hand, hedging at every turn to convince whites that Black Montgomery was doing anything but displaying cheek. This kind of argument would be seen as anathema in northern papers, but it represented a pragmatic calculation for helping convince white southerners to obey Supreme Court decisions.

For example, that same 1940 edition of the *Tribune* included a story about the deaths of three Black men at the hands of the Montgomery police. Two were shot while the third mysteriously developed a fractured skull while in police custody. The paper was clearly frustrated with the situation, but couched its criticisms of local law enforcement with quotes from "the fair-writing Montgomery Advertiser." That paper normally stood firmly on the side of white supremacy, but had responded to the violence by telling its readers that it was "not willing to see a handful of police officers bring [terror] to our citizens by wantonly abusing and humiliating people of color (only because people of color do not vote their strength in our elections)." Inherent in the *Advertiser*'s admonishment was the assumption that the color line and the sanitized voting bloc that came with it would suffer if such extralegal violence by policemen continued. The only way that the *Tribune* could take local police to task without repercussion was to use the words of whites who had bona fides on race issues. The paper worked within the constraints of a social system that placed boundaries on its ability to advocate where it could for what it could. The *Tribune* made a conscious choice not to breach the limits of that social acceptability because to do so would leave it powerless to do any advocacy in the future. This was another example of practical radicalism. When Police Commissioner William Preston Screws "came like a sinner to the mourner's bench" to meet with the *Advertiser*'s editor for its commentary on police brutality, the *Tribune* reveled, again through the words of its white counterpart, that cops were being held accountable by an "editor who asks only that every human being in this friendly old town by the river receive his just deserts in every circumstance."[39]

In 1941, the *Tribune* reported on the efforts of the Alabama attorney general to convince his white counterparts in other southern states to file amicus briefs in the suit of Black Illinois congressman Arthur W. Mitchell, which was scheduled to go before the Supreme Court and which challenged segregation on railroad cars coming south from northern areas where there was no such rule. Mitchell had brought the case in 1937 after he was compelled to leave his Pullman car for lesser quarters when his train, traveling from Illinois, reached the Arkansas line. Because there were no other media that could provide the *Tribune* with protective cover, its story was presented without comment, providing background on the case and quoting the attorney general's open letter to other white southern attorneys general, but not overtly denouncing them for siding against the Illinois congressman.[40]

In March 1941, a staff writer at the *Tribune* reported on Alabama's attempts to avoid paying equal salaries to Black teachers despite having been ordered to do so by the Supreme Court—a task being undertaken by many of its southern counterparts. White leaders in the state suggested "lowering the pay of white teachers, cutting the school term, or [requiring] an additional outlay of $2,000,000 by the State Legislature," all plans designed simply to create resentment among the white population, to make them feel slighted in what was presented as a zero sum game of rights. "All these 'tactics and schemes' have been detected by Negro educators," the paper reported. Teacher salaries were no longer just an issue for teachers. They were an issue for everyone: "Sentiment seems to be, to use the phrase of a Montgomery newspaper editorial, 'devoted to making the American schools absolutely free and equal.'" This was an important, racially divisive issue, but even in its clear stand on the side of pay equity, the article remained guarded, letting its reporting make the case and couching its complaints in quotation marks and attributions. Schemes by lawmakers to lower the pay of white teachers or cut the school term were "interpreted by Negro thinkers" as "appeals to resentment."[41] The paper made its case carefully and practically: explaining the issue to readers and pointing them in the direction of advocacy without expressly engaging in that advocacy itself.

The *Tribune* used the same strategy in May when describing the growth of resistance to the poll tax. "Today," one article explained, "the South is more disfranchised than solid." It described disagreement over the poll tax but noted that "anti–poll tax sentiment seems to be gathering support." The American Federation of Labor and the *Alabama Negro Baptist* were in favor of repealing it. White papers like the *Birmingham News* and the *Dothan Eagle* defended the tax. The *Tribune* clearly supported repeal. After all, "people, not poll tax[es], are the pillars of democracy."[42] But it obscured that advocacy in a demonstration of groups for and against, using their arguments to make its case.

The paper also looked across the border to neighboring Georgia and its race-baiting governor, Eugene Talmadge. Georgia was close enough to be a threat to overt advocacy, but when the local white daily, the *Montgomery Advertiser*, ran an editorial denouncing Talmadge's "demagogic effort to becloud all other issues" in favor of race, the *Tribune* reprinted the editorial with attribution. Opportunistically endorsing the attacks of others was safer than making those attacks.[43]

The *Tribune* was willing at times to go after white politicians in its own state. In 1942, Alabama governor Frank Dixon turned down a contract to bring more jobs to the state because "as long as he is Governor no white man will work under a Negro." A staff writer for the *Tribune*, tongue in cheek, took him to task, noting that daily "hundreds of white people crowd in" to the local American Federation of Labor office, run by a Black man, "and ask for a job. I am sure that Mr. Dixon doesn't know this." The story then compared Dixon to Mississippi's white board of education, which for years had neglected Black schooling. "We white people thought we were doing something when we failed to educate the Negro," one Mississippi editorial had explained, "and today our sons are being sent to war and many of them have already been killed while many Negroes have been turned down because of their [lack of] education." The point the *Tribune* labored to make was that Dixon's actions were fundamentally counterproductive to everyone in the state, including whites. "I voted for Governor Dixon and I thought at that time he was the man for the job," the author admitted. "But today he has reached back in trying to stir up all the Southern states."[44]

Later that year, Dixon's replacement, governor-elect Chauncey Sparks, met with a delegation of Black leaders from the state, including the presidents of the Birmingham and Montgomery NAACP branches, Emory O. Jackson, and his brother E. G. Jackson, editor of the *Tribune*. The paper was pleased that Sparks "believed that the Negro in Alabama had a right to demand justice" and that "he was in sympathy with the struggle of the Negro and would try to do something about bettering Negro conditions." That was a significant statement from an Alabama governor in the 1940s. Sparks would, of course, only go so far. He firmly held to his belief in "the rigid preservation of the tradition of independent development of the two races along segregated lines, and that there must be no 'social equality.'" Still, he conceded that something "could be worked out" to provide "an equal opportunity to live and make a living." It was an interesting line to draw, and cynics found it a disingenuous one. But Sparks told the delegation, "I am going to see that everybody gets justice during my administration."[45] That and the meeting itself were significant displays of legitimate concession that previous governors had been unwilling to make. Significantly, the *Tribune* didn't celebrate Sparks. It simply reported on the meeting. In openly criticizing Dixon's race policy and reporting favorably without fawning on the limited concessions made by Sparks, the paper was holding leaders accountable in a time and place that scholars generally assume to have been impossible.

On September 3, 1944, Recy Taylor was kidnapped while leaving church and then raped by six white men, who admitted the crime to police. Still, they were never indicted, igniting protests from the Black community in Alabama and across the country. E. G. Jackson teamed with Eugene Gordon from the communist *Daily Worker* to confront Governor Sparks and demand an investigation into the case. He helped organize meetings and generate petitions, along with allies such as E. D. Nixon, Rosa and Raymond Parks, Rufus Lewis, and Johnnie Carr, all of whom were important activists for Black rights in Alabama. This leadership group would, argues Danielle McGuire, "lift Martin Luther King, Jr., to international prominence a decade later, after their leading organizer was arrested on a Montgomery bus."[46] Jackson was not territorial about his newspaper's coverage, willingly speaking to reporters from the *Chicago Defender* about the case. He also spoke at public meetings and drove the protests forward outside the pages of his newspaper.[47]

Taylor's case was a symbol of the age. An all-white, all-male jury dismissed the case in October 1944. After months and months of activism led by the Black press and, in particular, by Rosa Parks, the attorney general finally sought a grand jury indictment. But that jury too was all white and all male, and in February 1945 it failed to indict any of the men who had confessed. The verdict stunned and frustrated Black Montgomery, and historian Danielle McGuire has described it as bringing "the building blocks of the Montgomery bus boycott together a decade earlier." Those building blocks, however, could only be gathered by the coverage of the Black press. The *Tribune* should have been the gatherer for the SNS, but as the case wore on, Jackson deferred to his brother's *Birmingham World*, worried about backlash in the racially charged air of the state's capital. "Decency calls for the protection of womanhood," wrote Emory Jackson in the *World*. "Permit womanhood anywhere to be abused, you leave it without sufficient protection everywhere. Erring men who escape punishment in one instance will feel no restraint against any woman anywhere. . . . in the interest of selfish idealism, the Grand Jury should feel impelled to indict the guilty."[48] In the absence of the *Tribune*'s ability to comment, the *World* made the case that allowing crimes against Black women was simply a gateway to crimes against white women.

Emory Jackson investigated the rape of Recy Taylor. In 1946, Jackson was "instrumental" in the creation of the Alabama Committee for Equal Justice along with E. D. Nixon, Rosa Parks, and others, a group formed specifically to organize efforts on behalf of Taylor. The committee maintained an office on the fourth floor of the city's Exchange Building, with Caroline Collier Ballin, "a known Communist," according to the FBI, as its secretary. More important for the bureau, the group "formed as a counterpart" to a similar organization in New York created by "writers of 'THE DAILY WORKER' and other Communists" in November 1944. An internal FBI memo noted efforts by the *Worker* to raise funds to pressure Alabama's governor and encourage an indictment and trial of the white rapists. The bureau had records of Jackson's meetings with various organizations, including the Southern Negro Youth Congress, in relation to the case.[49]

This situation was another example of practical radicalism. For all of Jackson's efforts on behalf of Taylor, neither her September rape nor the trial of her attackers in October ever received mention in the *Birmingham World*. Jackson worked diligently on her behalf, but he did not do it in the pages of his newspaper. The efforts of journalism and activism came together well in cases without a direct bearing on those who might want to cause the paper harm. When such events were closer to home, the printed grapevine gave way to organizing, lobbying, and fundraising through other channels. Though Jackson was an unapologetic fighter for Black rights, there was an affinity with the actions of Booker Washington for voting rights. Tuskegee's leader had financed efforts to end grandfather clauses in Louisiana and Alabama but never acknowledged that work. His was an earlier, even more cautious practical radicalism, tinged by the memory of slavery.[50]

Black soldiers who returned from the war expected more justice than Recy Taylor received, partly because they had just been fighting for democracy against tyranny abroad and partly because of overseas exposure to more accepting racial climates in France and the Philippines. They found upon return to the American South, however, that such expectations would not be satisfied with the kind of immediacy that came in battle. In January 1946, for example, Montgomery's *Alabama Tribune* reported that the Alabama Supreme Court had set aside a death sentence given to Black convicted rapist Johnnie B. Smith, who had been told during the trial to stand so that witnesses could "see him better for the purpose of identification," which constituted a violation of the defendant's right against self-incrimination.[51] This was a step in the direction of fair treatment for Black defendants in Alabama courts and surely gave *Tribune* and Syndicate readers a measure of confidence that they too had at least slightly less to fear from southern courts.

The court decision wasn't a war victory. It wasn't even a battle victory. But it was incremental progress. And there was further incremental progress in September when Clarence Norris, one of the Scottsboro Boys, was released on parole from Kilby Prison just outside Montgomery. This left only one of the men remaining in custody.[52]

World War II had been a major investment for Black America, but it was, like all investments, a beginning rather than an end. "Negroes must gird themselves for a mighty fight in the immediate future that recent gains will not be lost," an Atlanta pastor said to a Montgomery audience at an Emancipation Proclamation anniversary celebration in 1947. As it had since its inception, the paper was using quotes from an activist as a surrogate for its own advocacy, but that didn't make the statement any less true. The years following World War II were going to be a mighty fight, as more and more frustrated Black southerners found themselves settling for incremental progress and small battle victories in the war for equality at home.[53]

The *Tribune* noted that the Alabama NAACP, at its first session in June 1947, had urged Truman to veto the Taft-Hartley Act, which limited the power of labor unions, and stumped in favor of a federal antilynching law. At the group's second meeting in October, the right to vote was the principal issue, and the *Tribune* reported assiduously on that meeting, the group's call for suffrage, and the continued fight for it over the next year and a half. That fight centered on repeal of the Boswell Amendment, an addition to the Alabama Constitution enacted in 1946 in response to the Supreme Court's *Smith v. Allwright* decision outlawing white primaries. The amendment required any potential voter to explain a part of the constitution of the registrar's choosing before being allowed to sign up.[54]

These were important efforts, and the *Tribune*'s coverage spread the word throughout the city and the state, but victories were hard to come by. Taft-Hartley passed. A federal antilynching law never did. The Boswell Amendment survived until March 1949, and the Voting Rights Act wouldn't become reality until almost a generation later. When, for example, news emerged that six Black prisoners had been beaten for minor offenses in Alabama state prisons, the paper reported on Governor James Folsom's call for "a full scale investigation" into the prison system (which was progress), but the proposed study never managed to limit racial violence in those prisons (which was not).[55]

In 1948, the politics of race became the dominant national story, pushing beyond the bounds of Montgomery, of Alabama, and of the South. First there were Supreme Court decisions. When a Black St. Louis family was prevented from buying a house in a white neighborhood because of a restrictive covenant, they sued with the help of the NAACP, and the case eventually ended up at the Supreme Court as *Shelley v. Kraemer* (1948). The argument that the NAACP's Thurgood Marshall had to rebut was the same one used in the *Smith v. Allwright* decision concerning white primaries. Neighborhoods were essentially private entities, went the claim, and private entities could restrict whomever they wanted from being part of the group. The Court did appear somewhat sympathetic with that reasoning. Race-based restrictive covenants were, on their face, not invalid under the Fourteenth Amendment, the Court argued, continuing its decades-long dialogue with its earlier 1890s race decisions in *Plessy v. Ferguson* and *Williams v. Mississippi*. Private parties could voluntarily abide by the terms of a restrictive covenant, explained Chief Justice Fred Vinson, writing for the majority, but they couldn't seek judicial enforcement of such a covenant, because enforcement by the courts would constitute state action. That state action would necessarily be discriminatory, so enforcement of a restrictive covenant in a state court would violate the equal protection clause of the Fourteenth Amendment. And so while the Supreme Court did not specifically invalidate the "on-its-face" doctrine of the 1890s, it did find a way around it. The dictates of private entities did not matter if the state was prevented from enforcing those rules. Such would make the state complicit, and the state could not be part of discriminatory practices.[56]

The *Atlanta Daily World* saw the decision as the first step on the way to the "end of restricted communities and ghettos and slums." Austin Walden, the head of Georgia's NAACP, saw *Shelley* as a "milestone." It gave "flesh and substance to the Constitutional guarantee of equality under law." The *Tribune*'s news coverage of the event came from syndicated sources, fitting the SNS pattern, but its commentary was its own. The paper's editor, E. G. Jackson, celebrated the decision, which "knocked the props from under the unfair and undemocratic restrictive covenants," but reminded his readers that "in another sense, the decision fails to end all of the tribulations, heartaches and headaches" of the Black real estate market. "For individual property owners, chiefly whites, can continue to refuse, by common agreement and conspiracy to sell to Negroes, Jews, and others who may be deemed undesirable by white neighbors." Thus there was still more work to do, though "we rejoice in the decision and we congratulate the National Association for the Advancement of Colored People for one more victory in the endless chain which is being chalked up by its staff of lawyers."[57]

The issue of higher education also continued to be of concern to the Syndicate's readers. Regional segregated graduate education was far from equal, and there was no chance that Black southerners would support it. It was "the plainest type of folly to indulge Southerners in the thought that Negroes will be satisfied with this arrangement." But not satisfied with attacking the plan itself or its white promoters, the *Atlanta Daily World* also castigated the "heads of Negro institutions holding forth phony mediums of escape to those southerners who are grappling with the problems." The *Alabama Tribune* simply ran the same syndicated coverage from the *World*. The NAACP legal victories had clearly given almost all of the southern Syndicate papers, including the *Tribune*, a new belief that quality Black educational facilities wouldn't come from publicly funded entities when the funding for those schools was controlled by whites. What makes this all the more interesting is that the collusion with which the editors charged the Black college administrators was the same kind of charge that was often thrown at the Black editors before they moved to an integrationist position on education. Both professions served as connective tissue in the liminal space between the Black and white worlds: college administrators relied on funding from white legislators and knew that the only reason for their schools' existence was the maintenance of segregated education, while editors toed a racial line that ensured the safety and viability of their publications while interpreting news from white mainstream sources to a Black audience with decidedly different interests. The response of the Syndicate papers to the Meharry plan to fund a Black graduate school in Nashville put them through the looking glass, exposing the original arguments that bound them ideologically to the administrators of Black colleges.[58]

Meanwhile, Oklahoma had added a law school at Langston University to protect its white law school from integration. Ada Lois Sipuel Fisher (who had married during the intervening period) decided to apply to the University of Oklahoma again rather than attend the newly created Black law school at Langston. Another rejection. Another suit. This time, the U.S. Supreme Court denied her based on the fact that her argument was fundamentally different than that of her first suit, and the district court was responsible for such decisions. There was a Black law school now, the Court explained, so the argument was not based on unavailability. It was instead based on the inferiority of the Black institution. Again the Black press was dismayed, portraying the Supreme Court's decision as a technical cop-out or an attempt by the Democratic Party to shore up northern votes for the 1948 elections while still maintaining the loyalty of white southern Democrats.[59]

Looking on from Montgomery, the *Alabama Tribune* knew that such decisions could have repercussions all the way to the Deep South. In reporting on efforts to rehabilitate Black higher education in Alabama, the *Tribune* began its coverage using the surrogate advocacy approach. "'We can't dodge giving Negro citizens professional training any longer with the ruling of the United States Supreme Court in the 'Ada Lois Sipuel Case.' This was the advice given here today by Former Congressman Joe Starnes, newly elected chairman of the State Board of Education." When that board of education "evaded consideration" of a Black student's application to Alabama Polytechnic (now Auburn), the *Tribune* covered the incident and tied it to the broader regional college plan developed by white southern conservatives.[60] Adding to the argument, the student who had been denied, William Bell, was a World War II veteran and a strong student at Montgomery State Teachers College. The state board claimed it was "in process of making provisions for graduate and specialized training of Negro students." The superintendent argued that working with other southern states for regional Black schools was the best solution because "most Southern States are simply not financially equipped to provide separate facilities for both races in such fields." The hypocrisy of the statement was surely obvious to the *Tribune*'s readers. The argument for regional Black schools, thus shifting the financial burden to the more prosperous southern states, was also the argument for integration, which would save money for all of the states.[61]

For all of the emphasis on desegregating higher education in 1948, it was also an election year, and presidential politics intensified the substantial ramifications for national and regional race relations. Though Harry Truman was a war president who had won World War II by dropping atomic bombs on Japan and had initiated the Cold War, he was also a replacement president, having taken over for Roosevelt after his death in April 1945. He had not been elected in his own right. Thus in 1948, he was not only challenged by Republican Thomas Dewey, but also faced an opponent from the left, Henry Wallace, who denounced Truman's Cold War, stumped for universal healthcare, and argued for an end to segregation and voting discrimination. To shore up his base and make a play for the Black northern vote, a nervous Truman began talking publicly about the possibility of desegregating the military, about a federal antilynching law, and about other potential civil rights measures.[62]

And he did desegregate the military. When it looked like the Cold War could become a hot war very quickly in the wake of the announcement of the president's containment policy in March 1947, and with leaders like A. Philip Randolph publicly declaring that Black soldiers would not fight the Soviets in a segregated military, Truman was forced to live up to one of his promises. On July 26, 1948, Truman issued Executive Order 9981, mandating the "equality of treatment and opportunity for all persons in the armed services without regard to race, color, religion, or national origin," which officially ended segregation in the military. Full implementation did not happen until the onset of the Korean War in 1950, but it was clearly, if nothing else, a rhetorical victory in 1948.[63]

The *Tribune* was thrilled with the decision, arguing that the president "has nothing to lose. Negroes and all other minorities will back him in this to the limit." A segregated military "is one of the Nation's worst advertising cards in the eyes of foreign lands." This sentiment was echoed throughout the Syndicate and the Black press in general, but the *Tribune* also saw the military desegregation as secondary to Truman's adoption of a permanent version of the wartime Fair Employment Practices Committee to prevent racial discrimination in federal employment. Such could be an even more substantial boon domestically. In typical Syndicate fashion, the paper sought to justify its advocacy for Truman's proposal in unthreatening terms. "As to fair employment, there can be no reasonable objection since the order carries with it the selection of personnel solely on the basis of 'merit and without distinction' as to race or religion," the *Tribune* explained. "It would appear that such a law would be to the greatest advantage to white citizens, certainly in the more technical fields, since Negroes have been denied the privilege of training in those areas. In fact, man for man and job for job, the Negro worker, under the sole merit system, would always be at a greater disadvantage than whites."[64] It was a unique method of celebrating equality, and it demonstrated the practical radicalism the Syndicate papers employed. Unequivocal praise was followed by a justification largely geared toward white readers, even though there were no white readers. Or perhaps, there were no white readers other than those checking up on the radical stances of local Black residents.

Things hadn't changed much since Roosevelt died. The South was still the base of the Democratic Party, and white southerners were incredibly upset about the desegregation of the military. This was the reason the *Tribune* decided to phrase its celebratory defense the way it did. But Truman and pragmatic, nonsouthern Democrats saw that the Black vote, northern and southern, and the white liberal vote were too important to abandon in favor of the white South. At the 1948 convention, the Democrats even included a strong civil rights plank in their platform. White southern Democrats felt betrayed so they bolted from the convention and formed the States' Rights Democratic Party—the Dixiecrats—to better hew to the party's racist roots. The Dixiecrat candidate, Strom Thurmond, won the Deep South but wasn't able to stop Truman from winning the election. The effort served, however, as an opening salvo in the postwar white southern revolt against Black rights claims.[65]

The *Alabama Tribune* covered the Dixiecrat revolt at the Truman nominating convention in 1948, as well as Alabama governor Jim Folsom's decision, against the Dixiecrat mandate, to campaign for the sitting president. Truman "wants action, and not mere words, on Civil Rights legislation; on discrimination by reason of race[,] color or national origin, on protection of racial and religious minorities from discrimination in employment, the right to vote, the right to equal protection under the law," and he wanted them in direct contradiction to the southern wing of his party. "For this courageous and forthright leadership Americans and especially American Negroes, owe to Mr. Truman an undying debt of gratitude." This was the sort of commentary with which the paper could get away. It emphasized the positive benefits of Truman's platform rather than overtly denouncing the Dixiecrat campaign, which would have made it a target for angry Montgomery whites. When in May 1949, Folsom submitted his "36-point program" to the legislature, the *Tribune* reported specifically on the "seven measures of particular benefit and interest to Negro citizens of this state." Folsom wanted to abolish the poll tax and other restrictive measures in order to aid Black voting rights. He wanted recreational facilities for Black visitors to state parks, better educational facilities for Black students, and higher minimum salaries for teachers.[66] Again, the *Tribune* didn't editorialize, allowing the proposed measures themselves to do the work of advocacy.

But more advocacy was necessary. In May 1949, *Tribune* editor E. G. Jackson wrote of another in a long line of incidents of police brutality. He described how Montgomery's new police chief had entered as a reformer, but the latest Black man killed by law enforcement in the city brought the total to fifteen dead. Jackson reported that two white policemen had beaten an unarmed Black man named Henry Lee to death. He then reprinted the official story, which claimed Lee had a gun and was firing at the cops. "This is what they put in the paper Sunday night," he wrote. "I don't find any of it to be true." This was a marked departure from the paper's typical advocacy by proxy. Jackson was clearly frustrated. He went after the police and the story they concocted, and he included his name in the byline. The article was not a denunciation of policing, and it did not make calls for massive changes, but it did point out police culpability in the significant amount of blood and hypocrisy in the area. The paper was more muted in November, but Jackson did report that "a 12-man white jury yesterday had freed a white policeman" charged with killing an unarmed Black man in 1947. The officer had argued that he was being threatened, while the prosecuting attorneys had noted that the man was shot in the back. Jury deliberation lasted only thirty minutes. There was no screed that accompanied the tale in the paper, but the facts of the case provided their own denunciation.[67]

In January 1950, the paper reported on Folsom's appointment of an "all-veterans interracial 11-man committee organized by executive proclamation," which was tasked with investigating the wrongful rejection of military veterans applying to become electors. Some of those rejected were white, but the vast majority were Black. There was no direct advocacy in the article, and the committee ultimately died on the vine of a Jim Crow government ready to retrench against the coming onslaught of the civil rights movement. The paper's coverage did demonstrate, however, the use of military service as a cudgel against the denial of Black rights, a practical strategy that marshaled the time-honored effort to gain validation through overt patriotism.[68]

In August 1951, the *Tribune* reported on a poll tax modification bill that "would exempt 10 Black Belt counties" where the Black population "equals or excels that of the white segment." The paper explained that in Wilcox and Lowndes counties, two of those included in the bill, no Black votes had been tallied in fifty years. In December 1952, the *Tribune* covered the statement of E. D. Nixon, a Montgomery civil rights leader and president of the Montgomery Progressive Democratic Association, who charged that "quota-style racial restrictions on voting in several counties and a complete blackout in others" were evident across the state.[69] The paper used the words of Nixon to make what was a relatively obvious case.

While the country's eyes were focused on the Supreme Court in May 1954, the *Tribune* reported on "a vote denial suit alleging that the Bullock County Board of Registrars 'wrongfully and illegally failed to register' four Negro applicants," which had been filed in the U.S. District Court in Montgomery. In an exhaustive account, the description of the suit made the case against voting discrimination. Bullock County officials required Black applicants to have someone vouch for them, whereas white applicants did not. Black applicants waited hours before being ultimately rejected while white applicants registered immediately. When the court found the Bullock County Board of Registrars guilty in September, the *Birmingham World*'s Emory O. Jackson took the reins, describing the case in minute detail and clearly endorsing the findings.[70] Such was the synergy of the Syndicate's newspapers in Alabama, which worked together to produce a guardedly forceful message in the 1930s–1950s.

Emory Jackson also made efforts outside the *World* offices. In February 1945, he had worked for a federal investigation into the Jefferson County Board of Registrars for denying registrations to qualified Black voters. The following summer, he helped form the United Registration Committee to fight further discrimination against Black veterans trying to vote in the primary. A half-page advertisement in the white *Birmingham News* decried the denial of voting privileges to several Black veterans and encouraged Black registrations; it was sponsored by several Black groups, including the NAACP, the Southern Negro Youth Congress, and the Southern Conference for Human Welfare. "The Negro veterans are not asking for special favors," the ad explained. "They seek to exercise their citizenship right by registering on the basis of their qualifications—on the same basis as their former white comrades in arms." An FBI report credited Jackson—in his role as secretary of Birmingham's NAACP—with being instrumental in raising the advertising funds and bringing the various groups together for the effort. The one column inch the *World* gave to the registration denials was just a small fraction of the large advertisement in the *News*, and it quoted Jackson in his role with the NAACP, not mentioning his editorship of the paper. It was the NAACP secretary—not the editor—who wrote to the registrar, "It is an unworthy commentary on our times and our political system that men who fought for their country are being denied a chance to vote in their country."[71]

Jackson also was a member of the advisory council of the Committee for Alabama, an arm of the Southern Conference for Human Welfare, "a veiled Communist front organization," according to the FBI. The bureau spent much of its time linking various leaders of the Committee for Alabama to communist activity, but never placed Jackson in any of those roles. Thus the FBI charitably concluded that he was not an actual member of the Communist Party.[72] He was instead "an opportunist who is zealous in working for the advancement of the negro race and the overcoming of discrimination, segregation and other so-called injustices to which the negro race in the South is subjected." The bureau noted that labor leaders mistrusted him, viewing him as antilabor when it suited his racial aims. That was unquestionably true, but the FBI conveniently omitted that those labor leaders were white southerners.[73]

Jackson's sister Ruby Jackson Gainer was a teacher who helped lead the fight for pay equalization in Birmingham schools, a fight aided by the Southern Negro Youth Congress, another of the FBI's supposed "negro Communist front[s] in Birmingham." Gainer, the bureau noted thankfully, encouraged the Southern Negro Youth Congress committee working for equalization to remove two members because of their association with communism. The Jackson siblings were very involved in state and local politics and campaigned vigorously in the summer of 1946 for Pauline T. Dobbs for the state legislature, Luther Patrick for Congress, and James Folsom for governor. When Jackson found out that members of the Alabama State Committee of the Communist Party were campaigning for the slate, he spoke to local leaders of the party and asked them to stop. He "did not trust those people," claimed a bureau report, and Jackson told an informant that "it is all right for me to believe in certain things and sacrifice myself but those folks (Communists) go out and sacrifice everybody for their own cause and try to exploit (the election situation)."[74]

In October 1946, Jackson had been frustrated with the Syndicate, threatening to resign over printing problems and claiming that he "made this covenant with the newscarriers and advertisers" that they would get papers every Tuesday and Friday morning, which was not happening. "I will not be untrue to the newscarriers and the advertisers to whom I gave my word," he told Scott. In December, he wrote again with "a sense of outrage" over the late arrival of papers and said the paper "is worthless when it comes late." The delays fomented a sense in the city that "the Birmingham," as the paper was known in Syndicate correspondence, "has a bad name for keeping a schedule." Jackson challenged Scott to read an edition of the Birmingham paper. "If so," he told his boss, "you'll throw your hands up in horror. If you have any pride, you will hide behind a wall of your tears." His theory as to the reason for the problems was "that in Atlanta nobody wants it to approximate first-class journalism. So let the printing deteriorate. Blur the work. Fracture the grammar. Kink up the ads." He argued that "no other paper in the SNS chain has the competition facing the Birmingham World—Review, Informer, Voice, Leader." None had the circulation problems or staff problems. It was "a journalistic injustice to Birmingham."[75]

Jackson stayed, however, and continued with similar complaints throughout 1947 and 1948. "It is evident, as I have told you before, that it is the pattern to butcher, omit and batter Birmingham World news and advertising copy." In May 1949, a still-frustrated Jackson complained of those in Atlanta who "continue to de-grammar, de-journalize and de-grade our efforts on the Birmingham World." He cited an example where a column he submitted had used the phrase "salary rise," which was changed to "salary raise." He encouraged SNS officials to "check this construction and spelling with the English professors in some of your colleges over there," and "they will find me to be correct."[76]

He also directed much of his frustration at the race fights in the region. In September 1947, Thurgood Marshall contacted Jackson about the NAACP's attempt to overturn the state's infamous Boswell Amendment, enacted in 1946 in response to the Supreme Court's *Smith v. Allwright* decision in an effort to keep Black voters from registering. "I have never been more certain of the success in such a case than I am in a carefully worked out case against the Boswell Amendment," Marshall told Jackson. "We will be ready to move whenever you are." He explained that while there was a plan, he hesitated to share it publicly until a case was formally filed.[77]

In 1946, as secretary of the Alabama state conference of the NAACP, Jackson had been assigned along with physician and NAACP leader E. W. Taggart and attorney Arthur Shores to study the state constitution and the Boswell Amendment's place in it. A circular disseminated by the Alabama NAACP had lobbied against the amendment prior to its approval. It had provided a full reading of the proposed amendment and explained to potential voters, "Nine amendments to the Constitution will be voted on in the November election. The so-called Boswell Amendment is No. 4. If you are opposed to white supremacy make an X mark opposite the word 'NO' below proposed amendment No. 4."[78]

Meanwhile, Jackson's paper reported on the committee's work and the significance of the vote against the amendment. When the National Conference of Colored Railroad Firemen voted its opposition to the Boswell Amendment at the group's Birmingham meeting, the *World* covered it. It reported on the Alabama Negro Press Association's public statement against the amendment and noted that Jackson was chair of the group's Anti-Boswell Amendment Committee. In the days leading up to the election, the *World* published blistering editorials defending Black people's right to vote and noted the national embarrassment that the Boswell Amendment would bring to Alabama. Articles encouraged everyone to vote and announced a series of Cast Your Ballot rallies across the state. The "full vote" of minority groups, the *World* assured readers, would be against the "hated Boswell Amendment," which was "a 'white supremacy' device" that had to be defeated. It was not defeated, however, because Alabama had a white supremacist electorate, and Jackson's coverage was dutifully solemn after the failure while assuring readers that the fight was not yet complete.[79]

Jackson was the Alabama chair of the NAACP's membership drive and president of the Alabama state conference in 1947. He was heavily involved in the organization, giving speeches, producing reports, and attending committee meetings. When Harry Truman and Eleanor Roosevelt spoke at the closing meeting of the NAACP conference in June 1947, Walter White personally invited Jackson to sit on the dais. Jackson was integral to forming new branches of the NAACP in the state, aiding locals in 1947 in forming branches in both Selma and Huntsville.[80]

There was clearly synergy in these efforts, but that did not necessarily bring results. Jackson complained to NAACP president Gloster Current that "the Birmingham [membership] campaign is lagging," a reality made all the more frustrating by the fact that "our paper has thrown down an unprecedented barrage of NAACP publicity. That alone should have brought in over 5,000 membership[s]. Birmingham is discouraging" in "its so-called leadership." Membership was clearly a priority. Alabama had sixty-seven counties and twenty-three NAACP branches. "There is an imperative upon the militant leadership of the State of Alabama to conduct registration on a Statewide basis," pronounced a missive from the regional headquarters in New Orleans. "Especially this is true, since the Boswell Amendment, in order that the Negro vote will be felt at election time. To have the people organized in 23 communities, and unorganized in 44 communities, simply means that the objectives of the NAACP are being pushed further and further into the future."[81]

In May 1947, Oliver Harrington, the NAACP national public relations director, urged Jackson to send a reporter from the *World* to cover the NAACP's case on behalf of Herman Marion Sweatt in the Texas Civil Court of Appeals. Even before the arguments, the organization knew the case would be a watershed. Press coverage would be "of the utmost importance," Harrington told Jackson. "As you may well remember, the press, and particularly the presence of a host of correspondents in the courtroom during the Columbia 'riot' case in Lawrenceburg, Tennessee, had more to do with influencing the most sensational southern jury verdict than any other single factor."[82] Harrington was talking about the Mink Slide riot (see chapter 5), where the whites of Lawrenceburg attacked, but the Black residents of the town's Mink Slide district were arrested. Twenty-five Black defendants were tried for shooting local policemen, but only one was found guilty and served a relatively short jail sentence. Harrington credited the acquittals to press reporting and assumed that such public scrutiny would be necessary in Texas.

Jackson unquestionably saw the importance of the *Sweatt* case, but his resources were decidedly limited, so he saved his most ardent efforts for Alabama. Among his other work in 1947, Jackson spearheaded Operation Suffrage, a political planning committee of the Alabama NAACP, which was designed to catalog all of the Black political organizations in the state and collect comprehensive data on registered and qualified voters, along with a full list of "obstacles to voting" in each county. At the end of the year, Jackson told the organization that "there were times when it seemed that I couldn't make it because of the pressure of other duties," but despite his constant newspaper work, "to be an officer of the NAACP, I feel, is the highest honor that a community can confer upon a leader."[83]

In July 1947, the *Pittsburgh Courier* published an article on the plans of Birmingham's commissioner of public improvement. After reading it, Jackson wrote to the commissioner asking if he was behind a bill in the legislature that would ban unions and whether he opposed civil service protection for Black employees "and their uprating beyond the level of garbage collectors." This was an example of the synergistic relationship between the northern and southern Black press, but also an example of the willingness of the southern press to be active in holding its government officials to account. Jackson did not publish the story in the *World*, since he had already been scooped by the *Courier*, and the commissioner never responded to his letter, but the letter itself and its basis in the *Courier*'s reporting demonstrated a measure of symbiosis among competitors.[84]

While there was a mutually beneficial relationship between the NAACP and Jackson's paper, and a mutually beneficial relationship between the northern and southern Black presses, there was an even stronger bond between members of the Scott Syndicate. When the American Heritage Foundation's Freedom Train began its national tour in 1947, for example, taking a moving museum of U.S. historical artifacts across the country, it announced an integrated program at every stop. The planned events in Memphis and Birmingham, however, encountered officials unwilling to accommodate the violation of local segregation ordinances. Both cities proposed different versions of an alternative plan that called for separate visitation times for each race. Birmingham's plan, put forward by Public Safety Commissioner Eugene "Bull" Connor, required patrons to enter in alternating groups of roughly twenty spectators, with the next group entering after the previous group had moved to the next train car. Jackson helped lead the charge against this practice, developing plans to boycott the segregated event with the NAACP and using his role at the *World* to question Winthrop Aldrich, the foundation's chair, about the group's plan to deal with the controversy. Jackson asked whether the train's public stand against segregation had changed, but then went further. "The Birmingham World suggests," he wrote in a letter to Aldrich, "that if Birmingham officials insist on jimcrow plans that the American Heritage Foundation cancel the Birmingham schedule." This was not distanced journalism, but it was not supposed to be. Ultimately, the foundation canceled the Freedom Train's stops in Birmingham and Memphis.[85]

The *World* had reported on the scandal, including the "possibility of a county-wide attempt to boycott" the event if it remained segregated. Leaders of NAACP branches in Mobile, Montgomery, and Birmingham all rallied to the cause, though Jackson's coverage of himself always separated his two roles. He was always the "secretary of the NAACP" in such situations, never the author of the story itself. In editorials, however, those lines were blurred. "No good purpose can be served by the train exhibiting here under plans which are out of harmony with progressive, enlightened and rational race relations," wrote Jackson. "It is hard to see how any self-respecting Negro would care to view [the] Freedom Train on the basis of second-class citizenship." His editorial commended the NAACP's efforts and specifically stated, "The Birmingham World urges the American Heritage Foundation to withdraw the Birmingham Schedule." When the efforts succeeded, bold headlines above the masthead celebrated the victory, and articles argued that it was the "city's bigotry" that had "doomed [the] Freedom Train's appearance." It was an example of organizational activism and journalistic activism working together to generate momentum for successful change.[86]

After comments in a January 1948 *Birmingham Age-Herald* article by Charles V. Hendley of the Colored Masonic Temple praising two white police officers—"They don't come any better," said Hendley. "They are my idea of police officers."—Jackson wrote to Hendley and asked him "whether in your opinion Negro policemen could do as good or better job toward improving the posture of the so-called Negro business area in Birmingham than White policemen?" Considering the "unsuccessful attempt to attain Negro policemen" by activists in the city, the "political implications" of the story were significant, and "it is important that we have your reactions."[87] This demonstrated another mutually beneficial relationship, even if unintended, between the local white press, the local Black press, and the opportunity for activism.

Of course, that relationship could be intentional as well. In February 1948, Jackson wrote to the editor of the local white daily in Sheffield, Alabama, praising him for "commendable duties of progressive journalism" in his coverage of rape charges against two white Colbert County farmers accused of assaulting a local Black woman. He wasn't writing as a fellow journalist, but as secretary of the Birmingham NAACP. He told the editor that despite all of his good work, "we note that unlike newspapers in Birmingham you do not as yet capitalize the 'N' in Negro. We believe that in a course of time you will see fit to follow the practice."[88] He also wrote to the editor of the *Birmingham Post*, excoriating one of the paper's authors for his "distorted conclusions" about race and segregation. The *Post* article had claimed that unequal treatment in segregated facilities was the fault of the Black man, "because his actions do not deserve the same treatment." Jackson called the article's claims "reckless and libelous." There was no evidence presented for any of its assertions, and "none can be adduced."[89] Jackson was again writing in his leadership capacity with the NAACP, but his day job was no mystery in the city, and directly challenging white dailies on their race positions was a bold move for a fellow journalist, even when not responding as a journalist.

In April 1948, Jackson's NAACP sent a circular to community leaders in Birmingham for a meeting to create a plan "for dealing with the alarming and increasing police violence and terrorism against Negro citizens." In that month alone, three Black citizens had been killed by the police. Officers had pulled off NAACP membership buttons from people, stomping them and insulting the organization, and they had "beaten and intimidated" Black businessmen. This problem continued. In 1948, the Birmingham police killed a total of 14 Black people, and all of the slayings were ruled justifiable homicides. "Some of them may have been justifiable," Jackson put in his notes. "Some were obviously avoidable. Others were questionable. Two of them were unwarranted and could have been called lynchings." In 1949, the Birmingham police killed 16 more. More broadly, in 1948, there were 106 homicides of Black people and 13 white homicides. The Black population of Jefferson County was 41 percent of the total, but accounted for 89 percent of the violent deaths. In 1949, there were 68 Black homicides and 22 white homicides, with Black deaths accounting for 75 percent of the total.[90]

Violence was a problem that lingered, one without a simple fix, and so Jackson continued his program to remedy problems with available solutions. In February 1948, for example, Jackson wrote to Walter White that the Congress of Industrial Organizations was planning a separate test case of the Boswell Amendment without the cooperation of the NAACP, "giving lip service rather than living action to the question of Negro suffrage." The Southern Negro Youth Congress had done substantial work in voter registration efforts, but the fact remained that despite the "large number of qualified Negro applicant[s] for registration" who had been denied the opportunity, "it is unbelievable but true that as yet we can not find a single Negro in Alabama with nerve enough or interest enough to file a test suit" against the Boswell Amendment. The fear was real, and the potential for retributive violence was obvious in the homicide and police brutality figures.[91]

As of the summer of 1948, Jackson was coordinating with lawyers in Alabama, New York, and Illinois about initiating suits against the Boswell Amendment. "We must watch this situation most carefully for obvious reasons," Thurgood Marshall told him. "I am depending on you and the state conference to keep the state angle straight and we will keep the national angle straight." Marshall argued vigorously against taking action on any Boswell case "without full consultation, cooperation and approval" by Jackson and the Alabama branches of the NAACP. There were myriad instances "where cases have been brought by local groups without prior consultation with anyone and have resulted in the establishment of bad legal precedents which have harmed not only the individual case in the individual state but have done immeasurable harm to our entire program," Marshall explained. "That is the reason we have state conferences and a *national organization*."[92]

That summer was also the presidential nomination season, and the Dixiecrats ultimately walked out of the Democratic convention in protest of Truman and civil rights. The Dixiecrats then held their own nominating convention in Birmingham, and Jackson attempted to cover the event. In addition to all of his other duties, Jackson was integral in the organization of the Progressive Democratic Council, a group of Jefferson County voters that planned to send a delegation to the Dixiecrat convention, and served as its chair. Bull Connor, however, would have none of it. The police kicked Jackson out and told him to run. Jackson moved slowly, less to flout authority and more to ensure that he was not providing police with a reason to shoot him as he left.[93]

After the Dixiecrat revolt in the summer of 1948, the Alabama Progressive Democratic Association began a campaign against the new party, sending circulars and holding special meetings to convince people to vote for Harry Truman. "The choice is between Democracy and dixiecracy," one circular said. "In a dixiecracy, the Negro will be less than a slave. You can join the fight to save the dim freedom, harshly enjoyed in some parts of the South by Negro people, or let it go by default."[94]

In January and February 1949, with the Dixiecrats safely kept out of the White House, Jackson wrote to his circulation department, led by L. A. Scott, airing his frustrations about the paper's circulation in certain areas and other problems.[95] Part of the problem for Jackson was trying to coerce better productivity from employees who were directly related to the family that owned the company. It left Jackson feeling unable to cope with his situation and properly lead his office. Jackson's threats to leave the *World* were more than bluster. In December 1949, he wrote to Gloster B. Current about "any worthwhile position open on the National NAACP Staff which I can fill." He provided Current with his qualifications and noted that he could be ready to assume his new post soon after accepting. The only lag would be to "arrange my affairs at the Birmingham World so that my successor would not find the going too rough and complicated."[96]

Again, however, he stayed, taking on those rough and complicated tasks himself. One of the most pressing issues was securing advertising: keeping in contact with local businesses and convincing them of the benefits of advertising in the *World*. The vast majority of local advertising secured by the *World* was individual classified advertising, followed by that of local companies. The paper also profited from national advertising campaigns. In the summer of 1949, Pepsi purchased a series of large ads in the *Birmingham World*, facilitated by the Biow Company, a New York advertising firm. The advertisements featured notable Black people, like explorer Matthew Henson and conductor Dean Dixon, making the case that they were leaders in their fields, and Pepsi too was a leader in its field. Another campaign that summer came from Philip-Morris, which provided imagery that local advertisers could use in their own advertisements to highlight the fact that they sold Philip-Morris cigarettes.[97]

Those national ads were generally facilitated through term contracts. The Louisville and Nashville Railroad, for example, signed an advertising contract with the *Birmingham World* for the year spanning the summer of 1949 to the summer of 1950 in the amount of $244.80. When the railroad had additional advertising that went beyond the bounds of the original contract, it paid with "intra-state advertising passenger scrip." This was a beneficial arrangement, allowing Jackson and his reporters to travel at a discount, which made the paper more flexible. It could also cause problems, as in August 1948 when Jackson wrote in his paper and in a letter to the Birmingham L&N office that "card crooks" upset the passengers: "I hope that you will take the necessary steps to rectify this situation."[98] The incident demonstrated the ambiguous bond created by payment in company scrip, but it also demonstrated that Jackson was willing to publish his thoughts over and against the best editorial interests of his advertisers.

Jackson explained in March 1949 that an advertisement of two columns and four inches would cost six dollars per edition, making the cost twelve dollars per week for "the eight-inch display." A *World* flyer attempting to recruit new advertisers described the Black community of Birmingham as willing consumers. The Black population was more than 40 percent of the total, spending more than $140 million annually, and they spent their money at businesses that advertised in the local Black press. "THE WORLD is Birmingham's oldest Negro Newspaper and the state's only Negro semi-weekly."[99]

Jackson's role as managing editor made him a de facto advertising executive, but it also made him a de facto community leader. When the state announced that 155 new seats had been added to the gallery of the House and

Senate chambers, Jackson wrote to the director of Alabama Records and Reports asking about provisions "for Negroes to visit the gallery," since the *World* "plans to have reporters on hand during the session of the legislature." When students filed for admission to the University of Alabama law school and graduate school in January 1949, they wrote to Jackson to let him know. When a Birmingham woman wrote to Jackson in 1952 about being rejected by the Jefferson County Board of Registrars when attempting to register to vote, Jackson called the office and wrote to the woman encouraging her to return. "I had a long talk today with Mr. Thompson," he told her. "Let him know who you are, and I think that upon signing your application, you will be registered as a voter."[100] To be a Black southern editor was to be all things to all people.

In April and May 1949, Jackson wrote to the Justice Department urging federal action in Birmingham. His first request was about the unsolved and virtually uninvestigated bombings of three local houses. The second was about the denial of voter registrations by the Jefferson County Board of Registrars. Both responses from the U.S. assistant attorney general were politely dismissive. In July, Jackson wrote to C. Floyd Eddins, chief of the Birmingham Police Department, to explain that a local man had received a bomb threat. He denounced the action as a threat to organized government itself and urged Eddins, "a man of justice and courage, to rise to the challenge which the threat-warning has made." This was action on behalf of the NAACP, but it was also, though unstated, action by a Black editor focused on a white police chief. When a hooded mob invaded a local Black work camp, Jackson sent an immediate telegram to solicitor Howard Sullinger in Bessemer urging action. "You have an opportunity to show whether local law enforcement is able to cope with [a] klan mob," he wrote. "Mob law must not be allowed to replace legal law."[101]

In December 1949, Jackson wrote to Roy Wilkins, suggesting a plan for fighting Alabama Dixiecrats by having the Birmingham branch of the Justice Department "move in against these hostile board of registrars," while others worked to fight "registration apathy in Birmingham." He wanted to convince as many voters to register as possible and recruit organized labor to help in the endeavor.[102]

That summer and autumn, Jackson had worked with the NAACP to aid a zoning case in which fifteen Black property owners had filed a class action lawsuit "designed to make it possible for any citizen to live where he can rent, build, or buy." A group of Black citizens had been denied access to "the necessary expansion of homes for Negroes in desirable and wholesome surroundings," and the suit moved to federal court. When John Temple Graves criticized the suit in the *Birmingham Post*, Jackson wrote to explain his position and that of the NAACP, arguing that local solutions were everyone's choice, but "when all efforts to do this fail to bring satisfactory results there is no recourse other than that of seeking assistance through legal channels."[103]

The fight was important enough that Jackson placed a letter to the city commission on the front page of his newspaper. "The Birmingham World urges solution of the zoning problems within interpretations of the federal court decisions," he opened. "Negro people here correctly insist that one has the constitutional and American right to live where he is able to buy, to build and to rent." Beyond that, "we assert that it is the American way and the human impulse for a man to defend his home against peril and disrespect." Jackson explained constitutional law. He named the city commissioners. "In this vital hour no man with the American passion for respect for the courts and the law should be trapped on the side of those who would corrupt or subvert or distort court-interpreted law in a vain effort to limit democracy and to halt man's march down the freedom trail."[104]

Jackson also encouraged local pastors to take up a collection for the case in their congregations and bring the proceeds to the office of the Birmingham NAACP. "We must win this zoning fight," Jackson wrote in August, "because upon it rests the fate of the faint and declining leadership we have here." He was dispirited because "tensions are mounting in Birmingham. The local NAACP Branch has been weakened by the onslaughts of prejudice." Even more, "violence of all description is visited upon Negroes," and "I have been unable to investigate and report these evil things" because of illness.[105]

Still, it seemed that the violence had actually strengthened the resolve of the NAACP. In August, the local branch wrote to Attorney General Tom Clark in Washington, asking for an investigation into the August 12 bombing of the homes of two local ministers. There had been "six Negro home[s] bombed over [a] short period without [a] single arrest," and racial tensions remained high because of the "unfortunate utterances of public official[s]." The telegram explained that the NAACP had made repeated requests to the Justice Department for action, all of which had gone unanswered. The bombings were directly related to the zoning fight, and the NAACP made it known to authorities that its members clearly understood what was happening. A telegram to the president of the city commission condemned the violent actions and urged "day and night police protection for the Negro homedwellers in Smithfield area." Another to Public Safety Commissioner Bull Connor angrily explained that the latest bombings occurred "just three days after you allegedly warned that quote we're going to have bloodshed in this town unquote unless white citizens had their way about racial zoning." And naturally there had been no arrests. "It could be reasoned that such a statement as attributed to you [became] the signal for violence."[106]

The constant struggles took their toll on Jackson. "Physically I am but a worn out man," he also wrote in August 1949. "But with aching bones and a burning spirit I manage to totter on. Should I fall, or when I fall, let it be as the evangelist of social justice." Despite the difficulties, he never considered stopping his efforts: "I can now understand the addict who becomes a slave to dope. I try to quit, to give up, to turn back, even to forsake this cause. But I am a slave, a weakling, or something worse, without even the power to run away from the fight."[107]

In response to a February 1950 article in the *Birmingham News* on Black Belt politics and race relations, Jackson wrote to the paper's editor criticizing its denouncement of the "mass registration" of Black voters. "Why does 'mass registration' come up only in connection with the voting of qualified and responsible Negro citizens?" he asked. "The color and race of a group should not be allowed to victimize the personal rights of the individual who by the accident of birth is a member of that group." Jackson cited the Fifteenth Amendment, arguing that "for 49 long years the Negro individual has been denied the ballot in the Black Belt simply because he is viewed as a 'mass man' like a drop of water fallen into an ocean. He is seen as an ocean rather than as a drop." It was a problem that informative news articles could have a substantial role in remedying. "It would be a serviceable journalism," Jackson wrote, "for an enlightened reporter to do an honest and intelligent reportorial job on voting practices and opportunities in the Black Belt." And that was not happening in the city's white dailies.[108] Such a critique of his newspaper colleague was an overt shot across the bow, challenging not only the paper's racial views, but also its journalistic integrity.

Jackson also still had problems with his own paper. As of July 1950, he was still pressing for circulation improvements, including better recruiting of newsboys and efforts at expanding circulation. "You know Gus," Jackson said, referring to C. A. Scott by his nickname, "no matter what the program, I am going to do what I can to try to either hold or build our circulation." In August, he wrote to L. A. Scott, the Syndicate's circulation director, complaining again about recruiting problems for newsboys and continued delivery problems. The situation was made all the more egregious for Jackson because he had seen "an ad used by the Memphis World, our sister paper, to build circulation upon a promotional project." There was clearly a rivalry between the "sisters," and the perceived effort at circulation development for one of the papers only exacerbated the anger over various slights for the other.[109]

In the week ending August 17, 1950, the *World*'s weekly receipts rose to $604.96, with $361.55 coming from advertising. The business was clearly growing. The paper's circulation report was divided into deliveries for subscription holders and cash sales from newsboys. That week, subscribers received 1,193 deliveries on Tuesday and 1,231 on Friday. In addition, the paper sold 1,915 additional copies on Tuesday and 2,061 on Friday. That brought the total sales to 3,108 of the Tuesday edition and 3,292 of the Friday edition, earning the paper $452.48 (though much of that total was unpaid, owed by the salesmen distributing the papers, and thus limiting the week's receipts). The weekly totals throughout the autumn of 1950 remained relatively consistent with the week of August 17, vacillating up and down slightly with each week. Friday's edition always sold slightly better than Tuesday's, and daily sales always outstripped subscription deliveries.[110]

But revenue constancy did not mean that the problems were solved. In November, Jackson went further in his criticism of editing problems at the Syndicate, decrying the "unnecessary and, I suspect malicious errors, in the work of the Birmingham World." It was "a deliberate effort of the Central Office to mar" the paper and "keep us from making a good showing over here." The errors were so blatant that they must be intentional. Some news copy was not run, "stories were crossed up," and spelling and grammar were changed for the worse. Jackson was "disgusted and disillusioned" over the treatment of his paper.[111]

In February 1951, Jackson sent a letter to Scott from an advertiser complaining that his ad was buried at the bottom of a page. Jackson understood that Scott claimed that was the most efficient way to run advertisements, but the Birmingham editor countered that it was simply the easiest way, one that "requires no make-up man of any quality." This approach could lose advertisers and needed to be addressed. Circulation, he claimed, was down to around 3,500. "During 1949, possibly 1950, our circulation ha[d] ascended to over 5,300. We had two full-time workers then. Yet there was never the best operation and the returns were never satisfactory." In August 1951, Jackson again complained of mistreatment, arguing that Scott never followed up with the Birmingham office when "vital communications" were sent to Atlanta. "This is certainly out of line with sound business administration and tends to indicate that this office is not even worthy of the courtesy of a reply."[112]

The papers both within and outside the Syndicate were like sports teams in a professional league. They competed with one another within the confines of the industry, all the while aware that their best interests were served when all were successful. As of 1946, for example, Jackson was the official representative of the Associated Negro Press in Birmingham. He also served as a representative for the *Pittsburgh Courier* in Alabama. In 1948, the *Courier* assigned him to write a feature on Montgomery for a series on how state capitals were living up to the recommendations provided by Truman's Committee on Civil Rights. "This is certain to be one of the Courier's biggest features of the year," the paper's news editor told him. "It is a series that will touch every Negro in America." Jackson also wrote stories for the *Baltimore Afro-American* about lawsuits, the actions of Bull Connor, and other Birmingham issues. Through the National Negro Publishers Association, Jackson had a strong relationship with the *Chicago Defender*'s John Sengstacke. He was also in close contact with John McCray of the *Lighthouse and Informer*.[113] None of that writing was interpreted as a conflict of interest.

Jackson had been integral to the founding of the Alabama National Negro Publishers Association, which was always a political entity. The group's Public Relations Committee proposed using "bilbo," the last name of Mississippi's senior senator, as a common noun and verb, and sent the directive to all member papers.

> bilbo (bil-bo), v.; -boed (bod); -boing (boing); From United States Senator Theodore Gilbert [*sic*] Bilbo (Miss.) 1877–, notorious for slanderous public speeches against racial and religious minorities. 1. To hate in an unreasoning manner. 2. To give vent to spasms of slanderous prejudice against a person or race because of differences of color or creed. 3. To lie in order to discredit a racial or religious group.
>
> bilboer (bil-boer) n. 1. A hater of other persons or groups because of differences of race, creed or color. 2. A prejudiced person.
>
> Quisling got his. I don't see why we shouldn't give Bilbo what he has earned.[114]

In 1947, the NNPA created the Advertising Society to spread information about advertising agencies, discuss and solve problems related to newspaper advertising, and to publish a monthly newsletter. Though it was a subsidiary of the NNPA, it would act with complete autonomy. Also in 1947 the NNPA's news service broke away and formed the National Negro Press Association, which was designed to take pressure off the parent organization and to create a more complete service in line with the tenets of the Associated Press. It was administered by a committee consisting of Thomas Young of the *Norfolk Journal and Guide*, Carl Murphy of the *Afro-American*, and C. A. Scott, and its creation was another outgrowth of the competitive unity among Black newspapers.[115]

In October 1947, the NNPA planned for its executive committee to meet with representatives from the NAACP to discuss "a common front for prosecuting the cases having to do with equalization of educational opportunities." As part of that prospect, Thurgood Marshall had sent the group a statement of the NAACP's policy, vowing to fight school segregation and arguing that there was "no scientific basis for racial classification by the states" and that discriminatory segregation laws "were never intended to provide equal facilities but rather to set up a system of dual citizenship." It was, Marshall explained to the group, "impossible to have equality in a segregated school system."[116]

The move was seen as necessary to prevent infighting. Carl Murphy of the *Afro-American* noted that in Texas there was "an open fight between our good friend, Carter Wesley, and Thurgood Marshall" over the *Sweatt* case, which such a meeting could solve. "The most important thing that publishers and national organizations need is a common front," he argued.[117] It was an interesting statement because it pushed against assumptions of journalistic objectivity and also assumptions about the individual mind-set of each member editor. Such a policy meant that anyone not toeing the NNPA line or that of organizations like the NAACP, with which it was aligned, could be shunned as problematic traitors. That was certainly the case for Davis Lee, a Black journalist who stumped for segregation.

In September 1948, the president of the NNPA wrote to the editor of the white daily *Norfolk Ledger-Dispatch* about an article it had reprinted by Davis Lee, explaining that Lee "has no standing whatever in the National Negro Publishers Association" and that his paper "is not considered a competent journalistic endeavor." It was "packed solidly with the vilest and cheapest kind of filth and gossip which is gathered by morbid volunteer scandal mongers." The group wrote a similar letter to *Time* magazine. The *Norfolk Journal and Guide*'s Thomas Young expressed his frustration with Lee to Jackson: "Anything you can do to debunk this guy will be a help to the Negro Press and to the race generally."[118]

Lee's provocations made publications like Jackson's *World* a continued necessity. But in the week ending August 14, 1952, the paper's receipts were down to $414.29, only $160.52 of that coming from advertising. While there were other weeks in 1952 with higher totals and other weeks with lower, that week was a representative example of the *World*'s year. Rare were the weeks when advertising totals outpaced those from paper sales. The *World*'s profit profile had shifted, turned on its head from the late 1940s and 1950, when advertising was the greater source of income.[119] Still, the paper was dependent on advertising and focused on the needs of its advertisers.

Despite the revenue problems, the *World* had continued to fight for race rights in Birmingham. When a group of Black veterans pressed the issue after having their registrations rejected, for example, Jackson and the *World* sought to cover the hearing of the Folsom Vote Probe Committee, which was studying the case, in January 1950. He wrote to the committee's chair to ask about the hearing's location so that he could send a reporter, claiming that no one at the Birmingham courthouse would tell them where it would happen. "The Jefferson County Board of Registrars are using delaying tactics by engaging in lengthy conversation[s], numerous rest periods and extended questioning of applicants," he explained to the chair. "Negro applicants are being refused because they can't answer hazy and two-edged questions." What began as a location request on behalf of the paper became a letter of advocacy, an effort to get justice for the denied veterans.[120]

In another 1950 incident, Jackson wrote to Thurgood Marshall describing the case of Zack L. Gunn and included his sworn statement taken at the Birmingham NAACP. Gunn's case was emblematic of a series of incidents in Cleburne County, where Black drivers were stopped for minor traffic violations and then arrested. Alcohol in the car made the situation even worse, since Cleburne was a dry county. The prisoner was then beaten and threatened by law enforcement. If the victim had the money to post bond and pay whatever fine law enforcement imposed, officers would take the money and decline to press official charges, claiming that they wanted to save the victim the trouble. Others were encouraged to have money wired to fix the problem. It was then sent to the bank. As Jackson noted, "Never is money wired to law enforcement or officers of the court." Gunn was convicted and fined, and he knew that he was always susceptible to further shakedowns.[121]

Birmingham's WEDR radio station essentially banned discussion of any news dealing with the NAACP in September 1951. An angry Jackson wrote to the station, "It is unfortunate that a Radio station built on the Negro market and the Negro audience would by such censorship take an action which implies hostility to the aspirations and yearnings of Negro citizens for first-class citizenship." The station was "on the side of those forces which seek to suppress the NAACP by smothering news about the NAACP." Jackson reminded the station that "radio uses the air which is owned by all of the people and by the very nature of its operation is indebted to the people."[122] This screed demonstrated Jackson's determination when it came to his newspaper and his frustration that others could be intimidated into censoring themselves for some kind of local security when he risked so much every Tuesday and Friday. It also demonstrated the difference between his radicalism and the practical radicalism of his southern journalistic counterparts.

That radicalism continued. In January 1952, Jackson wrote to Congressman Laurie Battle about a series of bombings in Alabama, which destroyed a home in Phenix City and another in Sand Mountain. "Add to these new evil outbreaks the nine unsolved racial bombings in our own Ninth Congressional district together with two arsonic fires," Jackson reported, "and you get something of the picture of the widespread frequency, pattern and malignancy of these bombings." He hoped that Battle would introduce federal legislation to make such crimes federal offenses, taking jurisdictional control out of white southern hands.[123]

Later that year, one of Jackson's *Birmingham World* employees, Pollie Anne Myers, and her closest friend, Autherine Lucy, attempted to desegregate the University of Alabama by applying for enrollment without mentioning their race. When the school accepted them, the *World* ran a banner headline, making the university realize what it had done. It immediately began backtracking. As he did with so many other efforts, Jackson worked as an advocate through his editorials and through his activism, helping to shepherd the resulting lawsuit through the courts. Finally, in January 1956, Lucy was admitted by order of the court. But the school rejected Myers, the original instigator of the suit, hoping it would dissuade Lucy from deciding to attend. Jackson remained involved, raising money and finding student allies on campus. "The story of Lucy to attend the university," explain historians Gene Roberts and Hank Klibanoff, "is also the story of Emory Jackson's determination to live a life worthy of his journalistic ancestors, the men he so admired because they had made the Negro press the fighting press."[124]

In January 1953, C. A. Scott asked Jackson about writing some editorials to be included in the Atlanta and Memphis papers and enclosed a story on segregation in Alabama. The story cited the "growing concern among Alabama's [white] political and educational leaders" that the Supreme Court would eventually declare public school segregation unconstitutional. "Why not a good editorial pointing out the fallacy in detail and wage a consistent fight for prompt and continuous improvement of the schools until they are equalized, at least at the public school level," Scott suggested. "Our editorial position is still to advocate the entrance now of Negroes to the state schools at the professional and college level." Primary and secondary education cases were already working their way through the courts, yet the *World*'s editorial position was to argue for the equalization of segregated schools below the level of higher education. It was the simple pragmatism that fought for things achievable in the region. The suggestion was to take the premise in the original segregation story and work within its bounds to carve out a better position for Black students in Alabama. Still, in August 1953, the Syndicate planned a series of advertisements for a combined NNPA-NAACP project, and "all or some of the money from these ads would go to the NAACP Legal Defense Fund."[125]

In June 1953, William G. Nunn, the *World*'s managing editor, urged Emory Jackson to take over a project documenting educational inequality in the South. He wanted numbers on spending and school enrollment. There had to be more ammunition beyond the moral case. "In trying to prove to our reading public that the south's theory of 'separate but equal' will never work educationally," he argued, "we must get the facts and figures." Jackson responded by writing to C. G. Gomillion at Tuskegee, who sent him assembled data from 1936 to 1951. The numbers were stark, demonstrating massive disparities in enrollment, building values, and capital outlay per student. Spending for Black pupils was only 30 percent of spending for white pupils in the 1936–1937 school year. That disparity shrank through the remainder of the 1930s and 1940s, reaching just below 72 percent by the 1950–1951 school year. But even that progress left a vast spending gap that disadvantaged Alabama's Black students in immeasurable ways, particularly when broader capital outlays, building values, and other data became part of the calculus.[126]

Through March 1954, business remained steady, and weekly receipts hovered for the paper between $250 and $450. Both advertising and circulation surged, however, beginning in April 1954, a month prior to the Supreme Court's *Brown v. Board of Education* decision, most likely in anticipation of the decision. On April 8, weekly totals reached $564.69. On April 15, they reached $689.63. Perhaps more important, $302.56 of the latter total came from advertising. Against all of the caricatured timidity of the Black southern press when it came to civil rights issues, it was clear that civil rights issues were good for business. On May 6, less than two weeks from *Brown*, the paper's weekly receipts totaled $715.45, with $373.50 coming from advertising. That was the highest those totals would get through the summer, but the average income of the paper rose to over $500 weekly through the period, a demonstrable improvement over the previous two years.[127]

Civil rights paid the bills. And they paid them because Black southern newspapers had established a pattern of practical radicalism that led their readers to the conclusion that the time for such action had come. It wasn't overdue. Civil rights were a pragmatic response by the Supreme Court to the workmanlike progress of the NAACP's Legal Defense Fund, beginning with graduate school decisions and moving slowly along the chain of precedents. Responding in kind would be a pragmatic response by white southern school boards, ultimately saving states a significant amount of money. Black southern newspapers provided, in the words of Martin Luther King Jr., the "fierce urgency of now." And when the Black South became the focus of national attention, the Black press benefited from the reputation it had developed over the previous decades.

Still, friction with the Syndicate did not dissipate in the wake of financial solvency. In July and August 1953, Jackson's complaints to the home office continued. "We have no system and without system, routines, goals, standards and etc. you cannot build anything," he told Scott. This problem was exacerbated by the fact that "I make less money than a country school teacher." Later in August, a frustrated Scott responded. "Reason, logic and everything else should tell you and others concerned there that errors in your paper grieve me as much as they do you," he told Jackson. "But I don't think harsh statements help the situation."[128]

In September 1953, Jackson included in his paper's copy a letter to the editor originally sent to the local white *Post-Herald*. The letter took Birmingham's white papers to task for not including courtesy titles for Black women. It cited one article in particular where both a white woman and a Black woman were quoted, but only the white woman was referred to as "Miss." Jackson planned to run the letter with a note that it had also been sent to the *World*: "It is being published today in the interest of promoting respect for all womanhood and for good usage." Scott, however, returned it to Birmingham unpublished, telling Jackson that he didn't think it was "good policy for us to get into controversy with other papers."[129] But it was hard to ignore that those "other papers" were white dailies. Scott was continually worried about crossing the kinds of lines that would drive the Syndicate into legal or racial controversy. There had been plenty of discussion in Syndicate papers over the years about the use of terms of respect for all people, but they did not take on a local newspaper for the omission. Practical radicalism dictated that such discussions remain in the realm of theory rather than local praxis.

Jackson, however, was a man of praxis. In July 1953, the *Afro-American*'s Murphy wrote to Jackson to explain the plan of the NNPA to support the NAACP Legal Defense Fund in its Supreme Court segregation cases. All Black newspapers, he suggested, should raise money for the cause. Papers in larger cities should combine for massive rallies, culminating in a major event in October in Washington, D.C., sponsored by the NNPA. "We should make it crystal clear in our editorial comments and our news stories that ours is a fund-raising campaign," stated the report of William G. Nunn, the NNPA president. "We intend no picketing, no march on Washington, no hysterical demonstrations. We are willing to abide by whatever decision the Court makes based on the facts supplied by Thurgood and his associates." Murphy included questions for Jackson about the logistics of such a plan, but the broad contours were in place. It perfectly encapsulated the role of Black southern newspapers, an approach of practical radicalism that sought to raise funds through media advocacy, but stopped short of "hysterical demonstrations." The Black newspapers would, the report said, raise money for the legal challenge, and then let the chips fall where they may, because seeking clarification was not the threat to the white South that protesting was.[130]

This formula could be maddening for those willing to be more tangibly radical. In August 1953, for example, Jackson wrote to Walter White, frustrated about the position of John Temple Graves and other journalists who encouraged Birmingham's Black population to be conciliatory and work within the system, to be patient and cooperative. "White people haven't changed any," Roy Wilkins responded. "When they have the situation fully under local control they boot Negroes about unmercifully and turn a deaf ear to all pleas for justice, cooperation and decency."[131]

While white people's lack of mercy was not poised for any self-imposed correction in the near future, the work of Jackson and the *Birmingham World* ensured that an honest record of its manifestations would exist, along with an accounting of the justice, cooperation, and decency that continued to push back against it.

Chapter 5

Tennessee

The Great Migration Black Population Changes (%)

City	1910-1940	1940-1970
Chattanooga	7.4	−11.8
Knoxville	−1.7	−6.6
Memphis	−2.6	2.5
Nashville	−8.7	−4.8

The listed cities are the ones large enough to be included in Census statistical materials. "The Great Migration, 1910 to 1970," U.S. Census Bureau, 13 September 2012, https://www.census.gov/dataviz/visualizations/020/508.php.

The *Nashville Independent* joined the Scott Newspaper Syndicate in the same month that the *Birmingham World* was created in 1931, but it was not long for survival.[1] There was among Atlanta's Syndicate leadership a desire to get back to the Nashville market after the paper's collapse. Nashville was the state's second largest tiered market and a hub of Black cultural and university life, the home of Fisk, Meharry, American Baptist, and Tennessee State. And so in 1932, the SNS created the *Nashville World*. It was one of five Black newspapers in the city that attempted to compete with the long-standing *Nashville Globe* between 1910 and 1940.[2] But even though it had the financial backing of the Syndicate, the *Nashville World* proved to be just as unsuccessful as the others. It lasted less than six years. That eventual lack of viability, however, didn't affect its early message.

"Another World Is Started Today," the Syndicate announced hopefully in its Atlanta flagship. The *Nashville World* was to be a semiweekly, the fifth *World* paper following the creation less than three weeks earlier of its counterpart in Jacksonville. "With the establishing of this new paper, the Southern Newspaper Syndicate moves another step ahead in its plans to furnish the South with the latest news and best features," announced the SNS, "and to furnish employment to talented men and women of the race who could not otherwise find employment befitting their training." John R.

Patterson, formerly of the *Atlanta Daily World*'s advertising department, transferred to become editor and publisher of the new venture.³ The Scotts were not leaving this new publication to local contributors as in most markets, but sending their own representatives, demonstrating the importance of the market to the SNS.

The *Nashville World* looked much like its Birmingham counterpart, featuring crime and celebrity divorce stories on the front page, interspersed with civic and city news. Its editorial page, however, lamented the murder of Black men by police in Memphis and worried over the state of Tennessee prisons. It hoped for the end of lynching and the use of terms of respect like "Mrs." when Black women were addressed by local whites. It was "the only local newspaper," the editorial masthead proclaimed, "with exclusive SNS service."⁴

Netrel Wright, who wrote the *Atlanta Daily World*'s "Seen and Heard" column while still in high school (he was "a popular member of the local younger social set") left in January 1936 to run the circulation department of the *Nashville World* and to produce a similar column for that paper. Columnist Sam McKibben explained that the "Atlanta school boy journalist" had "engaged in a triumphal march toward recognition as circulation manager of the Nashville World." That year also witnessed another change as the paper struggled to survive. John Patterson was out as Wright's boss, ultimately replaced as the paper's general manager by Wittie Anna Biggins. Biggins was a former Indianapolis schoolteacher and stenographer who had come to Nashville in 1920 and eventually created the W. A. Biggins Commercial College, offering courses in sewing, millinery, artwork, "beauty culture," stenography, and secretarial bookkeeping. In 1931, the school added other courses, including accounting, dressmaking, and designing. By 1936, the business was running itself, allowing Biggins to take over the *World*.⁵

The paper was situated perfectly to cover the Sunday School Union, the publishing arm of the AME Church, which was headquartered in Nashville. It was also situated to cover any controversy coming out of the body. In June 1936, for example, Ira Bryant, the longtime secretary-treasurer of the AME and head of the Sunday School Union, was voted out by the national conference in New York in favor of E. A. Selby. Bryant, however, was not willing to relinquish his post, leading to lawsuits, court battles, and a series of recriminations that threatened a rift in the denomination. Selby claimed that the national conference vote had given him the post. Bryant claimed, correctly, that the Sunday School Union had its own board of directors that made such decisions. He argued, also correctly, that in two decades at the helm, he had grown the union into a profitable concern. It was the only profitable section in the denomination, he said, which had led to conspiracies for his ouster for years. The courts ultimately agreed with Bryant. The *World* chronicled all the machinations that led to his victory.[6]

The *Nashville World*'s editorial policy under both Patterson and Biggins supported the Roosevelts, both Franklin and Eleanor. It railed against police abuse in Black neighborhoods, explaining, for example, that "under the Code of Tennessee an officer has no authority whatever to arrest for a misdemeanor without a warrant, unless the offense is committed in his presence." It warned readers that "certain type[s] of policemen and duty sheriffs as a rule, care nothing about the law when the rights of colored people are involved." At the same time, when "the sheriff, the white physicians, and all who helped in any manner to ferret out the guilty" cooperated to catch a white man who had assaulted a "twelve year old Negro girl," the paper congratulated law enforcement. The *World* also used its editorial page for more esoteric arguments, warning, for example, against the dehumanizing and alienating effects of "civilization" and the urge for progress. Man "stands with the golden rule in one hand, while with the other, he builds a mechanism that tears its tenets into threads."[7]

To the west of Nashville, things were little better in Memphis, the state's largest Black market. "Living conditions for blacks in the urban South reflected their bleak occupational prospects," writes historian David Goldfield. They were "reminders of inferiority." In Memphis, Black residents lived in neighborhoods called Slippery Log Bottoms, Queen Bee Bottoms, and Shinertown, names that, in the words of Goldfield, "indicated their disadvantaged topographical position."[8] The people of Shinertown, who were already in such a disadvantaged position, were going to need a voice to help guide them through the worst economic catastrophe in U.S. history.

In July 1931, the Syndicate created the *Memphis World*, led in its early incarnation by editor and manager J. E. Oakes, giving the SNS a triweekly voice far from home on the Mississippi River. By September, Oakes had hired Lewis Ossie Swingler from nearby Crittenden, Arkansas, to be the paper's city editor, and Swingler would soon take over the *World* and steer it through the hard years of the Depression. The *World*, unlike its Tennessee counterparts, offered a full page of comics and littered its front page with lurid and sensational crime coverage. The paper "enters the field with no axe to grind or grudges to air in public print," it claimed in its inaugural edition. "The policy of the World will be one of sanity and fairmindedness. These columns will be no media for spite work." It argued that "the primary function of a newspaper is to print news. The Memphis World will not be content until it prints ALL the clean and constructive news originating here." The murder headlines and scandal coverage seemed to push against that claim, but the paper pushed back: "It is the mission of this newspaper to be a mirror. It strives to reflect the things happening." In one early February 1932 edition, for example, the paper grimly reported with no headline or fanfare that the single month that had passed in the new year had already witnessed ten homicides of Black people, putting the city on pace to exceed the seventy-five Black victims killed in 1931.[9]

Early in its history, the *Memphis World* encouraged Black ministers to become more active in the fight for racial justice. It encouraged Black businesses to stop gouging Black customers. It actively sought higher wages for Black teachers. Such were necessary fights. Black ministers in the South tended to cultivate a personal sense of salvation over and against the activism that was often a hallmark of Black Protestantism. Black businesses often took advantage of the fact that they had a relatively captive customer base in order to raise prices. Teacher salary disparity in Memphis, as throughout the country, left Black teachers making demonstrably less pay than white teachers. The *World*'s advocacy included a rebuke of the West Tennessee Teachers Association, which had been ineffective at bringing about any substantial change, in favor of a new, more militant organization.[10]

Even at its founding, the paper's lush layout included a comics page, a sports page, a society page, and a page of church news. The pages not reserved for such fare discussed local funerals, murders, traffic accidents, and robberies. The *World*'s service as "a mirror" reflected a Black population struggling with the same ephemeral pleasures and inherent dangers as many socially marginalized and economically limited groups, but it also showed the desire for upward mobility that was part of such a position. The paper's coverage of national race stories like Scottsboro and the effort for a federal antilynching law demonstrated that Memphis was also aware of broader obstacles to race progress.[11] This was the kind of self-awareness that belied criticisms of the Black press as trading in vice, since a mirror serves not only as a reflection, but as a visit from what is most familiar. Just as the pages of Joseph Pulitzer's *New York World* and William Randolph Hearst's *New York Journal* of the 1890s brought readers to the looking glass with scandal to prod them on civil service reform and ending government corruption, the *Memphis World* used society news, church information, sports, and crime to provide meaningful racial news that local white papers never offered. That the focus of that racial news tended to veer from local events in an effort at self-preservation didn't make the news any less relevant or meaningful to those moving toward the mirror.

In one September 1931 editorial, the paper castigated white Atlanta attorney Luke Arnold for welcoming a Baptist convention to the city by peppering his remarks with racial epithets. Arnold was a surrogate for Atlanta mayor James L. Key, who wasn't able to attend. "We do not believe Mayor Key himself would use such objectionable terminology," the paper claimed, but that didn't make "this pre-Lincoln psychology which fathers public uncouthness" any easier to swallow. Significantly, the paper argued, "the only consolation to be drawn from the affair is the fact that Negroes no longer are afraid to voice protests to such official insults."[12] That was not necessarily true, particularly when it came to criticisms directed specifically at locals, but it was a sentiment that remained vital to the survival of Black southern journalism.

There were worse indignities closer by. In March 1931, a car wreck between a Black Tennessean and a white Mississippian on the Mississippi side of the state border led the white driver and the local sheriff to hunt down the Black driver in Memphis. They murdered him in front of a local Black family. In the trial the following year, the sheriff concocted a story about self-defense that every Black witness denied, but it was enough for the all-white jury to acquit. "A cold blooded murder," the *World* reported, "a crime typical of Mississippi treatment toward Negroes of the Delta state, had its counterpart in Tennessee." The paper understood the risks it was taking but also was outraged at the trial's outcome. Its coverage denounced the murderer and his obviously false testimony because he came from across the border, committing a crime "typical of Mississippi." Left overtly unreported but obvious was criticism of the principal culprits of the failed indictment, the all-white jury that freed the murderer.[13] They were local and therefore could not be the focus of the coverage. The *World* reporters understood, however, that they did not need to be. Overt criticism of the murderer would lead to an all-too-familiar understanding of the local jury's failure by the paper's readers. Such were the coded references required of practical radicalism.

Like its Syndicate counterparts, the *World* spent significant advertising space ensuring that its readers understood the value of a southern press: "The newspaper in your community is the only way in which you can keep informed of local and round-the-world happenings among Negroes." A community paper "provides employment for men and women of our race who otherwise would not enter the field of their choice" because of "the steel bars of racial prejudice."[14] The message was clear. Newspapers "in your community" should take precedence over others, such as the *Chicago Defender* or *Pittsburgh Courier*, that might be available. Southern papers not only provided what readers needed, but also stood as a dam against racial prejudice.

Of course, there were better and worse southern papers. The *World* chided its local competition for "selling out to the white man" by offering weak editorials that didn't advocate strongly enough for the race. To bolster its own bona fides on that count, the *World* spent much of its early editions chronicling Black history and celebrating holidays like Carter Woodson's Negro History Week.[15] While stumping for Negro History Week had value, it wasn't exactly fire-eating. The *World* was arguing for a practical radicalism that advocated for the race without directly attacking local white southern values, which could draw the kinds of negative attention that ultimately led to retribution, violent or otherwise.

Practical radicalism, to be effective, required the coordination of papers across the state, which allowed the kind of deflective coverage that could provide plausible deniability in various markets that might be faced with immediate or violent racial antagonism. Memphis and Nashville weren't enough. The Syndicate next put its foothold in Knoxville, first with the short-lived *Knoxville Recorder* in February 1934, an effort replaced in September by the more durable *Public Guide*, published by Clarence Houston Graham, which survived until 1938.[16] Graham was a Knoxville native, a piano teacher by trade, whose paper seemed to better have its finger on the pulse of the city than did its brief predecessor. A December 1934 editorial, for example, lamented the debt being accrued by the federal government in the wake of the Depression while admitting that circumstances dictated that there was little choice. The writer remembered, however, that following the Civil War Black families were promised "forty acres of land and a mule. How is it that out of the multitude of suggestions for a panacea for our present ills, some ingenuous [sic] soul has not risen up to offer this as a way out of our present depression?" Another editorial questioned the Tennessee Valley Authority about the lack of hiring of Black workers. "It is true that Negroes comprise a relatively small per cent of the population in this area," the *Public Guide* explained, "but the percentage of Negroes dependent for subsistence upon purely manual labor is so much greater than among whites that this should be a factor to consider in giving employment at these great public works."[17]

Yet another editorial lamented the amount of Black crime in Knoxville, but along with the common southern editorial pleas for better behavior among Black citizens, the paper suggested that "more colored jurors would be of help," as would having "more Negroes as officers of the law to patrol Negro sections to prevent crime." The paper called on the city's Negro Voters League, which had done so much to register voters: "Why not accomplish something worthwhile as a result of that voting?"[18]

One worthwhile effort would be an end to lynching. In May 1936, the *Guide* lamented that the federal antilynching law had been set aside by Congress in favor of "measures regarded by them as more important." It encouraged readers to "make this lynching question the supreme issue in so far as they are concerned in the coming National campaign." It reminded readers that though Republican platforms continually promised action on lynching, the party had never done anything constructive about the problem. The issue demanded results, and if neither party was willing to take action, "it is the imperative duty of the Negro voters of the country to turn for relief to the Socialist or other party willing to fight to the finish this great national evil." It was rare for a southern paper that wasn't particularly radical to suggest the possibility of a turn toward socialism, but such was the power of lynching as a political issue. In October 1936, the paper described a narrow escape for an acquitted murder defendant in Anniston, Alabama, and one not so lucky in Dalton, Georgia. "It is high time that a stop be put to the practice of lynching in this country," the paper insisted. "While candidates for the Presidency are making their views known on social and economic issues they should be asked to state their views on a federal anti-lynching law."[19]

The *Public Guide* was a vigorous Republican organ, even supporting Alf Landon as the 1936 presidential candidate against Roosevelt. In Chattanooga, the Syndicate fostered the *Chattanooga Observer*, another decidedly Republican paper, which was founded by Pat Patterson, brother of Tuskegee Institute president Frederick Douglass Patterson, in November 1934. Patterson soon sold the paper to Walter C. Robinson, a former truant officer who left to run the *Observer*.[20]

Robinson's *Observer* had a relatively moderate voice that saved its passion for railing against the expansion of the Democratic Party. Robinson was accustomed to wielding significant power among area Republicans. He had organized the city's Negro Voters League and had worked for its "educational commission." In March 1935, however, he lost a local election. The Syndicate's John R. Patterson credited differences over specific issues, including the Tennessee Valley Authority, for the loss, but he mostly laid the blame at the feet of "Robinson's enemies." They had reasons for "their dissatisfaction with his leadership, most of which are trivial and characteristically political grudges."[21] Meanwhile, his paper argued that Black neighborhoods must be kept as clean and safe as possible. They needed to demonstrate to white Chattanooga what the Black community was capable of, and therefore there must be a coordinated effort to maintain cleanliness. In a rights game with whites, perception mattered.[22]

Of course, rights themselves were also important. Robinson consistently called for more equitable application of the voting laws and urged all of his Black readers to exercise the franchise.[23] He was willing at times to take on the city's sacred racial cows. "Mr. McMillan, Commissioner of Education of Chattanooga deliberately and willfully refuses to allow Negro mechanics to work on any of the school projects under c[o]nstruction in the city at the present time," explained the *Observer*, "which is costing all of the tax-payers irrespective of color approximately a million and one half dollars." It reprinted a lengthy statement by the local brickmasons organization to counter charges by T. H. McMillan that the lack of hirings for public works projects was the result of a lack of qualified Black workers.[24] This bold move not only publicly criticized the city's education commissioner, but also aligned the paper with the local masons union. Such was not the timeworn strategy for Black southern journalistic activism.

In April 1937, McMillan suspended John P. Greer, principal of the James A. Henry School, for "loosely handling of cafeteria funds, immorality and drunkenness." The municipal court dismissed the case because there was no real evidence for the charges, but McMillan fought anyway. The paper never interpreted McMillan's actions as retributive toward the Black population, but it did portray him as a racist. Greer was not the only "colored teacher who has been harassed by the McMillan administration since its inauguration."[25]

In a February 1935 editorial, the *Observer* had described accusations in a white Memphis daily that Chattanooga was part of a communist conspiracy that had developed from interracial contact on Black college campuses. The white paper equated "the struggle against lynching, against war and fa[s]cism, against the denial of constitutional rights and for the [disbanding] of the KKK" with a planned "Red Revolt." Sustained contact between "white and colored youth" was the real culprit, centered around hubs like "Fisk, Tuskegee, and Shaw University," all with "departments of Social Sciences" that fostered such activist thinking. The *Observer* argued in response for the importance of social sciences and the legitimacy of fights against lynching and other racial problems. "If thinking makes men red, then we are facing a red age, for the age in which we live is the one in which clear thinking and frank expression are doing more for humanity than all other forces put together."[26]

In April 1936, Robinson spoke at the Atlanta Political and Civic League. "He has organized the colored citizens of that city so well that now they hold the balance of power in the political equation," the *Atlanta Daily World* reported. "There are only 30,000 colored citizens in Chattanooga, but the colored people registered numbers well over 5,000." This was an interesting bar for holding the balance of power, but southern versions of progress were decidedly incremental. In January 1938, for example, Black citizens petitioned the city to include an appropriation for "colored physicians" to follow their patients to a new hospital being built in Chattanooga. A local judge agreed to a $200,000 plan so that "the old hospital can be reconditioned to permit the colored to practice therein." It was a plan "applauded by the crowd" and demonstrated that there could be at least some manner of racial cooperation in the city.[27]

The *Observer*'s work had clear benefit for the Syndicate. In April 1938, the second annual Southern Negro Youth Congress met in Chattanooga, and an SNS paper in the city provided the coverage. The Southern Negro Youth Congress had been founded the previous year to improve citizenship, jobs, education, and health in the Black South. Atlanta University's Rayford Logan told his audience to "stop living in a dream world of peace and re-adjust their thinking to the possible necessity of going to war to preserve democracy." He condemned collegiate peace campaigns and argued that democracy had often been "achieved largely through force of arms." Pauline Redmond, director of Chicago's Youth Department, emphasized domestic policy. "We live in the worst of slums. Our death rate is higher than that of our white brother. Too many of us contribute to illiteracy. We are discriminated against in the North and denied the right to vote in the South," she told them. "What are those but frontiers?"[28]

Syndication also provided a form of fact-checking. A December 1938 Syndicate article published with an Atlanta dateline mentioned that a John W. Schultz had been charged in Georgia for practicing medicine without a license. The article mentioned that he was a "leading physician" in Chattanooga. Two weeks later, a syndicated article from the *Observer* explained that "this Mr. Schultz (so-called Dr. Schultz) is no physician at all and is not recognized as such in the city of Chattanooga or the State of Tennessee."²⁹ This was another example of the syndicate working like a grapevine.

There was similar fare in another Syndicate paper, the *Jackson Times*, edited by William D. Holder in Jackson, Tennessee. Jackson was "the birthplace and General Headquarters of the CME Church," and the *Times* covered it extensively. There was also, however, substantive race politics in the paper. After the Supreme Court ruled that Black Alabamans were being systematically excluded from juries, thereby forcing retrials in the Scottsboro case, the *Times* ran an editorial by attorney P. L. Harden of Jackson, who celebrated the decision, noting that "Tennessee has taken the lead of practically all our states in reform and revolutionary movements." He was certain that judges in the state "will not need a proclamation from our governor but will fall in line with fair play to all citizens."³⁰ This was the kind of naïve optimism that frustrated so many about the South and the Black southern press. The *Times* and, by way of syndication, the other papers of the SNS interpreted such victories as ends rather than beginnings, trusting that white leaders would implement federal rulings instead of using those rulings as the genesis of fights for their implementation.

In May 1938, the *Knoxville Progress Post* was founded by editor Edwin A. Wilson, a recent graduate of Knoxville College, replacing the city's *Public Guide*.³¹ When the Ku Klux Klan that year warned a local contractor to fire a group of Black Georgian workers and send them home, the contractor defied the warning and continued building a stretch of highway between Chattanooga and Nashville with his entire workforce. The *Post* celebrated the courageous decision while reporting on the incident. The paper also covered in depth the 1938 testimony of Charles Hamilton Houston and Thurgood Marshall to a joint congressional investigating committee regarding discrimination in the administration of the Tennessee Valley Authority. The testimony ultimately led to the promise of further investigations, but even after those promises, discrimination in hiring, firing, and hourly wages continued in the New Deal program. So too did the *Post*'s reporting on every nuance of the race problems with the TVA and the efforts of the NAACP to address them.³² The paper didn't provide stinging editorials calling for integration, but it reported such incidents with a depth and interest that demonstrated a clear stake in the outcome. Again, this was advocacy without actually advocating. It was advocacy through reportage on the advocacy of others.

As the 1930s became the 1940s, that kind of advocacy remained the norm. The *Memphis World*, for example, often had to modify its coverage in response to white pressure. In the 1940s the paper's circulation rose to 16,300, and its influence was palpable, at least in relative terms. The circulation of its white counterparts stood at more than 200,000, but the *World* came under scrutiny anyway from Mayor Edward "Boss" Crump and Police Commissioner Joy Boyle. Boyle in particular targeted the paper's reports as agitators of racial hostility, so Crump personally demanded of the editor that such subversive pronouncements cease. Editor Lewis O. Swingler and his chief columnist, Nat D. Williams, had no choice but to comply. They still emphasized the fight for Black rights in the state, the nation, and the world. They celebrated along with the state's other Black newspapers the death of Tennessee's poll tax in 1943. They criticized the segregated World War II military and celebrated the accomplishments of Black soldiers. Their coverage of rights demands within the confines of Memphis, however, diminished to silence.[33]

Thus the 1940s *World* responded to racial violence by either calling for calm or endorsing the authorities outright. In the Detroit riots of 1943, for example, the *World* called for "no relaxation of vigilance on the part of police and local authorities to prevent mobs from forming," even though the police had killed seventeen Black protesters. Closer to home, the 1946 Mink Slide riot in Columbia, Tennessee, dominated the state's headlines after an altercation at a local department store led to charges of assault against a Black man for essentially defending his mother against a white aggressor. He was released on bond, which led to a white mob massing near the Black business district of Columbia, known as the Mink Slide. Black veterans and others gathered in response to protect the neighborhood, prompting white officials to arrest the locals, search homes without warrants, steal from residents, confiscate guns, and attack at will. At the end of the attack, four Black residents were dead. The police later killed two of the hundreds they had detained. The *World*, however, simply described the events as "inopportune" and urged caution in Maury County, lest the United States lose face in "the eyes of the United Nations."[34]

The paper even dismissed A. Philip Randolph's March on Washington for Jobs and Freedom, which was organized to protest a lack of defense jobs for Black applicants and the segregated military. The paper hoped that Randolph's "non-violent civil disobedience" would be "at once rejected by the rank and file of Negroes and Negro leaders throughout the country." This was a rare perspective, as the vast majority of Black newspapers in the country, and even in the South, supported the march. This editorial position, according to historian Samuel Shannon, was "prompted by a sense of survival."[35]

The Syndicate's *Chattanooga Observer*, which had also been publishing since the early 1930s, was in a similar position. In 1939, the *Observer* reported on a speech given by its founder and editor, W. C. Robinson, in Cleveland, Tennessee, where he presented a decidedly Washingtonian Republican line. "The predominating opinion among Negroes is that their color prevents them from succeeding in the world," but he believed that was untrue. He blamed instead "the prevelancy of crime among Negroes" and their unwillingness to create business organizations ("a race that refuses to be organized and follow leadership cannot be saved"). If a Black man "has what the world wants, and succeeds, the world will make a beaten path to his door." Race would not be a factor.[36] It was a decidedly shortsighted position, but it was also a decidedly southern position.

The *Observer*'s reporting was by no means uniform. In April 1939, the paper reported favorably on the sentencing of "a Negro to be electrocuted for killing another Negro" for the "first time in more than a quarter of a century." To the paper and those it interviewed, this was a certain sort of progress and would ultimately make the streets safer; the verdict demonstrated that the state was taking crime against Black victims seriously. In June, it reported that the Tennessee Valley Authority was discriminating against its Black employees by demoting them "from skilled labor to common labor," thus reducing their pay. At the same time, the Hod Carriers Union of the American Federation of Labor took Black union dues but wasn't defending Black labor interests against the TVA. When Robinson gave a speech at Atlanta's Hunter Street Baptist Church, he thrilled his audience by arguing for a legitimate Black labor movement in response to white union exclusion: "Some people respect religion, but all people respect power."[37]

The second annual Southern Conference for Human Welfare was held in Chattanooga in 1940, featuring, among others, Eleanor Roosevelt. Founded in November 1938, the Birmingham-based group brought together southern liberals, the majority of them white, to solve the economic and social problems of the region. While the group dedicated itself to voting rights and the elimination of the poll tax, it did not directly rebuke Jim Crow, choosing instead to work for better treatment within the segregated system. Robert H. Montgomery of the University of Texas told his audience at the meeting in Chattanooga that "the sharecropper should be a good scientist." After all, he explained, "he has an opportunity to study astronomy through the roof and geology through the floor." Syndicate coverage noted that F. D. Patterson, president of Tuskegee, "apparently just couldn't leave to get a full meal" because the sessions were "so interesting."[38]

On the conference's opening night, Mordecai W. Johnson, president of Howard University, argued that the South "has paid in the moral and spiritual degradation of four and one half million Negroes, and three and one half million white men, in the impoverishment of large areas of its farm land, in a heavy percentage of illiteracy and in a bloody cleavage between the north and the south. We just traveled down the wrong road." John B. Thompson of the University of Oklahoma was more wry: "Negroes are deprived of the citizenship so much that for some of us to say our oath of allegiance holding to equality and justice and liberty is to smile grimly." The Syndicate, by way of the *Observer*, was pleased to report that there was no segregation at the conference. "A pledge that there would be no Jim Crow in the treatment of delegates was exacted from the Chattanooga City Council by the conference," the SNS reported, "following unpleasant experiences at the first conference held in Birmingham."[39]

In January 1941, the *Observer* reported on the denial of jobs in "defense industries located in and near Chattanooga" and the organized letter-writing campaign to see that changed. The NAACP and other organizations led the protest, with the bulk of the letters going to President Roosevelt and Senator Estes Kefauver. "We are protesting against the discrimination being shown Negro workers in this area in the national defense program," one letter to Kefauver read. "As our Representative, we are insisting that you use your office to bring pressure on the industries which have been awarded contracts in the national defense program."[40]

One of the paper's other worries was the high murder rate in Black Chattanooga. To address that, the Monuments Baptist Church held a "thou shall not kill" mass meeting, where the community discussed ways to lessen Black crime. George W. Chamlee, a former Tennessee attorney general and Scottsboro lawyer, spoke at the meeting, advocating a profiling campaign allowing the "search and seizure" of anyone who looked "suspicious" after ten or eleven at night. All ideas were welcome as the community sought to stanch the flow of violent crime in the city.[41]

In March 1942, the *Observer* told the story of Mary Hamilton of East St. Louis, Illinois, who had responded to the call of a recruiter for workers on a Mississippi sugarcane plantation. The "75 or 80 [or] more men and women" were promised two dollars per day, along with room and board, "but we never got any money whatever." The workers were kept in a state of "semi-slavery." Along with sunup-to-sundown work, Hamilton claimed, poor behavior resulted in lashes and murders. "Young women who were considered capable of becoming mothers were thrown in a big house called the 'breeding house' with a big Negro man." It was a terrifying and harrowing ordeal, and Hamilton finally escaped with the help of "a good white woman" to Baton Rouge, and from there she "begged enough money to buy a ticket to Chattanooga."[42] This was a cautionary tale for those in the city and those within range of the Syndicate, a reminder of the cruelty of southern whites and Black people's vulnerability.

The paper celebrated in February 1943 when the Tennessee legislature repealed the state's poll tax, whose "only excuse" was "to disfranchise an element of the citizens of the state." It maintained an air of paternalism, however, reminding readers that the move now meant that "there can be no excuse for Tennesseans to fail to take advantage of their alienable right to vote; and Negroes in particular, should welcome the opportunity." When the target was out of state, however, the *Observer* could be more trenchant. In March 1944, for example, the paper took Mississippi senator Theodore Bilbo to task for arguing that the Washington, D.C., slums should be cleared of their roughly twenty thousand Black "alley dwellers," sending them instead to "be put to work on farms in Virginia and Maryland." The paper criticized Bilbo's race record (and thus his motives), as well as that of his state, arguing that if he "was forced into a contest in his home state where all of the citizens of that state were permitted to vote," he would not be Mississippi's senator.[43]

The following month, the Supreme Court issued its landmark *Smith v. Allwright* (1944) decision on another race crisis in another state. In *Smith v. Allwright*, a Texas man, Lonnie Smith, had argued that the white primary held by the Texas Democratic Party violated his constitutional rights. Primaries were technically private events, and southern states had always argued that their private nature meant that the Democrats could keep out whomever they wanted. That was what Texas had argued. But the NAACP's Legal Defense Fund, led by Thurgood Marshall, argued that since Texas was a one-party state, primary voting was tantamount to the final election, so excluding people from the primary violated their right to vote. The Court agreed, basing its ruling on the Fourteenth and Fifteenth Amendments and arguing that abridging "the right of citizens to vote on the basis of color" was prohibited by the Constitution. What made the case so important was not only that it invalidated the white primary, but also that it led the Court to agree that the effects of laws in practice were just as important as the laws' language, bringing the decision into direct conversation with the *Plessy* and *Williams* decisions of the 1890s.[44]

In the wake of *Smith v. Allwright*, the *Observer* acknowledged the declaration of the leader of Tennessee's Democratic Party that Black voters had always been able to vote in the state's primaries. The *Observer* agreed, appreciative that there had never been a white primary law in Tennessee. However, "of greatest concern to thoughtful Negro observers is the woeful indifference on the part of Negroes themselves." It didn't matter "how liberal Supreme Court decisions may be," an editorial noted. "If people exhibit downright lethargy and indifference concerning their own political interests by failing to go to the polls and vote for well qualified men and women for public office, the decisions may as well not be rendered."[45] The *Observer* had demonstrated this paternalism before, as had many other Black southern newspapers, and it turned a legal victory into an opportunity to chastise the race.

Paternalism was present in Tennessee Syndicate papers as well. From 1906 through the 1940s, the *East Tennessee News* served Black Knoxville, calling itself a conservative organ but consistently arguing for the vote and a more equitable pay scale for Black workers. It traded, like its Tennessee counterparts, in practical radicalism, quick to praise white officials for any moderate concessions to the Black community. A relatively uniform patriotism came from the *News*'s editorial page, with the exception of support for U.S. acceptance of European refugees. The paper argued that fixing the conditions of Black America was far more pressing than fixing those of overseas groups.[46]

The *News* had joined the Syndicate in December 1938, but the long-established organ retained the voice of its founder and publisher. Webster L. Porter was born in Marietta, Georgia, but moved with his parents to Knoxville when he was three. After his high school graduation, at only seventeen years old he founded the *East Tennessee News*, which he continued publishing for the next thirty-nine years.[47] The *News*'s emphasis changed little after its association with the SNS. Porter still edited the paper; it still made the same kinds of arguments. The only appreciable difference in its pages after contact with the Syndicate was more emphasis on stories emanating from Georgia and a liberal smattering of SNS reports to accompany local writing and articles from the Associated Negro Press.[48]

In April 1939, the *East Tennessee News* responded to an effort by the Republican Party to study why Black voters were leaving the party by hiring a professor from Howard to evaluate the trend. The *News* suggested that Republicans didn't need a professor. They should instead look "among the habitués of cross road country stores, who languish there, chew tobacco and get the news reports over the soap box radio." They would tell the party to support Black institutions, like President Roosevelt did, and to fight against discrimination, like his wife did. The paper was particularly proud of the First Lady for her denunciation of the Daughters of the American Revolution's treatment of famed contralto Marian Anderson. Without developing "fair and liberal attitudes" toward Black America, "all the efforts of experts in every university of the land will prove of little consequence in pulling away Negro support" from the party of Roosevelt.[49]

Closer to home, the *News* celebrated in February 1940 after the Knoxville school board voted to equalize the salaries of white and Black teachers, adding $14,700 to the 1940 budget to do so. The *News* chalked up the victory to the Negro Teachers League, a local group dedicated to the issue, and made the subtle case simply with the style of the rest of its coverage. Such gains—which were being demanded of many southern school districts in the early 1940s—came from the kind of practical, accommodating commentary that accompanied the paper's presentation of the news. One year later, for example, Porter spoke to Swift Memorial College in nearby Rogersville, arguing that "the sooner the minority racial group dispels the idea of an inferiority, just so soon will the racial group rise in the estimation of other races." That sounded like a Washingtonian self-help ethic, but Porter was making the claim that the races were fundamentally equal, that when Black students had the same facilities as whites, they had done equally as well or better than their counterparts. He compared Thomas Edison and George Washington Carver, arguing that if one had "placed them behind a screen and judged their accomplishments by comparison, it would have been utterly impossible to determine which was white and which was black."[50]

Still, the *News* did not support the NAACP. The paper admitted that the group "may have a purpose to serve in espousing the cause of the minority racial group nationally," but insisted that "in handling acts of discrimination and injustices in communities, especially [in the] South, there should be no outsider interference. Such situations should be left wholly in the hands of local leaders." The paper also noted the NAACP's inconsistencies and infighting as part of its "definite non-inclination to adopt the organization's program considering it as being of little worthwhile consequence." With that position clearly established, its flank clearly secured, the paper defended NAACP leader Walter White in a 1941 controversy involving his postponement of a hearing on defense industry discrimination. White had "worked earnestly, fearlessly and unselfishly in interest of the organization's program," but only received bickering and criticism for his troubles, the result of "a group of envious, selfish Negroes to bide their time for the opportunity to destroy one of their number who has made rapid strides of progress in the favor of his fellowmen." There was, it seemed, only one solution: "The Negro racial group is thoroughly in need of a house-cleaning from within." This was another instance of practical radicalism. The paper bookended a full-throated defense of White with a preamble rejecting the NAACP in favor of "local leaders" and an epilogue of calling for a Black housecleaning.[51]

The *Knoxville Journal*, the local white paper, advocated for Black rights during World War II. The *News* reprinted the *Journal*'s 1942 editorial in full. The *Journal* argued that one problem "that will inevitably come up for reexamination in light of our declaration of objectives will be the status of the American Negro." The editorial, written by the paper's editor, Guy Smith, wasn't calling for Black equality by any means, but it did note that "we cannot undertake the solution of problems in distant lands and shy away from those within our own."[52] This was the kind of generic, moderate proclamation that the *News* most appreciated.

Earlier in 1942, the *News* had reported that "Negro physicians and dentists have been placed on equal basis with white medics at the Knoxville General hospital." The Black doctors worked at the hospital's "Negro unit," but until this decision had not been allowed to practice unsupervised. The effort had been led by the East Tennessee Hospital Association and resulted in a legal ruling that declared, "No regularly licensed physician in the state of Tennessee can be deprived of his right, regardless as to race, color or creed, to practice medicine and surgery in any tax supported hospital in the aforesaid state, unsupervised."[53] There was still a Black ward, and full equality was still at least a generation away, but it was progress, and it was the kind of local progress that the *News* felt it could celebrate.

The paper's positions were more complicated than that, however. A 1943 article hailed Ralph Chandler, publisher of the *Mobile Press* and *Mobile Register*, who had criticized a local judge for releasing white men arrested after fomenting violence against Black stevedores because they had been promoted to skilled labor positions. The *News* hailed the publisher, arguing that the nation "is extremely fortunate in that there are numbered among its outstanding leaders men the type of Mr. Chandler."[54] Here, too, was an example of practical radicalism: praising an influential white southerner for an action rather than emphasizing the judge who released the perpetrators. By finding sympathetic white voices within the system (though Chandler was still a supporter of Jim Crow), a southern paper could sheathe its message in a different kind of white envelope.

The other side of that strategy was to criticize officers of the law for crimes against white people. In September 1943, the *News* discussed a New Orleans case where a white man convicted of raping a nine-year-old girl was shot and wounded by the girl's father. The police then shot and killed the father while he was in custody, claiming they were "viciously attacked" by their wounded prisoner. The paper called the incident a lynching, the policemen "guilty of flagrant dereliction of duty which savors much of lynch rule." Such, the *News* argued, was the logical extension of the disturbing American trend: "So long as the white leadership of our country tolerate[s] the lynching of defenseless Negroes, there is grave danger of the lynch rule being extended to include white men, and even women."[55] The paper once again used whiteness as a barometer of proper behavior.

In September 1944, the *News* railed against "the terrible lynchings that have been staged in Italy," where prisoners were "jerked from witness chairs in the courts hearing charges; and cruelly beaten to death by mobs that offered defiance to all constituted authority." Lynch law in any form, the paper argued, had to be stopped. Closer to home, in November a boy was lynched at the State Training and Agricultural School for Negro Boys at Pikeville; he had been sent to the reformatory after murdering two white women. The paper's extensive coverage emphasized official calls for an investigation into the incident, but also the need for reforms at the school, including possible relocation and the "hiring of Negro personnel, with a superintendent who has majored in social science."[56] The paper was able to advocate positively for those incarcerated at the reform school without appearing to sympathize with a double murderer.

The *News* also pushed back against the Great Migration, noting that the *Pittsburgh Courier* and other papers were urging Black southerners to move to northern and eastern cities. They "describe conditions in other sections [of the country] as the 'gold at the end of the rainbow.' And in so advising, are unquestionably doing a vast majority of those who follow such suggestions irreparable injury." The paper described the previous wave of migration in the 1910s, noting the racial violence that accompanied it: "Those who make changes in residence seeking to avoid annoying problems, both racial and economic, will find that all sections, north, south, east or west will furnish annoyances plenty." The *News* didn't deny that education and working conditions were superior up north, but "there are thousands of Negroes who were born in the South; have lived in the South and will continue their residences in the South until they answer the final summons." A better idea, the paper contended, was for able northerners to come to the South, where Black residents needed "the services of doctors, dentists, mechanics, lawyers and the like." Things would never get fixed in the South if its best and brightest absconded to other areas.[57]

And there were, without question, things that needed to be fixed. In June 1946, the *News* responded to George Schuyler's claim in his *Pittsburgh Courier* that "Negroes are not at all afraid of the sheet-like garb and flaming crosses" of the Ku Klux Klan. That was, the *News* admitted, essentially true. Such over-the-top gestures, however, masked more secretive efforts against minority groups. "Those of the anti-Klan groups who do not entertain fear and alarm over the ruthless depredations and insidious undercover program of the KKK are wholly unmindful of their own welfare." Keeping with its strategy of practical radicalism, the paper lauded "leading Baptist ministers of Knoxville" who "denounced the program of the KKK and such organizations in no uncertain terms." There was also "editorial opposition being registered by the daily newspapers," and all of it would help destroy the terror group.[58] By placing white leaders as the heroes against the Klan, the paper was able to denounce one secretive group of whites by praising other very public groups. Such was the strategy of the Tennessee Black press in microcosm.

Meanwhile, at the far west of the state, the *Memphis World* was playing out a similar strategy. "Look who's advising Negroes," started a February 1944 editorial in the Syndicate's *Memphis World*. "Senator Theodore Bilbo of Mississippi—the man who has made a perfect score in opposing every man and every principle, calculated to advance the cause of the Negro" both at home and abroad. "Judging by any test of measurement, Bilbo is the biggest failure the senate ever had." Bilbo had claimed that Black Americans could not be loyal in the fighting effort of World War II because they would always be the victims of discrimination and would always be inferior. The *World*, however disagreed: "Negro Americans do not need to be advised about the stakes they hold in this war for freedom. Their hearts are in this war, not because they are being given the kind of reception which first class citizens should be accorded, but because they hope for and envision such a day when this war is done." In August 1945, the *World* reprinted a *Lighthouse and Informer* editorial arguing that if "Bilbo were not so ignorant, he would not be of much value to you and to me. Out of his ignorance he is really helping Negroes. Bilbo is exposing to the world the entire South and its rotten political and social system."[59] The paper, like so many others, used the war as a catalyst for equality claims. Unlike many others, it was a southern paper in a large market on the border of an even more notoriously racist state. If practical radicalism made it difficult for the *World* to rage against the Memphis machine, it had a convenient foil just south of the city limits—in Mississippi.

The *World* also reported on nearby incidents within its own state, like the 1946 Mink Slide riot in Columbia. It reprinted stories from the Associated Negro Press and the Syndicate on investigations into violence, voting denials, and the murder of two Black citizens who had been jailed after the February event. But the riot was in Tennessee, which made the paper more reluctant to present public criticism. "Merely because of the foolish and inexcusable explosion of tempers which touched off a race riot at Columbia, Tenn. last Monday," the paper argued, "is no good reason to suppose that racial tensions in the South are growing more pronounced." It was clear that "race riots, lynchings, unfair economic and political practices" would alienate the Black population and keep the United States from living up to its democratic promise, but at the same time, the paper urged, "let every Negro be constantly careful that he does nothing to cause an interracial clash." The distance to Columbia from the *World*'s offices on Beale Street was more than double that to Oxford, Mississippi, home of lily-white Ole Miss, the pride of Senator Bilbo, but the location of the state line fundamentally changed the paper's willingness to criticize. The following week, for example, the paper reprinted an editorial from the *East Tennessee News* praising Governor Jim Nance McCord for sending Lynn Bomar, the chief of Tennessee's Highway Patrol, to stop the riot. It was not state officials who were at fault, or even necessarily the racist policies that they represented. Instead, it was "those officers of the law at Columbia" who "broke faith" with Bomar and decided to kill two Black prisoners. The paper assiduously covered the aftershocks of the event, but its editorials demonstrated a caution not present in its attacks on Bilbo.[60]

In August 1947, the *World* denounced Mississippi when only 281 Black votes were counted in the state's Democratic primary. In the same edition, an editorial admitted to being "completely awed in our admiration for the rapid strides which Negro educational institutions are beginning to take in our Southland." Tennessee State was undergoing a $3.5 million expansion. Alcorn A&M College was doing well, too, despite the fact that it was "away down in Bilbo's Mississippi." Such was the protective cover that borders provided. Alcorn was only sixty miles farther from Memphis than was Nashville's Tennessee State, but the mind-set created by those imagined lines put it "away down."[61]

Those lines, however, were most certainly imagined, and white southern ideology moved across them as easily as rural highways. The *Memphis World*, then, could not help but tread on local ideologies and was willing to do so when there was no direct attack on local whites. The paper endorsed Harry Truman in 1948, over and against the Dixiecrats, who were "waging a desperate battle to hold on to their age-long traditions to rule by terror and thus subject the Negro to second class citizenship." The paper was sure that "no sensible Negro will be fooled by southern congressmen who say they are not against the abolition of the poll tax but are against the invasion of states' rights. The plain and undeniable truth is that they are against a free and unrestricted ballot." The *World* was also a vigorous supporter and defender of the NAACP. Walter White was "the symbol of the hopes and aspirations" of Black citizens across the nation, "the race's greatest and most militant crusader for justice." The *World* even used editorial space in August 1948 to defend the organization's decision to double its membership fee from one dollar to two.[62] Its practicality did not signify an unwillingness to take positions unpopular with local whites; it simply refrained from direct assaults on them.

That understanding between the *World* and its readers, that knowledge of the boundaries that circumscribed the grapevine in the South, helped the paper grow. The *World*'s circulation continued to expand in the years following the war. It listed its 1947 circulation at sixteen thousand. By 1952, it had grown to twenty thousand.[63] And it continued to play by the same rules.

In April 1950, for example, the *World* warned against "the use of mass psychology to suggest that there is imminent danger of a Communist uprising, or that a few thousand Reds can take over the United States." From there, "it is easy to assume that every person who has ever talked to an admitted Communist is guilty by association." Red-baiting was a "monstrous doctrine" that needed to be defeated. In another column, the paper noted that the real danger to the U.S. democracy was not a stated communist, but instead "the double-talkers who sometimes give fervent lip service to the democratic idea but who at the same time say they would 'go to jail' before granting Negroes the same privileges as other citizens. The real saboteurs of democracy are those who would oppress others simply because of a racial difference." The following year, it excoriated Birmingham for its series of bombings and acts of police brutality, still maintaining its strategy of saving its direct attacks for those outside its borders.[64] A segment of its readership, however, was growing beyond the bounds of that strategy.

In 1947, pundits had predicted fewer Black newspapers but larger ones, a consolidation that would strengthen the market, the quality of the journalism, and the longevity of the papers. "The protest function of the Negro press will remain unimpaired or even will expand," predicted John Burma. Optimism was rampant, but proponents seemed to forget the dependency of such outlets on the very thing they were fighting against. As that fight became more sustained and more immediate in the 1950s, advertising declined and circulations dwindled.[65]

While there was a measure of cooperation among the various syndicates, and the NNPA served as an organizing body for them all, there were times of opposition when the caution of the South became too blatant for northern counterparts to ignore. Thus in 1951, just months after the *World* celebrated its twentieth anniversary in Memphis, the Sengstackes moved into the market, publishing the *Tri-State Defender*. Adding insult to injury, the *Chicago Defender*'s move into Memphis was facilitated by taking the *Memphis World*'s editor and a key Syndicate leader, Lewis Swingler, who either had become frustrated with his original paper's lack of militancy or was willing to jump ship for more money. "While the *Memphis World* was reserved, reluctant, and Republican," Gene Roberts and Hank Klibanoff have noted, "the *Tri-State Defender* was aggressive, gregarious, and Democrat[ic]." The new paper maintained what Roberts and Klibanoff describe as "a healthy sense of outrage," which poised the *Defender* chain perfectly to cover the investigation and subsequent trial of Emmett Till's murderers in 1955.[66]

"The job of a militant newspaper is more than just printing news," the *Tri-State Defender* stated in its first edition. "It gathers, shapes, and molds public opinion. It searches out the truth and brings justice to the innocent and punishment to the unjust by focusing the glaring light of the printed word on them." Like the *World*, it was well funded, but unlike the *World*, its money and editorial policy came from the North, and thus it was a far more militant voice for Black rights. The *World*'s conservative approach gave the Sengstacke syndicate entrée into Memphis, and as the 1950s wore on, that divergence in editorial policy continued to grow. The *Memphis World*—already the most conservative of the three principal members of the Scott Syndicate—consistently argued for a gradualist approach to Black rights, and the *Defender* vigorously criticized the Eisenhower administration for being gutless when it came to enforcing judicial decrees and policing a violent, disobedient white South.[67]

That gradualism did not keep the *World* and the Syndicate off the radar of law enforcement groups. In July 1953, the special agent in charge of the Memphis FBI office sent word to his superiors about an editorial in the *Memphis World* denigrating the House Un-American Activities Committee and suggesting the use of the FBI for investigatory tasks. The paper wrote that such efforts needed to be "conducted by the people and committees whose sole interest is that of the country's welfare and not one of political aspiration." The editorial complained that HUAC and other similar committees made no effort "to protect the innocent individual. Consequently, many people are ruined for life." The FBI could investigate without the public destruction, and its agents were actually trained for the work. "Most of all, they are not drunk with power and don't have to stoop to the level of common antics to keep their jobs."[68]

The agent in charge also reported that the paper was part of the Syndicate and run by "C. A. Scott, Negro." He noted that the paper was printed in Atlanta and that the Memphis FBI had no "derogatory information" on its editor, James H. Purdy. The *Memphis World*'s advertising manager, however, was Rosa Brown Bracy, who had "actively participated" in the Progressive Party campaign in St. Louis in 1948, the agent explained. She served as an elector for that party in Tennessee, which was dominated by local communists, in the 1952 election. Bracy was also "known to have subscribed to the 'Worker,' East Coast Communist publication." He did note that Bracy wasn't a member of the Communist Party and had "no part in the management or editorial policy of the Memphis World." Additionally, a redacted source had informed the bureau that "neither Purdy nor any other Memphian writes any editorials for the paper"; all editorials emanated from Atlanta and were carried in other Syndicate papers.[69]

The Memphis report prompted Atlanta's special agent in charge to report that the same editorial also ran in the *Atlanta Daily World*, fitting the dictates of syndication, and to note that C. A. Scott had attended a Southern Negro Youth Congress meeting in Columbia, South Carolina, in October 1946, where he watched a panel discussion on voting rights "led by Dr. James Edward Jackson who is presently a missing Smith Act subject." The Southern Negro Youth Congress, the agent reminded the director, was on the attorney general's list as a "subversive organization dominated and controlled by the Communist Party." When the group had met at Clark College in Atlanta in 1944, Scott spoke on "his experience of the Negro voting in Georgia." As of 1946, Scott was on the executive board of the Southern Conference for Human Welfare, which had been "cited as Communist Party Front by the House Committee on Un-American Activities." In May 1948, informants noted, Homer Bates Chase, a Communist Party organizer, had contacted Scott to explain the ramifications of the Mundt-Nixon communist registration bill being debated in Congress. The law would have forced all communists to register with the attorney general. In 1952, confidential sources advised, Scott was on a mailing list for the *Southern Patriot*, a publication of the Southern Conference Educational Fund, which itself was an integrationist outgrowth of the Southern Conference for Human Welfare.[70]

There was also a debate among the FBI offices about the possibility of writing a letter of appreciation to either the *Memphis World* or the Syndicate for the editorial, a possibility that was ultimately rejected because the editorial was "primarily an attack on Congressional investigating committees and apparently was not written for the purpose of praising the FBI." The home office also noted that the "derogatory information concerning C. A. Scott" (from Atlanta's special agent in charge) precluded sending any complimentary letters.[71]

In reality, there was little that the bureau needed to fear from the *World* and the Syndicate. In 1960, the *Memphis World* endorsed Richard Nixon for president, while the *Defender* supported John F. Kennedy. Simple longevity had kept the *World*'s circulation figures above those of the *Defender* through the 1950s. But by 1963, the *Defender*'s circulation figures had risen to twenty-four thousand, while the *World*'s had dropped to six thousand. As of the 1960s, Memphis readers were hungry for something more militant.[72]

When there was a rift in the Shelby County Republican Party, the *Defender* covered the fight. It urged readers to register to vote and to encourage others to register. When Memphis icon W. C. Handy insulted the NAACP, the paper criticized him. The *Defender* carried the same sensational criminal coverage; the same civic, church, and society news; and the same sports as the *World*, but it forwent, at least to some degree, the practical radicalism strategy that discouraged direct criticism of locals. "The average colored citizen of Memphis does not receive much courtesy from the average local white policeman," read one such effort. The paper encouraged better training as a solution to poor police behavior. It didn't rail against policing or the Memphis force. But it did directly critique local officers, something the *World* often seemed loath to do.[73]

The *Chattanooga Observer*, another longtime SNS newspaper, was far more *World* than *Defender* in outlook, but it fell somewhere between them. As World War II came to a close, for example, the *Chattanooga Observer* was vigorously anti-Truman. At the same time, the paper advocated for Black police, better schools, and well-funded health facilities for Black Chattanooga. When the city refused to build a new Black junior high school in the years following the war, editor W. C. Robinson used the paper to make an adamant argument in favor of directly electing members of the school board. Accountability, he argued, was the only remedy against neglect.[74]

In July 1947, the *Observer* described the passage of Taft-Hartley over the veto of Harry S. Truman. Whereas the *Alabama Tribune*, for example, was vigorously opposed to Taft-Hartley and had urged its veto, the *Observer* welcomed the override. "A part of the new law provides for an open shop which will redound to the good of many Negroes," the paper explained, "because no labor union can prevent him from exercising his God given rights to work whether he has a union card or not." Taft-Hartley was unquestionably designed to restrict the power of labor unions and to undo some of the work of Roosevelt's National Labor Relations Act. The *Observer*, however, argued that some of those restrictions would limit a union's ability to discriminate in the racial makeup of its membership. "Therefore, the vast majority of Negroes throughout America welcomes the new Labor Law," the paper claimed, perhaps disingenuously. "It is [their] second emancipation."[75]

Later that month, the paper described itself as "a public service institution" and argued that a Black newspaper should "reflect the attitudes, the wills, the determinations, the progress and the short comings of the community which it represents." This was a defense of itself, but also a defense of Black southern journalism. "Propaganda, ill-directed without any regard for the whole citizenship is damaging," the paper argued. The *Observer* "does not believe that the citizens of Tennessee can dictate to the citizens of Maine or Mississippi, nor do we believe that the people of New Hampshire or North Carolina can dictate to the citizens of Tennessee."[76] This argument represented a specific sensibility of the region. All meaningful journalism, the paper seemed to be saying, happened on the local level. True southernness required reading a Black southern newspaper. In its urgency, this was an echo of the Syndicate's earlier pronouncement that "Negroes are different in Dixie," and it demonstrated a pushback against the creeping horde of northern Black newspapers advocating more revolutionary or radical positions in the wake of World War II.

To that end, the next week's edition included a front-page letter from the mayor of Chattanooga supporting the publication. He noted that "the colored people of Chattanooga are fortunate in having a newspaper capable of providing leadership and of offering encouragement and initiative to the people it serves." If Chattanooga's Black community needed one thing, they "need[ed] more Negro leaders and they need[ed] more opportunities to demonstrate and develop their leadership ability."[77] In stumping for Taft-Hartley and defending Black southern journalism against the encroachment of papers like the *Chicago Defender*, the *Observer* was celebrated by the mayor as a paragon of what Black leadership in Chattanooga should look like.

Such is not to say that the paper ignored more racialized reporting. In July 1945, for example, a white police officer had been arrested and charged with murder for shooting and killing Edward Mays, a Black man, while chasing him down the street. In March 1946, the *Observer* reported on a "fiery cross" burned in the middle of Market Street in front of the Greyhound bus terminal in the heart of Black Chattanooga. In July, Eugene Talmadge, Georgia's Democratic gubernatorial nominee, came to Chattanooga on business and gave a speech announcing plans for a revised "white man's primary" to be established at the party's state convention. He was confident that placing primaries "under party control instead of under state control" would "satisfy the findings of federal courts," and he cited South Carolina's system as a successful example "to eliminate Negro voters from our primary."[78]

In November 1948, the *Observer* lamented the thirty-five Black murder victims in Tennessee that year and the hundreds over the previous decade. It acknowledged that the bulk of those deaths came at the hands of Black assailants, but "is not the Negro what the whites have made him? Who then is the real, honest to goodness killer? You answer that question. Don't think too hard. The answer is simple."[79] This was a striking change from the paternalistic tone that the paper normally took, implicating systemic racism for Black crime rather than poor behavior among Black citizens.

There had been some race progress in 1948. When the Supreme Court issued its *Shelley v. Kraemer* decision on racially restrictive covenants, the paper reported on the ruling with full SNS coverage. A Black St. Louis family had been restricted from buying a house in a white neighborhood because of one of those covenants, and they sued. The argument against them was the same as it was in *Smith v. Allwright*. Neighborhoods were essentially private entities, went the claim, and private entities could restrict whomever they wanted. The Court agreed with that to an extent. Racially based restrictive covenants were, on their face, not invalid under the Fourteenth Amendment, the justices argued. Private parties could voluntarily abide by the terms of a restrictive covenant, but they could not seek judicial enforcement of such a covenant, because enforcement by the courts would constitute state action. That state action would necessarily be discriminatory, so enforcement of a restrictive covenant in a state court would violate the equal protection clause of the Fourteenth Amendment. It was a technical equivocation, but it was a substantive victory, and the *Observer* covered it as such.[80]

Closer to home, and thus even more important to the paper and its readers, the *Observer* reported on the city's August hiring of seven Black policemen; banner headlines and photographs documented their every move. "The best thing that has happened to Chattanooga for a long time was the employment of Negro police and putting them on Ninth Street," the *Observer* claimed, "and they are working every minute they are out there." It was a victory, but it also required further effort. The paper acknowledged the "fine way that they have started their work," but reminded readers that the Black policemen were "shouldering a very weighty responsibility." It was their job to excel at police work, "and it's the responsibility of the Chattanooga public and particularly the Negroes to help them make good."[81] Black crime, the paper was contending, was an affront to civil rights. Attaching the success of Black Chattanooga and the future of further integration to the success of the Black police officers in the city meant that anything that made their jobs more difficult was an attack on the entire race.

In December one of those policemen, Thomas Patterson, was shot while apprehending a Black suspect. Though Patterson's leg was wounded, he maintained pursuit and caught his attacker, which exacerbated the *Observer*'s appreciation of his heroism. "Nine policemen out of ten, whether colored or white, would have used his gun under the circumstances, which he would have been perfectly justified in so doing," but Patterson was able to apprehend the suspect without firing. It was a demonstration of Patterson's ability as an officer, and thus the ability of the group of Black officers, but it was also a demonstration of the need for those Black officers in policing Black Chattanooga.[82] The implication in the *Observer*'s editorial was that a white officer would have responded by firing on the fleeing Black man. The paper never stated that claim explicitly, which would have cut against the practical radicalism it continuously cultivated, but there were decades of examples to prove the point. Patterson's action served as a demonstration of the violence that could be averted through policing that didn't come with the racial bigotry that often existed between white southern policemen and Black southerners.

Later in December, "two Negroes actually heard evidence as members of a jury in criminal court," the first time in the history of Hamilton County. The *Observer* noted that some saw the seating of the Black jurors as "an accident," but others saw a potential precedent. Court officials began discussing issues like the feeding of juries, normally done in nearby segregated restaurants. "Under law a jury may not be separated during trial of a case."[83] That wasn't an issue in the relatively swift deliberations for the breaking-and-entering case on which the two Black jurors served, but such were the kinds of questions that inevitably appeared when the possibility of regular Black jury service became a reality.

On the national level, the *Observer*'s most sustained coverage was devoted to lynching and the campaign to obtain a federal antilynching law, a long-sought goal that had been given all the more emphasis by Truman's campaign rhetoric during his 1948 run for president. "If the Democratic Party fails to keep its platform promises to the American Negroes," the paper claimed, "they cannot blame anyone but themselves since they control all branches of the Federal Government."[84] The paper wasn't alone in its frustration.

The attempts at a federal antilynching law had begun in the early 1880s, but one of the first potentially successful efforts came in 1917, when Leonidas C. Dyer, a Republican congressman from St. Louis, proposed a law that would make lynching a federal felony. It was stopped by a Democratic filibuster in the Senate, but the campaign continued. Pushed in particular by the NAACP, independent advocates like Ida B. Wells, and virtually every Black newspaper in the country, reformers lobbied for a law that would make racially motivated mob violence a federal offense, and thereby remove local law enforcement from responsibility for prosecuting the crimes. Unsuccessful efforts at such legislation continued for decades. (Finally, the Emmett Till Antilynching Act was secured in 2022.) The periodic efforts had been a rallying cry for crusaders, and in the mid-twentieth century they were a rare point of agreement for virtually all of the Black press, a demonstration by proxy of the need for the federal government to step in to police southern state governments and protect their Black citizens.[85]

Of course, violence didn't have to come in the technical form of lynching to be a constant danger to Black southerners. In June 1951, the *Observer* reported that a white city bus driver had shot and killed a Black passenger after an argument. The passenger's seven-year-old son was standing next to him. To their credit, police charged the driver with murder. The following year, a Black Baptist minister riding a bus to Chattanooga from Atlanta claimed that "two white men beat and strangled him" after he "refused to move to a rear seat." No one helped the sixty-seven-year-old man, and at the next stop in Acworth, Georgia, "police officers boarded the bus and threatened to jail him if he did not move to the rear of the vehicle." This was one story in a cacophony of others, but at least Cobb County officials claimed to be searching for the two men who had attacked the aged preacher.[86] They didn't find them, probably because they didn't really want to, but the claim of intent by the police, no matter how disingenuous, was more than Black victims usually received.

It was clear that such violence, combined with the failure of the Truman administration to pay off on its promises of progress, disillusioned Black journalists—and particularly those at the *Chattanooga Observer*, who were already predisposed to mistrust the president.[87] After Dwight D. Eisenhower's election, a jubilant *Observer* reported that two "Chattanooga business leaders" were being considered for cabinet positions. They were white, but they were Republicans from Chattanooga, and that was enough for the paper. In January 1953, W. C. Robinson represented his newspaper at Eisenhower's inauguration, one of "approximately 200 outstanding Negro Republican leaders from all over the United States." The syndicated report from the Republican newspaper described the event as "history-making," and in its way, it was.[88] White Democrats had been in power for the previous twenty years, and in the South, white Democrats were the party of white supremacy. Black representatives at a Republican inauguration were a powerful symbol, a harking back to Republican administrations a century prior. Robinson's presence only enhanced the event for the paper.

In April 1953, the paper celebrated Eisenhower's State of the Union address, which had proclaimed the need for "economic freedom" in relations with labor. It was a typical Republican anti-union message, and the *Observer* loved it, bemoaning "autocratic union leadership" that "made a cynical game of labor-government-management relations" and "a wicked cycle of strikes, nationalization, and government-forced wage increases." The paper simultaneously celebrated corporations, which formerly had conjured "visions of mysterious accumulations of wealth and dubious financial machinations." That caricature, "happily, seems doomed to abysmal failure." Corporations provided "an almost endless list" of goods, services, and jobs, and they paid the taxes that sustained the country and dividends that sustained a growing number of shareowners.[89] There was a slippery slope in supporting Republicans, but this was a demonstration of the class difference between publishers like Robinson and the Scotts and the bulk of their readers.

The following year, an *Observer* editorial analyzed Tennessee's upcoming election for governor and senator, including attempts to unseat incumbents Frank Clement and Estes Kefauver, respectively. The staunchly Republican paper celebrated the reelection of the Democrats because their opponents in the party primary, in an attempt to break the hold of incumbency, had "injected" the "race issue" into the campaigns, telling Tennessee voters that the election was essentially a referendum on the Supreme Court's *Brown v. Board* decision and that voters should support them because they would fight the implementation of school desegregation tooth and nail. Clement and Kefauver, no civil rights activists, still supported the constitutional system of checks and balances and argued that there was nothing to be done about the ruling but comply. Thus it really wasn't a political issue at all anymore, argued Kefauver, and its appearance in the campaign was solely "to fool people for their votes."[90]

The *Memphis World* and *Chattanooga Observer* were not the only two newspapers in the Syndicate's Tennessee stable at the time. In August 1950, the SNS had strengthened its position in the state when it added the *Nashville Sun*, published by local minister F. D. Coleman and edited by L. D. Williams. "We contend that, all things considered, and all of the facts of history taken into consideration," the paper wrote in its founding manifesto, "as much progress is being made in advancing the cause of the Negro in the South as is being made in the North, and that even more could be accomplished if the Southern Negro adopted his own strategy for advancement rather than let some 'eager-beaver' up North sell the Southern Negro a formula for advancement."[91] The *Observer* appeared almost militant by comparison.

With that position established, the *Sun* forwent bold crime coverage on its front page, opting instead for civic and religious news. While the paper did report on acts of discrimination and racial violence, its conciliatory stance never wavered. "A large and growing element of Southern white people are more than 'meeting the Negro half-way' in this matter of promoting better race relations," read one editorial. "This fact ought to be acknowledged boldly by those who claim to be leaders of the Negro race." Another editorial again castigated those "eager-beavers" who "have no patience with people who caution patience" in solving racial problems.

"Any one who confesses he is a 'gradualist' is called a reactionary by the eager-beavers." But patience, the *Sun* argued, was the best strategy. Once Black schools and colleges were made equal to their white counterparts, white people would "most certainly" want to attend them. "And once white people look in upon a colored school just as fine, with teachers as good as white teachers and as well paid, they will apply for admission to such schools and nobody will keep them out."[92] This position was almost sad in its folly, a caricature of the Black southern press that supported the dominant opinion of that press, even though it was a minority position.

In September 1950, Tennessee's attorney general, Roy Beeler, issued an opinion holding that "Negroes must be admitted to the lily-white University of Tennessee for graduate, dental and law studies." The *Sun* explained that Beeler had argued to both the university president and the governor that they "must bow to the inevitable" following the Supreme Court rulings, but added that the opinion did not apply to undergraduate education. Soon after the Court's opinion, the paper reported that "three colored students will enter UT soon," but it did not list the students. Instead, the article explained *Missouri ex rel. Gaines* and its role in the opinion. In June 1951, the *Sun* shared data from a survey of students at the University of Tennessee with the *Atlanta Daily World*. They demonstrated that a majority of those students would go along with the courts in "admitting Negroes to graduate schools," but "the majority is not definite and decisive enough to be enthusiastic."[93]

In April, the paper had covered the pending elevation of Tennessee A&I to a full-fledged university in the fall, and then it reported on the official change when Tennessee governor Gordon Browning spoke at the new university's convocation ceremonies. The coverage demonstrated no trepidation on the part of the *Sun* about the elevation being part of a *Gaines*-style attempt to avert the University of Tennessee's eventual desegregation, instead interpreting the move as a victory for Black students in and around Nashville.[94]

In July 1951, the *Sun* covered Fisk University's eighth annual Race Relations Institute, which featured a speech by M. E. Tilly, Atlanta field director of the Southern Regional Council and a member of the President's Committee on Civil Rights. Tilly expressed optimism about racial discrimination: "The minority groups are no longer taking it lying down." Fitting that analysis, the paper covered a December 1951 strike by "nonprofessional workers" at Hubbard Hospital, part of Meharry Medical College, in response to the "cancellation of their privilege of free meals." The drama continued throughout much of December, with some workers claiming that they now wanted an increase in pay of five dollars per week. After a meeting at the hospital, some of the striking workers refused to leave the building, leading to thirty-three arrests. The incident "had the Nashville public divided in sentiment," with the workers disorganized and hospital authorities claiming a deficit but agreeing to reinstate the free meal policy nonetheless.[95] It was a compromise, a partial concession, and demonstrated the problematic nature of administrations at historically Black colleges since the 1920s.

Black colleges had been founded in response to racism, but they were not necessarily a militant protest against it. Black private schools developed because access to better white schools was not available. Black public colleges were almost always created by white legislatures to defuse the potential for integration attempts at white universities. Black colleges thus sought to create a socially respectable middle class of their student bodies, which would protect the reputation and existence of the school itself. This allowed students to achieve some kind of financial security after graduation while making them largely unwilling to rock any of the racist boats that the universities depended on for their survival. But education doesn't work that way. Students who learned more and more about the history, economics, and sociology of their country and their region became more and more frustrated with the status quo. Southern Black colleges thus developed extremely authoritarian administrations designed to keep such contradictory norms in place.[96]

Segregated Black colleges, it seemed to many, were a failed idea. As early as the 1920s, student protests against the administration of Black colleges occurred at Howard, Hampton, and Fisk. Importantly, these were the country's elite Black schools and were located in urban settings that put students in frequent contact with white society. Black students could, in a way, see what they were missing. In the 1930s, as Joel Rosenthal has noted, white radical activism in the face of the Depression, led most forcefully by the National Student League, provided new fuel for such critiques, as did revelatory, sensationalistic cases like the Scottsboro trials in Alabama. Students at Virginia State protested against the "Victorian atmosphere and the convent-like restrictions" placed on them. When students at Fisk protested a local lynching and picketed the local segregated theater, President Thomas E. Jones expelled the leader of the protests for actions that were "detrimental to the best interests of the University." In the 1950s, when the student council president of the South Carolina College for Negroes helped organize a post-*Brown* desegregation petition, he was expelled, touching off campus-wide protests that culminated in the expulsion of more students and the dismissal of several members of the faculty and staff. "It must be reported as one of the bitter ironies in the civil rights movement in the South," wrote William P. Fidler, general secretary of the American Association of University Professors in 1965, "that the administrations of some Negro institutions have exercised autocratic control over the actions and utterances of their faculties and students."[97]

Black college students were not the only ones dissatisfied. In February 1952, the *Sun* published an article titled "What the Negro Veteran Wants" by Francis Young, a military public relations officer. The article served as a list of demands from Black veterans and was perhaps the most radical statement the *Sun* had produced. Young called for "unrestricted suffrage" and "justice in law and government." He called for better educational opportunities, a federal antilynching law, and the "removal of segregation in public places." He wanted better wages, universal terms of respect for Black citizens, and the "removal of objectionable advertising ridiculing Negroes or show[ing] the Negro as the inferior type." It was a strong statement, but it was presented by proxy and still directed largely at a Black readership. "Now that we know the facts of what the Negro Veterans want what are the readers going to do about it?" Young asked in closing.[98] Even when the rhetoric became more substantial, the onus for change was still on the Black population rather than the white.

The Syndicate's last attempt in Tennessee was the *Independent Call*, published by C. L. Hyatt in Knoxville beginning in February 1953. The month after its founding, the paper covered the effort of the local NAACP to recruit two thousand new adult members and five hundred new youth members into the organization. The next month, the *Call* covered the lawsuit of four Black golfers who filed a complaint against the city of Knoxville for the right to play on the city course, which at the time was leased to a local country club. The city's defense conceded Black people's right to use public land but argued that "this right was nullified because of the lease." In April, the Young Men's Civic Club of Knoxville began a fight to change the discriminatory policies of the *Knoxville City Directory*, asking the publishers to use the titles "Miss" and "Mrs." for Black women and to remove the "C" (for "colored") after the names of Black residents. The initial plan, as reported by the *Call*, was to convince Black residents not to give information to the company until there was an agreement on corrections.[99]

Knoxville, however, was not the sort of city to suffer such activism without a response. Also in April 1953, the Klan burned crosses on the lawns of Black attorney George McDade and a white employee, Beulah Boston. McDade and Boston had been charged with common-law lewdness after McDade was discovered in Boston's apartment. McDade contended that he was taking his employee food because she was sick and unable to work, and police admitted that he was fully clothed and she was in pajamas. But even the hint of an interracial tryst was too much for white Knoxville: the police responded with arrests, and the Klan responded with burning crosses. When the two were arraigned later that month, the defense charged and the prosecution admitted that the warrants used to enter the apartment were invalid, but the judge still refused to dismiss the case. There was no jail time for the coworkers, but the threat had been made, and the bar for proper behavior was set with both atavism and the law.[100]

Meanwhile, despite the *Nashville Sun*'s prediction, no Black students had yet entered the University of Tennessee. In April 1953, the *Independent Call* reported on the university's plan to sidestep the Supreme Court's graduate school orders. The only programs at the university that would be open to Black students were "programs not available in State owned and supported institutions elsewhere in the state." The paper covered the fight to integrate the graduate school and claimed that it was the opinion of those following the case that "this is the same old dodge that southern whites give to prevent Negroes from getting full benefits under the constitution."[101] And, of course, it was.

Every step forward was met with white hands attempting to push Black people two steps backward. This made the nexus of SNS papers in Tennessee all the more vital in checking white supremacy at the onset of the organized civil rights movement against it.

Chapter 6

Mississippi and Louisiana

The Great Migration Black Population Changes (%)

City	1910–1940	1940–1970
Baton Rouge, La.	−5.6	−19.5
Jackson, Miss.	0.6	−10.6
Meridian, Miss.	−3.7	−2.8
Natchez, Miss.	−1.8	−4.5
New Orleans, La.	14.9	3.8
Shreveport, La.	−2.5	−13.0
Vicksburg, Miss.	−1.8	−6.7

The listed cities are the ones large enough to be included in Census statistical materials. "The Great Migration, 1910 to 1970," U.S. Census Bureau, 13 September 2012, https://www.census.gov/dataviz/visualizations/020/508.php.

Mississippi

W. A. Scott was intimately connected to the founding of the *Jackson World*, as the "paper was founded in the state, which is the birthplace of Mr. Scott. He also received much of his education at Jackson college." He created the Jackson World Publishing Company to run the operation and hired local E. W. Banks to edit the paper. "It is ideally located," the Syndicate boasted, "in a state devoid of Negro newspapers."[1] That was undoubtedly true. The roar of the 1920s didn't really reach Black Mississippi, but the Depression of the 1930s certainly did, eroding a Black press that was already struggling. Only thirty-three Black periodicals existed in Mississippi in that decade, only fifteen of them commercial presses; most were housed in Jackson. It was a vast decline. In the 1890s, there were forty-six Black periodicals, in the 1910s, there were sixty-six.[2]

Most Black Mississippi editors did not seriously examine issues of segregation, lynching, or voting rights—due largely to intimidation and the violent consequences that might befall them. Still, papers carried plenty of reprints and wire stories that made those issues crystal clear.[3] Though the Mississippi papers were printing the news, if the story was written elsewhere, or if the reported event took place elsewhere, it seemed they felt their hands were clean. Such was the fundamental principle of practical radicalism: papers provided clarity on the race issues that mattered to readers without creating coverage that could result in retributive violence from angry whites.

Nell Irvin Painter argues that the two characteristics of the Black press most clearly definitive of the difference between it and its white counterpart are a racial orientation (as opposed to a "partisan orientation") and "a sense of supranational racial identity," exemplified by coverage of the West Indies and Africa. Small-town southern Black weeklies, however, often went against the Painter model of the Black press. The *Southern Advocate*, for example, founded in 1933 in Mound Bayou, Mississippi, was a four-page paper that emphasized religious issues and the activities of area churches, along with printing local social and entertainment news and some state news. There was little coverage of national or international politics. There was little of Painter's "supranational identity."[4]

Mississippi was a decidedly rural state without large media markets. It was rife with rural poverty, which was exacerbated by the Great Depression. And it was emblematic of the racial violence and Jim Crow restrictive racial culture that blanketed the entire South, which became known as the "closed society" in its efforts to defend white supremacy. The development of a viable network of Black newspapers in the state was understandably precarious, but it was inherently necessary. The coverage and editorials of these papers, then, encompassed a wide range of strategies. In early 1934, the Syndicate was involved in a push to expand its range by creating a series of *World* papers. The *Mississippi World* was published in Natchez by local Douglas W. Mozique. The paper's syndicated coverage included the doings of Natchez College, a historically Black junior college that would later be made famous by Anne Moody, who attended the school in the early 1960s before moving on to Tougaloo and working as an activist. There was also the nearly requisite crime and murder coverage. A boy was killed for the eighty-five cents in his pocket. A man was beaten and shot during a fight. This was the kind of scandalous coverage that Syndicate customers would always stop to read, whether in Natchez or in the other *World* papers created in 1934.[5]

There was also the *Weekly Echo* in Meridian, which was, according to its masthead, "A Home Paper with a Home Editor That Tells the State News Weekly." It was "Mississippi's Standard Negro Newspaper of Character,

Circulation and Opinion, with More than 10,000 Readers." Its editor and business manager was Roy L. Young, who employed an assistant editor and a circulation manager in a small operation.[6] An editorial from one late July 1932 edition began by noting the constant bemoaning of the "delinquency of our Negro youth," but instead of following the script of the well-worn Black southern jeremiad, it placed the blame for such problems, at least in part, on "the conditions of our city schools." The primary schools were severely underfunded, but the one high school in Meridian was even worse: "A condition of congestion that should not be associated with human beings exists in this building." Most of the editorials, however, didn't stray from the timeworn formula. The next week, for example, the lead editorial was an extended disquisition on the virtues of "home." Another encouraged readers in the face of difficult economic times: "I believe if we will cut the DE and I out of DEPRESSION and use the rest of the letters which will be 'PRESS ON' conditions will be better for all of us."[7]

While much of the *Echo*'s content was relatively religious and noncontroversial, the paper did cover the murder of seven Black firemen for the Illinois Central Railroad by white men attempting "to scare workers off the job so that their places could be filled by unemployed and needy whites." It covered the NAACP probes of "virtual slavery" in flood control camps on the Mississippi River. When three Rome, Georgia, policemen killed one Black man and wounded another in a dice game raid, the paper covered the story in detail, but its editorial on the subject emphasized that the curative to such ills was to turn to God. It emphasized that the "Negro has always been humble and submissive" and tried to make the case that "all that the Negro possesses has come to him because of his willingness to bow."[8] This was precisely the type of message the Black southern press was pilloried for sending.

Howard Thompson's *Corinthian Gazette* was similar, if on a slightly smaller scale. Its circulation was roughly three hundred, servicing Corinth, Mississippi, and its surrounds. One representative editorial complained about Black voting in the town. When a local white politician claimed that "there are such few Negroes who are interested in who governs them, while the majority can be bought for a pint of whiskey," the paper responded not by denouncing such white political rhetoric, but instead by using the insult to encourage better Black behavior. "Practically all Negro citizens pay some kind of tax," the paper stated, "but very few pay [the] poll tax, [and] there are numbers of Negroes who know what to vote for, but no one knows it, because their only conversations are based upon 'Which

Is the Fastest Car a Ford, Chevrolet or Pontiac.'" The paper hoped to "see if we can't vote by showing to candidates that we are governed by sound doctrine, talk business instead of frivolous things, support our leaders and quit kicking against them." The Black citizens of Corinth needed to "establish more business enterprises." They needed to save money and invest it: "Buy us some homes instead of automobiles. In short, try to get some capital: the whole world will recognize money." This was a distinctly Washingtonian flourish. Black voters needed to pay poll taxes, stop concerning themselves with the things they enjoyed, earn money, and "quit kicking against" white leaders so that the latter's impression of Black Corinth would improve. It was a decidedly different message than what was coming from the paper's northern counterparts. When the *Gazette* reported on a local car crash between a white driver and a Black driver, for example, it noted that the white driver was at fault, but the Black driver received the citation from white officers. "No one believes that justice was done in the case," the paper admitted, but it approvingly reported that the Black driver "did not try to resist anything that happened; he took everything with a smile." Its coverage closed by bragging, "It was the quietest case between a white and a colored that has ever happened in the south."[9]

Other contemporary Syndicate papers, like the *Vicksburg Tribune*, the *Meridian Progress*, and the *Greenville Leader*, provided similar messaging.[10] Founded in 1929, the *Leader* celebrated Black achievements and worried over Black causes of Black problems. There was no emphasis whatever on Black political participation and voting. Unions and labor movements were anti-American, problematic entities that Black people would do best to avoid. The *Leader* argued, "In all things that are purely social we can be as separate as the fingers, yet one as the hand in all things essential to mutual progress." But that Tuskegee model only worked if Black southerners stayed in the South. Mississippi papers, as a general rule, sought to keep Black residents in the state, arguing that African Americans were a southern people who did not belong in northern urban hubs like Chicago or Detroit.[11]

The most important Mississippi SNS addition in the early 1940s was the *Jackson Advocate*, headquartered in the state capital. The *Advocate*, under the leadership of editor Percy Greene, hewed to the same Washingtonian line as the *Leader*, but did make room in its pages for a decidedly southern version of activism. In June 1941, the paper reported on efforts of Black World War I veterans to join the Mississippi branch of the American Legion. Greene himself was among the veteran petitioners. That month the paper also covered state plans to organize a Mississippi Negro Defense Council; Governor Paul Johnson Sr. had called on "Negro leaders in all walks of life, and in all sections of the state" to attend a meeting in Jackson for the purpose.[12]

In August, Greene went further, explaining that the appointed officers of the Agricultural Adjustment Administration in the state were all white. But "with fifty-two per cent of its population Negroes, and largely a farming state," the paper reasoned, "one reaches the conclusion that a larger per cent of the farmers in the State are Negroes." Black farmers also had less education and less opportunity, and thus were "in much worse need of service and information to be given by these appointees." Sticking with practical radicalism, the *Advocate* didn't rail against the racist cronyism of the appointments nor lament the bigotry that would harm the fortunes of Black agricultural workers. Instead, it urged "the appointment of some Negro field officer in the state to explain the AAA to Negro farmers, lest more than half the farmers of the state get something less than a second hand idea of the meanings and benefits of the farm law."[13] Greene understood that he needn't engage in a quixotic attempt to gain an equal number of Black AAA executives. By asking for one and explaining his reasons, the same stark point was made.

In an extensive November 1941 editorial, the *Advocate* quoted heavily from the work of historian Herbert Agar, arguing that in comparison to the behavior of Nazis, "we Americans have no grounds for pride in our general treatment of the Negro." The comparison was a common but powerful one, but Agar continued by qualifying that it would be even worse under the Germans: "In a Hitlerized government there would be no hope." The *Advocate*, however, sensed the overcompensation in such statements. "With so much writing and speaking being done about the bad lot the Negro would fall into in a German dominated world," the paper explained, "we have begun to wonder if any one has been able to discover any wide-spread and growing pro-Nazi attitude and sentiment on the part of the American Negro."[14]

That same month, the paper celebrated as two Black convicted murderers were sent to the electric chair. They had killed Black victims, and the *Advocate* saw the verdicts as signs that white juries were beginning to take the loss of Black life seriously. "All throughout the state," the paper explained, "all thinking intelligent Negroes, will commend and congratulate Judge Guynes and the Juries who heard the above trials." The writer hoped that the case "presages the beginning of a time in all the courts of the State, when Negro murderers will be given the measure of punishment their crime deserves."[15] In a state with so many established bigotries in place, the emphasis on convicting Black criminals seemed a strange choice for the limited editorial space available to the paper, but the stand in favor of respect for Black victims of crime would not be generative of any white backlash.

In March 1942, the paper reported on the annual meeting of the Mississippi Commission on Interracial Cooperation. The group discussed the proposed creation of a school for "delinquent Negro youth" and the failed efforts of reformers to achieve the equalization of teachers' salaries, as had been attained in other states. The plenary address was made by Jessie Daniel Ames, general field secretary of the Commission on Interracial Cooperation. Ames, a vigorous and outspoken opponent of lynching, "called upon the white people to learn more about the Negro by reading the Negro papers and magazines to get a real understanding of their condition, which would in turn awaken them to greater efforts toward inter-racial tolerance."[16]

In October 1942, the paper railed against the lynching of two fourteen-year-old Black boys in Shubuta, Mississippi. The two had "allegedly confessed to the attempted rape of a thirteen-year-old white girl." A mob took the teens from the jail and hung them from a railroad bridge, where the supposed crime had taken place. The *Advocate* denounced the lynchings as "by far the worst to have blotted the fair name of the state," which was made more egregious since "Negroes are sending their sons to the armed forces" and "laboring to make the fullest contribution to the war effort on the home front." The paper lauded the state's governor for condemning the lynchings and claiming to work to apprehend those involved.[17] This was a sound strategy that had been used by southern newspapers for years. The editorial played to readers' patriotism and set itself on the side of the white Democratic governor in wanting justice for the victims, giving the *Advocate* the white envelope it needed for its denunciation.

In another article, the *Advocate* described a meeting between the governor and "a Negro delegation" about an uptick in racial violence in the state. It quoted statements from Congressman John Rankin and Senator Theodore Bilbo denouncing the federal legislation to eliminate poll taxes as a prerequisite for voting. Rankin claimed that the only ways to deal with Black people were segregation or "deportation, extermination, and amalgamation." The paper didn't directly attack the statements, but noted that "Negroes of Mississippi are resentful towards the expressed feelings" of the legislators. Combined with lynchings, discrimination, and segregation, they "foreshadow[ed] a dark and gloomy future for racial relations in the state."[18]

In January 1943, the paper reported on a federal grand jury indictment of five white men, "one of them a deputy sheriff-jailer," for the lynching of a Laurel farmhand, who was also hanged from a bridge. The *Advocate* didn't provide editorial comment, but did include, even before the description of the charges, the opinion of "several local white attorneys" who had been quoted in the local white daily "as saying they regarded the action 'as another attempted federal invasion of states' rights.'"[19] Such reporting in the local daily demonstrated the importance of the Black press, whose simple, factual coverage of the indictment (using civil liberties statutes in the absence of a federal antilynching law) acted as a counter to the biased coverage of its white counterpart.

The trial of the lynchers was set for April, and the *Advocate* stuck with the story, explaining that "maximum penalties under the civil liberties statutes provide a fine of not more than $5,000 and imprisonment for not more than 10 years." Howard Wash, the Laurel farmhand, had killed his employer in self-defense after being assaulted for arriving late to work. After a jury convicted him of second-degree murder and sentenced him to life imprisonment, a mob of angry whites—dissatisfied that there wasn't a capital verdict—took matters into their own hands. It was obviously illegal, an easily proved lynching. But it was also a white Mississippi jury. The lynchers were acquitted after a brief one-day trial.[20]

At the same time that the Laurel indictment was coming down, however, the *Advocate* was using its editorial space to denounce A. Philip Randolph's March on Washington movement as "revolutionary and radical," counterproductive in the face of an inevitable war. The paper admitted that Randolph's goal was "to focus the attention of American people upon the violation of the basic human, moral and citizenship rights of the Negro in this country," but despite that the writer hoped that "the proposal of nonviolent civil disobedience by Mr. Randolph will be at once rejected by the rank and file of Negroes and Negro leaders throughout the country." The United States, the *Advocate* argued, was not India, and it needed no Gandhian approach to securing Black people's rights. In a democracy, there were better, safer ways to earn rights and respect.[21] This was the kind of editorial that gave Black southern journalism its reputation for bowing to white domination, but at the same time it provided the paper with a national foil to demonstrate its patriotism and ultimately bolster efforts at earning rights locally in Mississippi.

Such was one of the cornerstones of practical radicalism, as was touting the successes of local Black citizens. A February 1943 editorial, for example, praised the accomplishment of Roddie Pridgett, a Black farmer from Rankin County, who "had become the first Negro farmer in the United States to pay back, in full, a loan obtained from the Farm Security Administration" a full thirty-six years before the final payment was due. The occasion allowed the paper to praise the FSA for the opportunities it provided to Black farmers. "In the cotton producing states, the share cropper system and the system of farm tenancy that has developed along with the development of cotton farming," the paper explained, "is largely responsible for the widespread illiteracy, poverty and general backwardness, that led to the designation of the south, in recent years, as the nation's Number One Economic Problem." By helping sharecroppers escape that system, the FSA allowed farmers to avoid "many of the major evils of the Share Cropper, Farm Tenancy System."[22]

In July, British economist Sir William Beveridge spoke in Jackson: "The Negro is peculiarly suited to Southern Agriculture, and particularly to the Mississippi Delta, and should be kept here rather than permitted to migrate to Detroit, Harlem, and others of the nation[']s industrial centers." Beveridge suggested improving Black living conditions "through better schools, homes, etc.," as a carrot to curb migration. The *Advocate* agreed that migration was hurting the economy of the South, but questioned Beveridge's knowledge of the region. The paper was frustrated that it always seemed "the very first remedy to be suggested is that of benevolent paternalism. Benevolent paternalism has been tried with the Negro. It failed." And it would always fail "because of the limitation, imposed by self-interest, on the part of those who administer it." The only way to change the conditions of southern agriculture and thus curb the Great Migration "lies in the Negro being given the right to vote and the opportunity to shoulder the full burden of the duties and responsibilities of Citizenship." Black people didn't need handouts, the paper explained, they needed to be given the rights and responsibilities of everyone else. Fair treatment would keep Black farmers in the South.[23]

But fair treatment was hard in coming. That same month, the paper covered the case of Elijah Parker, who had been sentenced to die for the murder of a white farmer in Madison County. In late June, Parker had received a stay of execution when his lawyers filed an appeal to the U.S. Supreme Court, charging that their client "was not granted Due Process of Law, and that threats, duress, and coercion were used in obtaining the confession upon which he was convicted." Those tactics were used by many law enforcement departments in the South and were a clear violation of due process, but there was little hope for a Black man convicted after confessing to killing a white man in Mississippi.[24] Parker was eventually executed, but the Supreme Court's original stay seemed like progress. So too did the civil rights charges against the Laurel lynchers, even though they were acquitted. Such failures, Greene's paper argued, could be turned to successes most easily through use of the franchise.

Voting had always been the cause célèbre of the paper, and it reacted angrily and in detail in July 1944 when "the Mississippi Democratic Party took advantage of its first opportunity to show the rest of the Nation its disregard for the recent decision of the United States Supreme Court giving Negroes the right to vote in the Democratic Primaries of the South" and denied ballots to dozens of qualified Black voters. That month, a Black man was killed by a plainclothes police officer on Jackson's Farish Street under suspicious circumstances. The man was in a dispute over a cotton crop with several local white men, who had threatened to kill him. The paper noted that "there was no apparent connection between his death and the crop circumstances," but explained the "coincidence" all the same, knowing its readers could draw the connections without the paper drawing the ire of local officials.[25]

In December 1944 the paper called disfranchisement the South's "wors[t] evil." It appreciated efforts to pass a law abolishing poll taxes. A widespread white rumor said that Adam Clayton Powell was claiming that he would move to Mississippi and run for governor if the tax were abolished. The *Advocate* doubted the speculation and denied that Black voters would use the franchise in a bloc as a way to thwart white efforts. Thus, while it appreciated the sentiment behind trying to remove the poll tax, the paper noted that "the real and therefore more important impediment in the pathway of the Negro of the south towards the franchise and the right to vote is the right of comparatively insignificant public officials to determine the right and qualification of the Negro citizens to vote, even after having paid the required poll tax." The paper reminded readers that working for the right to vote was to "attack the problem on all fronts," not simply in one ceremonial or representative issue.[26]

In June 1945, the *Advocate* ran a letter that had been sent to the paper from a group of Black noncommissioned officers serving in Germany. "We have come to the conclusion that the Negro will be given better opportunities once we return to civil life," the soldiers hopefully assessed, "but we will not dare satisfy ourselves with that. The Negro has got to fight for what he wants and not in a physical nature. We will never get that which we desire to demand by using physical force." They were fighting to keep the country free for democracy: "So in the final we are looking for what we fight for. We are expecting the rights of an American citizen because we are Americans." The letter was extensive, and the *Advocate* published it in full, hoping that the hopes of the soldiers would become reality in time.[27]

But this optimism was without evidence. There were approximately seventy thousand Black servicepeople from Mississippi, all of whom would have to readjust to life in the Jim Crow South. "In the case of a recently discharged Negro Veteran," the paper chronicled, he was "denied compensation for disabilities incurred in or aggravated during his military service." His appeal to the local board of the Veterans Administration had been heard without his presence, and "his interests had been represented by a man, whom he did not know, had never seen, who had never been to his home, who had never questioned [him] in any manner relative to his condition." As a solution to such problems, "we respectfully urge upon Governor Thomas L. Bailey the need of appointing a Negro Member to the State Service Commission," which was designed "to advise and assist returning veterans, in order to coordinate the efforts of Negro Citizens of the state on behalf of the returning Negro Veterans."[28] It was respectful. It was practical. And it was activism on behalf of Black soldiers.

In June 1946, the paper commented on an article in *Life* magazine by John Foster Dulles about Soviet foreign policy and how to respond. Among the weaknesses of "capitalistic centers, notably the British Empire and the U.S.," which made them vulnerable to the Soviets, was "imperialism with its by-product of racial intolerance." The paper pounced on the comparison. "In the simple matter of the Negro right to vote," it argued, "lies the dynamite with which Mississippi and the United States could make democracy the unchallenged idea and ideal of the world."[29]

There was, however, some progress on that front. In April, the *Advocate* had celebrated a new Supreme Court decision in a Georgia case that validated its original Texas decision invalidating the white primary. "A new age is being born," the paper suggested. "No person who takes an honest look at the situation can fail to see that many of the worst conditions of the South exist primarily because of the fact that the Negro Citizens of the South do not enjoy the right to vote." A real demonstration of democracy, it argued, "would be that the powers that be in Mississippi, without waiting to face the inevitable decision of the United States Supreme Court, would set in motion the right of qualified Negro Citizens of the state to vote in all elections along with other citizens of the state." This was a bold call in the one political area—voting rights—about which the paper was intransigent. And that bold call paid dividends. "One of the greatest victories for and in the name of democracy took place in Mississippi on Tuesday, July 2, 1946," the paper reported, "when for the first time in the state's history Negro citizens voted unmolested and without incident in the State Democratic Primary election." Bilbo had called on white Mississippians to "resort to violence to keep Negroes from the polls," but no violence was reported, and Black voters participated in the primary, "which is tantamount to [the] election."[30]

Still, the losses resonated more than the victories. In 1930s Mississippi, everything had been segregated, and Black schools, neighborhoods, and facilities were all unequivocally inferior to those of whites. From the 1880s to the 1930s, 463 Black Mississippians had been lynched, more than 5 per every 10,000. The majority of Black people in the state were tenant farmers and sharecroppers, suffering the inevitable problems that came with such positions: debtors' prison, the convict leasing system, and virtual reenslavement. There was also the attendant required social deference and unequal communication between white and Black people. This system was so inherent to the thinking of white Mississippi that Bilbo published a book on the subject in 1947: *Take Your Choice: Separation or Mongrelization*. It became—through decades of constant use, through the false remembrances of the "lost cause" and the inherent assumptions made daily about Black inferiority—the southern way of life, which was in essence a euphemism for the white southern way of life.[31] When combined with the dilapidated state of Black education in Mississippi and the closed door to almost every possibility of economic mobility, there was little room for Black Mississippians to maneuver in making claims against the system. The system served to keep the dictates of the philosophy that undergirded it in place, a circular fallacy and a self-fulfilling prophecy from which it was nearly impossible to escape. White supremacy and Jim Crow created a totalitarian system where criticism was tantamount to treason.

Mississippi history textbooks featured nothing about Black leaders, argued that Reconstruction was a corrupt disgrace, and gave the system an academic grounding. The focus of the educations of white and Black students remained different, as white Mississippi children were prepared for college, professional programs, and other opportunities. Black education was assumed to be wasted on those who would never reach such heights, and thus the self-fulfilling prophecy continued to spin its tautological wheel. The state had founded Alcorn A&M for potential Black collegians, but it offered an inadequate degree from a university that carried little weight. The overarching bigotry that enveloped the state led more than a million Black residents to leave Mississippi between 1910 and 1960.[32]

Those still in the state, however, needed newspapers that represented them. The Syndicate's *Jackson Banner* made an attempt, reporting in the early 1950s on the pending execution of Willie McGee, a "37-year old father of four children," for "an alleged rape he vehemently denies committing." The paper described the three convictions of McGee, the first overturned for a change of venue, and the second overturned because "Negroes had been systematically excluded from the juries." The third conviction, however, had not been overturned, despite the efforts of a substantial legal team trying to secure his release. When a last-minute plea for clemency was put to Governor Fielding Wright in early May 1951, police arrested forty-two people demonstrating outside the state capitol building in an effort to spare the life of McGee. The attempt failed, however, and McGee was executed.[33] Though the *Banner* was clearly opposed to McGee's execution, it provided no editorial comment, simply describing the facts of the case and the efforts to save his life in the tradition of the grapevine. To do any more would have been to curry the anger of white Jackson.[34]

In April 1951, after the regional coordinator for the NAACP announced that the organization was going to work to integrate Mississippi colleges, Governor Wright had vowed to keep Mississippi education segregated "regardless of costs or consequences." The *Banner* reported on Wright's statement and printed much of it, but again did so without editorial comment. In June, the paper reported on the creation of the Negro Womanhood Defense Committee, formed to help raise funds for the prosecution of a local white man accused of raping a fourteen-year-old Black girl. The group committed to raising $10,000 for the prosecution.[35] The effort demonstrated the clear disparity in criminal justice standards in Mississippi, particularly after the execution the previous month of the probably innocent McGee. The paper limited itself to coverage of the rape and the defense committee, as it had done with coverage of Fielding Wright and Willie McGee. When denunciations weren't feasible, the *Banner* was able to make its point by simply piling up basic evidence of the rampant inequality.

But the problems continued to haunt. When the NAACP tried to capitalize on post-*Brown* momentum by attempting to integrate five Mississippi school districts, for example, the White Citizens Council teamed with government officials and local outraged whites to stop the move. Both the white *Jackson State Times* and the *Jackson Daily News* took vigorous pro-council positions, defending the organization and encouraging membership. The white *Yazoo City Herald* ran a full-page ad submitted by the council. The NAACP's desegregation effort failed largely because of the collusion of mainstream newspapers. The white press in Mississippi continued to support the council, to accuse the NAACP and similar rights organizations of being tools of communism, and to validate segregation and racism with the legitimacy that comes with standard news coverage. All of this made the work of the Syndicate and its members even more important.[36]

Louisiana

The *Louisiana Weekly* was founded as the *New Orleans Herald* in September 1925 by Constant Charles Dejoie, who published the paper, and O. C. W. Taylor, a school principal who served as its first editor. (They changed its name a month later.) Dejoie was a wealthy businessman with ties to both the Black and Creole communities in New Orleans. As a young man he graduated from Southern University and worked in his family's drugstore before working for the U.S. Railway Mail Service. He then turned to publishing. Dejoie and Taylor worked out of a small office in the Knights of Pythias temple on Saratoga Street in New Orleans, attempting to create a militant voice against racial oppression in the Deep South. "There is only one course for a Negro newspaper to take in matters pertaining to Negro life," said the paper's first editorial, "and that is the right side. Any attempt to sidestep and to 'pussyfoot' is more harmful to the race than anything else. Negro papers are not the property of the individuals who have them in charge, but the property of the Negro public whose interests they should serve."[37]

It was a population that needed serving. By 1932, New Orleans ranked last out of thirty-one metropolitan areas in money spent for public relief. It made no provisions for family welfare or indigent mothers. It helped no indigent Black citizens. The only group New Orleans helped was blind people. This stood in contrast to other southern cities, including Atlanta, Memphis, Birmingham, and Charleston, all of which provided some measure of family welfare and categorically included needy African Americans. From

May 1933 to February 1934, the Federal Emergency Relief Administration provided nearly $32 million to Louisiana. Almost four hundred thousand Louisianans, white and Black, were on the rolls by January 1934, and FERA noted that the state had "a higher proportion of its citizens on relief than most States of the Union." Those citizens had little choice. Louisiana wasn't providing its own unemployment relief. Finally, in July 1934 the state legislature passed its first unemployment law, authorizing local taxes on entertainment to be used for relief efforts.[38]

In July 1932, in that troubling economic environment, the SNS announced the addition of the *Louisiana Weekly* to the fold. The *Weekly* became the first paper the Syndicate didn't actually own to be printed in Atlanta. The *Weekly* had, for its first seven years, been printed by a local white print shop; its transition to the SNS marked the first time it was printed by a Black company. The acquisition came on the heels of the Syndicate's founding of *World* papers in Jackson and Jacksonville and was facilitated by Delphine W. Taylor, a former Syndicate employee who had moved to work at the *Louisiana Weekly* as an executive in 1931. "The signing of the mutual agreement between Mr. C. C. Dejoie, president of the *Louisiana Weekly*, and Mr. W. A. Scott, founder and owner of the Southern Newspaper Syndicate, links the *Louisiana Weekly* with the only Negro Daily in the world, as well as the fastest and most spectacular newspaper syndicate ever attempted by Negro journalists," the *Weekly* announced. It bragged in particular about the rotogravure sheet that would now be added to the paper and the quality printing that the plant in Atlanta provided. Still, the paper was quick to remind readers that the extra features would not increase the paper's price, which would remain at five cents. "The affiliation," it added, "does not mean a merger of the two companies, but an association that will supply the readers of this section with the latest news, prepared in the most presentable form."[39]

It was an auspicious time to associate with a Louisiana newspaper. In the summer of 1932, Albert White, longtime editor of the *Shreveport Afro-American*, attempted to register Black voters to participate in the Democratic primary. In response, a white mob began to look for him, which forced him to flee the state. When they couldn't find him, members of the mob marched to Shreveport's Lakeside Auditorium, which was scheduled to host a meeting of a local Black voters' group. That meeting was canceled to prevent any possible violence, so the mob surrounded the building for hours to prevent any later meeting from happening. "While no blood was shed," one newspaper report explained, "Negro citizens spent an anxious night as leading white citizens were reported to have declared that the streets of their city would be drenched in blood before Negroes would be allowed their right to vote."[40]

Early in its history, the *Louisiana Weekly* had taken moderate stances for educational opportunities, better housing, more playgrounds, an end to "sectional differences," a "cohesion of business forces," and an effort to "minimize fun-loving." But at the onset of the Depression, it moved to the left, arguing for equal treatment for Black customers in local stores and urging unemployed Black workers to apply for relief. It encouraged voters to register and pay the poll tax. Beginning in 1930, the paper made the case to readers that they should only shop at stores that hired Black workers, calling it an "economic defense policy" against racist hiring and firing practices in New Orleans, a campaign borrowed from a similar effort by the *Chicago Defender*.[41]

By making the move to a more aggressive stance for Black rights, the *Weekly* positioned itself well to act as a gatekeeper for local Black politics and rights advocacy groups. It weighed in with full-throated praise for or concern about various presidents of the New Orleans branch of the NAACP, for example. When George Labat served as president in the early 1930s, the *Weekly* was loudly dissatisfied. When James Gayle took over in the middle of the decade, the paper showed its approval. Its standard was a leader who was active and willing to push the status quo. The *Weekly* treated groups like the NAACP as the paper's legs, doing the work that the paper's activism required. Rights groups only sometimes lived up to that standard.[42]

In response to the white *Newark Evening News*'s plan to "deport" the city's Black citizens to the South, the *Weekly* fired back in a syndicated column at "our Nordic friendly enemies," explaining that the migration that created Newark's Black population was the result of the demand brought by World War I. "The Negro was virtually lured to the North to aid the various industries in milling all kinds of commodities for making the world a safer and saner place in which to live." Black soldiers also fulfilled their patriotic duty by serving in the military, the paper explained: "Whereas these wily schemes are the sudden impulses of thoughtless individuals, it is meet to give these matters wholesome consideration if for no other purpose than to study the psychology of the American white man." This was the perfect way to handle such pronouncements, noting their base ridiculousness while still making a trenchant and serious case against them. After the *Weekly*'s analysis of the Great Migration, the war, and their consequences, it closed its editorial by noting, "Clowning should be an added feature to the Olympic games; the Americans would triumph with little difficulty." The *World* titled the editorial "Clowning in New Jersey." That kind of editorial gave the Syndicate the moral high ground; it argued from a position of seriousness while not taking its opposition seriously. It also conditioned readers to see threats even in the most cartoonish pronouncements of white supremacists. Most important, the *Weekly* could afford to be so biting because its target was far away. Practical radicalism dictated that a similar racist stand by, for example, a local politician could not be answered so caustically.[43]

When the Orleans Parish School Board cut teacher pay in the wake of a Depression-related budget deficit, for example, the *Weekly* endorsed the move and saw it as "fitting indeed that the Negro teacher bear his share of the load." The paper was quick to point out that Black workers bore similar loads in all industries, and thus "we sincerely hope that the Negro will not be forgotten when it comes to dispensing Louisiana's $12,000,000 Federal relief fund. We also hope that we will not be obliged to come around the 'back door' to get our share of relief." Again the paper was able to strike a balance, this time between conciliation and reasonable demands. "When it comes to 'cuts' and slashes in salary we must take it squarely on the chin," the editorial concluded. "And when the time comes to dispensing relief we would like to receive it as upstanding men and women." Similarly, after a series of murders of Black Mississippi workers by "white labor agitators" in hopes of scaring off Black employees and thus creating more jobs for unemployed white workers, the *Weekly* expressed the requisite outrage, but tailored its response not to incite its Black readers, but to convince whites of the folly of such a practice. "If irresponsible white men are allowed to murder Negroes and take their jobs and nothing is done about it, it will not be long before they will be killing one another for the same purpose," the paper reasoned. "To our thinking the trouble in Mississippi is not lack of legal machinery to put a stop to these outrages but deficiency in strength of determination to do so."[44]

The paper did sometimes engage in more direct local criticism. When an NAACP investigation revealed that federal spillway projects in Arkansas, Louisiana, and Mississippi were reviving all of the harshest practices of the convict leasing system, the *Weekly* urged a federal inquest. "The states lynch and the federal government aids or abets exploitation of Negro laborers," stated an editorial. "Of the two evils, the latter is by far the most inglorious because it has the sanction of a government of the people, for the people, and by the people." When a Black voter was refused registration in New Orleans, the *Weekly* again went on the offensive, arguing that mistreatment in the courts "is no indication that we should lie down on our rights and allow those (who are right only because they have might) to intimidate us to the extent that we undervalue the power of the ballot." This was interesting phraseology. Black citizens were apathetic about voting, which certainly hurt them, but that apathy was the result of consistent abuse in the courts. "You pay taxes; you own property, but you cannot vote," the paper told readers. "If you prize your value in the community register today and if you are turned down, go into the courts."[45] It was a call to arms by the *Weekly*—and by extension the Syndicate—on the federal level with the spillway project and the state level with voter registration. This was the radicalism that later southern papers would be accused of abandoning, and it was syndicated across the region.

The *Weekly* also weighed in on the mistreatment of Black students in public schools, on controversies in local businesses and municipal issues, and even on the celebration of the centennial of British abolition. It used its opinion page to comment on lynchings in Louisiana and throughout the South. After Franklin Roosevelt's electoral victory in November 1932, it argued, "Now that the Democrats will soon be in complete power of the national government, they will have an opportunity to wipe out the distrust with which [the party] has justly been regarded by many colored people." The paper made the case that in a world that featured the neglect of Black students, controversies of all kinds, and new lynching accounts every week, Black voters, who were in a state of party-loyalty transition, would choose a candidate pragmatically: "The thoughtful Negro will cast his ballot for the party that he thinks will safeguard his basic rights."[46]

After the end of the Syndicate's relationship with the *Louisiana Weekly*, the SNS helped James B. LaFourche create the *New Orleans Broadcast*, which began in May 1934 as a direct competitor for the *Weekly*. It survived for only a year, but it made its presence known.[47] In July 1934, for example, the *Broadcast* reported on a scandal that featured the pastor of St. James AME Church suing one of his parishioners, claiming that her diamond ring actually belonged to one of his daughters. The paper assumed the worst of the minister, arguing that the church was, unbeknown to its congregants, "indebted to a homestead association in the city here to the extent of nearly $10,000 dollars." Using anonymous sources, the paper then reported that the church had been able to make a "small payment" to stave off foreclosure, but it remained on shaky financial ground: "It is a known fact that the old historic church has been disorganized and that some of the old financial pillars have been removed."⁴⁸

The paper clearly reveled in this church scandal, so much so that "a group of ministers said to be representing the local Ministerial Alliance" took the *Broadcast* to task, condemning LaFourche and his paper for publishing articles about St. James AME and appointing a committee of elders to call on the editor to ask him to either retract his scandalmongering or apologize. LaFourche was unfazed. He noted that the ministers could have gone to court but chose instead to speak to him in person, "so it can be seen by their actions that their purpose was not to seek justice, but to take the law into their own hands by calling on the editor as a MOB in which a conspiracy existed to do 'bodily harm.'" The *Broadcast* called on the "laymen of all denominations" to undo the city's Black ministerial class: "The pulpits have so successfully divided our one time strong churches that whenever a laym[a]n has the courage to speak for right, he is called a preacher fighter by his best friends."⁴⁹ This response demonstrated a significant confidence: LaFourche was willing to take on a church in the South and assumed that his readers would take the side of the press. It was also a religious class fight that those among the working class would appreciate.

Whether or not that brash coverage was the reason for the paper's early demise, there was more to LaFourche's coverage than scandal. In September, the *Broadcast* puzzled over the "antics" of Louisiana senator Huey P. Long and whether his claims to be working for the poor and laboring classes included the state's Black residents. The answer seemed to be no. "There is scarcely a positive act in Senator Long's career to indicate that he has ever thought about the Negro citizens of the state," the paper reported. "He has been indifferent to lynching, to peonage and has been anything but liberal in according economic opportunities to the Negro." The paper launched into a litany of the politician's more public hypocrisies before admitting that "despite all this, the Negro figures to win some advantages from some of the moves Huey and his gang are making even though they are indifferent to him." Chief among them was the "free poll tax constitutional amendment," which would functionally eliminate the state's poll tax. "If this amendment is made into law," explained the *Broadcast*, "Negroes expect to win the ballot in this state."⁵⁰

Beginning in July 1937 and for much of the remaining year, the Syndicate fostered a similar practical radicalism in Monroe, Louisiana's *Southern*

Broadcast, published by Sherman Briscoe, a teacher and football coach at Monroe Colored High School. Briscoe's column, "The Week's," was syndicated by the SNS in August and September 1937. It provided nonthreatening, nonpolitical fare. New Orleans was dangerous and probably influenced by "voodoo." It was the anniversary of the national anthem. People should be kind to waitresses. Briscoe's complete lack of controversy aided his rise through the ranks of Black publishers. He later became the executive director of the Washington bureau of the NNPA. It also gave him clout within Louisiana. When Southern University hosted a meeting with federal officials charged with administering funds for the Agricultural Adjustment Act, for example, Briscoe was among those invited "to hear how colored people can participate in benefits from the $85,000,000 federal farm tenant appropriation."[51]

Even for someone as nonthreatening as Briscoe, however, consequences always existed for Black publishers. In January 1937, for example, Briscoe's *Broadcast* had misprinted an article about a fatal accident. In response to the printing mistake, Briscoe was arrested and held in the parish jail over a weekend before the paper corrected the error. Meanwhile, the white papers in the city deemed his arrest so pedestrian as to not even merit a mention, despite the fact that a journalist was being jailed and Black criminality was always a welcome story in white dailies. The incarceration was also a violation of Briscoe's habeas corpus rights since no charge was ever filed against him.[52] It was nothing more than an effort by white law enforcement to silence an influential Black voice in the city. The stakes for Black southern publishers could be exceedingly high.

Editions of the paper that survive from the summer of 1936 to the summer of 1937, just prior to its contract with the Syndicate, show that it was national in scope. These *Broadcast* editions tout the paper as "The Authentic Voice of the South—Printed in the South for America." Its front page covered race news from around the country and the world, publicizing lynchings and other serious fare, along with sensationalistic murder stories and civic boosterism. It then moved to lighter coverage of Louisiana news. The paper announced its platform as being devoted to "a conscious appreciation of ourselves to the extent that we shall command respect rather than demand it." It sought Black economic development, a revival of Christianity, better school facilities, and "to teach our people to look on the brighter side of Negro life." Briscoe, the paper's editor and general manager, told his readers, "We are a great people with strange dreams and a wonderful heritage lost somewhere in the years between. It is the duty of every Negro to help gather up the missing links." To that end, the paper featured a religious page that included a weekly Sunday school lesson.[53]

A July 1936 editorial reported a litany of lynchings and other crimes against Black people in just one representative week, and then explained how such outrages could be combated. "We can do something about it by keeping our homes and our person clean," the paper explained. "We can do something about it by sending our children to school and by seeing to it that they are trained to make a worthwhile living." It argued, "No boy or girl should be allowed to finish high school without knowing how to do some kind of work well enough to earn an independent living."[54] This was definitely a voice of the South, a Washingtonian message of self-help and industrial training that cut against many of the national messages with which it competed.

Another Syndicate paper came later in Monroe. The *Twin City Tribune* set up shop in February 1940 only a block away from what had been the home of the venerable *Southern Broadcast* two years prior. The *Tribune*'s syndicated coverage, however, seemed almost a caricature of its predecessor. It included stories of a husband and wife being murdered and the honoring of a local minister, mimicking the common crime and church coverage that called such papers into question. The paper's one syndicated opinion piece was an editorial extolling the virtue of patience.[55] This was not the kind of coverage that generated staying power in a local paper, and the *Tribune* folded before the end of 1941.

Farther south in Louisiana was the *Baton Rouge Post*, edited by William H. Mitchell, manager of the local YMCA. The paper was somewhat more radical than its Monroe counterpart, covering, for example, the December 1937 speech of NAACP field secretary William Pickens at St. Mark's ME Church as he stumped for a federal antilynching law.[56]

Federal antilynching law was always safe and popular territory. In January 1938, the *Post* reprinted an editorial from the *Catholic Review* in favor of the antilynching bill. It railed against Black Democrats who voted for pseudo populist congressmen who welcomed Black votes but maintained white supremacy. Throughout the month, the paper reported diligently on the antilynching bill and the Democratic filibuster against it. The *Post*'s editorials for the bill, however, remained cautiously in the practical radicalism lane. "The several states of the South have definitely shown in the past several years that they are unwilling or unable to cope with the Lynch evil of their states," the paper explained. "And since they cannot or will not protect the lives of citizens of their states, what is wrong in asking the Federal

Government to handle the situation for them?"[57] It was a good question, but it was more passive than aggressive, calculated to raise the issue without angering white southerners opposed to the law.

Louisiana's racial issues were amplified in the war years, particularly in places with a military presence, like Alexandria. Georgia M. Johnson was born in the city around 1894 and became a schoolteacher in the 1920s. The following decade, she worked as a Rapides Parish social worker, the first Black woman to do so. Ultimately, she took that sense of social responsibility into her leadership of the local NAACP, which had developed in fits and starts in Alexandria. Various attempts had occurred in 1921, 1927, and 1930, none lasting particularly long. But Alexandria was within five miles of five different military bases that specialized in basic training, and in 1941 the city's population exploded as a result. Before 1941, Alexandria had twenty-six thousand residents, eleven thousand of whom were Black. By the end of the year, the Black population itself stood at twenty-six thousand, with the total population at sixty-seven thousand. In response to that growth and in response to statewide campaigns to improve teacher salaries and register Black voters, Alexandria made its fourth attempt at a branch of the NAACP. Johnson chaired the Legal Redress and Legislation Committee, enduring both racism from white locals and sexism from within the organization itself to fight for the rights of Black people in central Louisiana. "The day will come," she stated, "that all men and women regardless of color will have their rightful place in this nation and that we will no longer be the foot mats of this American Country and will not be Semi-slaves as we are but Americans."[58]

To reinforce this work, Johnson started her own newspaper, the *Alexandria Observer*, in July 1941 and allied it with the Syndicate. Among the events the paper covered—and among the things Johnson investigated in her role with the NAACP—was the Alexandria riot of January 10, 1942, which began after a group of white MPs began "reportedly arresting intoxicated soldiers" from Camp Claiborne at a local civilian Black theater, at which point several hundred other soldiers joined the effort to prevent mistreatment of their fellows by the MPs as locals looked on. "An unidentified colored woman" was shot by a stray bullet. State patrolmen and Alexandria city police joined the MPs in the fight. Camp Claiborne, the *Observer* reported, was one of the camps listed by the NAACP "as sites where colored military policemen are needed." Both Black soldiers and Black locals expressed their frustration at Jim Crow in the military and the town, and for their trouble more than three thousand were arrested. The battle lasted two hours, and at least twenty-eight Black protesters were shot. There were reports, the paper said, that "several colored soldiers were killed."⁵⁹

In response to the "unwarranted attack upon unsuspecting Negro MPs, soldiers and civilians," the Baptist Ministers Alliance of Alexandria sent a letter to President Roosevelt bemoaning the poor treatment of Black soldiers in the area. It was supplemented by several missives sent to state and military leaders by the NAACP. The commanding officer at the base sent a letter to the head of the local branch of the NAACP "in which he deplored the crucial situation and the unfortunate occurrence" and promised a thorough investigation.⁶⁰

The *Observer* reported on the alarm of local whites following the incident. They feared reprisals by Black soldiers, feared that the city and county would be held financially liable for damages, feared potential jail time for white participants, and feared that Alexandria would be "put 'off limit' for the 30 or 40 thousands of soldiers in Camps Beauregard, Claiborne and Livingston who spend millions of dollars with local business firms." Those fears gained currency later in January when the War Department "placed tentative blame . . . on civilian policemen and one military policeman (all white)" for the riot. In a scathing letter to Secretary of War Henry Stimson, the NAACP argued that the Alexandria incident was "only one more in a succession of regrettable ones whose cumulative effect has been to demonstrate that the Army has abdicated in favor of local southern white sentiment in the handling of United States soldiers who happen to be colored."⁶¹ Johnson's coverage of the riot in her paper was practical. Her defense of Black Alexandria in her role with the local NAACP was radical. When the racial consequences were simmering in such close proximity, editors had little choice.

And the racial consequences seemed always to be simmering in the Deep South. As the Syndicate's relationship with states like Louisiana and Mississippi evolved through the 1930s and 1940s, the SNS also attempted to spread its reach farther.

Chapter 7

The Syndicate Moves West

The Great Migration Black Population Changes (%)

City	1910-1940	1940-1970
Amarillo, Tex.	-0.1	4.1
Austin, Tex.	-5.1	-8.1
Beaumont, Tex.	-1.4	-1.4
Des Moines, Iowa	1.7	0.6
El Paso, Tex.	0.0	-1.4
Fort Worth, Tex.	5.7	-3.9
Galveston, Tex.	4.0	3.6
Houston, Tex.	3.2	-7.9
Little Rock, Ark.	-0.1	-6.6
Milwaukee, Wis.	13.2	1.2
Minneapolis, Minn.	3.4	0.1
Muskogee, Okla.	-1.8	-10.6
Oklahoma City, Okla.	4.2	-0.7
Omaha, Nebr.	4.5	1.8
Phoenix, Ariz.	-1.7	3.6
Pine Bluff, Ark.	8.0	-7.7
St. Louis, Mo.	27.5	6.9
Topeka, Kans.	0.0	-2.0
Tulsa, Okla.	0.0	-0.1
Waco, Tex.	0.2	-3.3

The listed cities are the ones large enough to be included in Census statistical materials. "The Great Migration, 1910 to 1970," U.S. Census Bureau, 13 September 2012, https://www.census.gov/dataviz/visualizations/020/508.php.

Arkansas

W. A. Scott's original vision for the SNS was to create an organization that covered much of the country. This goal required, first and foremost, covering the farther reaches of the South, moving west before spreading beyond the bounds of the former Confederacy. To that end, though its presence would never be overwhelming, the Syndicate featured several smaller efforts from Arkansas. For example, Forrest City's *Southern Liberator* emphasized both labor and local Black news. The two articles that exist from the paper describe a "survey of economical, social and educational conditions of Negroes below the Mason and Dixon line" and a Southern Tenant Farmers Union strike in eastern Arkansas. Published by the Southern Liberal Organization, the paper was concerned with farm labor in particular. It was sympathetic to the problems of all poor southerners, including Black southerners, but it was not a fundamentally Black newspaper.[1] The *Liberator* was a legitimate demonstration of significant if simple (and temporary) racial progress.

In Pine Bluff, the Great Protective Association began publishing the *Sunlight* in 1937 and aligned the monthly paper with the Syndicate in December 1939. Its editor and business manager was P. K. Miller, who was also the president of the Great Protective Association. His editorial in the paper's one surviving edition was a plea for Mississippi to enforce its state antilynching law, practicing the practical radicalism of critiques on the actions of other states, even as the situations in those states mirrored what happened in the paper's home area. Even larger, however—more than a quarter page, double the size of the antilynching editorial—was a letter from Miller to the association's agents, encouraging them to "see your members who are in arrears and get them paid up."[2] Far from a radical agent of racial change, the *Sunlight*, though it certainly did have the best interests of Black people in mind, acted more as an agent for Miller and his association. The paper took the two most important Black businesses during the age of Jim Crow—journalism and insurance—and combined them in an effort to enhance the power of both. The bulk of the paper's coverage worked to those ends, which were not served well by controversial stances.

More substantial, and thus more long-lived, was the *Arkansas World*, published in Little Rock, the state's largest area of potential influence. It allied with the Syndicate for more than thirteen years beginning in March 1940. Over the course of its existence, the paper was able to develop a practical radicalism in line with many of its southern forebears.[3] In its early incarnation, the *World* was edited by C. H. Jones, a graduate of North Little Rock's Shorter College. He was a conservative opposed to the Congress of Industrial Organizations's 1941 attempt to organize Black domestic service and industrial workers in Little Rock. He argued that workers joining a union would only antagonize employers. The Associated Negro Press reported that Jones was "held to be work[ing] hand in glove with white opponents of the union's organizing efforts. Jones, it is said, receives his financial support from white planters and mill owners." But he also had the support of his publisher, A. G. Shields, cofounder of the National Negro Publishers Association and the group's western vice president. After the onset of World War II, Jones signed an NNPA resolution (along with others), declaring "loyalty to the United States and to President Roosevelt, who is charting our national course in this hour of crisis. Freedom and democracy must be saved for the world."[4]

The *World* had entered a market with an already established paper, the *Arkansas Survey-Journal*, with a similar philosophical bent and a much longer legacy, going back to the 1920s.[5] The *Survey-Journal* was a four-page weekly with two pages of advertisements. The *World* believed, rightly, that it could command the market with an eight-page weekly with a modern graphic design and a page of comic strips, which would give Black journalism in Arkansas's capital city the look of Black journalism in larger cities, like nearby Memphis. In the one surviving edition of the *Arkansas World*, the paper used that slick, professional style to frame syndicated articles about a lynching in Georgia and federal antilynching legislation in Washington, D.C. An editorial in September 1940 described the global conflict as "the crisis of the age," which was "making unprecedented demands on the great structure upon which our principles of government must rest." Because of those problems, "it is up to our group now to meet their end of the challenge."[6] The paper explained that the Black population always looked for chances to prove its equality, and rising to the occasion of the pending fight would do just that.

Then there was a move from sycophancy to fantasy. In April 1942, the *World* reprinted a story from a white Missouri paper that claimed a submarine had appeared in the Mississippi River and "took aboard a Negro farmer before disappearing." The paper admitted that it couldn't "vouch for the authenticity of this story. However, for the benefit of our many readers we are publishing the story." In September 1942, the paper ran an advertisement for the Psychiana Corporation, which claimed to be able to harness the spiritual power of the people "to bring about the downfall of Hitler, Mussolini, and Hirohito," and it encouraged readers to send their names and addresses for free information.[7]

Such was not the approach of a crusading paper, but the *World* did eventually hit its stride and found the radical side of its practical radicalism.[8] In October 1945, the *World* reported on the plight of Will Brown, a Black sharecropper on the plantation of J. A. McLendon in Mississippi County, Arkansas. McLendon, also a deputy sheriff in the county, accused Brown of "going with the wives of the Negro men" living on the plantation, and he led the cropper to a nearby building where he and a group of "henchmen" committed acts of "brutality and barbaric practices," almost killing Brown. He was "tortured in an indescribable manner," including the application of lye to his body. "Then a coat or blanket was tightened about my face in an attempt to smother me," Brown explained. He only escaped with his life after playing dead. The *World* reported that the farmer's story had been reported to both the NAACP and the FBI, and his attackers were not from the city.[9] Thus the cover existed that allowed the paper to provide an exhaustive exposé.

There were also urban issues with which to grapple. A September 1946 editorial, for example, railed against incidents of violence in the city. "It is high time," the paper stated, "that a halt be called to the number of crimes committed by the Little Rock Negroes against each other." The problem had reached epidemic levels, and the courts were partly to blame: "The menace of the indulgent judge who decides that 'since it happened among nothing but Negroes, it makes but little difference how I dispose of it' should be removed." With that exception, however, the paper was principally concerned with Black perpetrators, even advocating "condemnations to the electric chair, or a real stiff sentence to the penitentiary" as remedies to Black-on-Black crime.[10]

Still, in January 1947, the *World* published a letter from Willie Francis, a St. Martinville, Louisiana, inmate who had survived an attempted execution in 1946 and was scheduled to be executed again after losing his appeal to the Supreme Court. "I was sitting in my cell hoping for some good news," Francis wrote. "But when they told me that the Supreme Court of the United States said I have to go back to the chair, I just about gave up hope." Francis's letter was in aid of raising funds for a new appeal. "My lawyer never took a cent from me or my family because he knows we're poor," he reported. "If anybody who reads this paper wants to help save me from going back to the chair, I ask them to please send whatever money they can to me here at the jail. I'll answer and thank them all myself."[11]

A May 1947 editorial in the *Arkansas World* reminded readers that "one cannot expect Negro business to grow without the support of colored people" but also clearly put the onus for that growth on the businesses themselves. Black businesses needed to "compete favorably with other businesses in prices and quality of commodities" and avoid "slip-shop methods and careless service." Another editorial the next month denounced poor behavior on buses and in other public places. "Profanity, vulgarity, rowdyism are becoming common on our streets," the paper complained. And when people attended the theater, they were "offended and annoyed by the clownishness and boorishness of thoughtless young people" who would often "giggle, laugh, whistle" during moments of "tense tragedy or of moral significance." As in its chiding of Black customers and businesses the previous month, the paper explained that "other people measure all Negroes by the stupidity and coarseness of a few."[12] Given that assumption, there was a valid reason for the complaint, but such lectures seemed to many a tone-deaf fiddle solo during the burning of Rome. Such laments gave southern newspapers their conservative reputations.

This strategy continued in October, when the paper criticized those who admonished that Black citizens should "get together," organize as a united front, and begin thinking along the same lines. Such was an impossibility and needn't be desired, because there could be a multiplicity of valid ideas for progress within one racial group. The call "that colored people 'get together,'" the paper explained, "is an alibi for those who wish to obstruct or postpone action for the welfare of colored citizens."[13]

The paper's own actions for the welfare of Black citizens took a variety of forms. In March 1951, for example, the *World* reported on the plight of the Reverend Morris Alexander Curry of Idabel, Oklahoma, who had been ejected from his first-class train seat on the Kansas City Southern Railway "and forced into the jim crow section of the train." Curry told the paper that he had contacted an attorney and planned to file suit against the company. The *World* chronicled his story in intricate detail but without editorial comment. Curry's suit never materialized, but the paper's coverage of the incident did much the same publicity work that the suit would have done.[14]

In January 1952, the paper lauded Harry Truman's call for civil rights legislation, noting that he "will be opposed as usual by the coalition of traditional Southern Democrats and reactionary old line Republicans." At the same time, "the large and growing body of enlightened democratic Southern Democrats will support the President," as would "enlightened Republicans." This was an important concession, the kind of cover that allowed the paper to stump for rights legislation and another example of practical radicalism. That same month, a *World* editorial lambasted "ballyhoo orators" who "attribute insincerity to those who espouse programs in our behalf." It argued for pragmatism, for trusting the political leaders who claimed to have the best interests of Black people in mind. It railed against "the use of certain extravagant and meaningless phrases, such as, 'I am sick and tired of being represented by Uncle Toms,' or 'I will give as much as any man for my race,' or 'I am not afraid of threats or reprisals.'" Such a critique was a defense of the paper's editorial policy. Surely castigated as an "Uncle Tom" paper for its lack of radicalism, the *World* was making a case for practicality in the face of ongoing "threats or reprisals."[15] Whether actually trusting politicians was a good idea mattered less than the underpinning of the paper's defense of the practice. This is, the paper seemed to be saying, as radical as we can be.

The next month, the *World* argued that the paper was "fundamentally interested" in public schools, public health and sanitation, housing projects, law enforcement, transportation, employment, and civil rights: "We are unalterably opposed to any sort of race or religious discrimination in any of these basic needs." It encouraged voters not to be neutral: "Our loyalty should be only to those willing to stand with us and for our needs." This was a vague pronouncement by design but still demonstrated a willingness to advocate for the issues its readers cared about most. Another editorial that month reinforced the position, denigrating neutrality and encouraging readers to "take sides." It described the "millions of our people in the South who are sweltering under burdens of poverty, illiteracy and ignorance, superstition, immorality, and exploitation" and urged votes for candidates who "will be able to do something about those things."[16] This was another vague pronouncement, and only some of the listed burdens qualified as rights issues, but the editorial was a stand in theory against the problems haunting Black people on the western edge of the South.

Texas

That western edge was also composed of the largest land mass and one of the largest populations in the region, Texas, a market coveted by the Scott family. From 1934 to 1938, the SNS facilitated the publication of the *Fort Worth Mind*, edited by C. R. Wise and Raymond L. Melton. The duo was particularly sensitive to criticisms common in Texas and across the nation that the Black press emphasized salacious crime over stories that uplifted the race. "Why should we cover up our faults and iniquities?" the *Mind* asked, mirroring the ethos of the Harlem Renaissance of the previous decade. When white papers published stories about the improprieties of wealthy or influential Black citizens, "the Negro does not call up the white editor and fume," nor did people threaten to stop reading. "But just let the Negro editor publish the same news, then the trouble begins." There was, the *Mind* argued, a double standard. Crime stories were news, and Black editors had the same responsibility as their white counterparts to publish the news. The criticisms, however, didn't stop there. If an editor "is militant, the 'Uncle Tom' race-leaders will suggest that he 'ease up' on certain of their friends for fear of antagonizing them." The paper, however, was unapologetic. "It is the policy of the *Mind* to publish facts, regardless of the individual concerned."[17] The syndicated editorial defended the papers of the South, which often filled their pages with crime stories, and in the process took a proletarian stand. In describing "militancy," the *Mind* was actually discussing attacking upper-class Black leaders, and therefore endeared itself to lower-class readers without rocking any racial boats.

"There are more wholesale murders going on in the South than in any other part of the country," explained another syndicated *Mind* editorial. "The entire fault lies in the COURTS of the land." From there, a typical argument would have blamed southern law enforcement for complicity in those murders by not prosecuting the killers. The *Mind*, however, went in a different direction. "Any Negro can kill another Negro and, with the sum of fifty or one hundred dollars and the swearing to an audacious lie which will never be legally proven or disproven, be freed in the next two or three hours; yet, when he is caught practicing the art of stealing from some white person, which was taught and instilled into him by the whites, he is sentenced [to] twenty years in the penitentiary."[18] This was an interesting turn, one that the northern Black press typically didn't take. Black-on-Black murders were not given the proper concern by local law enforcement, allowing the flimsiest lie to free a killer. But even minor crimes against white people were aggressively prosecuted, destroying the life of the accused. What's more, those crimes against whites were "taught and instilled" by whites. This was an early media critique of the emphasis on Black criminality, but it was coming from a source that had recently defended its own publication of Black crime stories. While that earlier editorial emphasized the exposure of the behavior of elites, the later editorial demonstrated the fine line that such arguments walked. Exposing the crimes of the talented tenth was the responsibility of the southern Black press. Emphasizing the crimes of the other 90 percent was the purview of its white counterpart, which in the process "taught and instilled" criminality into the population.

The *Mind* also addressed those Black murders. When Fort Worth's police chief explained the city's high murder rate, he credited the figure to "a great many Negro slayings in Fort Worth." And so the *Mind* sought to teach him that "the huge murder rate among Negroes may be attributed to several causes—not that they are innately murderers. Some of those causes are: lack of education caused by the South's dual system of education; the need of Negro policemen in large gatherings of Negroes; and paramountly—the laxity of swift and suitable punishment when a Negro kills another Negro."[19] While the editorial's final reason echoed its earlier complaint about the relative lack of concern among policemen in relation to Black-on-Black crime, its connection of the South's segregated education system and lack of Black police officers to the high murder rate demonstrated remarkable insight into the root causes of the problem.

Earnest McCarty provided a strong case study. In March 1936, McCarty was charged with attacking a white woman and was sentenced to death in the electric chair. His accuser claimed that she was walking home from a nearby school one evening when a "Mexican-looking Negro" asked her directions before ultimately throwing a coat over her and raping her. There was no other evidence. The injustice sparked Black Fort Worth to action, including the creation of the Earnest McCarty Defense Fund Committee, which sought to raise money for lawyers for appeals. The *Mind* urged swift action to save him. R. L. Melton acted as secretary of the Defense Fund Committee. In Hattie Crooms's "Deep Water" column, published in the *Mind* but disseminated more widely through the Syndicate, she compared McCarty's case to that of the Scottsboro Boys and argued that citizens of Fort Worth and Tarrant County, Texas, should care just as much about the local version. "As the mongrel cringes before his master's whip, likewise does Earnest McCarty as he piteously faces the panging current of the electric chair."[20] McCarty ultimately was executed in 1937, but the *Mind*'s fight demonstrated its willingness to engage in activism close to home.

The paper urged readers to pay their poll tax and vote, for example, and castigated them when they did not. In 1934, the *Mind* had reminded citizens that it had made a poll tax request, "yet any number of Negroes did not do so, and they were not all broke." When the Texas Democratic Party decided to leave the question of Black primary voting "up to the discretion of the individual ballot box judges," the *Mind* read the statement as an act of intimidation intended to warn Black voters away because the party knew it couldn't legally bar them. "By all means, this paper urges all qualified voters to vote," an editorial stated, "or, at least, attempt to vote at all the various precinct boxes. Let the Judges turn you down. You then have other bridges to cross." In April 1937, the paper favorably covered the creation of a local NAACP Youth Council in Fort Worth. It also supported the Texas Commission on Interracial Cooperation when it sponsored a late 1937 bill in the Texas legislature to provide financial aid for Black students seeking higher education and professional training. The group argued that the vast majority of Black teachers in Texas came from out of state because Texas simply didn't have the infrastructure to educate Black educators. "A more worthy or timely bill could not be introduced in the Legislature for the benefit of our group," the *Mind* believed.[21]

The Syndicate's push into Texas included more papers than the *Mind*. In 1934, for example, there was the *Austin Messenger*, which covered, among other things, a federal court ruling that declared "the present practice of barring Negroes from democratic primary elections in Texas" unconstitutional. In response, the Austin Negro Citizens Council wired telegrams to the president of the Democratic National Committee and to the U.S. president himself, encouraging them to support Black primary voting. "Knowing your attitude of fairness," the council wrote to Roosevelt, "we would appreciate a word from you to the State Democratic Committee in our behalf, thereby avoiding court reaction on our part."[22] This message was conciliatory, hat-in-hand underlings asking their superiors for a measure of grace, but it was also a threat to relitigate Black primary participation and thus provide more negative press for the party. Roosevelt and James T. Farley, head of the Democratic National Committee, were surely unworried about coverage from individual Black papers, but coverage in the *Messenger*, syndicated by the SNS, put word of the voting fight of Black Texans into homes across the South and across the country.

The *Dallas Express* was a Syndicate rotogravure member. The *Express* was founded by William E. King in 1892. "So long as the Negro helps to support the government," he said, "so should he contend for his rights." King was anti-Washington and emphasized gaining political rights in his newspaper. He was a Republican, but was willing to criticize Republican politics when he felt it necessary. King was killed in 1919 by his fiancée, who attacked him for leaving her for another woman. The *Houston Informer*, another Syndicate paper, merged with the *Texas Freeman* in 1930, becoming the *Houston Informer and Texas Freeman*. Its publisher, Carter Wesley, soon developed local editions throughout east Texas. The *Informer* reached, in one form or another, Corpus Christi, Galveston, Longview, Marshall, Lovelady, Palestine, Tyler, Texarkana, and Austin. His success allowed him to purchase the *Dallas Express* in 1940, moving into Texas's other major market.[23]

Then there was the *Houston Guide*, the *Marshall Tribune*, and the *East Texas Times*, all mid-1930s efforts of the Scotts to enter the western market. The motto on the masthead of the Syndicate's *Galveston Voice* was emblematic of the local populism of these papers: "The Voice of the People Is the Voice of God."[24]

The Syndicate's *Waco Post-Dispatch* encouraged locals to pay their poll tax and saved its most trenchant statements for national concerns, like a federal antilynching law. One editorial noted that prior to 1932, the country's kidnapping laws were incredibly weak. "But something happened in March 1932 that opened the eyes of the nation," the paper explained, referring to the Lindbergh baby, "and today we have one of the strongest kidnap laws in the world. I wonder when will there be a baby born to a Negro that will be of such importance that we might get an Anti-Lynch law. I am sure the sacrifice of having him lynched would be worth the benefits of the law."[25] This was an inordinately powerful statement emanating from a place of frustration about the failure of federal policy. Many felt the same frustration, but not many were willing to publicly admit to hoping for a high-profile murder to push the polling in favor of an antilynching law.

The *San Angelo Enterprise* was edited and published by Van Pell Evans, who was also the San Angelo manager of the Universal Relief Insurance Company. He was "a man of vigorous determination and with all of the energy of one's soul is giving West Texas its first and only Negro newspaper." He was also working to develop "the outstanding insurance company in West Texas. With an unsubdued spirit and undepressed mind, he is overcoming all obstacles to reach the uppermost rounds in the ladder of success."[26] That kind of success was common since the insurance and newspaper businesses interacted constantly in the Depression years, but it also emphasized the fine line that such businessmen and editors had to walk.

The *East Texas Times* was published in Big Sandy. The *Amarillo Herald* was published by a local music teacher named Kathryn Olive Hines, one of the few western Black papers produced by a woman. William Howard Wilburn ran the *Tyler Tribune*. Albert White was responsible for the Houston-based *Texas Examiner*, which was billed as the first semiweekly paper in Texas history.[27] All had short but significant runs; exemplary of such efforts was the *Galveston Guide*, which replaced the *Voice* in 1937.

The *Galveston Guide* was from its inception a Syndicate paper. It was "Galveston's Largest Circulated Negro Weekly Newspaper," but only a small portion of its coverage was local. The paper seems to have been founded after a Syndicate advertisement encouraging people to start papers by sending in a little content and having the SNS prepare a newspaper for their town. The message of the Syndicate spread to southeastern Texas simply by recruiting someone to "publish" a paper. That publisher was

H. L. Law. His front-page editorial in the *Guide*'s debut edition sounded a hopeful note for a Galveston recovering from the Depression and urged readers to "stand solidly for the City Party." That was the only political party that had openly welcomed Black residents of Galveston. "So we are for the City Party. All the way. We cannot vote any other way." The paper's aim, it promised readers, was "to give the citizens of Galveston a weekly publication featuring Local and National news that will inspire, encourage, and enlighten individual citizenry."[28]

The SNS also had a newspaper farther west in El Paso, Texas, the *Southwestern Torch*, which was founded in 1937 by Marvin E. Williams and joined the Syndicate in 1940.[29] In one blistering September 1940 editorial, the *Torch* blasted the Great Migration, arguing that economically, Black northerners and southerners were essentially equal. In the South, however, the Black person "at least learns to be self-reliant. He learns to think; to master situations." The southern Black resident "gains social graces" from his experience in the region. Furthermore, "northern mixed schools afford no opportunity for social contact and development for Negroes." There were still problems—"prejudice, discrimination, biased enforcement of the law and making out with less than his portion of Federal appropriations"—but the region "has produced more noteworthy citizens than any section of our great nation." The paper described icons from Sojourner Truth and Frederick Douglass to Joe Louis, "a southerner by birth." It was the pressures of the region that have "given the Negro ZEAL, created VISION and aroused HOPE! He started from the plantations of the South. Shall a child forget its parents? No. Never!"[30] This was an interesting document, the paper's ode to the "motherland," and it stemmed naturally from regional pride and fears about the demographic shift resulting from mass migration and the resulting vulnerability of those left behind. Perhaps most important, the *Torch* interpreted migration to the American West as something fundamentally different than migration to northern urban industrial hubs. Either that or it interpreted El Paso as part of the South. In either case, the paper did not sugarcoat the racial problems in the region.

An editorial the following month, for example, described a local Selective Service board that had developed a plan to honor the first man called to service, until one board member worried, "Supposing he were a Negro?" The *Torch* explained that this wasn't simply a racial question: "This is Racism, to use a phrase recently clarified by Dr. Ruth Benedict." By asking that question, the board member "was saying that white people were better than other people. He was guilty of Racism."[31] It was an important editorial because it took an academic concept and translated it with a very specific and relatable example to all of the paper's readers and, through syndication, to readers throughout the South and the nation.

Oklahoma

In Oklahoma, the Syndicate had the *Bartlesville Voice*, published by Thomas S. Smith. A *Voice* editorial from March 1935 recounted with frustration the complaints "from the pulpit, the schoolroom, the theatre and the market place about the conduct of our people." Church leaders worried that the young no longer cared sufficiently about the sanctity of religious services. School authorities complained that Black children were dirty and unkempt; theater managers thought that Black behavior was "unsocial." Store owners claimed that Black customers were too boisterous and entered places of business with offensive clothing and a lack of basic hygiene. Instead of coming to the defense of its readers, the *Voice* sounded its alarm in the other direction, fitting the Black southern journalism model. "The above traits reflect your character," it chided. "For God's sake, let's stop it!"[32]

Less than 100 miles away was the *Muskogee Lantern*, published by A. K. Chandler, and 150 miles from there was the *Oklahoma Defender*, published in the state's capital city to compete with the more established *Oklahoma Black Dispatch*.[33] Competition, however, was always secondary to race unity in the cause of equality. One of the proposed federal antilynching bills, for example, imposed a penalty on counties where such crimes occurred, which would be used to pay the victim's surviving relatives. When it was defeated in 1938, some of its congressional opponents compared the bill to Nazi policy, noting a situation where a German representative had been killed in Paris by a Jewish radical, and Hitler responded by fining the German Jewish population $400 million. Roscoe Dunjee, editor of the *Oklahoma Black Dispatch*, called out the argument for its obvious absurdity: "The failure of American communities to apprehend, prosecute, and convict mobs, proves collusion and guilt on the part of entire community life. On the other hand there is no better example of the present-day German complex and ideology than in the American attitude toward its Negro citizens." Turning the Nazi analogy on its head was important work, and the *Oklahoma Defender*, edited by C. Nelson Moran, saw in the argument enough value to celebrate the *Black Dispatch*'s editorial in its pages and, after syndication, in the pages of the other papers of the SNS.[34]

Iowa

The *Iowa Bystander* was created by Atlanta native James B. Morris, the son of formerly enslaved people. As a teenager, his best friend was lynched after being falsely accused of raping a white woman. The event both radicalized Morris and made him eager to study law. "The first Negro lawyer I ever saw was during an Emancipation Proclamation celebration back in 1905," he said. "His idea was that Negroes should fight for their rights but continue to maintain their dignity." To live up to that creed, Morris attended Hampton Institute and then Howard Law. While at Hampton, he befriended a fellow student, George Woodson from Des Moines, Iowa, and in 1916 he made his way to Des Moines to spend time with his friend. Morris stayed and was admitted to the bar in 1917, then began practicing law two years later after serving in World War I. He led the Des Moines chapter of the NAACP, and in 1925 he cofounded the Negro Bar Association. In 1922, he bought the *Bystander*, the oldest surviving Black newspaper in Iowa, for $1,700. The paper first had appeared in 1894. It was, remembered Morris, "the brainchild of several forward thinking Negroes in Des Moines who realized that the existing daily press left the Negro out in the production of the papers and the news about them generally."[35]

The Black residents of Des Moines had seen a couple of efforts at a Black press in the nineteenth century, both of them halting and young at the time of their deaths. The *Bystander* broke that mold, and in 1936, its rival, the *Iowa Observer*, broke it as well, serving as a progressive competitor to the rock-ribbed Republican *Bystander*. Both of them aligned with the Syndicate at various points in their existence.[36]

Along with the growth of Black press in the state, however, there were more dangerous developments. The Klan grew in Iowa as it did in many northern areas, pushed in part by the Great Migration, which increased the number of Black southerners in the state. When the Klan came to Morris's house to protest his paper's participation in a federal antilynching campaign, he and his brother Clyde ran them off with shotguns. But there was also significant positive white contact. The *Bystander* had difficult times during the Depression, but Harvey Ingram, publisher of the white *Des Moines Register*, donated $100 to the *Bystander*'s coffers and gave

Morris a list of white businessmen who were committed to the paper's survival.³⁷

In 1934, Des Moines district judge Frank S. Shankland granted parole to a Black man convicted of the manslaughter of a white man. Despite the protests of the prosecutor, Shankland released Thomas Rowland because he was the sole support of his family, because the verdict was questionable, and because petitions from both the community and the jury asked for his parole. "Seldom in the annals of American courts has a Negro been paroled for killing a white man," the *Bystander* reported. Like the *Bystander*'s coverage of Angelo Herndon addressing Des Moines citizens at the Jewish Community Center on behalf of the International Labor Defense, this was the kind of story that showed to Black southern citizens reading the syndicated coverage a world they simply did not know at home.³⁸

Herndon's case was the perfect example of the diaspora in reverse. He had traveled from Ohio for work and discovered communism in Alabama in 1930, soon becoming an organizer for the party. After moving to Atlanta, he was arrested and charged with "inciting insurrection" under an obscure antebellum slave statute—simply for attempting to organize Black workers in the city. The ILD came to his aid, but though he avoided the death penalty, he received a twenty-year sentence from an all-white jury in January 1933. After a series of appeals, Herndon finally secured his freedom in a U.S. Supreme Court ruling in 1937. His case became a signpost representing the standards of "southern justice" and the ties white southerners sought to make between civil rights activism and the specter of communism, as well as a symbol of the dangers of the migration of people and ideas.³⁹

The editor and publisher of the *Iowa Observer* in Des Moines was Charles P. Howard, who was an attorney in the city. His three sons worked for the paper, and the family also soon developed the *Waterloo Observer* and the *Tri-City Observer*. Howard's original connection to the Syndicate might have been Cliff MacKay, the *Atlanta Daily World*'s managing editor, who was from Des Moines and whose family still lived there. Or he might have had no original connection at all, like Alberta Gibson, simply wanting to join his paper to the roots of Iowa's particular grapevine.⁴⁰

In January 1940, on the first anniversary of the *Observer*'s founding, Helen Dameron Beshears, a leader in the Iowa Federation of Colored Women's Clubs, described the paper as dedicated to distributing news "necessary and beneficial to the reading public, to the protection of the civic rights and awakening and maintenance of social and legal justice on all fronts." One of Howard's columns, for example, took apart the Democratic national platform as it related to Black citizens, criticizing its attempt to sound as if the party had strived and would continue to strive for educational and economic opportunities. Howard didn't deny that such programs existed, but he argued that no one could "successfully contend that the Negro has had a fair participation in any one of these projects." The party pledged "to strive for complete legislative safeguards against discrimination in government service and benefits," but Howard and the *Observer* were not fooled: "If they wanted to give us safeguards against discrimination, they could give it." He ultimately ruled the platform "woefully disappointing. It does not begin to be as definite as the Republican platform." This was the kind of systematic critique of Democratic Party hypocrisy that the paper's small southern counterparts could never get away with writing themselves. At the same time, it was not the kind of radical denunciation that would put anyone in danger for republishing. In May 1941, another Howard column advocated for Black defense jobs, calling the treatment of Black workers in the defense program "practically a national scandal." He encouraged everyone interested in defense employment to write to the paper stating their qualifications and experience. "To get employment," he told readers, "we are going to have to unite, organize and stick together." A. Philip Randolph's March on Washington compromise in January was supposed to remedy some of the problems, but there was clearly more work ahead.[41]

In February 1943, an Iowa minister returned from the National Baptist Convention in Shreveport, Louisiana, and told the *Observer* about Black sharecroppers in that state moving west. "Representatives from California farming interests are in Louisiana hiring and moving all those who wish to go to this new field of agricultural endeavor," the paper had learned.[42] This was the kind of coverage that Black Iowans wanted, the children of migration learning about the continued growth of the grapevine out west. At the same time, it was an advertisement for the possibility of further migration should the elections not go well or if Iowa discrimination continued.

Of course, the second major wave of the Great Migration was a significant story, but so was World War II. *Observer* articles covered the Women's Army Auxiliary Corps training station at Fort Des Moines, noting with pleasure in July 1942 that the first arrival was a Black woman. Mary McLeod Bethune met with the women trainees that month in her role with the War Department. In February 1943, Eleanor Roosevelt visited the base, and the paper was effusive in its coverage of her visit to "the colored WAACs in their dining room, their quarters and their company headquarters. She beamed with pride as she headed the inspection party." As late as April 1945, the paper was reporting favorably on integrated fighting units in Europe and a new policy of integration in the Army Nurse Corps, using those examples to call for a full integration policy throughout the military.[43] This was a bold stance, exemplary of many of the paper's positions, but like its southern counterparts, the paper took aim at racial problems outside the bounds of its home. When dealing with local military matters, the paper was largely celebratory, even devoting a new column fawning over the female soldiers at Fort Des Moines. Such was the calling card of practical radicalism. That southern strategy ensured the *Observer*'s ability to make equality claims without running afoul of local whites.

Nebraska

The Syndicate also moved into Nebraska. John Benjamin Horton's *Omaha Chronicle* was not Omaha's first Black newspaper. Throughout the 1920s, the city had four different Black newspapers, including the *Omaha Guide*, which was still published in the 1930s, competing with Horton's *Chronicle*. In December 1936, Horton, along with four other Black candidates, entered the race for Omaha mayor, demonstrating a range that most southern editors would have found completely foreign in their particular sphere of influence.

The *Omaha Guide* was published by C. C. Galloway. The other Black Omaha papers were the *Omaha Progress*, published by Fred L. Barnett; the *Omaha Enterprise*, published by T. P. Mahammitt; and the *Monitor*, published by John Albert Williams.[44]

Arizona

The Syndicate pushed even farther west, following a Black southern population that had migrated (and was migrating) toward the Pacific coast. Alberta Gibson had moved in 1912 to Phoenix, Arizona, from Texas by way of California, where she became a laundress, working to support her mother and young son. By 1937, she had taken over the local newspaper, the *Phoenix Index*, founded in 1936 by the Reverend W. Gray. There was no long history of Black newspapers in Arizona because the Black population there was small. The state's first paper, the *Phoenix Tribune*, had begun in 1918, a child of the first wartime wave of the Great Migration. It was followed by the short-lived *Western Dispatch* and the more established *Arizona Gleam* before the creation of the *Index*.⁴⁵ Gibson wasn't a native of Arizona, and she knew that most of her readers weren't either. So after taking over the paper from Gray, Gibson aligned her paper with the Scott Newspaper Syndicate. In a town of migrants, she assumed, the news of Phoenix needed to be leavened with news of the South. The Arizona capital would be the westernmost point in the SNS orbit.

Gibson called her *Index* "A Paper with a Purpose," and she urged readers in another slogan, "Don't Spend Your Money Where Your People Are Not Welcome." The paper claimed to be politically independent and vowed that it "shall at all times, regardless of any set rulings or regulations, present the news completely, impartially and free from hatred." In every edition it listed its detailed platform:

1. To give to the colored people a race paper that they can feel proud of and in which they may express their views on all political, social, religious and economic questions which face the race.
2. To awaken racial conscience, especially in business, to the extent that we must become job makers as well as job seekers.
3. To instruct boys and girls in the art of thrift.
4. To promote the Fatherhood of God and the brotherhood of man.
5. To build a firmer racial foundation for prosperity.⁴⁶

This platform demonstrated a stretching of the grapevine to a far-flung state. Distance from the South clearly gave Gibson's paper an ability to be more radical, "to awaken racial conscience," but the listed aims also demonstrated that the vine had yet to break. The paper's goals emphasized thrift and religion in a decidedly southern way.

The ties that bound, of course, were there in more pragmatic ways as well. SNS affiliation ensured that news of Atlanta and other member towns and cities would be prominent in the *Index*'s pages. Advertisements for North Carolina Mutual Life Insurance, Atlanta Life Insurance, and other businesses were in every edition of the paper. Xavier University of Louisiana encouraged *Index* readers to attend, as did the Atlanta College of Mortuary Science and Tuskegee.⁴⁷

The paper's news, too, was national in scope, using syndication to cover the region held so dear by many *Index* readers. One August 1939 front page, for example, covered Prairie View A&M's master's degree graduation. The paper covered policy changes with the WPA and the possibility that Roosevelt would appoint a Black judge to the federal bench within the next year. The *Index* gave the most page space in that edition to a Farm Security Administration report demonstrating that 95 percent of Black farmers lived in the South and that half of all tenant farmers were Black, vastly greater than the racial population ratio. Page allocation in that edition and those succeeding it kept a large focus on the nation more broadly and the South in particular, bringing readers back to the roots of the grapevine. Editorials extolled the virtues of the southern accent and evaluated the state of the Republican Party. Through Scott syndication, the paper also reprinted editorials from southern newspapers, further connecting its readers with the region.[48]

Minnesota

From Arizona the grapevine moved to Minneapolis, where the *Twin City Herald* joined the Syndicate in December 1939. The *Herald* had been founded in 1927 by Minneapolis publisher Cecil E. Newman, who was born in 1903. "Cecil was a small, brown-skinned man of perpetual motion and tremendous spirit," wrote photographer Gordon Parks. The *Herald* was Newman's first effort, but he soon branched out, in 1934 founding the *Spokesman* and the *St. Paul Recorder*. When he did, local J. E. Perry took over the *Herald*.[49]

Perry owned a printing company and published the paper along with posters, business cards, letterhead, handbills, and anything else a customer might need. The *Herald* was a small four-page effort with a simple linear layout; two of its pages were devoted to advertisements. Its news content was dominated by civic and church stories, with editorials explaining and denouncing discrimination when the publisher found it fitting. An April 1939 editorial, for example, bemoaned the Minneapolis administration of the New Deal's Home Owners Loan Corporation, which was requiring larger down payments on corporation properties and a higher monthly rate on loan payments for Black applicants. "Economically, the Negro of this area is not so well situated that it is possible for them to own homes without being treated with an element of fairness," the paper explained. "If the statements regarding the aforesaid discrimination are true, and we have heard of them too often to accept them as wholly untrue, vigorous action should be taken at once."[50] This wasn't a stirring denunciation, not a fiery attack on specific officials accused of racial discrimination, but it was a clear statement and demanded recompense, however that recompense might look. This was practical radicalism.

After the paper aligned itself with the Syndicate in December 1939, more news of the South made its way into each small edition. Southern senators were outraged in January 1940 when a federal antilynching law passed the House. A group of students from Atlanta University's School of Social Work were coming to Minneapolis to train at Phyllis Wheatley House, a Community Fund agency that worked with the city's Black population. When a series of lawsuits challenging southern universities to enroll Black applicants made the news, the *Twin City Herald* remembered "a situation in Minneapolis that occurred a short time ago when students applying at our Vocational High School were not allowed to enroll in courses of their choice by student advisors." Though such did not seem as fully recalcitrant as keeping out Black students entirely, the paper was not so sure. "One of the stock excuses used by the other group for not employing Negroes is the scarcity or total lack of trained persons among them," the *Herald* explained. "Yet we are informed that the advisors refused, in some cases, to allow Negro girls to enroll in such courses as beauty culture and even stenography, and discouraged our boys from taking many courses likewise." These obstructions created a ceiling on potential employment that kept the Black population artificially ignorant and artificially poor, and they demonstrated that integration was only equality when all students were treated equally.[51]

The Syndicate never printed the *Herald* in Atlanta. It remained a small four-page weekly with a layout that never really veered from its original form. The Scotts were not a printing service for this paper; they were just a supplier of syndicated news. That was, of course, the most important part of the service, the tie that bound communities together and connected those migrating north with the home they left behind. Such a relationship lessened the cost for the *Herald*, lessened the effort for the SNS, and still provided that connective tissue of information so vital to diasporic stability.[52]

Chapter 8

From the Upper South to the Midwest

The Great Migration Black Population Changes (%)

City	1910-1940	1940-1970
Charleston, W.Va.	0.0	-3.1
Cincinnati, Ohio	15.4	6.8
Cleveland, Ohio	28.7	8.1
Columbus, Ohio	6.8	4.7
Dayton, Ohio	20.9	5.5
Evansville, Ind.	0.2	-1.9
Gary, Ind.	34.6	16.0
Hampton, Va.	-4.4	-9.9
Huntington, W.Va.	0.2	-1.2
Indianapolis, Ind.	4.8	3.9
Lexington, Ky.	-9.2	-5.2
Louisville, Ky.	9.0	-3.3
Peoria, Ill.	8.8	0.3
Richmond, Va.	10.2	-4.9
Roanoke, Va.	0.8	-4.2
South Bend, Ind.	10.6	2.4
Toledo, Ohio	8.6	4.1
Youngstown, Ohio	16.5	6.3

The listed cities are the ones large enough to be included in Census statistical materials. "The Great Migration, 1910 to 1970," U.S. Census Bureau, 13 September 2012, https://www.census.gov/dataviz/visualizations/020/508.php.

Kentucky

At the same time the Syndicate was creating its own newspapers from the ground up, it was also signing established papers to SNS contracts, including the *Louisville Leader*. That paper was led by publisher I. Willis Cole from Memphis, who had graduated from LeMoyne Junior College before coming to Louisville in 1915 to sell Bibles. That was a traveling job, but he liked the city, decided to stay, and founded a newspaper, publishing the first edition of the *Leader* in November 1917. It quickly became the most popular Black newspaper in the city, protesting discrimination and urging boycotts of businesses that treated Black customers poorly. He was frustrated with both the Republican Party's assumption of Black support (and its corresponding lack of action) and Black political apathy. Further, "Negroes will never amount to anything," he stated, "until the leaders among them stop so much bickering, and throw into the wastebasket their personal differences." His paper constituted the radical wing of Black Louisville, critics urging more work with white leaders in the Republican Party and a more measured stance on local race relations. The *Atlanta Daily World* described Cole as "a consistent fighter for the rights of the Negro."[1]

But there were limits, even for Cole, which made connection to the Syndicate beneficial for the *Leader*. In September 1932, for example, eighteen-year-old Leroy Cunningham was killed by a white Louisville police officer, "the 18th such victim of police brutality in the last few years." The *Leader* did not even mention the case, instead publicizing it outside the region through Scott syndication, ensuring that the murder would be documented and known despite local fears of police reprisal. This demonstrated that the Syndicate could be a vehicle for Black journalists to disseminate news that might be too controversial or dangerous for them to publish locally. The *Leader*'s principal connection to the Syndicate was through its subscription to and participation in the weekly rotogravure section. The paper got the eight-page "brown sheet" in its weekly edition; that and syndication were the carrots that had brought the Louisville paper to the SNS.[2]

There were also tangible benefits for the Syndicate as the Scotts pushed the SNS farther north at the same time as they moved into more western venues. Establishing a foothold in Kentucky and the upper South was vital to that effort. To get that foothold, the Syndicate was far more accommodating to radical content. In 1935, for example, the *Louisville Independent News*, edited by William "Fighting Bill" Warley, briefly joined the SNS. In 1933, Warley had been arrested along with AME Zion minister and lawyer Charles Eubank Tucker on a charge of criminal libel for reporting on "alleged indecency exhibited by a colored girl at a party attended by certain white and colored politicians." Warley, a Louisville native, had founded the paper in 1912 and used it for radical activism, deriding those in his own community who went along with racial segregation or depended on the racial status quo for their livelihoods.[3] Such radical stances often put him at odds with the Black elites of Louisville, who would rather he not make waves. It also put him at odds with the Republican Party. When Warley attempted to run for the state senate in 1919, the party had refused to back him. A riot enflamed by Republican Party opposition to an independent Black party in the Louisville elections of 1921 led to the destruction of Warley's printing press, but he continued publishing.[4]

Louisville was, far and away, the largest tiered market in Kentucky, making it the cornerstone of the SNS strategy. The *Louisville Herald Tribune*, published by attorney and minister Tucker, began its relationship with the Syndicate in the summer of 1937. It was less controversial than Warley's paper, but it did serve as an advocate for Black people. In a November 1937 editorial, the paper compared the budding dictatorships of Europe to their Democratic counterparts, arguing that the lack of an antilynching law in the United States put it on a dangerous path toward a version of the former: "The greatest lesson that history teaches is that no nation founded on injustice ever has or ever can stand." It was true that dictatorships "take life by summary proceedings," but they justified their actions by arguing that they were undertaken for the greater good. Meanwhile, "lynching has only to acknowledge that it is done to satisfy private malice, passion or prejudice." If the country wasn't able to "destroy the dragon of lynch law," it would ultimately "undermine the foundation of our government until its pillars crumble and engulf us all in anarchy and ruin."[5] And that would prove the dictators right.

The *Herald Tribune* was replaced in the ranks of the Syndicate in March 1938 by another incarnation of Warley's paper, now known simply as the *Louisville News*. It was, unsurprisingly, just as activist as its founder. In March 1938, the *News* responded to reports that local bellboys were not receiving wages and instead were only working for tips. This briefly became a small scandal in the city, and the *News* came to the aid of the bellboys, but noted that those complaining were "almost assuredly white, since Negroes seldom ever kick."[6]

The *Louisville News* changed its name to the *Falls City News* in November 1939, but kept its local coverage on racial disparities in the city and in Kentucky.[7] In December 1939, the paper covered the report of a special committee appointed by Kentucky governor Happy Chandler to study equal education in the state. That committee recognized the legal right of Black students to attend the University of Kentucky and other institutions of higher learning, including the University of Louisville, "harmonizing our state laws with the United States Constitution." Plans for the transition, however, moved slowly. In October 1941, almost two years after the Chandler committee's report, student Charles Eubanks filed his second complaint against the University of Kentucky, suing for undergraduate admission. To stop him from enrolling and to conform to the Supreme Court's opinion in *Missouri ex rel. Gaines*, the Kentucky legislature established Kentucky State College as his case was pending, hoping to provide a Black alternative to the all-white institution. Though Charles Hamilton Houston and Thurgood Marshall worked diligently on his behalf, the case dragged on for years, and Eubanks eventually dropped it in 1945. The *News* covered it until the end, rightly interpreting Eubanks as a symbol of the racial divisions in Kentucky higher education and the failure of the government to live up to its promises.[8]

In April 1940, Chandler, now a senator, voted against a federal antilynching law, and the paper railed against him, arguing that though he "has received thousands of Negro votes in the past," he would get "few if any" in the future. The paper asked Black leaders all over the city about their reaction, printing an exhaustive list of quotes damning Chandler for his vote.[9] It was a direct attack on the senator's politics, a militant response that required the paper and the city's leading Black citizens to put their names on fierce criticism of a popular white leader. This response simply couldn't happen south of Louisville. Similarly, in July 1940, the *News* reported on a traffic case in a local court where the defendant was referred to by the prosecutor as a "darkie." The accused's lawyer vigorously objected, reminding the court that his client was an American citizen and entitled to respect. The prosecutor withdrew "his repulsive statement." The paper applauded the defense attorney, arguing that such efforts were "needed in all instances where deprecating remarks are made concerning the race."[10] Those in Atlanta who had watched the failed prosecution of W. A. Scott's probable murderer would not have recognized such contrition.

In July 1941, a *News* editorial attacked Georgia's Eugene Talmadge for firing the dean of the University of Georgia College of Education for advocating integrated schooling: "It is discouraging to anyone possessed with a mind for fairness and the upholding of democratic principles to be forced to tolerate parasites" like the governor. The paper denounced the white leader as "Herr Talmadge of Georgia." When such editorials were syndicated by the SNS, they allowed southern papers, and Georgia papers in particular, to say through the cover of a Louisville dateline what they might not otherwise be able to say. Syndication was an act of surrogacy. Another editorial in September, for example, denounced a local store's window display for caricaturing a Black train porter. It was "the kind of display you would expect to find in Tennessee or in Georgia but not in Louisville."[11]

In April 1942, the paper ran a powerful editorial denouncing classism among the Black population. It quoted General Douglas MacArthur's pronouncement: "It is that indescribable consanguinity of race which causes us to have the same aspirations, the same hopes and desires, the same ideals and the same dreams of future destiny." That "consanguinity of race" should remind Black readers that "it matters not how high in wealth or intelligence or character a Colored American may rise" because "he still faces the same prejudices the lowest Negro faces." The editorial encouraged unity among the classes, arguing that "the simple ability to stand together and to work together" could provide Black people with the equality they wanted. It encouraged shopping at Black businesses and hiring Black employees. Above all, "that means loving each other."[12]

The *News* reported proudly in September 1942 that Black waiters from Negro Waiters Union Local 415 refused to replace white waitresses after an increase in the minimum wage for women and children led restaurant owners to revolt against the decision. In November, the paper ridiculed a white woman charging a Black man with raping her after she was unable to positively identify him, claiming, "All Negroes look alike to me."[13] Such was the nature of life on the northern border of the South.

In June 1943, the National Negro Publishers Association held its annual conference in Louisville, and the paper covered it assiduously. The SNS delegation to the conference was large, and the Syndicate reported on the doings, including a formal protest to the War Department from the NNPA, challenging the drafting of the Syndicate and the *Southwest Georgian*'s A. C. Searles.[14] The *News*'s location on the border between the South and the Midwest was a place where more radical declamations met with traditional southern segregation.

Back in the 1930s outside Louisville, papers like Lucy J. Cochran's *Lexington Record* also signed up with the Syndicate; the *Record* stayed with the group from 1934 to 1936. Cochran's paper launched a particularly scathing attack during that period on the white southern use of Black women's first names, rather than addressing them with a respectful honorific like "Mrs." "The practice of addressing all colored women by their first names is vulgar," the paper noted. "Colored women who in any way belong in public life chafe more under this injustice than others." It was one reminder of social difference that was constantly in their faces. Segregation only affected someone when attending an interracial event, but such marks of perceived inferiority came every day and often. The *Record* insisted that the practice should change, even reminding whites that using "Mrs." was "not a title showing social equality. It is simply a form of address that goes with a marriage license." You don't actually have to respect Black women, the paper seemed to be saying, to be polite. This perspective situated the paper at the intersection of race and gender, its Black woman editor representing the needs and aspirations of her full identity.[15]

That identity was always concerned with voting. In July 1935, the paper reported that the Negro Voters League of Lexington had reelected its officers, and the next month it celebrated that "for the first time in the history of Fayette county [the] election commission selected and approved Negro election officers in four precincts" in Lexington. All did not go well, however, as Cochran, one of the election officers for the Elm Tree Lane precinct, "was unlawfully excused without her request to do so and was not notified of her dismissal because two or three white women in the precinct complained of Negro election officers serving in the booth with them." Cochran's article on the subject noted that one of the white women had lived across the street from her for the previous six years.[16] Such was the nature of life in the upper South. Black women wouldn't have had an opportunity to serve as election officers in the Deep South, but they also wouldn't have had to face the indignity of racist dismissal.

In Owensboro, Kentucky, William H. Robinson was an insurance salesman and high school teacher who also edited the *Owensboro Eagle*. Its publisher was Louis McHenry, a Hopkinsville lawyer and Owensboro native, who eventually went on to legal consulting jobs with the NAACP. "Each day in this community," he would remark in a 1966 speech in Hopkinsville, "the Negro is reminded that he is a 'Second Class Citizen,' and is faced with many denials of the basic right of a citizen, but, yet we are expected to be patient and not speak out, because certain people or groups are not ready for the Negro to have all his rights."[17] Black people didn't have all their rights in other states as well. And so, from Kentucky, the Syndicate grapevine branched again.

West Virginia

The *West Virginia Weekly*, based in Charleston, the state's largest tiered market, was part of the Scott group from the end of 1933 through 1934. The paper's masthead described it as the "Official Negro Press of West Virginia."[18] The *Weekly* was "the biggest newspaper ever published in this vicinity," a laudable feat considering that "the history of Negro newspapers in West Virginia has been a tragic one." There was a society page, a women's page, and a page of short stories and serials. One editorial promised that the paper "will be absolutely fearless." After the paper's first six pages came the gravure weekly, then an "SNS Feature Section" that was, essentially, a Syndicate weekly, an eight-page composite of content from the Syndicate and the *Atlanta Daily World*, including national material from the ANP, other sources, and member papers. Advertisements for Atlanta Life Insurance and North Carolina Mutual were prominent. There were also the requisite advertisements for skin whiteners, hair straighteners, and patent medicines found in the pages of most southern Black newspapers.[19]

A Syndicate advertisement in the *Weekly* encouraged readers to "Start a Newspaper Next Week." Like similar ads in other member papers, the *Weekly* listed a series of cities throughout the South and in New Jersey, Indiana, and Ohio. "Publish a paper in your town or in any town listed below—we will print it." Despite the Depression, the advertisement claimed, there was an "upturn" in business. "Dozens are making real money following this plan—Get in the parade—It is growing." Another SNS ad encouraged readers, "Make a touchdown for yourself!! Get into the newspaper business today," and again included a list of potential cities. "Many men are earning good money by this plan. You assemble the news and mail it to us and we mail you a newspaper supplemented with features, rotogravure, editorials and news highlights!"[20]

In Huntington, West Virginia, the *Tri-State News* was founded by J. Carl Mitchell. A Milledgeville, Georgia, native and Morehouse graduate, Mitchell was the pastor of Huntington's Sixteenth Street Baptist Church and head of the city's NAACP chapter. It came as no surprise, then, that the *News* wrote positively about the Virginia NAACP's fight for making Black teachers' salaries equivalent with their white counterparts'. When police arrested two picketers among a group of young men protesting the exclusionary policies of Huntington's Virginia Market under the auspices of the NAACP in July 1942, the paper covered that scandal too. Mitchell, acting as president of the local NAACP, attempted to negotiate with the police. His paper was quick to report the inspectors' disingenuousness in their promises. When the pickets resumed in August, the authorities arrived again, and the paper was clearly frustrated. "Unjust, and ignorant of the law, city police and practically every constable in Cabell county came upon the scene and intimidated the pickets until they were forced, momentarily, to stop," the *News* reported, "but the signs had already done the damage, for business at the market [was] cut almost to nothing." Mitchell's paper then called for a Black boycott of the market: "Those who continue to go, and some people are, will lose their self respect and race pride by doing so." The paper quoted its leader in his capacity as president of the local NAACP. "This organization has just begun its fight," he said. "Anywhere injustice, or racial discrimination toward any race, creed, or color prevails, we are there doing everything in our power to destroy it."[21]

The *Tri-State News* and Mitchell criticized the owner of the market and the police who were involved. The rest of their statements were carefully broad, referring to "anywhere" there was "injustice." It was more radical than many of its counterparts, but it was still a proximate radicalism, which focused on individual perpetrators rather than indicting the entire local white population. In a volatile situation where the organization chaired by the paper's leader was involved in a racial fight, the *News* walked a fine line, seeking justice for Black Huntington while hoping to ensure its own survival to continue such fights.

Indiana

In July 1932, W. A. Scott traveled around the Midwest on "a 16 day auto tour" in preparation for the spread of the Syndicate, the national circulation of the *Atlanta Daily World*, and the expansion of the rotogravure section. Along with traveling to SNS offices in Birmingham, Nashville, and Memphis, Scott visited the *Louisiana Weekly*, *Louisville Leader*, *St. Louis Argus*, and *Indianapolis Recorder*.[22]

It is no coincidence that the *Recorder* joined the Syndicate's ranks in August 1932.[23] Kelly Miller describes the *Recorder* as politically independent as the pivotal 1932 presidential election approached, and that seems to have been the case. In an October editorial syndicated through the SNS, the *Recorder* endorsed careful civic participation and patriotism, casting "ballots conscientiously, courageously, intelligently, progressively and constructively in the interest of the administrative welfare of the nation as a whole," but it did not suggest one candidate or political party over another.[24]

Such was the norm for the Black press in 1932, and Republicans, who had always assumed the consistency of the Black vote, were not happy. Republicans castigated the *Pittsburgh Courier*, for example, for selling advertising space to both parties. Its editorial pages supported Roosevelt, as did those of the *Afro-American*. Typically Republican papers, like the *New York Age* and *Washington Tribune*, refused to endorse Hoover, the Republican incumbent, as did the *Boston Guardian*. The *Chicago Defender* took the *Recorder*'s neutral stance. Only the *New York Amsterdam News* and *Philadelphia Tribune* maintained their Republican endorsements, but as Kelly Miller observed in the *World*, "only feebly and apologetically after swallowing many previous complaints with painful gurgitation." Even more interesting to Miller was the turn of southern Black newspapers away from the party of emancipation: "Between the regular Democrats and the lily white Republicans of the South they find themselves between the Devil and the deep sea. The limited choice is between drowning or burning." The *Norfolk Journal and Guide*, *Louisville News*, *Houston Informer*, and *Kansas City Call* all turned from the Republicans to endorse Roosevelt.[25] The turn to the Democrats was by no means complete, but the 1932 election was a pivotal first step in the turn of Black America and Black media to Democratic support.

By 1938, the Syndicate had established a foothold in southern Indiana with the *Struggle*, a monthly attempting to compete with the established local *Evansville Argus*. The rivalry between the two demonstrated that established northern entities often felt threatened by southern papers' encroachment into their territory. "It Is Our Desire to State That Mr. Bertrand Jeffries, Editor of the Struggle, a Monthly Sheet, IS NOT Connected with the EVANSVILLE ARGUS in Any Capacity," the *Argus* explained in a particularly trenchant editorial. "The ARGUS Is a Weekly Associated Negro Press Newspaper and Not an Advertising or Begging Sheet." The *Argus* was "Not a Throw Away Sheet" like its Syndicate rival.[26] Of course, such commentary ignored the fact that the bulk of SNS papers included ANP content, some because they subscribed and some because the Scotts in Atlanta included ANP material when setting and printing their member papers. It also didn't account for the fact that the Atlanta syndicate had been a regular presence in the Midwest since the early 1930s.

North of Evansville in Indianapolis, the Syndicate began publishing the *World Telegram* in May 1939. It was originally run by Wittie Anna Biggins, an Indianapolis native who had begun her relationship with the SNS during her time with the *Nashville World* in the mid-1930s. But the *World Telegram* was taken over in short order by local G. L. Porter.[27]

Porter's paper was devoted to Roosevelt, who "was above partisanship when the safety and well being of the people of America is the first consideration." In August 1940, the paper excoriated Wendell Willkie, a "life-long Democrat, who turned Republican over night in a spirit of transient resentment over his wounded vanity." Willkie, the paper claimed, had changed parties because the government sought to rein in his gouging of power customers in the Tennessee Valley. Willkie claimed that the TVA was an affront to private enterprise, and after changing political parties he became the Republican nominee for president in 1940. "In writing your acceptance speech, Mr. Willkie, please explain how government interference in private enterprise has boosted the profits of the first 300 companies to report for the second quarter of 1940," the *World Telegram* condescended. "Also please explain the increase in department store sales." The paper issued a litany of examples of New Deal policies aiding private enterprise, including coal, steel, crude oil, and even electricity.[28]

That devotion to New Deal policies was nearly absolute. "Despite the difficulties offered to its program," the paper proclaimed, "the New Deal is conquering in its fight against unemployment." The "privileged interests" were trying to stop it, as was a recalcitrant Congress, but "Indiana is slowly, but surely, meeting its problems of unemployment." Meanwhile, the "talk of the Republican leadership and of Republican candidates" was "incomprehensible and without sense or meaning." In fact, the paper argued, it was the red-baiters themselves who were actually responsible for creating a communist menace. "No one who owns property, or owns a home subscribes to the theories of communism," the *World Telegram* explained. "But for two decades, the Republican capitalistic leadership made it almost impossible for a worker to own his own home, or for a farmer to buy or keep his farm."[29]

In July 1940, racial controversy came to Indianapolis when Dr. Clarence Lucas, Indianapolis City Hospital's "only Negro intern," was fired for "eating in the white interns' dining room." When a Black laboratory orderly protested the decision, he too was fired on the charge of "creating discord." The *World Telegram* interviewed the superintendent of the hospital, who was unapologetic, calling the orderly "an inveterate gambler" and claiming that he was trying to organize a strike of hospital employees. The scandal was significant for southern readers of the paper's syndicated coverage, not for the racism of the hospital, but instead for the hospital's integration and its superintendent's willingness to talk to the Black press.[30]

For residents of Indianapolis, the paper chronicled through Scott syndication the violence of the Ku Klux Klan in the South, fights for teacher pay equalization, the effort for a federal antilynching law, and other struggles against the indignities of the southern version of discrimination. The *World Telegram* also attacked racism and the income inequality it generated more broadly. One editorial described the leaps and bounds in medical achievements over the course of the previous decade. "So what?" the paper asked. "Of what use is this great advancement in medical science to this staggering percentage of our citizens who cannot derive the benefits of new discoveries and of practical medical assistance, first—because of their financial plight, and second, because the distribution of medical service has not kept pace?"[31]

Farther north was the *South Bend Citizen*, whose smaller, more rural market than the Indiana capital made the paper reminiscent of its SNS counterparts in the South. The *Citizen* was not the first Black paper in the city, however. The *South Bend Forum* had been a Black weekly edited in the early 1920s by the Reverend B. F. Gordon. That was during the flush times in the decade prior to the onset of the Great Depression.[32]

Illinois

The *Peoria Informer* was edited by William H. Evans. In a January 1936 editorial, Evans discussed the lynching figures for the previous year. There had been twenty people lynched. There had been seventy-one over the previous four years. It was "the greatest sin that can be committed against the human race." Though the incident had occurred almost twenty years prior in 1918, and though he didn't mention her by name, Evans told the story of Mary Turner, a Valdosta, Georgia, woman whose "unborn babe was torn from her womb and then she was put to death," all because she had the gall to speak out against the lynching of her husband. Most important for Evans and the *Informer*, "something could have been done about murdering people in this fashion." Roosevelt's Congress had been a "rubber stamp" for his policies, and "had he asked Congress for an anti-lynching bill, he could have gotten it at the word." But he didn't ask. "A Democratic Congress and a Democratic President, and lynching picked up," Evans reported with obvious frustration. "Hatred and extreme wickedness found a way out."[33]

His editor, the Reverend M. D. Dickson, issued his own editorial later that month, which wondered about Depression relief. "We know that a Christian country would not allow the people to starve, if such could be prevented," he wrote. "But, is not getting something for nothing hurtful to an industrious people? Will they not desire to continue to get something for nothing?"[34] This was a reminder that while lynchings were a crime that everyone could bemoan, the *Informer* was still unflinchingly conservative. Through the lens of Dickson's editorial, Evans's criticism of the Roosevelt administration seems more an attempt to cast blame on the Democrats for lynching, rather than using bureaucratic apathy in an attempt to denounce lynching.

Later that year, Dickson launched an attack on "naked women" who were driving society to Gomorrah. "It is Satan who causes people to present nude bodies," he explained. Women were "the standard of the social order," but "in this generation it seems that women are determined to go as nearly naked as society will permit." This was garden variety moralizing, but it did matter. The *Jacksonville Mirror*, for example, had described Peoria as "divided into many camps," as voting a "split ticket," and had argued that political unity could bring the city's Black population far more consideration.[35] As it stood, however, the city had a Black newspaper that blamed the beloved Roosevelt for lynching and bemoaned the diminishing morals of its readers. Unity was far from near.

Danville was a similar smaller market, and its *Illinois Times* had affinities with the *Informer*.[36] Edgar G. Harris, editor of the *Times*, was originally from North Carolina, but he registered as a teacher in Illinois in 1933. He worked with the adult education program of the federal school in Vermilion County and was a devoted member of the local Elks. He had founded the paper with his wife, Blanche, who served as circulation manager and city editor for the small venture. "They decided to start their own paper because they felt that the papers in town did not cover enough of the news in the black community," remembered Blanche's brother. But Harris was also a member of Baha'i, certainly a rare faith for the American Midwest. And fittingly, his paper demonstrated more radicalism and more willingness to buck local trends than its Peoria counterpart did. When a local minister was arrested by FBI agents in September 1940 for "selling copies of the *Chicago Defender* carrying the feature story of Adolf Hitler's Blitzkrieg over Savannah, Georgia," the *Illinois Times* was incensed and covered the arrest and the protests against it in detail. Officials brought the minister to the state attorney's office and questioned him for hours, saying that the false claim was a seditious act. The *Defender*, meanwhile, made calls to local authorities on the minister's behalf, noting that no law had been broken in the publication of the satirical piece and that the detention was simply a scare tactic to keep the *Defender* from circulating in Danville. Meanwhile, the *Times*'s angry coverage demonstrated that the *Defender* was not the only paper that authorities wanting to stanch Black voices needed to worry about.[37]

In September 1941, the paper covered two significant civil rights cases "very important to the Negro race in Downstate Illinois." One dealt with the rights of Black customers to be served in restaurants, and the other was "to decide whether Negro women will be allowed to try on hats and dresses in Department stores." The paper didn't attempt to raise funds for the cases directly, but it did report on fundraising efforts, letting readers know that "it takes funds to fight these cases." This type of syndicated reporting modeled for southerners the kinds of legal fights they would face a generation later. Still, that type of coverage could attract unwelcome attention in a town like Danville, and soon the *Times* moved to Champaign. It was replaced in Danville by another Syndicate paper, *What's News*, which featured tamer fare.[38]

Ohio

Black weekly newspapers in Ohio expanded as a result of the migration of Black southerners following World War I. Established papers like the *Cincinnati Union*, edited by Wendell P. Dabney, and the *Dayton Forum*, edited by John Rives, were able to thrive through the decade, and they were joined by dozens of new efforts, some lasting throughout the 1920s, others only existing briefly. The *Columbus Voice* was one of several Black weeklies published in Columbus, along with the *Ohio Torch*, *Ohio Recorder*, and *Columbus Weekly News*.[39]

The *Voice* provided the Syndicate with news of a northern capital city. In September 1932, for example, Cleveland Civil Service commissioner Harry E. Davis, who was also a member of the NAACP board of directors, spoke to the Columbus Board of Education, warning that the NAACP would sue if the body continued a program of redistricting to maintain segregated schools. "Separate schools invariably mean inferior colored schools," he told the board. Public schools were "the great training ground for democracy. The action of this Board tells 35,000 white children that their colored schoolmates are different, that is, inferior. Children have no innate prejudices but parents persist in transmitting their own prejudices to children and thus warping their minds and spirits."[40] This was a powerful message to the Columbus Board of Education, but it was also a powerful message to readers of Syndicate newspapers, most of whom were still three decades from any similar successful arguments. This kind of coverage laid the groundwork for similar arguments from the succeeding generation.

At the same time, the *Voice* also modeled real failure and bigotry. In 1934, a judge ruled that local politicians could force a property owner to evict Black renters. A neighborhood agreement existed that pledged to keep Columbus's Eastwood Addition neighborhood white, except when a Black resident was "a servant working for any white family." Despite a two-year court battle, the Black residents had lost. They were evicted.[41] Here again was a model for post-*Brown* southern activism, demonstrating that while court battles were productive, they were ineffectual without social protest (and vice versa).

The *Columbus Advocate* later took the place of the *Voice*.[42] The *Advocate*'s editorial policy was both a call to arms and a trenchant commentary on the disconnect between Black northerners and Black southerners. When Black Republican election officials in the city's Seventh Ward denied their fellow Black voters Democratic ballots, "browbeating and intimidating voters into accepting the Republican ballot" instead, the *Advocate* compared the scandal to "scenes of the Texas Primaries." On one hand, having Black poll workers and an assumption of voting so ingrained that corruption could take place were true benefits that southerners simply couldn't fathom. On the other, the willingness of Black officials to deny Black Columbus residents the right to vote when so many of those southerners, the vast majority of the Black population, never even had the chance, was obscene. "In any struggle for self determination," an editorial argued, "our so-called leaders, most of them receiving much or all of their money from sources other than Negro, must be considered as out of the fight." Echoing what would later become a clarion call of the Black Power movement, the paper blamed those leaders for being too comfortable to disrupt the status quo. "It would take a flock of sub-machine artillery and the gleam of a gangster's eye to make them say one word in behalf of their many Black brothers." The *Advocate* also lauded unions and the labor movement for, if nothing else, staying united and working for each other's interests. Such was not the case with the movement for Black rights. "The American Negro has turned out to be the most detached and painstaking absorber of punishment the world has ever seen," the *Advocate* railed. There was a class divide and a political divide, but there was also a regional divide. "Lynch a Negro in Texas and observe the reaction of the act on the placid countenance of an Ohio Negro," the paper said. "There is none, for as far as the Ohioan is concerned the Negro lynched in Texas might have inhabited the moon."[43]

Ormond Adolphus Forte's *Cleveland Eagle*, a competitor with the city's more established *Call and Post* in the state's largest market, aligned with the Syndicate in 1934 and 1935.[44] The *Eagle*'s devotion to investigative journalism and challenging the white establishment emphasized the differences between northern and southern journalism. An *Eagle* writer, for example, reported on a fiasco where two white police officers responded to an altercation in the tuberculosis ward of Cleveland City Hospital and gave a "brutal beating" to one of the Black patients. After publishing the story, which was one of several reports of hospital neglect that the *Eagle* exposed in its time with the Syndicate, the paper promised to furnish full details to the authorities. This was the kind of reporting in which southern papers couldn't or wouldn't engage. Around the same time, an *Eagle* investigation discovered that Black women registering with the local employment bureau were being segregated, and its exposé led to a city council meeting where the authorities promised to change the policy.[45]

Such cases, syndicated through the SNS, provided examples of successful activism that Black southerners couldn't find at home. While historical analyses of the Great Migration tend to emphasize the pull of available northern work or the push of apartheid conditions in the South as the dominant generators of movement in the years between the world wars, the presence of such syndicated news coverage, which provided an aspirational model of the power Black people could have, limited as it was, surely drove new migrants northward. Police and hospital mistreatment or employment bureau discrimination were not rarities that would have sparked southern awe. It was, instead, the successful responses of the northern press and its people that drew the eyes of Black southerners. Thus articles about mistreatment at hospitals or government agencies could actually drive southern migration rather than deter it.

There were other Ohio Syndicate papers, including William S. Vaughn's *Youngstown Challenger*; the *Cincinnati News*; the *Toledo Press*, published by Georgia native Alberta Kertz Jackson; and the *Dayton Progress*, published by Avery D. Watson.[46] The *Progress* was a crusading paper that was frustrated, for example, that the city and county had made provisions for caring for white transients, while not acknowledging their Black counterparts. The Salvation Army had consistently refused to help Black transients, and the paper assumed that officials were taking the attitude of the chief of police: "Right, wrong, respectful, or otherwise—if Negroid you belong in Jail." The police, in an attempt to crack down on the numbers racket, were "stopping and searching Negroes indiscriminately." The *Progress* explained that numbers writers and runners were just seeking "the 25 per cent paid as commission by the Banker." The police knew those higher up in the hierarchy. "Why not begin at the source?" the paper asked. "Because the Bankers are WHITE and will not stand for any molesting, but NEGROES will stand for anything."[47]

When Dayton began building a Black housing project in the city, the *Progress* reminded readers that "those who find work on the project so far are white union men." The least the "Jim Crow Committee" could have done, it argued, was hire some of those slated to live in the project for work on the building site.[48] This was legitimately radical writing, the kind not usually possible in the South, and yet it was syndicated across the region through the SNS.

The *Cleveland Guide* was published by Eugene Francis Cheeks who, like Jackson and so many others, was a southerner (from Virginia) and had moved north with the Great Migration. Cheeks was a printer by trade, and in 1930 he used that experience to found and edit the *Guide*. Cheeks also fought actively for civil rights, filing several lawsuits to check discrimination in Cleveland. For example, in September 1936, Cheeks sought the arrest of the white manager of the Great Lakes Expedition after a white waitress, Viola Dirst, refused to serve him in the cafeteria. Publicity from the case reached the mayor of Cleveland, Harold H. Burton, who stated that he planned to investigate the incident with the intention of upholding Ohio's civil rights law and opposing racial discrimination. The mayor scheduled a conference with his legal team, including Perry B. Jackson, the city's Black assistant police prosecutor. Jackson then issued the arrest warrant demanded by Cheeks, and the editor later successfully obtained a settlement for the case.[49]

This was a signal victory, but it was not Cheeks's first venture in lawsuits. Prior to the expedition incident, Cheeks had filed a civil suit against Par Three Golf Course after he was denied access to play. In another case, Cheeks obtained the arrest of a restaurant manager in downtown Cleveland after he was refused service. In June 1949, he initiated a $10,000 lawsuit against Thomas Burke, the mayor of Cleveland, along with the city's safety director and the chief of police, for denying him access to criminal records at the Cleveland police station.[50]

Cheeks celebrated when Tennessee repealed its poll tax, "reduc[ing] to seven the number of southern states still requiring a tax on the privilege of voting." He also reported on a petition presented by white residents of the Detroit suburb of Inkster to secede from the Black section of town. It was a racist response to the creation of a new housing development that would add five hundred more Black families inside the town's limits. Cheeks decried the "fascist elements of Inkster" and recognized similar attitudes in elements of Cleveland society. There was also more traditionally conservative coverage in the paper. The *Guide* reported heavily on church news, for example. It reported with sympathy when bandleaders protested the trend of turning spirituals into swing songs for dancing. They were tunes that should be considered "as sacred music."[51]

There was also interaction between the paper and its city counterparts. The *Guide* reported in January 1943 that the editor of the rival *Cleveland Call and Post* and president of the National Negro Publishers Association, William O. Walker, had turned a common argument against critics of the Black press. There were many who argued that the press was overly preoccupied with "the volume of crime news published." Walker, however, saw the criticism as a red herring. "What they are really concerned about are the constant stories that we carry week after week about racial discrimination in the army, in industry and in the government and the stories about the one-sided law enforcement in the south, about the poll tax and other such matters," he wrote. "They don't mind Negroes killing and cutting each other, but they do mind Negroes intelligently and determinedly demanding their rights as citizens." The criticism of crime coverage meant fewer readers for all of the other stories that meant so much more to urban Black populations. The *Guide* agreed, endorsing the message on principle as well as on the self-serving pragmatism that justified its own coverage. It wasn't, however, only reprinting material from its Black rival. When a major serving in North Africa wrote to the white *Plaindealer* that urban race riots during the war presented "a picture of conditions in our country that is manna from heaven to the Axis," the *Guide* reprinted that as well.[52] This was the kind of engagement with the local white press that Black southern newspapers could never have, but they could reprint these stories through syndication, fighting via surrogates.

Another northern surrogate was the *Toledo Voice*, edited by Al Roman, which joined the Syndicate in June 1939. It reported that month on the ouster of ten local Black firemen, who had been removed after the Ohio Supreme Court "refused to review a Court of Appeals ruling that the ten men were not eligible for appointment under civil service rules." The court adjudged that "the city illegally passed over men higher on the civil service eligibility list in appointing the colored men" after a suit was brought by a group of white Toledo taxpayers.[53] Toledo racists wouldn't burn crosses on the yards of Black firemen, as might be expected in the South, but they were bothered enough by their presence to sue to have them removed.

In January 1940, however, the *Voice* was able to report that the Ohio

State Highway Patrol had hired three Black employees, "the first time that Negroes have ever been made members of the highway patrol." They were low-level hires—a clerk, an assistant storekeeper, and a caretaker—but the symbolism mattered. Ohio governor John Bricker had ordered the hirings after a letter from the state superintendent stated that "Negroes would not be employed by him in the patrol organization." In August, the highway patrol went even further when leaders appointed Sanford Roan to be a patrolman, "the first time anywhere in the United States that a Negro has been appointed a patrolman in a state highway patrol," the paper crowed. At the end of 1941, the *Voice* reported with pride that the year had featured "a substantial increase" in the employment of "Negro workers" in Toledo, so many in fact that twenty-eight tenants in public housing were ordered to move "because their incomes now exceed government limitations."[54]

But this seems to have been a temporary hiatus in the racial discrimination permeating hiring in the city. In October 1942, for example, a local minister and rights activist, A. C. Powell, claimed that "there is discrimination against Negroes in Macombe Vocational High School," arguing that "colored boys were discouraged from undertaking certain courses because their teacher told them there would be no jobs for them after graduation." The president of the Toledo Board of Education denied the charges, noting that "Negro students have access to any and all courses" at the school, and "there is absolutely no racial discrimination in the Toledo system."[55] This was a problem that southern readers wouldn't experience until a generation later after integrated schools appeared in the region; it was a foreshadowing of things to come in the South.

Closer to the upper South was the *Cincinnati Independent*, founded in 1937 by Mary M. Norris Andrews, who also served as the paper's editor and publisher. Andrews, a mortician, had attended Spelman College before enrolling in the embalming school at the University of Cincinnati. Her move to journalism was auspicious. She was the first Black woman in the city to own and publish a weekly newspaper and the first to own a linotype printer. Andrews was born in Jackson, Georgia and raised in Atlanta. Her mother died when Mary was five years old, and she was raised by her father to compete in a world dominated by men. "My father told me that I could do anything that I wanted to do," she told an interviewer, "and I guess I was dumb enough to believe him." As described in the *Cincinnati Enquirer*, the *Cincinnati Independent* was devoted to "equality of citizenship, equality of opportunity and respect on the part of the Negro."[56]

In June 1943, the National Sunday School and Baptist Training Union

Congress held its annual convention in Cincinnati. The *Cincinnati Independent* reported on the speech of the organization's president, which echoed the *Pittsburgh Courier*'s Double-V campaign: "Our destiny is not only to fight for freedom of all mankind, our destiny is as well to win freedom for ourselves." There had been talk about freedom and equality after World War I, but that had been nothing more than "empty mockery." The convention also denounced race riots and "the fact that policemen are killing our people during these riots."[57] That was, to be sure, a denunciation focused on Detroit, another SNS stronghold, which experienced the worst race riot during World War II in June 1943. Such commentary was necessary. It was valuable. But it did not mean that the locals were free from racial problems.

In September 1943, the paper found itself having to quash rumors circulated by whites that Black women were involved in a "Push 'Em Club," where they took days off work to "spend their afternoons off jostling white passengers in crowded street cars, trying on dresses they have no intention of buying, or cluttering up cosmetic counters and annoying saleswomen behind them."[58] This wasn't the immediate trauma of Detroit, but it was the kind of absurd allegation that served as one of many in a death by a thousand cuts.

In October 1944, an *Independent* editorial discussed "the ambition of most people to own a home" and the danger of that ambition. The paper had witnessed "many Negro families rushing to put their meager savings into a home, leaving no reserve to take care of emergencies." They made themselves "suckers for real estate boards and shyster real estate dealers." The paper was sure to acknowledge that it approved of Black homeownership, but not "chump" purchases that drove homeowners into financial ruin. In August 1945, the paper again emphasized finances, describing layoffs at a local plant as wartime production had run its course, and the applications for relief by those who had lost their jobs. "No one likes to be told that 'I told you so,'" the paper inappropriately crowed, "but this is too much of an occasion to miss." The *Independent* explained that it had encouraged better financial decisions: "Negroes cannot say that they have not been advised to save." It seemed an odd choice to add salt to a fresh wound in the Black community, but "it is a well-known adage that 'you cannot accept charity and expect equality.' If we expect our rights, we must share our responsibilities and we cannot go about with our hands out."[59] It was a decidedly southern message.

But there were Cincinnati messages as well. After the war ended, in June 1947 the paper extensively covered every at-bat of Jackie Robinson's first trip to Cincinnati to face the Reds. Two years later, the paper reported on the vaudeville show of bandleader Louis Jordan. After the announcement of a week-long run of Jordan's program in Cincinnati, "some prejudiced city officials went to work and dug up an old, dust-covered ordinance that prohibited white and colored performers from appearing on the same stage together." Jordan refused to get rid of his white performers and threatened to cancel the shows, at which point the city officials backed down. "It's about time Negro headline artists stopped bowing to Jim Crow in order to make a dollar," the bandleader said.[60]

The increasing presence of northern papers in the Syndicate made it easier for member papers in the Deep South to emphasize the more radical elements of practical radicalism. Using bylines from northern climes could serve to deflect negative reactions from angry, retributive whites. The move of the SNS north benefited readers who had been part of the Great Migration, and it benefited the southern Syndicate papers by giving them sources for more unapologetic editorial content. Everybody won, and so the push north continued.

Chapter 9

The North

The Great Migration Black Population Changes (%)

City	1910–1940	1940–1970
Buffalo, N.Y.	17.3	2.7
Detroit, Mich.	34.5	8.0
Flint, Mich.	23.7	3.3
Grand Rapids, Mich.	9.7	1.0
Hartford, Conn.	23.6	2.5
Lansing, Mich.	7.2	0.9
Newark, N.J.	43.6	7.9
New York, N.Y.	15.0	4.2
Pittsburgh, Pa.	10.9	4.5
Trenton, N.J.	30.4	4.8

The listed cities are the ones large enough to be included in Census statistical materials. "The Great Migration, 1910 to 1970," U.S. Census Bureau, 13 September 2012, https://www.census.gov/dataviz/visualizations/020/508.php.

New York

Expansion was the Scotts' goal, but it could also cause problems. The burden on resources that necessarily resulted from the constant expansion in the mid-1930s led the Syndicate to sign a deal with the Crusader News Agency, headquartered in New York, for additional content. It was an interesting choice. Beginning as the press organ of the Hamitic League of the World and subsequently the African Blood Brotherhood for African Liberation and Redemption, the *Crusader* newspaper was part of the broader development of Black socialism in post–World War I Harlem and part of what historian Fred Carroll has called the "alternative black press."[1] The paper was founded by pan-Africanist thinker George Wells Parker in Omaha, Nebraska, but it soon moved to New York, led by the Caribbean-born radical Cyril Briggs, a former journalist for the *New York Amsterdam News*. It was a radical paper (the voice, along with A. Philip Randolph's *Messenger*, of Black socialism), which advocated for armed self-defense in the wake of Red Summer. The *Crusader* originally supported Marcus Garvey and the Universal Negro Improvement Association (UNIA) but turned critical of the leader after his Black Star shipping line failed. The paper stopped publishing in February 1922, after Garvey's indictment, but Briggs continued to operate what he called the Crusader News Service, designed to be a communist alternative to the Associated Negro Press. Also affiliated with the *Crusader* was Black lawyer and communist activist Loren Miller. In 1934, he and Ben Davis Jr., a Black communist leader from Atlanta who was the son of Benjamin Davis Sr., founder of the *Atlanta Independent*, took the editorial reins of the news service. It was the relationship of Miller and Davis with Atlanta and the SNS that created the bond between the Syndicate and the Crusader News Agency.[2]

Crusader articles began appearing in Syndicate papers in November 1932, reporting on hungry children marching to demand more relief in Washington, D.C.; the International Labor Defense working on behalf of Euel Lee, who had been forced through police brutality into a confession to four murders he did not commit; and a "group of 22 Negro men and women who went to Soviet Russia last spring to take part in the making of a film of Negro life." Stories distributed by the Crusader News Agency throughout 1933 and 1934 provided information about lynchings and strikes, along with nearly ubiquitous coverage of Scottsboro.[3]

This reporting provided supplemental content during a period of overexpansion, as the Syndicate attempted to keep pace with the Great Migration. It was also incredibly radical content for the Syndicate, too radical to be sustainable. Practical southern radicalism dictated more strategic efforts in rights fights than the Crusader News Agency would ever make. The *Memphis World*, for example, could never have stomached such fare. "No special evidence is needed to make out a case against the South for her religious intolerance, political bigotry and the race hatred which are more conclusive than were the statute books of the slave states," one *World* editorial began, before launching into a history of slavery, racism, voting restrictions, and lynching. The "South became the laughing stock of the Nation." In choosing race hatred over its own economic best interest, it doomed itself to being "a sorry spectacle," with people "walking about hungry above rich soil pregnant with stinking weeds and shrubbery." This is where the Crusader would have stopped, its historical case made that the South's bigotry had done the work of committing a version of suicide. Practical radicalism, however, dictated that such a declension narrative could not be left without something redemptive. The *World*'s editorial closed, "If the younger generation now in the colleges and those daily papers edited by intelligent whites had not become aware of conditions as they actually are throughout the South, the cause of Dixie as a section to inspire pride would be forever lost."[4] It was almost as if the paper was winking at its readers, all aware of the code required for maintaining the grapevine amid hostile and potentially prying eyes.

Meanwhile, the Syndicate's expansion into New York also took the form of recruiting new member newspapers. The *Buffalo Star* was published by Andrew J. Smitherman, who grew up in Gilded Age Oklahoma, where he first worked for W. H. Twine's *Muscogee Cimiter*. In 1912, Smitherman developed his own paper, the *Muscogee Star*, before moving it to Tulsa the following year. He was a devoted Democrat and a militant activist against lynching and other violations of Black rights. He was even chosen by Oklahoma's white governor, J. B. A. Robertson, to participate in an interracial conference on lynching following a spate of such murders in the state in 1920. His press was destroyed during the Tulsa race massacre of 1921, when simmering bitterness over Black economic success in the city combined with the more immediate charge that a Black man had raped a local white woman, leading white Tulsa to destroy more than four square blocks of the Black section of town and to kill as many as three hundred Black victims. It was the last major convulsion of what had begun as the Red Summer of race riots in 1919. White Tulsa blamed Smitherman and his paper for inciting the riot, and the white courts charged him, so he moved east, first stopping in Springfield, Massachusetts, before making his way to Buffalo. He worked at other papers there before borrowing $100 to start the *Buffalo Star* in 1932. That name was less a nod to Smitherman's time in Muscogee and more a nod to Buffalo's history with Black presses; its first paper was published in 1834 as the *Western Star*.[5]

Only part of the *Buffalo Star*'s long life—the paper continued into the 1950s—was spent with the Syndicate (from 1939 to 1940), and there are several editions of it that survive from beyond the bounds of its SNS run. They provide another example of a relatively consistent pattern. The *Star* emphasized civic news on its front page, along with salacious crime coverage. Its editorial page reminded readers, "Life is not long enough for us to live exclusively for ourselves," and it took on the corruption of Tammany Hall and stumped for comprehensive labor law reform. It vehemently urged passage of a permanent Fair Employment Practices Committee (FEPC) and resented the politicians attempting to stifle it. "Arrogance and bigotry rode high, wide and handsome in the Senate of the United States last week," the *Star* explained in January 1946, "when W. Lee (Pass the Biscuit, Pappy) O'Daniel from Texas, a so-called Democrat (but this is a misnomer) temporarily (dis)graced the chair of the Senate (maybe by prearrangement) and wielded the gavel to the tempo of Southern psychology and, for the time being at least, succeeded in carrying out the diabolical scheme of his equally pusillanimous Dixie colleagues to filibuster the FEPC bill." When the southern senators' filibuster defeated the bill in early February, the paper declared that the failure demonstrated that "we are not yet a nation of true democracy." The powerful pen would ultimately help slay such congressional attacks on equality, but the paper's approach was also a vestige of the practical radicalism that Smitherman had learned in Oklahoma. Tammany Hall, labor reform, and the FEPC were outside the local bounds of Buffalo, and all of the paper's most biting attacks focused attention away from Lake Erie.[6]

New Jersey

From Buffalo, the grapevine spread to Trenton, New Jersey, in the form of the *Trenton Record* from late 1939 to early 1940, which was rebranded as the *Trenton World* in February 1940. Its publisher was Joseph A. Clarke, an advocate for Black rights in the city. A syndicated article from January 1940 covered the pending attempt of a local committee "to form a colored national guard regiment" in New Jersey. In a February 1941 feature, the paper's general manager, Aroy R. Evans, interviewed former New Jersey governor Harold Hoffman, who was serving as director of the state's Unemployment Compensation Commission. It was a minor coup for an upstart Black newspaper and an opportunity that simply wouldn't be available in the South. Clarke used the pages of his paper to advocate for the appointment of Black lawyer Robert Queen to the city counselor's office, and in June 1941 the campaign paid dividends.[7]

Another of the expansion papers was the *Newark Herald*. J. Franklin King was city editor of the *Herald*, president of the National Negro Business Progressive Association, and manager of the Progress News Service, providing news of Black citizens throughout New Jersey. The paper's association with the Syndicate meant that the SNS was able to run *Herald* stories about Newark businesses thriving in troubling economic times and other reports coming from the Progress News Service.[8]

The only editions of the paper that survive were published in the late 1930s and 1940s, after the *Herald*'s time with the Syndicate, but those editions demonstrate the greater radicalism of the Great Migration papers. By that time, the *Herald* was under the leadership of Merrill Biddle. Its editorial masthead claimed to advocate for "equal political and civil rights for all American citizens regardless of race, creed or religion" and "federal action to abolish disfranchisement of Negroes in the Southern States." Its front page included all of the same salacious stories as its southern counterparts, but its reporting on voter rights, unequal housing, and job discrimination was far less cautious and far more willing to engage with those the paper saw as the problem in such situations. Its editorial page called for federal action against lynching, demanded equal distribution of federal resources for relief during poor economic conditions, and urged equal rights for Black citizens in New Jersey and the nation.[9] Northern Black papers still catered to a population dealing with rampant discrimination, but the less omnipresent, less atavistic version of that discrimination led to a willingness to be less compromising or cautious in editorial policy.

Morris M. Ward, an African Methodist Episcopal (AME) minister, walked a similar line while publishing his *Ideal Review* in Bridgeton, New Jersey.[10] The paper mostly covered AME news, little surprise considering the vocation of its editor. A small story from Bridgeton, however, reported on a local farmer who charged that a Black man had attacked a white woman, and thus led "a posse of 100 men scouring the countryside." That posse dissolved, however, when the farmer "admitted a colored man had only pushed his wife in a quarrel."[11] The account was one with which Syndicate readers would have been all too familiar—both the reaction of the white posse and the farmer's original lie. That the *Ideal Review* took for granted that the search was called off after the farmer admitted that a Black man "had only pushed his wife in a quarrel," however, inverted the narrative that most southern readers would have understood. In the South, there was no such thing as "only pushed his wife in a quarrel." That was a death sentence. And so the paper's simple assumption of white behavior did subtle work in generating new expectations for Black readers far from Bridgeton.

The *Atlantic City Eagle*, published by Frank W. Canty, was less subtle than its Bridgeton counterpart. In late May and early June 1935, poor whites in and around Atlantic City showed their racial fangs, frustrated at the growth of the Black population as southern migrants moved north looking for work. In late May, whites burned down the Macedonia Baptist Church and a gymnasium where Black children played basketball. On June 2, they killed two Black Civilian Conservation Corps workers. These crimes seemed to be committed without any meaningful investigation or punishment. The Atlantic County prosecutor claimed, against the conclusion of the coroner, that the deaths were the result of a hit-and-run accident. The *Eagle* wired New Jersey governor Harold G. Hoffman, explaining the murders and the blatant racism in the prosecutor's office and calling for an inquiry. Hoffman responded by launching a state investigation into the murders. "Governor Hoffman believes in that kind of Americanism that makes all citizens safe upon the highways of the state," the paper reported.[12] More interesting than the coverage, however, was the paper's role in wiring the governor and launching the state investigation, seeking justice for Black murder victims when the local prosecutor wouldn't provide it. This was temerity that the southern press largely did not have, but it was also an avenue closed to them, even if they had the stomach to try.

An *Eagle* editorial in September 1935 served as a call to action. "The great white race sees life in an attitude of sovereignty," the paper explained, "sees that he is master and owner and possessor of everything that God has created in this world." Viewing their own behavior as divinely inspired served to justify white people's existence. The *Eagle* wanted its readers to see themselves as children of God, as did whites: "When we allow ourselves to be subjected by and create others as our superior, we hurl an insult at our Creator who made us in the fullness of ourselves." In that way, the *Eagle* tied religion to rights and to activism, rather than to meek passivity. It encouraged Black readers to be more like whites, not in a self-hating assimilationist manner, but in an attitude that exemplified the ideas that "we will think of nations as our servants; that we will think of men as our partners through life, that we will strive to break down all industrial, economic and political barriers."[13] The syndication of this kind of editorial was significant because it turned the typical southern journalistic rhetoric about religion and activism on its head, providing a model that many southern readers typically couldn't see in their local paper. And regardless of the genesis of such an editorial, there was a resonance when readers saw such a formulation in the local paper over and against seeing it from the far-flung *Chicago Defender* or *Pittsburgh Courier*.

In the summer of 1936, the secretary of Atlantic City's board of trade sent a letter to the Metropolitan Life Insurance Company seeking employment for Black insurance agents in the city. Met Life responded that the company believed, "based on observations of the industrial business that the best type of service which that business requires for all its policy holders, of whatever race or creed, cannot be obtained through the employment of colored collectors." The *Eagle* obtained a copy of the letter and published it. The Syndicate followed, using a large bold headline: "'Metropolitan' Official Admits Segregation." While what Met Life was doing was not necessarily segregation, segregation was the language southern readers understood.[14]

Connecticut

The willingness to confront discrimination directly seemed to grow as the grapevine moved north, but the formula didn't hold as it stretched into New England. The *Hartford Advocate*, for example, was published by Cecil A. Davis, a native of the Virgin Islands who also served as a mail clerk for National Fire Insurance. One editorial from the *Advocate* provided "constructive criticism" about the indifference of "our professional trained men and women." It described the disconnect between the educated and uneducated Black residents of Hartford and tried to explain that the problem was based on a misinterpretation among the lower classes that the educated were apathetic. It was a timeworn criticism that the upper classes were "getting white." The *Advocate* was sympathetic: "Hartford needs all of the leadership of the right type that it can get."[15]

In the spring of 1936, Angelo Herndon went to Hartford to help organize a youth committee of the National Negro Congress, designed to study "the Negro's problems and to help better his social and economical status." Another representative of the congress told the *Advocate*, "We hope the Negro people in Hartford will not take the Youth committee for a Communistic organization because Herndon is connected with it." The congress was about equal rights for Black America and included members of all parties: "What we want is the NEGROES to join together and fight for what belongs to them, and that is EQUAL RIGHTS."[16]

Michigan

The northern state with the strongest ties to the Syndicate was Michigan, a relationship that began in August 1932 with the *Detroit Independent*. Affiliating with the *Independent* positioned the Syndicate perfectly when seven different Black candidates, representing both parties, appeared on the Michigan state primary ballot that month. It was the kind of story that demonstrated the possibilities that existed in the North. And there were others. The City Cab Company of Detroit, for example, a Black institution, operated more than a hundred taxis in the city. While poverty reigned in much of Black Detroit, the city's Booker T. Washington Trade Association and its members represented the potential for "Negro business" and modeled what could only be seen as the infinite opportunities of the North.[17]

The one available edition of the *Independent* from January 1923 trumpeted the arrival of Mary White Ovington, a white cofounder of the NAACP, for a speech in Detroit, and it also covered the NAACP conference in New York. Still, its stated platform seemed to fit the southern moralizing model. "Independent's platform for Detroit: 100% Americanism," the paper proclaimed. "Not more churches but better churches. Complete eradication of gambling and betting." Its lead editorial discussed the ballot and its power, not hoping that the possibility of voting would arrive—as would editorials in the South from that era—but instead hoping that Black voters in Detroit would "examine the promises and the qualifications of candidates with free minds" before casting their votes. "Detroit Negroes must awaken," the paper urged. There were also the requisite advertisements for hair straighteners and skin whiteners along with a heady local advertising presence.[18] Though the content of the paper a decade prior to its relationship with the Syndicate doesn't demonstrate any specific fit with Atlanta policies, the existing evidence shows a paper that evinced a northern approximation of the SNS ideal.[19]

The *Detroit World*'s managing editor, Golee B. Bryant, was a crusader and the founder, along with Morris Lewis, secretary to Congressman Oscar DePriest, of the Congress of Youth, "a national Negro youth movement" that helped to mentor kids and make them more successful. Bryant's paper reflected his activist bent. When the white students of Hamtramck High School and St. Florian Roman Catholic Church combined to plan a moonlight dance and bar the Black students from attending, Leroy G. White, the *World*'s Hamtramck editor, and Leonard Troutman, president of the *World*'s Jovial Juniors Club of Hamtramck, immediately protested to the principal, who responded by announcing that "every student in the High School should be welcome to attend any affair bearing the school's name."[20] It was a victory against the creeping horde of Jim Crow, and it was a demonstration of the kind of activism some Black reporters undertook. Instead of keeping a measured distance and reporting on the crisis, White and Troutman acted to stop the discriminatory practice and then reported objectively on what they did. It was, in a sense, New Journalism two generations before Tom Wolfe and his coterie made it popular. In the more immediate context, it was a demonstration of the activism of White, who became central both to the Syndicate and to Michigan Black journalism in the years to come.

The *Detroit World*—and thus its southern syndicate—covered the kind of news stories that southern journalists rarely had the opportunity to cover: the UNIA restructured its Detroit branch in February 1934; a local white-owned movie theater hired a full-time Black ticket taker and concession stand worker after complaints from its Black clientele.[21] For readers in Detroit these were informative stories that demonstrated the growing power that came with increasing numbers as the Great Migration continued. For readers in the South, however, such stories were aspirational, where groups like the UNIA thrived, and Black customers were served by Black employees because they had fought for the opportunity to be served in integrated settings by people who looked more like themselves. In the South, where white supremacy reigned, the UNIA could never thrive, and segregation gave Black theatergoers no choice but to be served by Black employees.

The *World* underwent a change in management in the summer of 1934, changing its name to the *Michigan World* in August. The paper's new managing editor was Petry Fisher, a deputy sheriff in Detroit, one of seventeen Black deputies in the city. Before that, Fisher had served in the State Highway Department and as an investigator for Michigan's Liquor Control. He also had attempted an unsuccessful run for state senate.[22] This wasn't necessarily the resume of a crusader, though it was clear that Fisher had managed through mainstream activities to become an important advocate for Black people in Michigan.

The state's most influential race advocate, of course, was not a journalist. In one syndicated *Michigan World* editorial, Fisher celebrated Detroit's own Joe Louis and told the story of his manager, John Roxborough, who gave his time and money to help take Louis from a prospect to a boxing champion. "So often young men of our race have all the makings, they lack nothing except the power to purchase the proper equipment that will mean going forward to success." Louis, of course, was a popular topic in the paper. Black Detroit reveled in its hometown hero, and the SNS seemed to revel in having a line to that coverage through syndication. That became all the more true as Louis prepared for his June 1937 heavyweight title fight with James Braddock at Chicago's Comiskey Park.[23]

Joe Louis, like so many others in Detroit, was a product of the Great Migration, an Alabama native whose family had moved to Detroit while Louis was a boy. He became a successful amateur fighter in the early 1930s before making his professional debut in 1934. Though he was talented, white boxing leaders were paranoid about another Black boxer in the style of Jack Johnson, the Black heavyweight champion from the 1910s, whose bluster, willingness to cross racial lines in sexual relationships, and overt displays of masculinity threatened notions of white supremacy. Louis's early career, explains historian Gerald Astor, was "stalked by the specter of Jack Johnson." Louis's handlers thus worked to ensure that his reputation would be one of deference and politeness, learning from the reactions to Johnson's earlier reign.[24]

Ultimately, however, his fights made Louis's name. He came to national prominence after defeating Max Baer in 1935, though he lost to Max Schmeling in 1936. The notoriety from those fights and Louis's continued success earned him a title shot in June 1937, when he knocked out James Braddock for the heavyweight championship. The *World* and other Michigan papers followed his every move in preparation for the championship assiduously, but no amount of coverage could match the celebration among Black America when he won the title. Louis became the Black argument against white supremacy, the pride and obsession of millions in the country. When he defeated Max Schmeling in 1938, he also became a representation of American patriotism against the Nazis. Serving in the army during World War II only further boosted that reputation. He maintained his championship throughout the 1930s and 1940s until he announced his retirement in March 1949. Louis was more than a boxer for Black Detroit and for Black America. He was a symbol of possibility, a representation of greatness, a point of pride whose image always loomed over all defenses of Black life and Black rights, a sports figure who embodied so much more than sports. The *Michigan World*'s coverage was matched by every Detroit and Michigan newspaper, and that reporting was syndicated throughout the country via the SNS and every other Black press syndication service. His visible presence during World War II served as a powerful argument for Black Detroit's and Black America's demand for equal rights.[25]

Fisher's *Michigan World* was in the camp of Louis, and it was also decidedly in the camp of Franklin Roosevelt by the close of the president's first term in office. The paper excoriated the policy positions of Republican challenger and Kansas governor Alf Landon and Landon's criticisms of the incumbent in an extended September 1936 editorial. The following year, the NAACP annual conference was in Detroit, and the *World* was thrilled to report the president's "message of greeting" to the group, reprinting the message in full and highlighting Roosevelt's emphasis on "the progress which we as citizens in a democracy have a right to expect."[26]

The paper's coverage of the NAACP conference also included the speech of writer and activist James Weldon Johnson, who was frustrated with the notion of one powerful organizer to lead the race, "a Moses who will surely deliver us out of the hands of the Egyptians. The day for that type of leadership is past." Johnson saw the need for a diverse leadership to fight bigotry on a variety of fronts. That kind of diversity would require coordination, of course, and the NAACP was well placed to provide it. The *World* had watched hopefully in the spring of 1936 as its correspondents learned that a federal bill might be in the works, endorsed by the NAACP, to fund an investigation into the Black Legion, a Ku Klux Klan splinter group founded in Ohio but centering the bulk of its terrorist nightriding in Detroit. "The Black Legionnaires oppose Negroes, Jews and Catholics bitterly," the paper reported, "and do not permit withdrawal from their society of any member."[27] This surely sounded all too familiar to southern readers of Syndicate papers.

Other syndicates saw opportunity in the *World*'s success. In April 1936, the Sengstacke family sent the *Chicago Defender*'s executive director, Lucius Harper, to Detroit to create a sister paper for the *Defender* and a competitor for the *World*. The *Defender* already had a Detroit edition, but it wasn't specific to the city. Thus the Sengstackes created the *Michigan Chronicle*, first edited by Louis Martin. It wasn't the *World*'s only competition. The *Paradise Valley News*, published by Roy Lightfoot, a Port Huron native, World War I veteran, and local club owner, had a longer history in the city. Both Fisher and Lightfoot saw the Sengstackes' new effort as a legitimate threat to their survival, and thus in July 1937, they decided to join forces, creating the *News World*, a combination of the *Michigan World* and *Paradise Valley News*, and the Fisher-Lightfoot Publishing Company. The merger was called by the SNS "the greatest and most sensational newspaper consolidation in the history of Detroit journalism."[28]

Fisher, still working in law enforcement, met with Syndicate leaders in Atlanta in August 1937 while in the city to consult with members of the Atlanta Police Department. Lightfoot, however, was new to the SNS. He was a former musician and the owner of the B and C Nightclub, the *News World* newspaper, and the Paradise Valley Consumers Association (named, as was his original publication, for the Paradise Valley section of Detroit). His was a profile more radical than that of his new partner. In 1937 and 1938, for example, Lightfoot led a boycott of Stroh's Brewing Company. "The Stroh

Brewing Company does one-half million dollars worth of business with Negroes annually and puts nothing back," he argued. "We wanted representation in proportion to the amount of money we were spending so we formed the Paradise Valley Consumers Association and asked Stroh's to hire Negroes as salesmen since all other breweries did." Stroh's unequivocally refused, so Lightfoot and the association began a boycott. There were pickets, banners, and other efforts to convince Detroit residents not to drink Stroh's beer. Lightfoot was also elected "mayor" of the Black section of Detroit, an unofficial tradition inaugurated in Chicago by the *Defender*. Sunnie Wilson described him as "a big, jovial man, weighing three hundred pounds." Lightfoot knew what he was doing. He also owned Long's Drug Store and used it as an information hub; residents called the local store when breaking news happened. That, in turn, created content for his newspaper.[29]

Fitting that kind of information-gathering strategy, the *News World* covered groups tasked with advocating for "its goal of social and economic advancement for Negroes." When Lightfoot's Paradise Valley Consumers Association was able to convince Goebel Brewing that it needed a Black sales representative, the paper covered the success, placing it in the context of broader potential success for Black employees. But it also necessarily provided positive publicity for Goebel, using its coverage as a carrot for corporations' willingness to include Black employees and to cater to Black customers. It also continued Fisher's civic tradition.[30]

In September 1937, Detroit's police commissioner attempted to segregate the police force, placing Black policemen in one special squad led by white officers and using them to police Black neighborhoods. The backlash the department received from leading Black officials and the Black press in the city forced the program's abandonment after one week. The *News World* explained that there had been only one previous attempt to segregate a special squad to deal with "one particular racial group. That was the Black Hand Squad which came to be known as the 'Dago' Squad before it met a similar fate."[31] This was the kind of coverage that would be expected of a paper trying to compete with the Sengstackes' *Michigan Chronicle*, but it was a policing problem that would be completely foreign to Black southerners reading about the incident through syndication. Most of those southerners would have relished the opportunity to argue about segregating police because that would mean there were Black policemen to segregate.

At a dinner program sponsored by the North Detroit NAACP Youth Council, the principal speaker, Gladys Brown, a Wayne State University student who had previously been a student at Louisiana State University in Baton Rouge, denounced race prejudice in the South but said that migration out of the region was not the answer. "Don't immigrate Negroes from the South," she argued. "That does not solve the problem in the South. Likewise Detroit as an individual community has its various situations to be remedied," situations that would not be helped by a new influx of southern migrants. The stakes for such problems were incredibly high: a Bureau of Labor Statistics study in May 1938 found that the cost of living for low-income Americans was highest in Detroit, making a precarious position even more dangerous.[32]

Meanwhile, the *News World* found itself in its own precarious position, struggling to survive against the better-funded *Chronicle*, which was financed by its founding entity in Chicago. The Sengstackes' top-down publishing approach was a powerful thing. They had founded the *Louisville Defender*, found it remarkably successful, and began implementing a new business strategy based on that success. Next was the *Michigan Chronicle*, where the Sengstacke company sought to take advantage of a Black population that had grown to more than 130,000. The *Chronicle* was written in Detroit, as was its Louisville counterpart, but it was printed in Chicago on days when the *Defender*'s presses would normally be lying dormant. Despite the offices in Michigan and Kentucky, the printing and the syndicated information flowed downward from the fount in Chicago.[33] Meanwhile, the Scott papers received printing services and syndicated material from the company's various publications, but the papers set their own scope and editorial policy. By the end of 1938, the *News World* was unable to survive.

The Scott Syndicate's presence in Michigan, however, was only beginning, fueled by the *Detroit World*'s original Hamtramck editor. Leroy G. White had a vision of empire much like that of W. A. Scott—the creation of a newspaper chain across his home state of Michigan. He began in March 1938 with his first publication, the *Michigan State Echo*, headquartered ninety miles from his hometown in Lansing. Syndicated articles from the state capital emphasized civic boosterism. The *Echo* reported in 1938 on the success of local singers and boxers and on the city's plans for celebrating the seventy-fifth anniversary of emancipation.[34] It was a decidedly southern strategy for coverage, but the paper would need more substantial fare to compete with the *Michigan Chronicle*. Thus the *Echo* also covered state elections and crime, using its proximity to the state government to report on legislative issues important to Black citizens. When newly elected officials came to the capital in January 1939, for example, the *Echo* reported angrily when those senators refused to reappoint Lawrence Stewart, the "first Negro Committee Clerk of the Senate." The Republicans, chided the paper, "gave notice to colored citizens of Michigan the course that its party intends to pursue during the coming two years" with the firing. When that body passed legislation "to transform Detroit's slum areas within two years" by creating a uniform housing standard, the paper reported neutrally on the change.[35]

The *Echo*'s positioning in the state capital would also be beneficial to readers around the state. White knew this, which is why he started in Lansing rather than Hamtramck or Detroit. In the summer following the *Echo*'s founding, just three months after the paper's first edition, White founded a second sheet, the *Jackson Echo*, followed the next month by the *Grand Rapids Echo* and the *Hamtramck Echo*. In August he founded the *Mc-Comb County Echo*, in September the *Pontiac Echo*. White was creating a Michigan version of the Scotts' national syndicate, and he was using the SNS to do it. The grounding principle of the SNS was that it democratized the news, that it allowed anyone with the wherewithal to start a newspaper by using the Syndicate as typesetter, publisher, syndicator, and printer. It thus stood to reason that someone with slightly more resources than the bellhops and laundresses who were heeding that call in the rural South could conceivably use the model to create a series of papers, a syndicate within the Syndicate, to serve, for example, an entire state almost eight hundred miles away from Atlanta. And so all coverage from Michigan included in SNS newspapers was presented as coming from the White Newspaper Syndicate.[36]

The *Echo*s from Jackson and Grand Rapids lasted less than a year, and it is clear that White was finding his footing as a publisher. In September 1938, the National Urban League held its annual conference near Jackson, Michigan, and the *Echo* followed its doings. At the same time, other syndicated coverage urged readers to believe in God and hard work as a recipe for success. Again White was using a southern strategy to ingratiate himself and his newspapers to a Black population dominated by southern migrants.[37] It was tame coverage, to be sure, and the paper grew more activist to better mirror its founder as time passed. But even in the early stages of the White Syndicate's development, southern readers of Scott Syndicate papers would have seen Urban League conferences and Black political organizations as decidedly progressive. Even though White's intended audience was the flower of the grapevine, not its root, his work was modeling for southerners the advantages of leaving the region.

That was apparent in his effort in his hometown, the *Hamtramck Echo*. Founded in July 1938 and lasting until 1942, that paper became the center of the White Syndicate's universe. Hamtramck was an interesting place, a two-square-mile city within the city of Detroit. Hamtramck's fortune was made in 1914 when the Dodge Brothers automobile plant opened there, encouraging a flood of migrants to arrive for the newly available work. Most of those immigrants were Polish, but they intermingled with people from Germany and Eastern Europe, along with a much smaller group of Black migrants from the Deep South. That could be a tense mix, particularly in a small, densely populated area, and White and his newspaper were the chief advocates for the minority Black population within those boundaries.[38]

When the local superintendent of schools failed to recommend any Black women as school clerks or stenographers when making his annual recommendations to the board of trustees in 1938, the paper angrily covered the omission, noting that though his list was not doctrine, "his recommendations carry much weight with the ruling body." When the mayor neglected to include a Black member on the Hamtramck Housing Commission the following year, protests didn't change the mayor's appointments, but they did force him to make a statement defending himself. Such stories demonstrated the clear differences in racial problems between the North and the South.[39]

Housing was a particular emphasis for White and the *Echo*. Controversy erupted over a 1939 Hamtramck housing project when white citizens complained about decreased property values, and Black citizens, in the form of the Negro Steering Committee for Better Housing, took the mayor to task for a veiled "attack" on Leroy White, who led the group. The committee "urged a thorough investigation of the rumored discrimination against the Negro in the proposed project." The issue seemed largely political, but the danger became real two years later. After White, in his role as chair of the Negro Steering Committee for Better Housing, wrote a public letter protesting racist actions of local Catholic priests, a note arrived for him: "If you don't behave you will be sent back to Africa. KKK." It was a reminder that advocacy for Black people could be dangerous anywhere. But AME minister C. M. Metcalf, White's ally in the housing fight, doubted the existence of the Klan in Hamtramck: "This has all the earmarks of being directly incited by the Hamtramck Tax Payers Association and the Catholic Priests of Hamtramck." White was emphatic: "No Ku Klux Klan, Catholic priest, or any other group will stop the *Hamtramck-Detroit Echo*, the Reverend C. M. Metcalf and myself from battling for the rights of Negroes in Hamtramck."[40] Southern readers of such syndicated stories would recognize the discrimination and the threatening notes, but the bold responses that included promises of Black press advocacy were less common. This report was a demonstration of the ubiquitous nature of racism, but also the opportunity available up north.

And such coverage was, more than anything else, a reflection of its publisher. White was an editor, but also an activist for Black rights. In 1938, he "led the fight for jobs in Michigan State Hospital at Hopewell," which was ultimately successful in securing Black positions at the facility. As of December 1941, White was the chair of the Hamtramck Negro Housing Committee, an updated version of the Negro Steering Committee for Better Housing. In February 1941, he organized efforts for a new $175,000 housing project for the city from the office of the White Newspaper Syndicate on Joseph Campau Avenue in Hamtramck. When enthusiasm for the struggle began to wane, White rallied the troops. "The housing fight is not won," he told supporters, "until the first Negro family moves in the colonel Hamtramck home project." Eventually, White sued the Hamtramck Housing Commission. He also worked closely with Metcalf "to establish bi-racial occupancy of Colonel Hamtramck Homes Federal Project."[41]

For all of his work as a community organizer, White's principal project was his syndicate, and the month after creating the *Hamtramck Echo*, he also founded a newspaper twenty-five miles up Lake St. Clair in the small resort town of Mt. Clemens, tapping his friend and colleague Prince Drewry to serve as editor and publisher of the *McComb County Echo*. Mt. Clemens, though it was Macomb County's seat, was, like Hamtramck, a city within a city, surrounded by Clinton Township. Drewry also served as a member of Clinton Township's school board—the first Black man in Michigan to serve on a local school board—and as a deputy sheriff for the county. He seemed as though he would be a leader who could guide the new member of the White Syndicate into the next decade. The paper, however, only survived until the end of 1939, and its work was far from stable. In January 1939, Drewry, acting in his role as a deputy sheriff, shot Willie Johnson during a scuffle while trying to arrest him. Ultimately the publisher was put on trial for the shooting after city officials determined that his term as deputy had expired. "A jury composed entirely of white persons" returned a "not guilty" verdict, and Drewry's paper crowed about the result: "Approximately 50 Colored spectators were in the courtroom. They applauded heartily when the favorable decision was given."[42] This type of situation was, to be sure, an interesting problem for editors and publishers, emphasizing the tenuousness of their positions and the many hats they wore in addition to the labor of love that was their journalistic endeavor.

There was occasional synergy, however. In July 1939, Drewry was running for reelection to the school board and publicized his candidacy in his paper, encouraging readers to vote. He also encouraged them to fight for Black rights more broadly. That summer, a case of discrimination in licensing a Black man to run a tavern brought the Mt. Clemens City Commission and the mayor to the U.S. District Court. "This means that the Mayor and the Commissioners are going to have to go on the witness stand and face a cross-examination concerning their treatment of colored people," the *Echo* explained. "For the first time in the history of the Macomb County, city officials are going to face the action of a Federal Court for trampling on colored people." The paper encouraged everyone to attend a mass meeting at a local Christian Methodist Episcopal church. "Victory depends on united action. The final victory will be a telling blow when struck for the rights of colored people. It will be your victory. You must help to win it."[43]

White continued his march through the state by moving next to Flint. In September 1938, Magnus Clark, representing the White Syndicate, began publishing the *Brownsville Weekly News*. The paper was the following year taken over by Henry G. Reynolds, who changed its name to the *Flint-Brownsville News* in November 1939.[44] Reynolds was a leading figure in Black Flint, elected president in late 1938 of the Club 25, "a group of young men of Flint who are accomplishing great things." A mortician by trade, Reynolds was willing to stir up things in Flint and was even offered a $200 bribe by racketeers to stop an exposé series he was publishing. "I told them to get out and don't come back," he wrote in his paper, courting more potential problems and demonstrating his willingness to put himself in harm's way.[45]

"Let us reaffirm the policy of the White Newspaper Syndicate," explained a front-page, above-the-masthead editorial in 1939, "that we are a non-partisan organization which is standing on guard for Negro rights throughout the State of Michigan. Whether our position may affect either the Democratic or Republican party is immaterial to us. Our fight will not be a personal one, but a fight that will be in the interest of all colored citizens of Michigan." Another editorial, written by White himself, encouraged Black workers to join Black unions and castigated the American Federation of Labor for excluding Black workers from certain jobs in certain areas of Flint and Detroit.[46]

Labor news was understandably substantial in these papers, as was coverage of civil rights and social equality in Flint and other White Syndicate paper locations. The *News* covered NAACP meetings, for example, whenever they occurred. When the organization's headquarters called for a national day of meetings in January 1941 to discuss the role of "the Negro in National Defense," the discrimination that accompanied that relationship, and potential remedies for it, the paper reported on the initiative and chronicled a litany of abuses in all branches of the military and in civilian defense jobs. This report dovetailed with A. Philip Randolph's March on Washington for Jobs and Freedom, pushing the notion that the war was an opportunity for the country to demonstrate its differences from fascism by providing democracy for its Black citizens.[47]

The year prior, Reynolds had written a letter to Republican Michigan senator Arthur Vandenberg, urging him to support the antilynching bill making its way through Congress. He published his letter, naturally, and also published Vandenberg's reply, which pledged support for the bill. Through its SNS affiliation, the paper covered teacher salary equalization fights throughout the South. It covered the southern Ku Klux Klan. It covered the plight of rural sharecroppers. Along with stories from the regions represented by the broader Scott Syndicate, the *Flint-Brownsville News* also maintained sections of news from each of the territories of the White Syndicate, covering Detroit, Hamtramck, Pontiac, and Lansing.[48]

Such is not to say that the two syndicates maintained a functionally equal relationship with Flint. The *News* abandoned its connection with White in the fall of 1940 but remained with the Scott Syndicate until April 1942. The scope of the paper's coverage did not change after leaving the more radical White. "We would dare to say that the unions mean more than anything else to the Negro in industry," opened one post-White editorial. Gone were sections reporting on the local happenings in Hamtramck and Pontiac after the paper aligned with the SNS separately, but everything else remained much the same.[49]

While Reynolds's publication remained a force in Flint, White's publications continued to make a broader impact across the state. In April 1939, he founded the *Detroit World Echo*, which became the largest paper in White's sub-syndicate, emanating from the state's largest city and the home of its largest Black population. Detroit was also the home of the rival *Michigan Chronicle*. Efforts to compete required more than civic news and church updates. Thus, when the secretary of the navy wrote to the vice chair of the local draft board in Detroit in March 1941, reaffirming the naval policy of refusing to "accept applicants for enlistment from Negroes in any but the messman branch," the paper reported on the policy as openly discriminatory.[50]

The next month, a massive strike at Ford's River Rouge plant led the company to use Black workers as strikebreakers. The *Detroit World Echo* covered the incident in depth, including the NAACP's denunciation of Ford's actions. Walter White traveled to Detroit and encouraged the scabs to leave the job. The paper reported that "racial tension had been injected so strongly into the struggle between Ford and the strikers that a riot might be staged." White issued a statement acknowledging that Ford had "hired more Negroes than any other Detroit employer," but the company had rarely given them a chance to advance through the ranks. Furthermore, "the attempt to use Negroes as a club over the heads of those who wish to organize themselves in unions in the Ford plants . . . is a dangerous move in times like these." White excoriated the American Federation of Labor for its "attempt to dupe Negro workers" and praised the United Auto Workers of the Congress of Industrial Organizations, which "conducted itself admirably in trying to remove the color line in this strike." After conferring with UAW representatives and leaders of the Detroit NAACP, White got in a truck and spoke over loudspeakers as the vehicle circled the River Rouge plant, hoping to convince Black workers inside to leave. In November, the union went further, electing a Black autoworker as an official and publicly denouncing the Ku Klux Klan.[51]

It was an important fight, but Leroy White's principal battle had always been housing such workers. In February 1942, Detroit's defense housing coordinator publicly decided to "uphold Negro occupancy" of defense housing, but he continued to delay action in response to pressure from angry local whites. The controversy led to rioting later that month, leaving fourteen people injured and twenty in jail.[52] In April 1942, the *World Echo* reported on the federal government's plan to "place Negroes in the Sojourner Truth Defense Housing Project." Leroy White was on the interracial Sojourner Truth Citizens Committee, which was calling on the mayor to put those plans in place. Upon the announcement of the federal order, the Detroit police commissioner, Frank Eamans, resigned. "It was under Eamans' direction that police prevented Negroes from occupying the project on February 28th which precipitated the resulting riot." The government order had followed a mass demonstration of roughly ten thousand at the statue of Truth in Detroit's Cadillac Square. In addition, a federal grand jury indicted three of the white leaders who had incited the earlier riot attempting to block Black entry into the project. Meanwhile, Black Detroit waited for the federal housing to open to them. Protesters marched in front of city hall with signs reading "Negroes have landed in Australia, when do we land in Sojourner Truth?" Finally, at the end of April, Black tenants entered the housing project under armed guard and amid the taunts and protests of angry whites.[53]

In March 1943, a new controversy developed when the federal public housing authority refused to "rescind the ban against Negroes at Willow Lodge Housing project," leading to a protest letter "from 20 leading citizens" to Roosevelt, asking him to correct the decision. While Emory O. Jackson was in the city for the June NAACP conference, he "had a highway view" of the Willow Lodge housing project war. "Housing is a fighting word here," he wrote. "People are living as thick as the sands of Florida."[54]

Tensions over housing boiled over again in June, and the *World Echo* was perfectly placed to cover the violence—and the Syndicate was perfectly placed to spread the news through its member papers. The setting was Belle Isle, the segregated city beaches on the Detroit River. When Black swimmers moved into the "white" part of the river, the whites attacked. Soon more than two hundred sailors from a nearby naval base joined them. Word of the battle spread through the city; particularly concerning was the fact that whites were attacking individual Black swimmers. (One account had a baby being thrown over a bridge.) That, of course, spread the riot all over town, with Black neighborhoods fuming and white mobs roaming the business districts looking for new victims. Ultimately more than six thousand federal troops calmed the violence, and at its end, there were thirty-four dead and more than seven hundred injured. Property damage ran into the millions. Twenty-five of the dead were Black, and seventeen of those were killed by white policemen tasked with stopping the violence. Along with the dead and wounded, the property destroyed, and the federal troops in the city, thirteen hundred people had been arrested and sat in lockup.[55]

The paper both covered the tragedy and called for calm. It described the immediate cause—"a widespread rumor that a colored woman and a child had been killed by whites at a beach"—and the broader stated cause by civic leaders: "an organized national fifth-column conspiracy to break our national unity and disrupt the home production front." The paper's coverage was comprehensive, from the incidents at Belle Isle to eulogies for the dead to the statement on the rioting from President Roosevelt. White men were beating Black men near city hall. Tear gas canisters were flying all over the city. The police had killed two "at an apartment hotel where, police said, Negro snipers were firing from upper windows. Gunfire and gas grenades from the police drove out all occupants." The *World Echo*'s coverage was also sure to mention that White was among the leaders who "issued appeals calling upon the rioters to stop fighting." Days after the riot, the city named a committee of twenty-five people tasked with bettering racial issues and working to "prevent a recurrence of riots."[56]

As the White Syndicate had already demonstrated, Detroit was not the only housing fight in the state as Michigan struggled to deal with Black southern migrants arriving for war work. In that tumultuous June 1943, the *World Echo* also reported on efforts to raise money to carry on housing fights in nearby Hamtramck, noting in particular Leroy White's suit against the Hamtramck Housing Commission, whose "final outcome will have great bearing on the entire question of segregated housing in northern states."[57] As southerners would learn in the decades to come, protest and legal challenges went hand in hand.

The NAACP held an emergency conference early in June on "the Negro in the War," with Walter White returning to Detroit to give the keynote address. Roosevelt sent a message, which was read at the opening of the session: "Nowhere has support of the war effort been more evident than in the case of our largest racial minority." The NAACP, however, saw little evidence of gratitude, citing the poor treatment of Black soldiers and civilians in the war effort. The group was "appalled at the wide discrepancy between our professed war aims of democracy and freedom and the treatment meted out to Negroes in nearly every part of our national life."[58]

It was no coincidence that the emergency conference happened in embattled Detroit. A variety of groups, including the American Civil Liberties Union and the Metropolitan Detroit Youth Council, called on the governor to investigate those responsible for causing the disastrous riots. The pressure for an investigation only rose when NAACP officials in the city began pushing for charges against a local white police officer who shot an unarmed Black man on the steps of the local YMCA in early July. The association investigated the riot independently, and Thurgood Marshall submitted his report to the governor around the same time. The group knew that the tension in the city was still simmering, so at the NAACP's urging, the troops securing peace in Detroit remained until August.[59]

As if to put an exclamation point on the turmoil, the International Association of Chiefs of Police held its annual convention in Detroit in August, keynoted by J. Edgar Hoover. The FBI director denounced "civil violence, race riots, and insidious campaigns against minority groups," calling events like those in Detroit "a national disgrace and a reflection upon all Americans." That Hoover was speaking with any sincerity or that White and his newspaper believed anything he had to say were equally unlikely, but the statement appeared in the paper as good faith reporting.[60] There was, in other words, a limit on any activist stance based on what a given editor saw as responsible journalism.

The White Syndicate remained strong through the early 1940s. Leroy White returned to Lansing in 1940, creating the *Lansing Echo*. He had less success that year in creating a stable paper in Saginaw. By the end of the war, the White Syndicate had largely dissipated. Meanwhile, the *Michigan Chronicle*, the *Defender*'s original competitive effort in Detroit, maintained its presence. It still publishes today. Though the White Syndicate ultimately lost that particular contest, it did provide a palpable influence on the wartime SNS, spreading news of the South into the upper Midwest and providing southern readers with information about one of the most important and combustible destinations for Black people during the last major wave of the Great Migration.[61]

That the Syndicate could absorb and sustain a sub-syndicate far from the warmth of the southern sun demonstrated its power and influence over the course of the 1930s, 1940s, and 1950s. Its geographical reach provided a nexus for Black readers in both rural South Carolina and urban Michigan, uniting through shared information and content syndication a diaspora willing itself north, on one hand, and willing itself toward a civil rights revolution, on the other.

Conclusion

The Twilight of the Scott Syndicate

"I do not know just how I will face the future," Emory O. Jackson confided in 1955. "My best days have been sacrificed on the Birmingham World and I see no opportunity for progress. Few men have had to give up as much as I have trying to live the things they believe. Could be that I have been mistaken in a number of those beliefs." At the end of the typed letter, Jackson concluded in pencil: "I have no plans for the future. I am finished."[1]

Jackson constantly worried about his role in journalism and in Alabama, and he was subject to persistent yet unfounded doubts. But he was decidedly not finished. He continued to edit the *World*, continued to work for Black rights in Birmingham, and continued to be the most radical voice in the internal structure of the Scott enterprise until his death in 1975. Jackson and the *World* were perfectly positioned to cover the arrest of Rosa Parks and the Montgomery bus boycott. Jackson had worked with E. D. Nixon for years. He covered the Montgomery Improvement Association's strategy sessions and was the first to report on the Reverend Martin Luther King Jr.'s nonviolent passive resistance strategy, which was appropriated from Mohandas Gandhi. Jackson's work had secured his activist bona fides and gained him an ideal vantage point from which to cover the burgeoning movement.[2] His work was a demonstration of the possibilities and platform of Black southern editors in the postwar period, and it made him the conscience of the SNS.

The Scott Newspaper Syndicate, however, demonstrated through its growth across the South and the nation through the 1930s, 1940s, and early 1950s that its conscience was not a static entity. It changed with time and place, couching activism in a practicality that sought to keep the individual newspapers afloat. This was no easy feat, and hundreds of newspapers associated with the SNS rose and fell in the quarter century of the organization's existence. Those papers, despite their varying longevity, served through syndication across the growing diaspora as vehicles of information, a modern kinship network that spread Black news and commentary to compensate for all that white media outlets ignored or distorted. They were the grapevine of the New South.

That grapevine was a Great Migration built of ink and paper, a movement out of the former Confederacy into regions without the kinds of Jim Crow systems and racial violence of the region Black people had left behind. It was built from a base of practical radicalism in editorial policy, which carefully negotiated opportunities to push back against white supremacy without incurring the financial or physical wrath of the white community in which a given paper was located. As the Syndicate spread beyond the bounds of the South, more papers were free of the stranglehold that forced editors into such practical positions, providing those down south with a particular and useful lifeline. More traditionally radical syndicated editorials from northern or western areas under the banner of the SNS allowed the more cloistered newspapers in southern states to say through the cover of an out-of-state dateline what was potentially too risky to say for themselves. Syndication, then, as it spread outward, became a medium of surrogacy; the Syndicate could direct editorial messages where they had the possibility of doing the most good.

And doing good was, of course, necessary. There was a long tradition of the white southern press defending white southern attitudes on race against any opponent, including abolitionists and northerners in the antebellum period and anti–Jim Crow advocates as the century turned. The white southern press was largely responsible for building the momentum for post-Reconstruction disfranchisement laws and for promoting a solid white South. This consistent defense, in harsher or softer tones, depending on the location and the paper, continued to validate the messages white southerners received in their history lessons, their family discussions, and their public lives. They believed that there was a significant cabal of outside agitators "bent on destroying the southern way of life." The list of opponents was long and multiracial, as white liberal politicians, judges, unions, communists, and the NAACP all fell under the harsh light of such scrutiny.[3]

That made the Black press, particularly in the South, all the more important. "The mass communications media have, over the past forty years, changed America into a mass society," Harold Cruse explained in 1967. "And on the bottom where this mass society emerges stands the Negro, not quite passive as of now, but still subject to manipulation and still politically fragmented, if not more so than ever." Cruse interpreted this reality as a "default of the Negro intelligentsia," but the Black press, serving as a constituent part of that intelligentsia, became a vital binding agent in the creation of that mass society, just as the grapevine had bound disparate groups of enslaved and freed people through the power of information in the generations past.[4]

"The Negro press is by far the most effective communication channel leading directly to the Negro people," wrote communist educator Doxey Wilkerson in 1947. "Whoever would influence the economic, political or civic beliefs and behavior of Negro citizens must necessarily approach his audience through the increasingly effective newspapers and magazines." The Black press was a "special-interest" press, a "fighting people's press" engaged in "championing the freedom and full democratic rights of the Negro people, stimulating and organizing their struggles, and helping to build an increasingly unified Negro people's liberation movement." As sociologist Benjamin Singer explained in reference to the proliferation of television in a later generation, mass media often serve power as a way to mollify a citizenry. Still, "although mass media may have a conformative potential for majority groups, it possesses a transformative function for minority group identities."[5] What was true for television and Black Power was also true for Black journalism and the early push against Jim Crow.

"From Harlem to Tougaloo, the Negro press is the most loudly impatient agency for immediate, fundamental change in the status of the race," argues Roi Ottley. "At times, in its honest fury against injustice to black men, it is a kibitzer on the sidelines of American life; and at other times, especially in periods of moral inertia, it is a noisy wailing-wall." Vanderbilt English professor Edwin Mims, writing in 1926 a call to action for progressives in the South, called the Black press "the single greatest power in the Negro race." Asa Gordon, writing about Georgia in the following decade, described Black newspapers as "moulders of opinion, mediums of expression, and developers of racial solidarity."[6]

The newspapers involved in the Scott Newspaper Syndicate did their work pragmatically. That practicality could manifest in coverage that sought to attack broader racial disparities without including direct attacks on local white citizens and institutions, which might cause physical or financial retribution for the paper. That practicality could also be financial. Newspapers in the North, like the *Defender* and *Courier*, or on the East Coast, like the *Norfolk Journal and Guide* and the *Afro*, had the resources to send reporters to various events important to Black people. In the Deep South, that simply wasn't the case. Limited financial resources made syndication even more vital. Having a newspaper in or near the area of a newsworthy event became the cost-effective equivalent of sending a reporter to the scene.[7]

Combined with the Scotts' willingness to effectively bilk the Associated Negro Press out of reprinting rights by sharing news with the Syndicate's member papers, that strategy helped solidify the grapevine and make it cost effective for small southern communities to have viable Black media outlets, even if only temporarily.

Albert Lee Kreiling has argued that the northern Black press's role in denouncing racial abuse was a ritual, a metaphysical act of atonement by northern papers and for northern readers who had left the South for other climes.[8] The Black press in the South had a more immediate job, a more visceral response to the segregation, violence, and disfranchisement that surrounded it. If the survival of a newspaper was a test of victory in those struggles, then most southern papers clearly lost, but the process of syndication allowed them to exist, even for a short time, to document the collection of large tragedies and small triumphs that constituted southern race relations. Though the life of most of the newspapers was limited to a span of months, the continuity generated by the Syndicate provided uniformity and stability to Black southern newspaper readers and to northern readers as it followed the trajectory of the Great Migration. In the process, it helped unify communities and provided information unavailable in other venues. The Scott Newspaper Syndicate survived depression, war, and bigotry with a practical radicalism that kept it viable in the liminal space between white authority and Black need in the quarter century prior to *Brown v. Board of Education*, the Montgomery bus boycott, and the civil rights movement that followed.

Beginning in 1954, fitting a new era brought by *Brown*, a biracial group of journalists and educators founded the Southern Education Reporting Service to report "factually and objectively on developments in Southern education stemming from the Supreme Court decision outlawing segregation in the public schools." Correspondents throughout the region collected clippings and investigated local stories of compliance and noncompliance, publishing the results in the monthly *Southern School News*, a journal of interest to everyone with a stake in the integration fight. That the SERS developed as the SNS faltered, however, was merely fortuitous timing. The former was not a continuation of the latter. The Southern Education Reporting Service was simply creating a nonbiased compendium of information, and while that did in a sense create another bond—like the uniformity of information provided earlier by the Syndicate—there was no opinion page, no banner headlines, no move beyond reporting stories related specifically to southern school desegregation. Members of both the Ku Klux

Klan and the NAACP were subscribers to *Southern School News*, for example, each looking for updates on the progress of southern responses to *Brown*. There were even staunch segregationists on the SERS board of directors, which demonstrated the pitfalls of such interracial contact—even in reporting on desegregation—since white members were able to appropriate much of the control of SERS from their Black colleagues. Still, in the effort to bind the South through uniform news coverage of integration, there were traces of the Syndicate in the SERS endeavor.[9]

The Scott Syndicate dissolved in 1955, a victim of infrastructure change more than anything else; a reduction in train service to and from Atlanta had made inexpensive, timely shipping virtually impossible. More symbolically, the Syndicate's replacement in the region by SERS represented the end of an era, made all the more evident by the *Atlanta Daily World*'s often troubled later civil rights record. When the Syndicate died, the *World*'s practical radicalism died with it; the paper made a decidedly conservative turn. It infamously criticized the city's student sit-ins and economic boycotts in the early 1960s as economically disastrous acts of artificial forcing of integration.[10] The later stance of the Scotts was simple conservatism, something fundamentally different than the pre-1960s strategy of practical radicalism. Unfortunately, the paper's overtly reactionary editorial policy after the onset of the civil rights movement has left a caricature of the southern Black press that doesn't fit either the Syndicate's earlier editorial positions or its sheer scope and size.[11]

Even in the Victorian era, well before the Scott Syndicate saw the light of day, historian Emma Lou Thornbrough notes, one of the most conspicuous characteristics of Black newspapers was "the large number which were started and their low rate of survival. Many were so ephemeral that only their names survive; others were so obscure that not even this evidence of their existence remains."[12] This reality did not change in the years following World War I, particularly in the South, where racism, financial hindrances, and educational deficiencies conspired to keep so many publications small and short lived.

To be sure, many of the SNS publications were also small and short lived, but their reliance on the Scott Syndicate in Atlanta allowed most to leave at least a light historical footprint. The influence of this group of southern papers has been given short shrift in evaluations of Black media of the pre–civil rights movement generation, but more credit is due. The Syndicate in its earliest days sold itself by arguing, "Negroes are different in Dixie." And as it turned out, the slogan was right.

Appendix A

Maps of the Geographic Growth of the Syndicate

1931–1935

1. Asheville Record
2. Atlanta Daily World
3. Atlantic City Eagle
4. Austin Messenger
5. Bartlesville Voice
6. Birmingham World
7. Brunswick Herald
8. Buckeye Tribune
9. Cape Fear Journal
10. Carolina Eagle
11. Carolina Enterprise
12. Charleston Telegram
13. Chattanooga Dispatch
14. Chattanooga Observer
15. Chattanooga Tribune
16. Cincinnati News
17. Clarksville World
18. Cleveland Eagle
19. Columbus Advocate
20. Columbus World
21. Crusader
22. Dayton Progress
23. Detroit World
24. Durham Dispatch
25. East Arkansas World
26. East Texas Messenger
27. Flashlight Herald
28. Fort Worth Mind
29. Galveston Voice
30. Globe Dispatch
31. Greenville World
32. Hampton Tribune
33. Hannibal Register
34. Hot Springs Mirror
35. Hub City News
36. Iowa Bystander
37. Jackson Times
38. Jackson World
39. Jacksonville Mirror
40. Jacksonville Tribune
41. Knoxville Recorder
42. Louisville Independent News
43. Memphis World
44. Michigan World
45. Mississippi Weekly
46. Mississippi World
47. Mobile Sun
48. Mobile World
49. Montgomery World
50. Muskogee Lantern
51. Nashville Independent
52. Nashville World
53. Natchez Journal
54. National Negro World
55. New Bern World
56. Oklahoma Defender
57. Okmulgee World
58. Pee Dee Weekly
59. Peoria Informer
60. Pittsburgh Criterion
61. Public Guide
62. Public Informer
63. Richmond Broadcast
64. Richmond Planet
65. Roanoke Enquirer
66. Rome Sentinel
67. Selma World
68. Spokesman
69. St. Louis News
70. Tampa World
71. Temple Times
72. Toledo Enquirer
73. Tropical Dispatch
74. Vox Populi
75. Waco Messenger
76. Youngstown Challenger

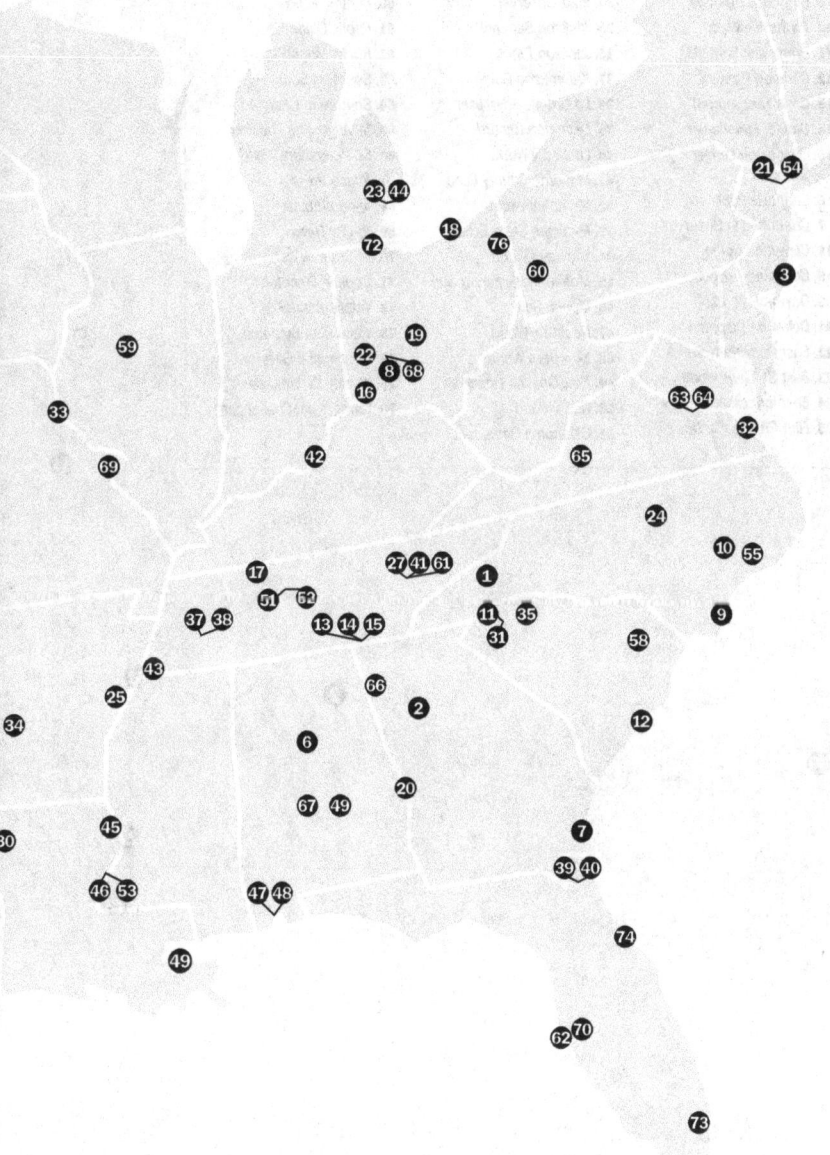

1936–1939

1. Alabama Tribune
2. Amarillo Herald
3. Anderson Messenger
4. Atlanta Daily World
5. Atlantic City Eagle
6. Augusta Journal
7. Bay County Bulletin
8. Birmingham World
9. Blue Grass Tribune
10. Blytheville World
11. Brunswick Sentinel
12. Camden Express
13. Cape Fear Journal
14. Capitol Plaindealer
15. Charleston Ledger Dispatch
16. Charlotte Post
17. Chattanooga Observer
18. Cleveland Guide
19. Columbus Advocate
20. Dayton Progress
21. Delaware Dispatch
22. East Carolina News
23. East St. Louis World
24. East Tennessee News
25. Flint-Brownsville News
26. Florida Tribune
27. Fort Worth Mind
28. Greensboro Tribune
29. Hamtramck Echo
30. Hannibal Register
31. Hartford Advocate
32. Helena Informer
33. Ideal Review
34. Iowa Observer
35. Jackson Sentinel
36. Jackson Times
37. Kalamazoo Guide
38. La Grange Advertiser
39. Lexington Record
40. Louisville News
41. McComb County Echo
42. Memphis World
43. Michigan State Echo
44. Michigan World
45. Mobile Press Forum Sun
46. Mobile Sun
47. Nashville World
48. New Bern World
49. New Orleans Observer
50. News World
51. Oklahoma Defender
52. Omaha Chronicle
53. Orlando Sun
54. Panama City World
55. Pee Dee Weekly
56. Pensacola Courier
57. People's News
58. Peoria Informer
59. Phoenix Index
60. Pontiac Echo
61. Public Guide
62. Rocky Mount Gazette
63. Southern Sun
64. Southwest Georgian
65. St. Augustine Enquirer
66. St. Petersburg World
67. Toledo Press
68. Toledo Tribune
69. Tri-City News
70. Tri-State News
71. Tropical Dispatch
72. Vidalia Banner
73. Waco Post-Dispatch
74. Washington Gazette
75. Weekly Commander
76. Youngstown Challenger

1940–1943

1. Alabama Tribune
2. Alexandria Observer
3. Arkansas World
4. Atlanta Daily World
5. Atlantic City Eagle
6. Atlantic City Tribune
7. Austin Item
8. Birmingham World
9. Brunswick Sentinel
10. Capital City Post
11. Carolina Lighthouse
12. Chattanooga Observer
13. Cincinnati Independent
14. Cleveland Guide
15. Columbus Advocate
16. Columbus World
17. Danville Star
18. Detroit World Echo
19. District Baptist
20. East Carolina News
21. East Tennessee News
22. Falls City News
23. Flint-Brownsville News
24. Galveston Examiner
25. Galveston Voice
26. Illinois Times
27. Industrial Era
28. Iowa Observer
29. Jackson Advocate
30. Jacksonville Progressive News
31. Lansing Echo
32. Lighthouse and Informer
33. Macon Broadcast
34. Memphis World
35. North Carolina Citizen
36. Palm Beach Record
37. Pensacola Courier
38. Phoenix Index
39. Pontiac Echo
40. Port Arthur Flash
41. Saginaw Echo
42. Savannah Journal
43. Shreveport World
44. South Bend Citizen
45. Southwest Georgian
46. Southwestern Torch
47. Struggle
48. Sunlight
49. Tampa Reformer
50. Toledo Voice
51. Trenton World
52. Tri-State News
53. Tropical Dispatch
54. Twin City Journal
55. Twin City Tribune
56. Universal Brotherhood
57. Vicksburg American
58. Vicksburg Tribune
59. Winston-Salem Post
60. World Telegram
61. Youngstown Challenger

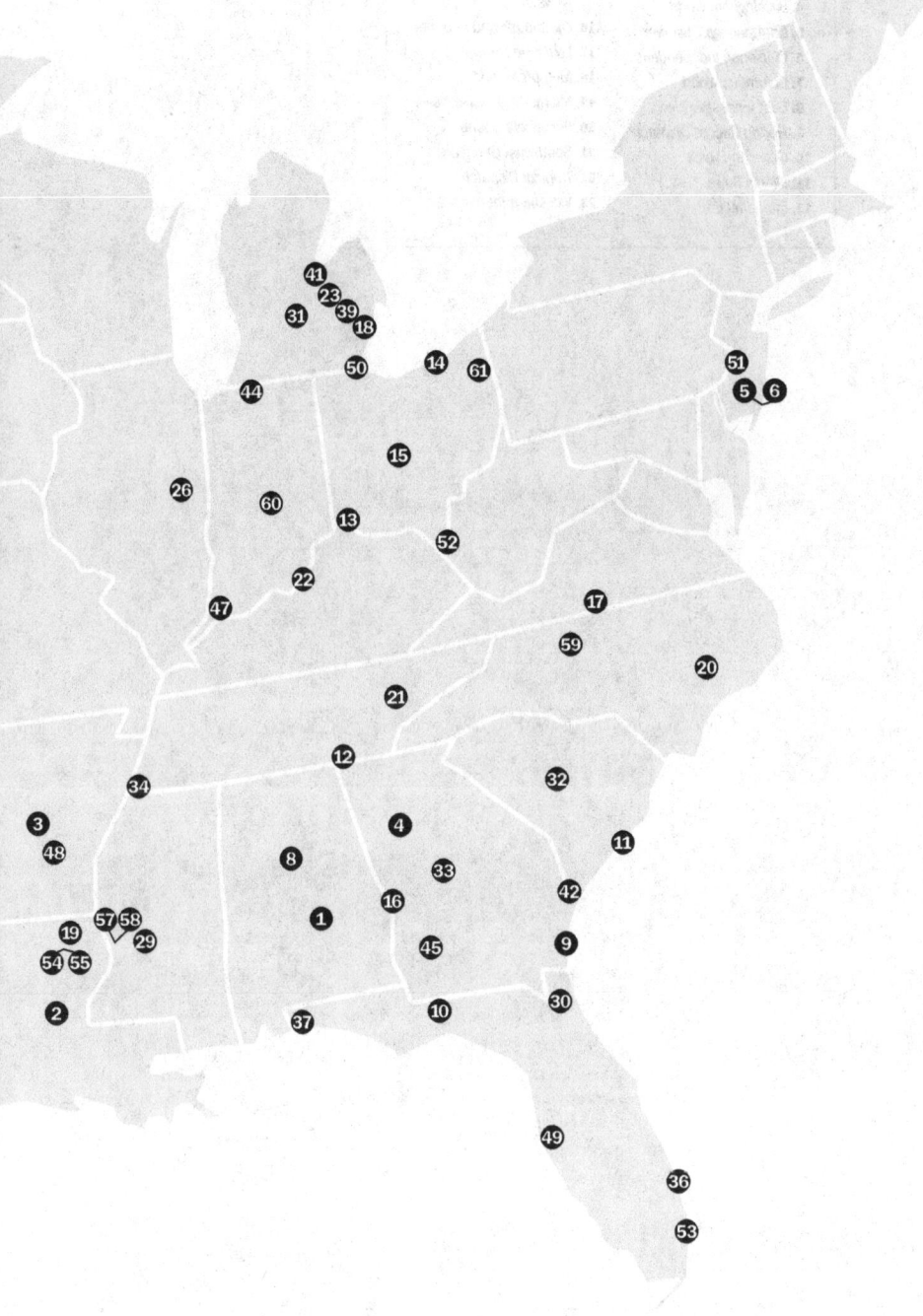

1944–1947

1. Alabama Tribune
2. Arkansas World
3. Atlanta Daily World
4. Birmingham World
5. Chattanooga Observer
6. Cincinnati Independent
7. Columbus World
8. East Tennessee News
9. Florida Record Dispatch
10. Galveston Voice
11. Illinois Times
12. Industrial Era
13. Iowa Observer
14. Jackson Advocate
15. Jacksonville Progressive News
16. Lighthouse and Informer
17. Louisville News
18. Memphis World
19. Miami Progressive News
20. Pensacola Courier
21. Southwest Georgian
22. Tropical Dispatch
23. Vicksburg Tribune

1948–1951

1. *Alabama Tribune*
2. *Arkansas World*
3. *Atlanta Daily World*
4. *Birmingham World*
5. *Chattanooga Observer*
6. *Cincinnati Independent*
7. *Columbus World*
8. *Florida Record Dispatch*
9. *Jackson Banner*
10. *Lighthouse and Informer*
11. *Memphis World*
12. *Nashville Sun*
13. *Pensacola Courier*
14. *Southwest Georgian*
15. *Tropical Dispatch*

1952–1955

1. *Alabama Tribune*
2. *Arkansas World*
3. *Atlanta Daily World*
4. *Birmingham World*
5. *Chattanooga Observer*
6. *Cincinnati Independent*
7. *Columbus World*
8. *Florida Record Dispatch*
9. *Florida Spur*
10. *Independent Call*
11. *Marion County Citizen*
12. *Memphis World*
13. *Nashville Sun*
14. *Northside Home News*
15. *Pensacola Courier*
16. *Southwest Georgian*

Appendix B

Newspapers and Their Time with the Syndicate

There were at least 241 newspapers associated with the Syndicate. Proof of the existence of most of these papers and their time as part of the Scott Syndicate comes from a methodical evaluation of the *Atlanta Daily World*'s cash receipt books from 1931 to 1955, which have notations for every month a given paper sent payment to Atlanta (OBV1 through OBV45, Atlanta Daily World Records, 1931–1996, Manuscript Collection no. 1092, Manuscript, Archives, and Rare Book Library, Emory University, Atlanta, Georgia). These notations are not always a reflection of the complete runs with the Syndicate. The *West Virginia Weekly*, for example, was listed in the cash receipt books as beginning with the SNS in the summer of 1934, but research in the West Virginia State Archives revealed that its run with the Syndicate actually began in October 1933. The *Spokesman* (Xenia, Ohio) was never listed in the cash receipt books at all, but it did make an appearance in a separate SNS ledger and thus was added to the list below.

The newspapers are listed by state in the order they were created, though they may not have joined the Syndicate in the same order. When newspapers share the same date span, they are listed in the order in which they appear in the *World*'s log books. There are four papers (*Globe Dispatch*, *Selma World*, *East Arkansas World*, and the first incarnation of the *Chattanooga World*) whose existence was demonstrated either by a separate Scott Syndicate ledger or a mention in the *World* itself, but the period in which they existed (between October 1932 and January 1934) is missing from the archival record (OBV136 through OBV138, Atlanta Daily World Records). This is one of three gaps in archival coverage; the others are November 1931–March 1932 and December 1940–May 1941. When a recorded existence of a newspaper was found in the last month prior to a gap or the first month after it, thereby indicating that its existence most likely included time within that undocumented period, the final date of the maximum possible span of the paper's life is included parenthetically.

Additionally, some papers changed their name (for example, the *Bartlesville Voice* became the *Tulsa Voice*, before reforming again several months later with its original name), and in those instances each incarnation of the paper has its own entry. Continuity additions were made when spans of one or two months separated constituent months in a series. Empty spans of more than two months were considered to be a stoppage in the paper's activity. Lone payments made by papers more than three months after the continuous set have been viewed as late payments for former services rendered. When there were only two mentions of a paper spaced more than two months apart, the record has been left untouched and is included here.

Newspapers marked with an asterisk (*) were part of the White Newspaper Syndicate in Michigan, which was recorded separately in the SNS cash receipt books. The White Syndicate's payment tenure is the final entry.

Newspaper	Time with the Syndicate
GEORGIA	
Atlanta Daily World	flagship
Columbus World	March 1931–October 1931 (March 1932) (December 1940) May 1941–March 1955
Brunswick Herald	(October 1932) February 1934–September 1934
Rome Sentinel	March–September 1935
Augusta Journal	May 1935–June 1936
Vidalia Banner	April 1936
Columbus Advocate	June 1937 November 1940 (May 1941)
Brunswick Sentinel	July 1938–September 1940
Southwest Georgian	November 1938–January 1944 August 1946–March 1955
La Grange Advertiser	December 1938–October 1939
Macon Broadcast	May 1939–November 1940 (May 1941)
Savannah Journal	(December 1940) June 1941–December 1942
FLORIDA	
Jacksonville World	June 1932–February 1934
Public Informer (St. Petersburg)	August 1932–July 1935
Miami Times	August–September 1932 (January 1934)
Tampa World	(October 1932) February 1934–January 1936
Tropical Dispatch (Miami)	(October 1932) February 1934–June 1950
Jacksonville Tribune	(October 1932) February 1934–August 1934
Palm Beach Tribune (West Palm Beach)	August–October 1934
Jacksonville Mirror	December 1934–April 1935
Broadcast (Bradenton)	May–August 1935
Vox Populi (Daytona Beach)	July–September 1935

Newspaper	Time with the Syndicate
FLORIDA (CONTINUED)	
Orlando Sun	August 1935–December 1936
	January–June 1938
St. Petersburg World	September 1935–November 1936
Ft. Myers World	December 1935
Panama City World	February 1936–January 1938
Florida Crusade (Tallahassee)	May–September 1936
Florida Guardian (Ft. Lauderdale)	June–August 1936
Tampa Journal	May 1937–October 1937
Florida American (Gainesville)	December 1937–August 1938
St. Augustine Enquirer	March–April 1938
Pensacola Courier	March 1938–December 1941
	July 1943–February 1947
	October 1947–March 1955
People's News (Tampa)	April–October 1938
Florida Tribune (Jacksonville)	June–August 1938
Bay County Bulletin (Panama City)	June–August 1939
Colored Citizen (Pensacola)	July 1939
Palm Beach Record	August 1939–May 1940
Capital City Post (Tallahassee)	(December 1940) June 1941
	October 1941
Tampa Reformer	(December 1940) June 1941–July 1941
Jacksonville Progressive News	(December 1940) June 1941–May 1946
Miami Progressive News	June–September 1946
Florida Record Dispatch (West Palm Beach, then Tallahassee)	February 1947–March 1948
	February–March 1949
	August 1951–June 1952
Marion County Citizen (Ocala)	December 1952–March 1953
Florida Spur (Ft. Lauderdale)	January 1954–March 1955
SOUTH CAROLINA	
Carolina Enterprise (Greenville)	March–October 1931
Charleston Messenger	August–September 1932 (January 1934)
Pee Dee Weekly (Florence)	(October 1932) February 1934–April 1936
Carolina World (Greenville)	May–September 1934
	January–February 1935
Charleston Telegram	August 1934–October 1935
Greenville World	October 1934–June 1935
Anderson Messenger	May 1935–June 1936
Hub City News (Spartanburg)	July–September 1935
Carolina Lighthouse (Charleston)	February–April 1940
Lighthouse and Informer (Columbia)	July 1940–January 1949

Newspaper	Time with the Syndicate
NORTH CAROLINA	
Charlotte Post	August–September 1932 (January 1934)
	October 1934–June 1939
Cape Fear Journal (Wilmington)	August 1932–July 1936
	July–September 1941
Carolina Times (Durham)	August–September 1932 (January 1934)
Durham Dispatch	(October 1932) February 1934–August 1934
Carolina Eagle (Kinston)	(October 1932) February 1934–May 1934
New Bern World	(October 1932) February 1934–July 1939
Asheville World	(October 1932)–February 1934
Asheville Record	July 1934–November 1935
Cuttings (Greensboro)	July 1936–December 1936
Washington Gazette	December 1936
Rocky Mount Gazette	January 1937
Greensboro Tribune	January–November 1937
East Carolina News (Kinston)	December 1938–July 1940
Winston-Salem Post	April 1939–March 1940
	September–November 1940 (May 1941)
North Carolina Citizen	October 1940–June 1941
ALABAMA	
Birmingham World	March 1931–March 1955
Montgomery World	September 1931
	(October 1932) February 1934–December 1935
Selma World	(October 1932–January 1934)
Mobile Sun	(October 1932) February 1934–April 1930
Mobile World	April 1934
Selma Post	April–May 1934
Mobile Press Forum Sun	May 1936–September 1938
Alabama Tribune (Montgomery)	June 1936–March 1955
Birmingham World (Bessemer edition)	May–June 1937
TENNESSEE	
Nashville Independent	March–April 1931
Chattanooga Tribune	March 1931
Memphis World	July 1931–March 1955
Nashville World	July 1932–November 1937
Flashlight Herald (Knoxville)	August 1932 (possibly through January 1934)
Chattanooga World	(October 1932–January 1934)
Knoxville Recorder	(October 1932) February 1934–August 1934
Jackson World	March–April 1934
Clarksville World	March 1934–July 1934
Chattanooga Dispatch	March–April 1934
Chattanooga World	April 1934 and October 1934

Newspaper	Time with the Syndicate
TENNESSEE (*CONTINUED*)	
Public Guide (Knoxville)	September 1934–April 1938
Chattanooga Observer	November 1934–March 1955
Jackson Times	March 1935–September 1936
Knoxville Progress Post	May–August 1938
East Tennessee News (Knoxville)	December 1938–February 1947
Nashville Sun (Clarksville)	August 1950–May 1952
Independent Call (Knoxville)	February 1953–March 1955
MISSISSIPPI	
Jackson World	July–September 1932 (January 1934)
Greenville Leader	August–September 1932 (January 1934) September–October 1934
Weekly Echo (Meridian)	August 1932
Mississippi World (Natchez)	(October 1932) February 1934–March 1935
Mississippi Weekly (Vicksburg)	March–August 1934
Mississippi Tribune (Vicksburg)	September 1934–January 1935
Corinthian Gazette (Corinth)	April–June 1935
Natchez Journal	April–May 1935
Jackson Sentinel	September 1936
Weekly Commander (Clarksdale)	August–October 1937
Southern Sun (Greenwood)	June–September 1939
Vicksburg American	July 1940–August 1941
Jackson Advocate	October 1940–July 1946
Meridian Progress	August–October 1941
Vicksburg Tribune	November 1941–October 1944
Jackson Banner	October 1949–June 1951
LOUISIANA	
Louisiana Weekly (New Orleans)	July–September 1932 (January 1934)
Globe Dispatch (Shreveport)	(October 1932–January 1934)
New Orleans Broadcast	May–September 1934 May–June 1935
Southern Broadcast (Monroe)	July–October 1937
Baton Rouge Post	August 1937–May 1938
New Orleans Observer	December 1938–December 1939
Twin City Journal (Monroe)	August 1939–July 1940
Twin City Tribune (Monroe)	February 1940–November 1941
Shreveport World	July 1940–October 1941
District Baptist (Bastrop)	October–November 1940 (May 1941)
Alexandria Observer	July 1941–December 1943
Bayou State Register (Grambling)	May–July 1951
ARKANSAS	
East Arkansas World (Marianna)	(October 1932–January 1934)
Hot Springs Mirror	June–July 1935

Newspaper	Time with the Syndicate
Southern Liberator (Forrest City)	December 1935
Blytheville World	January 1936
Camden Express	April 1938–October 1939
Helena Informer	September–December 1938
Universal Brotherhood (Texarkana)	May 1939–May 1940
	October 1940
	November 1941–December 1942
Sunlight (Pine Bluff)	December 1939–February 1942
Arkansas World (Little Rock)	March 1940–May 1953
TEXAS	
Dallas Express	August–September 1932 (January 1934)
Waco Messenger	August–September 1932 (January 1934)
Fort Worth Mind	(October 1932) February 1934–May 1938
Austin Messenger	(October 1932) February 1934–March 1934
Galveston Voice	(October 1932) February 1934–June 1935
Houston Guide	April 1934 and July 1934
Marshall Tribune	April 1934–January 1935
East Texas Messenger (Huntsville)	September–December 1934
Temple Times	July–November 1935
Waco Post-Dispatch	December 1935–June 1936
San Angelo Enterprise	April–December 1936
Amarillo Herald	March–August 1937
Galveston Guide	April–June 1937
East Texas Times (Big Sandy)	May 1937
Tyler Tribune	May–September 1937
Texas Examiner (Houston)	August 1937
Port Arthur Flash	October 1939–April 1940
Austin Item	January–March 1940
Southwestern Torch (El Paso)	February 1940–July 1941
Galveston Examiner	March–June 1940
Industrial Era (Beaumont)	August 1941–June 1945
OKLAHOMA	
Okmulgee World	March–May 1934.
Oklahoma Defender	March 1935–December 1939
Muskogee Lantern	March 1935
Bartlesville Voice	March–May 1935
	October–November 1935
	October 1936–January 1937
Tulsa Voice	June–July 1935
MISSOURI	
St. Louis Argus	July–September 1932 (January 1934)
Hannibal Register	(October 1932) February 1934–April 1937
St. Louis News	August–November 1935

Appendix B

Newspaper	Time with the Syndicate
KANSAS	
Capitol Plaindealer (Topeka)	September 1936–March 1937
	July–September 1937
NEBRASKA	
Omaha Chronicle	July 1936–September 1937
IOWA	
Iowa Bystander (Des Moines)	(October 1932) February 1934–October 1935
Iowa Observer (Des Moines)	January 1939–August 1941
	April 1942–December 1945
ARIZONA	
Phoenix Index	March–August 1937
	April 1938–October 1942
MINNESOTA	
Twin City Herald (Minneapolis)	December 1939–February 1940
WISCONSIN	
Milwaukee Observer	April 1940
KENTUCKY	
Louisville Leader	July–September 1932 (January 1934)
Lexington Record	September 1934–April 1936
Louisville Independent News	February–November 1935
Owensboro Eagle	November 1935–February 1936
Louisville Herald Tribune	June 1937–January 1938
Louisville News	March 1938–October 1939
	December 1942 and February 1943
	July 1943–February 1945
Blue Grass Tribune (Frankfort)	October 1939
Falls City News (Louisville)	November 1939–June 1943
VIRGINIA	
Hampton Tribune	August 1932
Richmond Planet	August–September 1932 (January 1934)
Richmond Broadcast	(October 1932) February 1934–June 1934
Roanoke Enquirer	(October 1932) February 1934–January 1936
Danville Star	April 1942–March 1943
DELAWARE	
Delaware Dispatch (Rehoboth Beach)	May–September 1938
WEST VIRGINIA	
West Virginia Weekly (Charleston)	October 1933–December 1934
Tri-State News (Huntington)	May 1938–August 1942
Charleston Ledger Dispatch	January–April 1939

Newspaper	Time with the Syndicate
INDIANA	
Indianapolis Recorder	August-September 1932 (January 1934)
Gary American	August 1932 (possibly through January 1934)
Struggle (Evansville)	September-December 1938
	December 1939-June 1940
World Telegram (Indianapolis)	May 1939-August 1940
Indianapolis World	November 1939-January 1940
South Bend Citizen	January-April 1940
ILLINOIS	
Peoria Informer	November 1934-April 1939
East St. Louis World	February-April 1937
Tri-City News (Moline)	April-May 1939
Illinois Times (Danville/Champaign)	September 1939-April 1945
What's News (Danville)	July-August 1940
OHIO	
Columbus Voice	August-September 1932 (January 1934)
Columbus Advocate	(October 1932) February 1934-October 1934
Cleveland Eagle	(October 1932) February 1934-November 1935
Youngstown Challenger	(October 1932) February 1934-November 1940 (May 1941)
Cincinnati News	March-August 1934
Spokesman (Wilberforce/Xenia)	February-March 1935
Dayton Progress	March 1935-January 1940
Buckeye Tribune (Wilberforce/Xenia)	April-June 1935
Toledo Enquirer	May-June 1935
Forum (Dayton)	November 1935-January 1936
Toledo Press	December 1935-July 1936
	December 1938-July 1939
Cleveland Guide	July 1936-January 1944
Toledo Tribune	March-April 1937
	April-November 1938
Toledo Voice	June 1939-August 1943
Cincinnati Independent	November 1939-March 1949
	September 1949 and March 1950
NEW YORK	
Crusader (New York City)	(October 1932) February 1934-May 1934
National Negro World (New York City)	March-April 1934
Buffalo Star	December 1939-January 1940
NEW JERSEY	
Newark Herald	August-September 1932 (January 1934)
	September-October 1934
Atlantic City Eagle	March 1935-November 1940 (May 1941)

Newspaper	Time with the Syndicate
NEW JERSEY (*CONTINUED*)	
Ideal Review (Bridgeton)	January–April 1936
Trenton Record	December 1939–January 1940
Trenton World	February 1940–June 1941
Atlantic City Tribune	January–October 1942
Northside Home News (Atlantic City)	March–June 1952
PENNSYLVANIA	
Pittsburgh Criterion	April–November 1934
CONNECTICUT	
Hartford Advocate	February 1936–April 1937
Connecticut Labor News (Hartford)	July–September 1937
MICHIGAN	
Detroit Independent	August 1932
Detroit World	(October 1932) February 1934–July 1934
Michigan World (Detroit)	August 1934–August 1937
News World (Detroit)	August 1937–November 1938
Michigan State Echo* (Lansing)	March 1938–May 1939
Jackson Echo*	June 1938
	November 1938–February 1939
Grand Rapids Echo*	July–October 1938
Hamtramck Echo*	July–October 1938
	March–June and December 1939
	May 1940
	August–September 1941
	March 1942
McComb County Echo* (Mt. Clemens)	August 1938–October 1939
Pontiac Echo*	September 1938–September 1939
	February–April 1940
Brownsville Weekly News* (Flint)	September 1938–October 1939
Flint-Brownsville News* (Flint)	November 1939
	(December 1940) June 1941–April 1942
Kalamazoo Guide	February–March 1939
Detroit World Echo*	April 1939–October 1940
	October 1941
	March 1942–March 1943
	November–December 1943
Battle Creek Tribune	August 1939
Lansing Echo*	January–July 1940
Saginaw Echo*	August 1940
*White Syndicate (Detroit)	March 1939–December 1943

Notes

Introduction. The Migration of the Scott Syndicate

1. Blakeney, "Sociological Analysis," 7.
2. This volume, *Practical Radicalism and the Great Migration*, is a companion to Aiello, *Grapevine of the Black South*.
3. Hahn, *Nation under Our Feet*, 69, 85.
4. Egerton, *Speak Now against the Day*, 285. In large measure, these first few paragraphs are the same as the opening paragraphs in the companion volume to this work, *The Grapevine of the Black South*, partly to ground the narrative at the same starting point as its predecessor before it veers in decidedly different directions. While there are additions, it is important to note the dependency.
5. This is similar to the ideology of managed race relations presented in works like Chafe, *Civilities and Civil Rights*; and J. Douglas Smith, *Managing White Supremacy*.
6. *Atlanta World*, 28 February 1932, 6.
7. Quoted in Detweiler, "Negro Press Today," 393.
8. Strother, "Race-Advocacy Function," 92, 94; and Michaeli, *Defender*.
9. Strother, "Race-Advocacy Function," 92, 94, 97; Detweiler, "Negro Press Today," 395–396, 400; O'Kelly, "Black Newspapers," 14; and Frazier, *Black Bourgeoisie*, 179. As Nell Irvin Painter has discussed, such criticisms dated to the nineteenth century. Papers focused too much on gossip and "society news." They often failed to emphasize more important political issues in favor of salacious stories that would drive circulation. They often didn't produce their own news or maintain any consistent editorial policy. In 1890, the Associated Correspondents of Race Newspapers formed in an attempt to meet some of this criticism, but it never established any satisfactory permanent standards. Painter, "Black Journalism," 32.
10. "Transcript of Evidence, Testimony for Plaintiff: C. A. Scott on Cross-Examination," Transcript of Record, U.S. Circuit Court of Appeals for the Fifth Circuit, *Tademy v. Scott*, no. 2701, Civil Action, 29.
11. "Transcript of Evidence, Testimony for Plaintiff: C. A. Scott on Cross-Examination," 29–32; and Atlanta Daily World Records, 1931–1996, Manuscript Collection no. 1092, box 25, Manuscript, Archives, and Rare Book Library, Emory University, Atlanta, Ga. That explanation, though true, was made galling by Scott's abuse of his own ANP subscription to fill content space in the Syndicate's member papers. See Aiello, *Grapevine of the Black South*.
12. Payment for such services would vary according to the work per week, "so much per hundred copies, so much per column inch for local composition, and so much per inch for advertising composition, and of course so much for make-up, if we had to do some special make-up, extra make-up we charged them." "Transcript of Ev-

idence, Testimony for Plaintiff," 33–38. See also Aiello, *Grapevine of the Black South*, 132–133.

13. Hogan, *Black National News Service*, 28, 56–74; and Gerald Horne, *Rise and Fall*. See also Aiello, *Grapevine of the Black South*, 133.

14. Douglass, *Life and Times of Frederick Douglass*, 531.

15. For more on the Great Migration, see Cohen, *At Freedom's Edge*; Grossman, *Land of Hope*; and Isabel Wilkerson, *Warmth of Other Suns*.

16. Burke quoted in Terkel, *Hard Times*, 82.

17. Thomas, *Human Exploitation*, xiv–xv; Lanctot, *Negro League Baseball*, 6; Hogan, *Shades of Glory*, 224–225; Frederickson, *Dixiecrat Revolt*, 13; and Warren, *Herbert Hoover*, 241–242.

18. See McKenzie et al., "Transmission Network Analysis," 470.

19. Department of Commerce, "Negro Newspapers and Periodicals in the United States: 1937," 1. The following year, the local reported total increased to 68.2 percent, but the point remained the same. Department of Commerce, "Negro Newspapers and Periodicals in the United States: 1938," 1.

20. Statistics about the Black populations of the various SNS cities, counties, and states come from my own data mining of the Fifteenth, Sixteenth, and Seventeenth Censuses of the United States. See Fifteenth Census of the United States, 1930: Alabama–Missouri, Montana–Wyoming; Sixteenth Census of the United States, 1940: United States Summary, Alabama–District of Columbia, Florida–Iowa, Kansas–Michigan, Minnesota–New Mexico, New York–Oregon, Pennsylvania–Texas, Utah–Wyoming; and Seventeenth Census of the United States, 1950.

21. Kessler, *Dissident Press*, 43.

22. Aiello, *Grapevine of the Black South*, 61–82.

23. Hahn, *Nation under Our Feet*.

24. Ibid., 387.

25. Gilmore, *Defying Dixie*, 4–6, quote 6. See also Egerton, *Speak Now against the Day*, 3–197.

26. Black et al., "Impact of the Great Migration."

27. Doreski, *Writing America Black*, xv, xviii, xxiii.

28. *Sipuel v. Board of Regents of the University of Oklahoma*, 332 U.S. 631 (1948); and Weaver and Page, "Black Press and the Drive," 21. See also Wattley, *Step toward Brown v. Board*.

29. *Chicago Defender*, 24 January 1948, 1, 14; *St. Louis Argus*, 16 January 1948, 1, 12, 23 January 1948, 12; *Philadelphia Tribune*, 20 January 1948, 4; *Michigan Chronicle*, 31 January 1948, 6; Weaver and Page, "Black Press and the Drive," 22; and *Atlanta Daily World*, 21 January 1948, 1, 3.

30. Weaver and Page, "Black Press and the Drive"; and *Atlanta Daily World*, 13 January 1948, 1, 14 January 1948, 6 (quotes), 21 January 1948, 3.

31. Brown-Nagin, *Courage to Dissent*, 2; and *Alabama Tribune*, 16 January 1948, 1, 23 January 1948, 1, 30 January 1948, 8.

32. *New York Amsterdam News*, 28 February 1948, 1, 10; *Chicago Defender*, 31 January 1948, 1, 15; *Pittsburgh Courier*, 31 January 1948, 1, 6; *St. Louis Argus*, 6 February 1948, 1; Weaver and Page, "Black Press and the Drive," 22–24; and deShazo and Lampton, "Educational Struggles," 189–190.

33. *Tropical Dispatch*, 1 January 1949, 8, 22 January 1949, 8.

34. Sullivan, *Lift Every Voice*, 380–381; Weaver and Page, "Black Press and the Drive," 24–26; and *McLaurin v. Oklahoma State Regents*, 339 U.S. 637 (1950). See also M. Christopher Brown II, "Collegiate Desegregation as Progenitor."

35. Even when the Black law school developed a little more, the quality was obviously unequal: more than 850 students in the white school compared to 23 students in the Black school, and more than sixty-five thousand library volumes compared to sixteen thousand. Only one graduate of the Black law school was admitted to the Texas Bar. Weaver and Page, "Black Press and the Drive," 25–26; Sullivan, *Lift Every Voice*, 380; *Henderson v. U.S.*, 339 U.S. 816 (1950); and *Sweatt v. Painter*, 339 U.S. 629 (1950).

36. *Michigan Chronicle*, 10 June 1950, 1; *Afro-American*, 10 June 1950, 1, 2; *Indianapolis Recorder*, 17 June 1950, 1; *Chicago Defender*, 17 June 1950, 1; *Los Angeles Sentinel*, 15 June 1950, 1; *St. Louis Argus*, 9 June 1950, 1, 2; and Weaver and Page, "Black Press and the Drive," 27–28.

37. *Atlanta Daily World*, 6 June 1950, 1, 6.

38. *Chattanooga Observer*, 17 February 1950, 1.

39. Poston, "Negro Press," 14. For more on Poston, see Hauke, *Ted Poston*.

40. Fred Carroll, *Race News*, 6.

41. *Philadelphia Tribune*, 10 June 1950, 4; and Weaver and Page, "Black Press and the Drive," 28.

Chapter 1. Georgia

1. For more on Georgia during the Great Depression, see Lorence, *Unemployed People's Movement*; Carlton and Coclanis, *Confronting Southern Poverty*; and Montgomery, Schmier, and Williams, "Other Depression."

2. The *Advocate*'s relationship with Tuskegee was more than theoretical, and Lewis even corresponded with the institute's George Washington Carver. *Atlanta Daily World*, 10 July 1937, 4, 17 July 1937, 4, 4 August 1939, 4, 11 January 1940, 5; *Pittsburgh Courier*, 19 October 1940, 14; and George Washington Carver to J. J. Lewis, 12 November 1938, George Washington Carver Correspondence, 1932–1939, unprocessed collection, Amistad Research Center, Tulane University, New Orleans, La.

3. *Atlanta Daily World*, 31 August 1937, 1.

4. *Atlanta Daily World*, 4 July 1938, 5.

5. *Atlanta Daily World*, 14 February 1940, 1, 28 June 1942, 5.

6. *Atlanta Daily World*, 10 November 1938, 1, 6 January 1939, 6.

7. *Atlanta Daily World*, 14 March 1940, 1, 31 July 1941, 1, 1 August 1941, 6, 7 August 1941, 1, 8 August 1941, 2.

8. Weaver and Page, "Black Press and the Drive," 15; and Egerton, *Speak Now against the Day*, 150–153.

9. Kelleher, "Case of Lloyd Lionel Gaines"; and Weaver and Page, "Black Press and the Drive," 15–16.

10. *Missouri ex rel. Gaines v. Canada*, 305 U.S. 337 (1938); Weaver and Page, "Black Press and the Drive," 16, 20; James, *Root and Branch*, 103–122; McNeil, *Groundwork*, 150–151; and Fenderson, "Negro Press," 184.

11. *Pittsburgh Courier*, 24 December 1938, 11; *New York Amsterdam News*, 24 December 1938, 1; *Indianapolis Recorder*, 31 December 1938, 9; *Cleveland Gazette*, 17 December 1938, 6; *Chicago Defender*, 24 December 1938, 16; and Weaver and Page, "Black Press and the Drive," 17–18.

12. Weaver and Page, "Black Press and the Drive," 19; and *Atlanta Daily World*, 19 December 1938, 6.

13. *Atlanta Daily World*, 11 February 1940, 1, 12 February 1940, 1, 13 February 1940, 1, 14 February 1940, 1, 17 February 1940, 1, 2, 18 February 1940, 1, 20 February 1940, 1, 21 February 1940, 1, 22 February 1940, 1, 25 February 1940, 1, 28 February 1940, 1, 3 March 1940, 1, 17 March 1940, 1, 5 April 1940, 6, 26 May 1940, 5.

14. *Atlanta Daily World*, 10 June 1943, 1.

15. *Atlanta Daily World*, 5 February 1943, 1, 10 June 1943, 1, 15 June 1943, 1, 22 June 1943, 1, 23 June 1943, 6, 25 July 1943, 1; and Gilmore, *Defying Dixie*, 355, 393. While under indictment, Baker County sheriff M. Claude Screws was shot by a white farmer resisting arrest in July. *Atlanta Daily World*, 9 July 1943, 1, 10 July 1943, 1. The trial of the law enforcement officers occurred in October, and they were convicted of violating civil liberties statutes and sentenced to three years in prison and $1,000 fines. The U.S. Supreme Court, however, granted them a new trial based on a technicality. It took place two years later in October 1945. In that trial, an all-white jury absolved Screws of responsibility. *Atlanta Daily World*, 7 October 1943, 1, 31 October 1945, 1, 1 November 1945, 1, 2 November 1945, 1. In April 1952, the *Southwest Georgian* merged with its competitor, the *Albany Enterprise*, making it the only Black newspaper in Albany. Despite the consolidation, the new paper kept the *Georgian* name, Searles as publisher and editor, and its association with the SNS. Later that year, however, Searles gave up his post to become special division manager for the Atlanta branch of the Mutual Benefit, Health and Accident Association headquartered in Omaha, Nebraska. *Atlanta Daily World*, 16 January 1952, 1, 20 January 1952, 5, 10 April 1952, 6.

16. *Atlanta Daily World*, 5 February 1948, 1, 11 February 1948, 1, 28 February 1948, 4, 3 March 1948, 1, 10 March 1948, 6, 14 March 1948, 1, 26 March 1948, 1.

17. *Atlanta Daily World*, 8 May 1948, 4, 4 August 1948, 1, 11 August 1948, 1.

18. Tubbs was, according to one society column, "quite as suave as ever—and quite as popular." *Atlanta Daily World*, 29 May 1939, 6, 9 July 1939, 4, 25 February 1940, 5.

19. *Atlanta Daily World*, 26 September 1939, 6.

20. *Atlanta Daily World*, 28 October 1939, 1, 7 November 1939, 6. The paper often covered the goings-on at the college. See, for example, 26 February 1940, 2.

21. *Atlanta Daily World*, 6 February 1940, 6, 1 February 1940, 7.

22. R. H. Hubert was the paper's original manager in 1931, but he was promoted in December 1931 to district traveling manager for the *Atlanta World*. His place as manager was taken by A. O. Bomar. William H. Spencer was, even at this early date, associated with the paper, and he met with the employees in December 1931. (In 1941, the *Atlanta Daily World*, in making the announcement of the new paper, did not mention Spencer's earlier association with its first incarnation.) The Syndicate reprinted *Columbus World* articles about William Spencer High School, the city's Black high school named after W. H. Spencer's father, who had advocated tirelessly for its creation, and the doings of Black soldiers at nearby Fort Benning. Gordon, *Georgia Negro*, 262; and *Atlanta Daily World*, 2 December 1931, 5, 18 December 1931, 6, 10 February 1932, 8, 21 February 1932, 11, 13 March 1932, 2.

23. The *Columbus World*'s publisher was Percy Lee Taylor, who was also the general manager for the Bishop Theater chain. The paper's 1024 First Avenue address was the Dixie Theater building. The Syndicate regularly reproduced a *Columbus World* column titled "News of Mighty Fort Benning," written by several authors

throughout the course of the war. *Atlanta Daily World*, 19 March 1941, 2, 21 August 1942, 5, 8 September 1941, 1, 3, 21 August 1942, 2, 4 September 1942, 2, 5, 9 July 1943, 2, 28 January 1944, 2, 25 February 1944, 2, 4 June 1944, 6, 9 June 1944, 2; Oak, *Negro Newspaper*, 155; Twelfth Census of the United States, 1900: Columbus City, Ga., sheet 2B; Fourteenth Census of the United States, 1920: Columbus City, Ga., sheet 5A; *Columbus City Directory* (Columbus, Ga.: R. L. Polk & Co., 1923), 1420; "History," Spencer High School, http://www.spencerhighga.org/About/history.asp, accessed 19 October 2014; and *Western Outlook*, 21 August 1915, 1.

24. *Atlanta Daily World*, 25 October 1941, 4, 21 April 1944, 6.

25. *Atlanta Daily World*, 17 August 1942, 6 (quote), 23 October 1942, 6, 3 November 1942, 2, 26 January 1943, 6, 15 February 1943, 6, 8 June 1943, 6 (quote).

26. *Atlanta Daily World*, 27 February 1946, 6, 28 November 1947, 5, 20 May 1948, 6, 7 July 1949, 2, 15 September 1949, 5, 11 January 1951, 4.

27. *Atlanta Daily World*, 19 April 1951, 2, 10 August 1951, 1, 6 December 1951, 3, 17 January 1952, 2, 29 June 1954, 1.

28. *Savannah Journal*, 29 September 1934 (available from the University of Georgia, Athens).

29. *Atlanta Daily World*, 20 March 1941, 1, 25 August 1941, 2, 30 November 1941, 1, 5 December 1941, 3. For more on this particular fight, see Aiello, *Grapevine of the Black South*, ch. 4.

30. *Atlanta Daily World*, 15 January 1941, 1, 1 July 1941, 1.

31. *Atlanta Daily World*, 29 August 1941, 6.

32. *Atlanta Daily World*, 11 August 1941, 2; and Aiello, *Grapevine of the Black South*, ch. 4.

33. *Atlanta Daily World*, 11 August 1941, 2.

34. *Atlanta Daily World*, 22 September 1942, 6.

35. While my data are taken from the U.S. Census, there are also other powerful resources, including Richard Sterner's *The Negro's Share*, which evaluates "the problem of the Negro's economic position in American society" (3). I largely take for granted the tenuous economic position of the Black population, but the spread of news was not necessarily reliant on money, and Black weekly newspapers were priced with a readership at or below the poverty line often assumed.

36. *Atlanta Daily World*, 1 May 1942, 2, 6 October 1942, 2.

37. "Fortune Press Analysis," 233, 235–236, 238.

38. Regardless, the endorsement was functionally ineffective in convincing a populace who mostly couldn't vote. Marvin Griffin won the election without the necessity of a runoff. *Atlanta Daily World*, 18 August 1954, 1, 21 August 1954, 1.

Chapter 2. Florida

1. *Atlanta Daily World*, 24 June 1932, 1. The *Jacksonville World* was published by Edward T. Gore.

2. See, for example, Knowlton, *Bubble in the Sun*; and Nelson, *How the New Deal Built*.

3. *Atlanta Daily World*, 24 June 1932, 3.

4. See Aiello, *Grapevine of the Black South*, 17–20.

5. Wynne, "Brownsville," 153–155, 160. Davis quote from *Atlanta Independent*, 17 November 1906, reprinted in Wynne, 155.

6. The paper also reported on the ousting of the general manager of the People's

Insurance Company by its board of directors. The insurance industry was central to the lives of the Black South, and its news remained prominent. *Atlanta Daily World*, 19 July 1932, 1A, 24 August 1932, 2, 7 September 1932, 2A, 28 October 1932, 1A, 30 October 1932, 1.

7. *Atlanta Daily World*, 2 October 1932, 6. Charles Augustus Lindbergh Jr., the only son of the most famous person in the United States, was kidnapped from his family's home on March 1, 1932, and a ransom note was left in his place. The $50,000 demand ushered in hurried negotiations and intrigue that would consume the family for the next two months. It also ushered in speculation, discussion, and concern in the pages of every newspaper and on every radio program in the country. On May 12, the baby's body was discovered by a Black truck driver, William Allen. "I just hope they get the man that did it," said Allen. "Nothing would be too bad to do to him." The headline of the *Houston Informer*'s coverage of the find read, "Negro Finds Lindbergh Baby." Jesse O. Thomas, a columnist for the *Informer*, expressed his sorrow and sympathy for the Lindberghs and the baby, but also noted the unique concern of the public about the case. "If we would be at all consistent, we must be as much concerned about the safety, the well-being of all the children of all the people," he wrote. "The kidnaping of the most humble and abject child in an Atlanta alley, be it white or colored, must loom up to the aspect of challenging our fervent prayers or we run the danger of being inconsistent." *Houston Informer*, 19 March 1932, 7, 21 May 1932, 1. See also Berg, *Lindbergh*, 239, 271; Fisher, *Lindbergh Case*, 7–14; Waller, *Kidnap*, 3–19; and Milton, *Loss of Eden*, 237, 249. The Jacksonville SNS paper became the *Jacksonville Tribune* in February 1934.

8. Reeves was born in April 1883 in Nassau, Bahamas, where he completed high school and began working as a printer. In August 1920, he sailed from Havana, Cuba, to Key West aboard the SS *Mascotta* before moving later that year to Miami, where he worked at Magic Printing Company and ultimately founded his own paper. Florida Passenger Lists, 1898–1951, U.S. Citizen Passenger Lists of Vessels Arriving at Key West, Florida, Records of the Immigration and Naturalization Service, 1787–2004; Florida Population Census, 1945, Dade County, Precinct 57, Negro; Fourteenth Census of the United States, 1920: Miami City, Fla., sheet 20A; *Miami City Directory, 1922* (Miami, Fla.: R. L. Polk & Co., 1922), 998; *Miami City Directory, 1928* (Jacksonville, Fla.: R. L. Polk & Co., 1928), 970; and *Miami City Directory, 1932* (Jacksonville, Fla.: R. L. Polk & Co., 1932), 588.

9. *Atlanta Daily World*, 16 January 1934, 2, 20 January 1934, 3; and Shofner, "Florida," 112.

10. *Atlanta Daily World*, 14 April 1934, 5, 17 March 1935, A2, 10 October 1937, 3; "Scott Newspaper Service [syndicating service], 1935," OBV136, Atlanta Daily World Records, 1931–1996, Manuscript Collection no. 1092, Manuscript, Archives, and Rare Book Library, Emory University, Atlanta, Ga. (hereinafter "Scott Newspaper Service, 1935"); and "Scott Newspaper Service [syndicating service], 1936," OBV137, ibid. (hereinafter "Scott Newspaper Service, 1936"). The advertisement listed cities that the SNS deemed ready for a newspaper, and it provides insight into the Scotts' vision of expansion as of early 1934: Alabama: Decatur, Florence, Huntsville, Anniston, Dothan, Gadsden, Selma, Tuscaloosa; Arkansas: Ft. Smith, Hot Springs, Little Rock, Helena, Pine Bluff; Florida: Gainesville, Sanford, Daytona Beach, Orlando, Pensacola, West Palm Beach; Georgia: Gainesville, Rome, Athens, Augusta,

Columbus, Macon, Savannah, Valdosta, Waycross; Kentucky: Lexington, Louisville, Paducah; Louisiana: Baton Rouge, New Orleans; Mississippi: Clarksdale, Hattiesburg, Jackson, Meridian, Vicksburg; North Carolina: Charlotte, Fayetteville, Goldsboro, Greensboro, Raleigh, Rocky Mount, Wilson, Winston-Salem; South Carolina: Charleston, Columbia, Florence, Sumter; Tennessee: Clarksville; Texas: Tyler, Beaumont, Marshall, Dallas, Port Arthur, San Antonio; Virginia: Danville, Lynchburg; West Virginia: Huntington, Charleston. The cities were both small and large, but all were in the South. It is clear that the Syndicate, though it had changed names, wanted to dominate in its home region.

11. When the *Tampa World* failed in 1936, Mason moved on to work with the *Houston Informer*. He also worked for the *St. Louis Call*. *Tampa City Directory, 1926* (Jacksonville, Fla.: R. L. Polk & Co., 1926), 773; *Tampa City Directory, 1934* (Jacksonville, Fla.: R. L. Polk & Co., 1934), 387; *Tampa City Directory, 1935* (Jacksonville, Fla.: R. L. Polk & Co., 1935), 413; Fifteenth Census of the United States, 1930, Tampa City, Fla., sheet 17A; "Scott Newspaper Service, 1935"; and "Scott Newspaper Service, 1936."

12. *Atlanta Daily World*, 31 January 1934, 1, 2 February 1934, 1, 10 February 1934, 2, 21 September 1934, 4, 8 September 1935, 1, 29 September 1935, 5, 21 October 1935, 6, 4 December 1935, 1, 20 February 1936, 2, 17 June 1937, 1.

13. Shofner, "Florida," 112–113; *Miami City Directory, 1929* (Jacksonville, Fla.: R. L. Polk & Co., 1929), 708, 1930; *Miami City Directory, 1934* (Jacksonville, Fla.: R. L. Polk & Co., 1934), 648; *Miami City Directory, 1935* (Jacksonville, Fla.: R. L. Polk & Co., 1935), 726; *Miami City Directory, 1937* (Jacksonville, Fla.: R. L. Polk & Co., 1937), 1066; and Sixteenth Census of the United States, 1940, Miami, Fla., sheet 6A.

14. The *Dispatch*'s religious editor, the Reverend E. L. Patterson, "the only Negro Bishop in the American Catholic Church," wrote a column called "The Spiritual Life" that was syndicated by the Scotts. Other *Dispatch* articles evaluated topics such as friendliness as the foremost quality to make a popular young man. *Atlanta Daily World*, 10 August 1934, 6, 2 February 1935, 4, 27 February 1937, 2. The benefits of syndication were often subtle. For example, when a Bahamian minister came to speak at Martin Luther King Sr.'s Ebenezer Baptist Church in 1935, the *World* was able to provide more information on the speaker by excerpting a profile originally published in the *Dispatch*. *Atlanta Daily World*, 1 August 1935, 1.

15. Langston Hughes, "Battle of the Ballot," 118; Rose, *Struggle for Black Freedom*, 63–65; Goldfield, *Black, White, and Southern*, 45–49; and "Masquerade Is Over," 179.

16. *Atlanta Daily World*, 17 May 1939, 1; *Indianapolis Recorder*, 20 May 1939, 16; and *U.S. v. Classic*, 313 U.S. 299 (1941). See also Connolly, *World More Concrete*, 173. I am not saying that all of South Florida journalism was uniformly activist. The *Palm Beach Record* also functioned as an SNS paper from 1939 to 1940 and did not engage in that kind of radicalism. *Atlanta Daily World*, 29 April 1940, 1, 3 May 1940, 6.

17. Shofner, "Florida," 112–113.

18. *Tropical Dispatch*, 11 May 1940, 8 (available from the Black Archives History and Research Foundation of South Florida, Miami); and *Atlanta Daily World*, 2 October 1941, 1, 3 October 1941, 2.

19. *Atlanta Daily World*, 11 January 1942, 1, 21 February 1942, 1, 18 January 1943, 6 (quote), 3 March 1944, 2, 3 September 1944, 4 (quote), 8 September 1944, 1, 3 November 1945, 4.

20. *Atlanta Daily World*, 4 October 1946, 4.
21. *Tropical Dispatch*, 14 April 1945, 1, 19 January 1946, 8.
22. *Tropical Dispatch*, 8 June 1946, 8.
23. *Tropical Dispatch*, 13 March 1946, 1.
24. *Tropical Dispatch*, 10 August 1946, 8, 17 August 1946, 1, 14 September 1946, 1.
25. *Tropical Dispatch*, 28 February 1948, 1.
26. *Tropical Dispatch*, 27 March 1948, 1.
27. *Tropical Dispatch*, 15 June 1948, 8.
28. The paper welcomed to the city a new Black entertainment periodical, *Nite-Life*, which promised that "its efforts will not be worthy of competitive seriousness." The new paper was edited by Stanley Sweeting and Charles C. North, and its masthead promised, "Not to Compete–But to Serve." Similarly, when Henry E. S. Reeves, publisher of the rival *Miami Times*, was honored in 1949 with a testimonial dinner, Daniel Francis was part of the committee to organize and publicize the event. *Tropical Dispatch*, 7 February 1948, 8, 26 March 1949, 1; *Miami Times*, 26 March 1949, 1; and *Nite-Life*, 16 October 1948, 2.
29. *Tropical Dispatch*, 26 March 1949, 4.
30. *Tropical Dispatch*, 19 February 1949, 1.
31. Francis was born in 1925 in the Caribbean. On 29 April 1946, he sailed from Nassau, Bahamas, to Miami aboard the SS *Captain Roberts*, and soon he had secured a position with the *Tropical Dispatch*. List or Manifest of Alien Passengers for the United States, SS Captain Roberts, list 18, 29 April 1946, Records of the Immigration and Naturalization Service, no. 85, Passenger Lists of Vessels Arriving at Miami, Florida, National Archives and Records Administration, Washington, D.C.
32. *Tropical Dispatch*, 7 February 1948, 1; and *Atlanta Daily World*, 15 May 1947, 4, 24 July 1947, 2, 17 September 1947, 5.
33. *Atlanta Daily World*, 26 October 1948, 4, 27 October 1948, 4.
34. *Atlanta Daily World*, 16 August 1934, 2, 20 November 1935, 2, 11 March 1949, 2.
35. *Atlanta Daily World*, 31 January 1947, 3.
36. *Atlanta Daily World*, 4 August 1948, 2, 11 March 1949, 6.
37. *Atlanta Daily World*, 17 October 1948, 1.
38. Shofner, "Florida," 112–113; *N. W. Ayer & Son's Directory, 1946*, 159; *N. W. Ayer & Son's Directory, 1947*, 165, 167; *N. W. Ayer & Son's Directory, 1948*, 169, 170; *N. W. Ayer & Son's Directory, 1949*, 172, 174; *N. W. Ayer & Son's Directory, 1950*, 174, 176; *N. W. Ayer & Son's Directory, 1951*, 175; *N. W. Ayer & Son's Directory, 1952*, 176; and *N. W. Ayer & Son's Directory, 1953*, 173. For more on the *Jacksonville Progressive News* and its time with the Syndicate, see chapter 6; *Atlanta Daily World*, 14 May 1946, 2; and Oak, *Negro Newspaper*, 154.
39. Shofner, "Florida," 111; and *Atlanta Daily World*, 31 August 1934, 5, 13 September 1934, 6 (quote), 8 October 1934, 1.
40. In the north of the state, the *Jacksonville Tribune*, another Syndicate paper, was edited by Florida attorney George G. DeVaughn, a close friend of the Atlanta group. DeVaughn was a strong writer, and prior to the creation of his *Tribune*, his work had appeared in larger papers, including the *Pittsburgh Courier*. After founding his own paper in Florida, DeVaughn began republishing some of his satirical writing from the *Courier*, featuring first-person accounts of "King Depression," "King Lynch," "King Inferiority Complex," "King Ingratitude," and "King Bossism." "I am King Lynch," one

of DeVaughn's soliloquies began, "one of the oldest and most brutal monarchs the world has ever known." It was certainly not new for Black commentators to castigate lynching, political machines, the Depression, or self-defeating Black attitudes and behaviors, but it was new to embody those things and denounce them as a first-person narrator.

In June 1934, the *Palm Beach Tribune* reported that Jacksonville resident Sylvanus H. Hart had brought suit against the county supervisor of registration to challenge the white primary. The Florida Supreme Court had already ruled against the white primary, and the *Tribune* reported on the efforts of locals and the Florida NAACP to end the practice in Jacksonville, one of its last bastions in the state. The Pensacola branch of the NAACP led by J. E. Sheppard, which was responsible for the Florida Supreme Court white primary case, sent lawyer J. E. Lenord to Jacksonville for Hart's case. *Atlanta Daily World*, 21 February 1934, 2, 6 March 1934, 2 (quote), 16 March 1934, 2, 6 April 1934, 2, 20 April 1934, 2, 13 June 1934, 1, 16 July 1934, 3. There is one edition of a *Jacksonville Tribune* that survives, but it is a white paper from 1939. See *Jacksonville Tribune*, 17 February 1939, 1 (available from Special and Area Studies Collections, George A. Smathers Libraries, University of Florida, Gainesville).

41. Shofner, "Florida," 111; Pride, "Register and History," 213; Fifteenth Census of the United States, 1930: Orlando City, Fla., sheet 8B; Florida Population Census, 1935, Orange County, Precinct 21, sheet 70; *Orlando City Directory and Orange County Gazetteer, 1928* (Orlando, Fla.: Miller Press, 1928), 137; *Orlando City Directory, 1932* (Orlando, Fla.: Miller Press, 1932), 129; *Orlando City Directory, 1936* (Jacksonville, Fla.: R. L. Polk & Co., 1936), 76; *Orlando City Directory, 1938* (Jacksonville, Fla.: R. L. Polk & Co., 1938), 72; *Atlanta Daily World*, 8 September 1935, A2, 28 March 1936, 1, 25 July 1936, A2, 29 January 1938, 4, 23 April 1938, 2, 30 August 1935, 1; and "Scott Newspaper Service, 1935." There was a *Florida Sun* emanating from Orlando beginning in 1924, but it was a white publication. See *Florida Sun*, 11 April 1925, 1 (available from Special and Area Studies Collections, George A. Smathers Libraries, University of Florida, Gainesville).

42. *Atlanta Daily World*, 19 December 1935, 1, 31 December 1935, 6, 16 March 1936, 1; "Scott Newspaper Service, 1936"; and "Scott Newspaper Service [syndicating service], 1937," OBV138, Atlanta Daily World Records, 1931–1996, Manuscript Collection no. 1092, Manuscript, Archives, and Rare Book Library, Emory University, Atlanta, Ga. (hereinafter "Scott Newspaper Service, 1937").

43. Grillo, *Black Cuban, Black American*, 3–17, quote 16. See also Lopez, *Unbecoming Blackness*, 214–216; Slate, *Colored Cosmopolitanism*, 153; "Scott Newspaper Service, 1935"; "Scott Newspaper Service, 1936"; and "Scott Newspaper Service, 1937."

44. Gerald Horne, *Rise and Fall*, 6–8.

45. The *Pensacola Courier* was still around as late as 1960, with a circulation of around four thousand. Nathaniel N. Baker was born on 30 May 1907 in Florida. From at least 1940 until 1960, he lived at 513 Reus Street with Cora, while serving as editor of the *Courier* and making an annual salary of $1,200. He died on 18 March 1960. Fifteenth Census of the United States, 1930: Pensacola City, Fla., sheet 22B; *Pensacola City Directory, 1936* (Jacksonville, Fla.: R. L. Polk & Co., 1936), 53; *Pensacola City Directory, 1938* (Jacksonville, Fla.: R. L. Polk & Co., 1938), 33; *Pensacola City Directory, 1946* (Richmond, Va.: R. L. Polk & Co., 1946), 43; *Pensacola City Directory, 1948* (Richmond, Va.: R. L. Polk & Co., 1948), 40; *Pensacola City Directory, 1950* (Rich-

mond, Va.: R. L. Polk & Co., 1950), 39; *Pensacola City Directory, 1954* (Richmond, Va.: R. L. Polk & Co., 1954), 241; *Pensacola City Directory, 1956* (Richmond, Va.: R. L. Polk & Co., 1956), 269; *Pensacola City Directory, 1957* (Richmond, Va.: R. L. Polk & Co., 1957), 35; Sixteenth Census of the United States, 1940: Pensacola, Fla., sheet 3B; Florida Population Census, 1945, Pensacola, Escambia County, Colored Race, Precinct 55; Shofner, "Florida," 110; and Pride, "Register and History," 213.

46. Brown-Nagin, *Courage to Dissent*, 87–88. Brown-Nagin also makes the case that this struggle led to the fight for school equalization, which became a pragmatic alternative to desegregation after *Brown*. See 88–113. For more on the fight for salary equalization, see Aiello, *Grapevine of the Black South*, 83–106.

47. *Atlanta Daily World*, 9 July 1941, 1, 9 April 1942, 1, 11 April 1944, 1. See also Kirk, "NAACP Campaign."

48. *Atlanta Daily World*, 25 August 1946, 4. For more on the lynchings, see Wexler, *Fire in a Canebrake*.

49. *Atlanta Daily World*, 5 September 1946, 4, 11 October 1946, 6. The location of Pensacola was significant. For at least a brief time in 1939, the Syndicate supported the *Colored Citizen*, another paper from the city. F. E. Washington had formed the *Colored Citizen* in 1918, but he always used 1913 as the year of its founding. Historian Jerrell H. Shofner has concluded that the paper was likely a continuation of the *Pensacola Brotherhood*, founded around 1910 by J. T. Spann. Its run with the SNS, however, was under the watch of Washington and seemed to only last through the summer of 1939. The *Colored Citizen* was a four-page weekly that kept its coverage to local civic dealings, church programs and updates, and the academic schedule at Florida A&M. Surviving editions include no syndicated stories, no controversial content, and no journalism that would be recognizable in the modern era as actual news. There were several Pensacola SNS datelines in June, however, and they fit with the pattern established by the *Citizen*'s competitor in Pensacola. One chronicled a local Black doctor leaving the city to "enter Harvard University to continue his studies in internal medicine. He enters there every two years to keep pace with the rapid changes and developments which scientific discoveries are adding to the medical profession." Another covered a "militant address" in the city given by Mary McLeod Bethune, a "noted educator and chairman of the Negro Division of the National Youth Administration." Her speech compared the plights of Black southerners and the Jews of Germany and advocated for "education and cooperation with one another." Washington edited his creation until at least 1942. When the paper closed its doors in 1965, Alberta Hannon was editing it. *Colored Citizen*, 26 May 1939, 1–4, 26 September 1941, 1–4 (available from the University of West Florida, Pensacola). The University of Florida lists an edition of the *Colored Citizen* from October 1948 in its collection, but that edition has been lost. *Atlanta Daily World*, 14 June 1939, 2, 17 June 1939, 1, 29 June 1939, 2; Shofner, "Florida," 104, 110; and Pride, "Register and History," 213.

50. *Chambers v. Florida*, 309 U.S. 227 (1940); Sullivan, *Lift Every Voice*, 247; and *Atlanta Daily World*, 30 December 1941, 2, 17 March 1942, 6.

51. *Atlanta Daily World*, 22 May 1942, 2.

52. Ibid.

53. *Atlanta Daily World*, 6 May 1944.

54. *Atlanta Daily World*, 20 February 1946, 6.

55. *Atlanta Daily World*, 14 May 1946, 2.

56. Davis Lee to Carl Murphy, 31 January 1940, Marshall:15:07, folder 72, Afro-American Newspapers Archives and Research Center, Baltimore, Md.

57. Sixteenth Census of the United States, 1940: West Palm Beach, Fla., sheet 17B; *West Palm Beach, Palm Beach, and Lake Worth City Directory, 1926* (West Palm Beach, Fla.: Clarified Directory Co., 1926), 654; and Shofner, "Florida," 110.

58. Correspondence from Loyal Compton, Press Secretary to Governor Fuller Warren, to Cullen E. McCoy, Editor of the Tallahassee Record Dispatch, 28 December 1951, Papers of Governor Fuller Warren, ser. 253, box 64, folder 6, State Archives of Florida, Tallahassee; and *Atlanta Daily World*, 1 March 1951, 4.

59. *Atlanta Daily World*, 22 January 1953, 4.

60. Shofner, "Florida," 111; and *Atlanta Daily World*, 14 February 1948, 2, 29 July 1948, 1, 27 May 1954, 4, 19 December 1954, 8, 24 July 1973, 2.

61. Doreski, *Writing America Black*, 61. Tolson quote, ibid.

62. *Atlanta Daily World*, 27 May 1954, 4. See Green, *Before His Time*.

63. King, *Devil in the Grove*, 103–108, 273–282.

Chapter 3. The Carolinas

1. Tindall, *South Carolina Negroes*, 150; and Hemmingway, "South Carolina," 291, 293 (quote), 297–298. Daniel Joseph Jenkins was born in 1864 in Buford Bridge, South Carolina, and lived in Charleston for fifty years. He served as president of the Orphans Aid Society and as the minister and president of Jenkins' Colored Orphanage. The orphanage ran entirely on "Faith and Voluntary Contributions" (Hemmingway, "South Carolina," 293). "Daniel Joseph Jenkins," file no. 10220, Standard Certificate of Death, State of South Carolina, Bureau of Vital Statistics, Columbia; *Charleston City Directory, 1893* (Charleston, S.C.: Southern Directory and Publishing Co., 1893), 430; *Charleston City Directory, 1895* (Charleston, S.C.: Lucas & Richardson Co., 1895), 433; *Charleston City Directory, 1904* (Charleston, S.C.: W. H. Walsh Directory Co., 1904), 440; *Walsh's 1924 Charleston City Directory* (Asheville, N.C.: Miller Press, 1924), 832; and Fifteenth Census of the United States, 1930: Charleston City, S.C., sheet 9B.

2. *Charleston Messenger*, 20 October 1917, 5 January 1918, 22 September 1928 (available from South Caroliniana Library, University of South Carolina, Columbia).

3. Fifteenth Census of the United States, 1930: Florence City, S.C., sheet 18A; Sixteenth Census of the United States, 1940: Florence City, S.C., sheet 15B; *Atlanta Daily World*, 4 November 1934, A3, 28 January 1934, 12; "Scott Newspaper Service [syndicating service], 1935," OBV136, Atlanta Daily World Records, 1931–1996, Manuscript Collection no. 1092, Manuscript, Archives, and Rare Book Library, Emory University, Atlanta, Ga. (hereinafter "Scott Newspaper Service, 1935"); and "Scott Newspaper Service [syndicating service], 1936," OBV137, ibid. (hereinafter "Scott Newspaper Service, 1936"). No editions of the *Pee Dee Weekly* survive. There was a paper published in nearby Bennettsville called the *Pee Dee Advocate*, but it was a white paper with a decidedly different outlook. See *Pee Dee Advocate*, 1 February 1934, 1 (available at South Caroliniana Library, University of South Carolina, Columbia).

4. For examples of the *Weekly*'s church and crime news, see *Atlanta Daily World*, 5 April 1934, 1, 21 April 1934, 2, 26 April 1934, 2, 2 November 1934, 1, 9 November 1934, 6, 30 November 1934, 6, 8 July 1935, 2.

5. *Atlanta Daily World*, 20 January 1934, 5.

6. Eugene Jack Smith was the "founder and editor" of the *Greenville World* and aimed, according to the Syndicate, "to place a copy of his paper on the door step of every home in S.C." In November 1934, the *World*'s business manager wrote a letter to the *Atlanta Daily World*, thanking the Syndicate for "the very fine way they have cooperated with us since we have been running the Greenville World." The letter praised "Mr. Scott," who "is always ready to correct any errors, and he does in a very kind way. We do appreciate everything that they have done for us, and with their continued cooperation, we are certain that the Greenville World will carry on." It did carry on, maintaining a modest circulation of between 500 and 750 copies. "Mr. Scott has a fine force of office ladies and workmen. They seem to work together, and we have been largely helped by this cooperative force, since they have been handling our paper." "Scott Newspaper Service, 1935"; "Eugene Jack Smith," serial no. 2156, order no. 1963, North Carolina World War II Draft Registration Cards, RG 147, box 339, Records of the Selective Service System, 1926–1975, National Archives Southeast Region, Atlanta, Ga.; *Greenville City Directory, 1935* (Richmond, Va.: Hill Directory Co., 1935), 703; *Greenville City Directory, 1941* (Richmond, Va.: Hill Directory Co., 1941), 354; and Hemmingway, "South Carolina," 296. Hemmingway is using Pride's "Register and History" and Behling's "South Carolina Negro Newspapers."

7. *Atlanta Daily World*, 7 July 1934, 6, 14 July 1934, 3.

8. *Atlanta Daily World*, 8 November 1934, 3, 9 November 1934, 4, 8 June 1935, 6.

9. The paper had a listed circulation of between 500 and 700 copies. "Scott Newspaper Service, 1935"; "Scott Newspaper Service, 1936"; and *Atlanta Daily World*, 30 August 1934, 2, 18 October 1934, 2, 16 February 1935, 1, 27 April 1935, 1.

10. *Atlanta Daily World*, 8 November 1934, 8.

11. Branch later became an insurance agent, then a grocer. *Atlanta Daily World*, 26 September 1935, 1, 20 January 1936, 4, 21 January 1936, 5, 7 February 1936, 2, 14 May 1936, 1; *Anderson City Directory, 1936* (Richmond, Va.: Hill Directory Co., 1936), 65; *Anderson City Directory, 1940* (Richmond, Va.: Hill Directory Co., 1940), 57; *Anderson City Directory, 1947–48* (Richmond, Va.: Hill Directory Co., 1947), 66; *Anderson City Directory, 1956* (Richmond, Va.: Hill Directory Co., 1956), 31; Pride, "Register and History," 347; "Scott Newspaper Service, 1935"; and "Scott Newspaper Service, 1936."

12. *Carolina Lighthouse*, 14 May 1939, 1, 3, 8 (available from South Caroliniana Library, University of South Carolina, Columbia).

13. Pride, "Register and History," 348. For more on Davis Lee, see Aiello, *Grapevine of the Black South*, 140–159.

14. *Columbia City Directory, 1943* (Richmond, Va.: Hill Directory Co., 1943), 579; *Columbia City Directory, 1948* (Richmond, Va.: Hill Directory Co., 1948), 499; *Columbia City Directory, 1953* (Richmond, Va.: Hill Directory Co., 1953), 453; *Columbia City Directory, 1956* (Richmond, Va.: Hill Directory Co., 1956), 508; McCray, "World Peace"; McCray, "In Defense of Student Education"; McCray, "Talladega Beauties"; McCray, "Arraignment of Student Inertia"; and Interview with John McCray.

15. Lau, *Democracy Rising*, 136–144; Egerton, *Speak Now against the Day*, 227–228, 287–288; Clayton and Salmond, *Southern History*, 68; and McGuire, "It Was Like All," 909, 930.

16. Bedingfield, "John H. McCray, Accom[m]odationism," 91 (quotes); and Hemmingway, "South Carolina," 291, 293. See also Bedingfield, *Newspaper Wars*.

17. Hemmingway, "South Carolina," 301; Egerton, *Speak Now against the Day*, 549–

550; Crespino, *Strom Thurmond's America*, 92–93; *Spartanburg Herald*, 20 June 1950, 1; and "Greenwood County, S.C. (libel case), 1950–1959," folders 45–47, box 4, John Henry McCray Papers, R1347–R1364, South Caroliniana Library, University of South Carolina, Columbia.

18. *Atlanta Daily World*, 1 May 1942, 6.

19. Olin D. Johnston to John H. McCray, 20 March 1943, R1347A (45), John H. McCray Papers, 11294, South Caroliniana Library, University of South Carolina, Columbia. Similar correspondence arrived from the mayor of Columbia. Fred D. Marshall to John H. McCray, 20 March 1943, ibid.

20. Jesse E. Beard to John H. McCray, 12 October 1942, Rebecca E. Louis to John H. McCray, 6 December 1942, J. Clarence Colclough to John H. McCray, 5 April 1943, and J. B. Drake to John McCray, 7 May 1943, all in R1347A (41–44), John H. McCray Papers, 11294, South Caroliniana Library, University of South Carolina, Columbia.

21. W. H. Knight to John McCray, 22 June 1943, R1347A (41–44), John H. McCray Papers, 11294, South Caroliniana Library, University of South Carolina, Columbia.

22. *Lighthouse and Informer*, circular letter, 23 August 1943, and C. A. Scott to John McCray, 2 September 1943, R1347A (41–44), John H. McCray Papers, 11294, South Caroliniana Library, University of South Carolina, Columbia.

23. *Atlanta Daily World*, 27 January 1944, 6, 21 April 1944, 1.

24. "Explanation of the Plan for 'Beating the Primary,'" A. J. Clement Jr. to John McCray, 15 April 1944, J. Bates Gerald to John H. McCray, 25 and 30 April 1944, all in R1347A (41–44), John H. McCray Papers, 11294, South Caroliniana Library, University of South Carolina, Columbia.

25. "The Lighthouse and Informer, 1944 Policies and Programs," R1347A (41–44), and Ira De A. Reid to John H. McCray, 6 June 1945, R1347A (45), John H. McCray Papers, 11294, South Caroliniana Library, University of South Carolina, Columbia.

26. C. A. Scott and Carter Wesley, NNPA circular letter, 5 March 1945, John H. McCray and C. A. Scott, 10 March 1945, and C. A. Scott, "Combined Report of the Southern and Western Vice-Presidents: Minutes of the Limited War-Time Conference of the NNPA," 27–29 July 1945, all in R1347A (45), John H. McCray Papers, 11294, South Caroliniana Library, University of South Carolina, Columbia.

27. Totals calculated from "Circulation Analysis," R1347A (45), John H. McCray Papers, 11294, South Caroliniana Library, University of South Carolina, Columbia.

28. John H. McCray to James J. Foster, 3 March 1945, John H. McCray to James W. Nesmith, 3 March 1945, and John H. McCray to Gibb G. Dorsey, 18 April 1945, all in R1347A (45), John H. McCray Papers, 11294, South Caroliniana Library, University of South Carolina, Columbia.

29. Joe Louis to John H. McCray, 14 December 1945, R1347A (45), John H. McCray Papers, 11294, South Caroliniana Library, University of South Carolina, Columbia. Other southern editors were also praised. At the August 1941 African Methodist Episcopal (AME) Sunday School Convention in Shreveport, Louisiana, for example, the presiding bishop praised the Reverend S. L. Jones for his editorship of the *Shreveport World*, another Syndicate paper, citing "his crusading efforts in promoting interracial goodwill and the outstanding work done here thru his efforts as publisher of the state's leading Negro paper." Jones's paper covered that convention. "The black man is not afraid of Hitler, Mussolini, or Japan," the bishop argued, "but is afraid of what America may do to [him] from within." The paper's account was sure to mention that

the minister "paid high tribute to the editor and manager of the Shreveport World, Rev. S. L. Jones." It wasn't Joe Louis, but the acknowledgment mattered to Jones. *Atlanta Daily World*, 29 July 1940, 3, 22 August 1941, 2.

30. Behling, "South Carolina Negro Newspapers," 80; and Hemmingway, "South Carolina," 291, 293.

31. Secrest, "In Black and White," 100.

32. "The Newspaper employed what William Gamson has identified as a 'collective action frame' to spur black political engagement," Bedingfield explained. Bedingfield, "John H. McCray, Accom[m]odationism," 91. For more on Gamson's collective action frames, see Gamson and Wolfsfeld, "Movements and Media."

33. *Atlanta Daily World*, 26 October 1945, 6.

34. *Atlanta Daily World*, 23 November 1945, 6.

35. *Atlanta Daily World*, 1 January 1946, 6.

36. *Atlanta Daily World*, 25 January 1946, 6.

37. *Lighthouse and Informer*, 19 January 1947, 8 (available from the South Caroliniana Library, University of South Carolina, Columbia). This was a common tactic for McCray. Later that year, he used the successful hiring of Black policemen in Miami, Tampa, St. Petersburg, Daytona Beach, and Ocala as a demonstration that Black policemen should be hired in South Carolina. He did the same thing in May when Savannah hired its first Black policemen. *Lighthouse and Informer*, 14 March 1947, 8, 18 May 1947, 8 (ibid.).

38. *Lighthouse and Informer*, 2 February 1947, 1, 9 February 1947, 8, 2 March 1947, 1, 25 May 1947, 8.

39. The attack is now infamous as South Carolina's "last lynching." *Lighthouse and Informer*, 2 March 1947, 1, 8, 14 March 1947, 1, 8, 4 May 1947, 1, 18 May 1947, 1, 8, 1 June 1947, 1; and "South Carolina: Trial by Jury," *Time*, 26 May 1947, 27.

40. *Lighthouse and Informer*, 1 June 1947, 8.

41. *Lighthouse and Informer*, 27 April 1947, 8. Despite the Southern Regional Council's problematic racial positions, it did work to document the Black press. See Durr, *Negro Press*.

42. The historiography on the life and career of Jackie Robinson is voluminous, but in particular see Eig, *Opening Day*; Lamb, *Blackout*; Long, *First Class Citizenship*; Rampersad, *Jackie Robinson*; and Tygiel, *Baseball's Great Experiment*.

43. *Lighthouse and Informer*, 13 April 1947, 7, 27 April 1947, 7, 8, 4 May 1947, 7, 11 May 1947, 7, 18 May 1947, 7, 25 May 1947, 6, 15 June 1947, 6. The paper was just as excited in July when Larry Doby signed a contract with the Cleveland Indians, demonstrating that Robinson had been the beginning of change rather than the exception to an established rule. *Lighthouse and Informer*, 13 July 1947, 7.

44. Simons, "Jackie Robinson," 54–55, quote 54.

45. Brian Carroll, *When to Stop the Cheering?*, 2–17, quote 4. By 1978 only 3.95 percent of employees of U.S. daily newspapers were minorities, and just over half of those workers were Black. Biagi and Kern-Foxworth, *Facing Difference*, 149–151.

46. For more on the death of the Negro Leagues, see Lanctot, *Negro League Baseball*, among many others.

47. *Lighthouse and Informer*, 11 May 1947, 8.

48. *Atlanta Daily World*, 14 May 1948, 4; Egerton, *Speak Now against the Day*, 497; and Frederickson, *Dixiecrat Revolt*.

49. *Lighthouse and Informer*, 5 March 1949, 1, 2, 5.

50. Egerton, *Speak Now against the Day*, 549–550; and Crespino, *Strom Thurmond's America*, 92–93.

51. Cora L. Bennett, "Henry Houston (Negro Newspaperman)," 29 August 1939, U.S. Works Progress Administration, Federal Writers' Project, Folklore Project, Life Histories, 1936–1939, Manuscript Division, Library of Congress, Washington, D.C., http://www.loc.gov/item/wpalh001755/, accessed 30 October 2014; Sixteenth Census of the United States, 1940: Charlotte, N.C., sheet 13A; "Houston, Henry," Certificate of Death, 11 August 1952, 17297, North Carolina State Board of Health, Bureau of Vital Statistics, Charlotte; and *Charlotte City Directory, 1932* (Richmond, Va.: Hill Directory Co., 1932), 270.

52. Bennett, "Henry Houston (Negro Newspaperman)." According to Ayer, the paper's circulation began at roughly 2,500 and finished in the late 1940s at just over 3,000, with a high of 4,260 during World War II. Those numbers, however, seem inflated. Syndicate records list the paper's 1935 and 1936 circulation at between 300 and 400. Certainly, a weekly circulation of 42,000 was vastly inflated. *N. W. Ayer & Son's Directory, 1933*, 694; *N. W. Ayer & Son's Directory, 1938*, 664; *N. W. Ayer & Son's Directory, 1941*, 699; *N. W. Ayer & Son's Directory, 1944*, 675; *N. W. Ayer & Son's Directory, 1946*, 681; *N. W. Ayer & Son's Directory, 1948*, 728; "Scott Newspaper Service, 1935"; "Scott Newspaper Service, 1936"; and "Scott Newspaper Service, 1937."

53. *Afro-American*, 26 July 1952, 5; and *Atlanta Daily World*, 22 September 1932, A1.

54. *Atlanta Daily World*, 16 July 1935, 1, 20 July 1935, 1, 23 July 1935, 1. For more on the plight of Black Charlotte during this period, see Newkirk, "Development of the National Association"; and Willie J. Griffin, "Indigenous Civil Rights Movement."

55. Covington and Ellis, *North Carolina Century*, 318–320.

56. Suggs and Duncan, "North Carolina," 267. While the paper faltered for several months in 1930 as a result of the early throes of the Depression, it returned in October of that year.

57. In 1940, Paul fully took over the *Tribune* from his mentor, changing its name to the *Carolinian* and maintaining its strength through the civil rights movement. Paul Jervay married Brenda Yancey of Atlanta, and his father-in-law, A. H. Yancey, helped finance the purchase of land for a new operations building in 1954. Covington and Ellis, *North Carolina Century*, 318–320; and Suggs and Duncan, "North Carolina," 267.

58. The *Journal* was so uncompromising that in 1973, a white supremacist named Lawrence Little bombed the paper's headquarters. Both the *Wilmington Journal* and the *Carolinian* survived into the twenty-first century. Covington and Ellis, *North Carolina Century*, 318–320; "Jervay, T. C."; "The History of R. S. Jervay Printers, the *Cape Fear Journal* and the *Wilmington Journal*," *Wilmington Journal*, 5 June 2008, 2C; and Suggs and Duncan, "North Carolina," 267.

59. *Atlanta Daily World*, 26 December 1941, 1; and *Cape Fear Journal*, 4 September 1943, 1–8 (available from the Office of Archives and History, State Archives of North Carolina, Raleigh).

60. Gershenhorn, *Louis Austin*, 21–23; Suggs and Duncan, "North Carolina," 267–269; Gilmore, *Defying Dixie*, 19; and *Atlanta Daily World*, 4 August 1932, A2, 30 August 1932, A6.

61. *Atlanta Daily World*, 22 November 1932, A6. Many editions of the *Carolina Times* survive, but none from the period of its association with the Syndicate. Still, later issues, beginning in 1937, demonstrate a similar fighting position from the paper and its editor against terroristic race violence. See, for example, *Carolina Times*,

12 June 1937, 1, 2, 17 July 1937, 1, 2, 13 November 1937, 1, 2. Editions survive from 1937 to the 1980s. Historian Glenda Gilmore describes a radical *Times*, still led by Louis Austin, that published editorials by communist organizer Don West and fought vigorously to desegregate several programs at the University of North Carolina. Gilmore, *Defying Dixie*, 202, 213, 255–260, 262, 264–273, 280, 284–285.

62. *Atlanta Daily World*, 15 February 1934, 4. Though the *Times* ceased to be part of the Syndicate, Austin and his newspaper continued to be a loud voice for Black rights in North Carolina through the classical civil rights movement. Gershenhorn, *Louis Austin*, 60–207.

63. *Atlanta Daily World*, 10 March 1934, 1; and *Southern Worker*, 25 March 1934, 2.

64. Spaulding was born in 1874 in Columbus County, North Carolina, descended from a family that had been free for generations. Spaulding left for Durham in 1894, completed high school, and became the manager of a Black grocery cooperative in 1898. His success there won him a managerial position two years later at another business founded in 1898, North Carolina Mutual Life. That company was founded by seven Black businessmen in Durham as the North Carolina Mutual and Provident Association, each investing fifty dollars. One of the founders, A. M. Moore, was Spaulding's uncle, with whom he lived while finishing his studies in Durham. The fledgling outfit was on the brink of failure when Spaulding began as a manager (he was actually the company's only employee at the time), but he turned its fortunes. He expanded throughout the state, then into South Carolina and eleven other states, making it the largest Black insurer and the largest Black business in the entire country. In 1919, he renamed the venture the North Carolina Mutual Life Insurance Company, and he ran the business until his death in 1952. *Atlanta—You Ought to Know*, 22; Weare, "Charles Clinton Spaulding"; Marie Garrett, "Charles Clinton Spaulding"; and *New York Times*, 2 August 1952, 15. See also Kennedy, *North Carolina Mutual Story*; Weare, *Black Business*; and C. C. [Charles Clinton] Spaulding Papers, 1905–1985, Rare Book, Manuscript, and Special Collections Library, Duke University, Durham, N.C.

65. *Atlanta Daily World*, 15 October 1932, 6, 17 October 1932, A2, 23 October 1932, A1, A3.

66. *Atlanta Daily World*, 23 October 1932, B2, 28 October 1932, B2, 16 November 1932, A1, 26 November 1932, 6, 27 November 1932, 3, 7 January 1934, 8, 14 January 1934, 8, 28 January 1934, 8, 1 March 1934, 1, 30 June 1934, 1, 1 July 1934, 1, 30 August 1934, 1.

67. *Atlanta Daily World*, 9 February 1934, 6, 26 June 1934, 6.

68. Martinez was a devoted Republican, even working diligently for the reelection of Herbert Hoover in 1932. "The Rev. Martinez," said Ohio senator Simeon D. Fess, "in our campaign for the re-election of President Hoover, proved himself a speaker of much force and power." Like so many others, however, the work of Roosevelt would ultimately change Martinez's party affiliation. He returned to Memphis in the late 1930s and worked as a correspondent for both the ANP and the SNS's *Memphis World*. By that time, he was a loyal Democrat, a "staunch supporter of President Franklin D. Roosevelt and his New Deal Administration." He also worked for Governor Clyde R. Hoey's North Carolina Commission on Interracial Cooperation. *New Bern City Directory, 1937* (Charleston, S.C.: Baldwin Directory Co., 1937), 149; *Atlanta Daily World*, 21 January 1934, 10 (first quote in note), 2 December 1934, 10, 16 November 1938, 3 (second quote in note); "Scott Newspaper Service, 1935"; *N. W. Ayer & Son's Directory,*

1935, 676; *N. W. Ayer & Son's Directory, 1936*, 673, 827; and *N. W. Ayer & Son's Directory, 1937*, 678.

69. *Atlanta Daily World*, 3 January 1934, 6.

70. *Atlanta Daily World*, 8 August 1935, 6, 21 August 1935, 1, 28 August 1935, 6. The following year, for example, Martinez celebrated as a Craven County judge ordered an end to gambling in the region. *Atlanta Daily World*, 27 October 1936, 4.

71. *Atlanta Daily World*, 14 January 1937, 1, 13 September 1937, 1.

72. *Atlanta Daily World*, 20 August 1936, 6; *Greensboro City Directory, 1936* (Greensboro, N.C.: R. L. Polk & Co., 1936), 573; *Greensboro City Directory, 1937* (Greensboro, N.C.: R. L. Polk & Co., 1937), 24; *Greensboro City Directory, 1939* (Greensboro, N.C.: R. L. Polk & Co., 1939), 24; "Joseph L. Alexander," Certificate of Death, 21037, North Carolina State Board of Health, Bureau of Vital Statistics, North Carolina Death Certificates, 1909–1975, microfilm S.123, rolls 19–242, 280, 313–682, 1040–1297, North Carolina State Archives, Raleigh; and "Scott Newspaper Service, 1936."

73. Dyreson, "Jesse Owens"; and Dyreson, "American Ideas about Race." See also William J. Baker, *Jesse Owens*.

74. Welky, "Viking Girls, Mermaids," 36–38, quote 38. See also Dyreson, "Marketing National Identity."

75. *Atlanta Daily World*, 19 March 1937, 6, 21 June 1937, 6.

76. *Atlanta Daily World*, 16 December 1938, 6, 17 December 1938, 5, 22 December 1938, 5, 4 January 1939, 2, 10 February 1939, 2, 18 August 1939, 6, 9 November 1939, 6. In another instance in June 1940, the paper expressed consternation when Jones County officials announced "the startling information that not one Negro in the county is qualified to vote." *Atlanta Daily World*, 12 June 1940, 1.

77. *Atlanta Daily World*, 3 March 1939, 6, 14 April 1939, 3, 20 July 1939, 6.

Chapter 4. Alabama

1. Quote from Allen Woodrow Jones, "Alabama," 31. There was a *Selma Post* in the 1880s, which was either a Black paper or a white paper with Republican sympathies, but it was entirely separate from the 1934 *Post*. The *Dallas Post*, founded in 1884 by AME minister W. H. Mixon, was the first secular Black newspaper published in Selma and Dallas County, but it doesn't seem to have lasted very long. Mixon went on to found the *Pensacola Enterprise* in 1887. *Atlanta Daily World*, 25 March 1934, 3; Robinson, "Black New South," 190; Allen Woodrow Jones, "Alabama," 31; Shofner, "Florida," 103; Pride, "Register and History," 182; *Tuscaloosa Gazette*, 15 August 1889, 1; and Allen W. Jones, "Black Press," 220.

2. Agee and Evans, *Let Us Now Praise*; Brown, *Up before Daylight*; Flynt, *Poor but Proud*; and Kelly, *Hammer and Hoe*.

3. *Atlanta Daily World*, 20 January 1934, 2, 3 February 1934, 2, 22 July 1934, 11, 11 August 1935, A1; "Scott Newspaper Service [syndicating service], 1935," OBV136, Atlanta Daily World Records, 1931–1996, Manuscript Collection no. 1092, Manuscript, Archives, and Rare Book Library, Emory University, Atlanta, Ga. (hereinafter "Scott Newspaper Service, 1935"); "Scott Newspaper Service [syndicating service], 1936," OBV137, ibid. (hereinafter "Scott Newspaper Service, 1936"); and "Scott Newspaper Service [syndicating service], 1937," OBV138, ibid. (hereinafter "Scott Newspaper Service, 1937"). For more on the philological argument about the Americas' African origins, see Weiner, *Africa and the Discovery of America*, vols. 1–3.

4. *Atlanta Daily World*, 17 February 1934, 2, 15 July 1935, 6.

5. *Atlanta Daily World*, 14 April 1936, 2, 29 June 1935, 2.

6. Fourteenth Census of the United States, 1920: Mobile, Ala., sheet 16A; Sixteenth Census of the United States, 1940: Mobile, Ala., sheet 4B; *Mobile City Directory, 1926* (Birmingham, Ala.: R. L. Polk & Co., 1926), 637; and *Mobile City Directory, 1932* (Birmingham, Ala.: R. L. Polk & Co., 1932), 585. The paper under its various names lasted for more than twenty years. The *Mobile Weekly Press*, edited by A. N. Johnson, actively opposed disfranchisement laws and urged the citizens of Mobile to move away if they were enacted. The paper collapsed during the Depression, combined with the *Forum*, and then eventually became the *Press Forum Sun*. Suggs, "Origins of the Black Press," 4; Allen Woodrow Jones, "Alabama," 38; and Suggs, "Conclusion," 427.

7. *Atlanta Daily World*, 12 December 1936, 2, 8 May 1937, 4.

8. The editor of the original *Press Forum* was C. W. Allen; its tagline was "A Square Deal for All the People." *Mobile Press Forum Weekly*, 9 November 1929, 1, 24 October 1931, 2, 29 October 1932, 2, 12 November 1932, 1. *Press Forum* editions exist sporadically from 1929 to 1934 (available from the Alabama Department of Archives and History, Montgomery). A 1941 edition of the *Press Forum Sun* survives as well. Though it was published after the paper had ended its relationship with the Syndicate, it demonstrates that the nonconfrontational bent emerging from the merger had not gone away. Allen was by 1941 listed as the president of the paper, C. E. Vaughn was the business manager, and H. R. Williams was the editor. *Mobile Press Forum Sun*, 17 January 1941, 1–4 (available from the Alabama Department of Archives and History, Montgomery).

9. Allen Woodrow Jones, "Alabama," 43–44; *Montgomery City Directory, 1928* (Richmond, Va.: R. L. Polk & Co., 1928), 276; *Montgomery City Directory, 1929* (Birmingham, Ala.: R. L. Polk & Co., 1929), 258; *Montgomery City Directory, 1931* (Birmingham, Ala.: R. L. Polk & Co., 1931), 287; *Montgomery City Directory, 1933* (Birmingham, Ala.: R. L. Polk & Co., 1933), 217; *Montgomery City Directory, 1935* (Birmingham, Ala.: R. L. Polk & Co., 1935), 250; Fifteenth Census of the United States, 1930: Montgomery City, Ala., sheet 18A; "Scott Newspaper Service, 1935"; "Scott Newspaper Service, 1936"; and "Scott Newspaper Service, 1937."

10. In the 1934 Alabama Democratic primary, for example, leading Black officials (the president of Alabama State Teachers College and members of the Montgomery Civic League) attempted to vote and were refused. "Sentiment is in favor of bringing a test case in the courts to force the Democratic party to permit Negroes to vote in its primary," one article reported. *Atlanta Daily World*, 28 December 1932, A1, 3 February 1934, 2, 17 February 1934, 2, 11 May 1934, 1, 26 May 1934, 2, 8 August 1935, 1, 2, 21 September 1935, 1, 18 December 1935, 2.

11. Allen W. Jones, "Black Press," 216, 219, 225; Gatson, *New South Creed*.

12. Roy Wright was also found guilty, but his age, twelve or thirteen, spared him from the death penalty. The other defendants were Olin Montgomery, Clarence Norris, Haywood Patterson, Ozie Powell, Willie Roberson, Charlie Weems, Eugene Williams, and Andy Wright. Dan T. Carter, *Scottsboro*, 3–50; and Norris and Washington, *Last of the Scottsboro Boys*, 17–26, 249. See also James Goodman, *Stories of Scottsboro*.

13. Dan T. Carter, *Scottsboro*, 51–103, 160–163; *Houston Informer*, 26 March 1932, 1, 30 April 1932, 8; *Oklahoma Black Dispatch*, 11 June 1932, 1, 2; Murray, "NAACP versus

the Communist Party"; Norris and Washington, *Last of the Scottsboro Boys*, 57–61; and *Atlanta Daily World*, 23 November 1932, A4, 29 June 1934, 1.

14. That same month, the Syndicate reported on the claim of Victoria Price, the Scottsboro accuser who had not recanted her statement (Bates had recanted her accusation), that she was offered $500 and later $1,000 to change her testimony. Two men were arrested for the crime in Nashville before being extradited to Montgomery. *Atlanta Daily World*, 4 October 1934, 6, 2 October 1934, 1, 17 November 1934, 1, 6 April 1935, 1, 16 June 1935, 1.

15. *Atlanta Daily World*, 24 September 1935, 1, 16 October 1935, 1, 24 October 1935, 2, 7 November 1935.

16. *Atlanta Daily World*, 9 January 1934, 1, 14 March 1934, 1, 21 March 1934, 1.

17. Hornsby, "Georgia," 128–129.

18. The *Tribune* was published by E. G. Jackson and in this early incarnation was edited by L. M. Haughton. Allen Woodrow Jones, "Alabama," 43–44; *N. W. Ayer & Son's Directory, 1937*, 41; and *N. W. Ayer & Son's Directory, 1938*, 41.

19. *Atlanta Daily World*, 27 May 1937, 1, 16 June 1937, 1.

20. They were not released, the defendants applied again in January 1940, and a hearing was scheduled for the following month. Again Heflin campaigned against them, and again they were denied. *Atlanta Daily World*, 23 March 1938, 1, 18 August 1938, 1, 1 November 1938, 1, 6 January 1940, 1, 24 January 1940, 1, 9 March 1940, 1.

21. *Atlanta Daily World*, 7 June 1937, 1.

22. For more on Dickson's relationship with Jackson, see Mangun, *Editor Emory O. Jackson*, 241; and Roberts and Klibanoff, *Race Beat*, 50.

23. Mangun, *Editor Emory O. Jackson*, 7–12; Allen Woodrow Jones, "Alabama," 44; Marty Stanton, "Emory Overton Jackson," in *Encyclopedia of Alabama*, http://www.encyclopediaofalabama.org/face/Article.jsp?id=h-1837, accessed 25 October 2014; and 1944 Desk Planner, box 7, Emory O. Jackson Papers, A423, Birmingham Civil Rights Institute, Birmingham, Ala.

24. Allen Woodrow Jones, "Alabama," 43, 44; and *Birmingham World*, 16 April 1933, 1. For Dadeville, see Beecher, "Sharecroppers Union in Alabama"; *New York Times*, 18 July 1931, 1; *Chicago Daily Tribune*, 18 July 1931, 3; *Tuscaloosa News*, 23 April 1933, 2; *Birmingham World*, 31 December 1932, 1, 7 January 1933, 1; *Birmingham Post*, 20 December 1932, 1; *Birmingham Age-Herald*, 20 December 1932, 1; and *Birmingham News*, 20 December 1932, 1.

25. Allen Woodrow Jones, "Alabama," 44–45; and *Birmingham World*, 21 May 1954, 1.

26. For more on Dickson's relationship with Jackson, see Mangun, *Editor Emory O. Jackson*, 241. There is a plaque dedicated to Emory O. Jackson at the former office of the *Birmingham World* at Seventeenth Street and Fourth Avenue North, placed there in 2012 after lobbying by Lovell Jackson, Emory's younger brother (who died in 2014).

27. *Atlanta Daily World*, 23 October 1939, 6; and Mangun, *Editor Emory O. Jackson*, 113–134.

28. *Atlanta Daily World*, 14 January 1940, 6; and Emory O. Jackson to John Anderson, 27 August 1948, box 6, Correspondence-NAACP, Emory O. Jackson Papers, A423, Birmingham Civil Rights Institute, Birmingham, Ala.

29. *Atlanta Daily World*, 24 April 1940, 2.

30. *Atlanta Daily World*, 31 March 1944, 1, 5 April 1944, 1.

31. "Bombing Report," in Periodicals (unnamed box), Emory O. Jackson Papers, A423, Birmingham Civil Rights Institute, Birmingham, Ala.; Eskew, *But for Birmingham*, 260–261; McWhorter, *Carry Me Home*, 95, 107, 274, 313; and *Atlanta Daily World*, 22 September 1945, 1. Jackson later initially supported the activism of groups like Martin Luther King Jr.'s Southern Christian Leadership Conference, but when the emphasis of such groups turned almost exclusively to integration, he stopped supporting them, arguing that voting rights and political power were the only way of securing long-term gains for Black rights.

32. Box–Subscribers, Emory O. Jackson Papers, A423, Birmingham Civil Rights Institute, Birmingham, Ala..

33. Emory O. Jackson to C. A. Scott, 21 and 31 July 1945, 1102.1.5.1, Birmingham World Office Files, Department of Archives and Manuscripts, Birmingham Public Library, Birmingham, Ala.; and Roberts and Klibanoff, *Race Beat*, 51. The United Sons of Dixie was founded during the war in nearby Chattanooga. The White Supremacy League was older, a creature of the resurgent Klan activity of the post–World War I era, founded in Indianapolis in January 1923. For more on the White Supremacy League, see Pierce, *Polite Protest*, 6–7.

34. Emory O. Jackson to C. A. Scott, n.d., 1102.1.5.1, Birmingham World Office Files, Department of Archives and Manuscripts, Birmingham Public Library, Birmingham, Ala.

35. Theron L. Caudle to Emory O. Jackson, 21 March 1946, Bernice E. Brile to Emory O. Jackson, 20 February 1946, Herbert Brownell to Birmingham World, 11 February 1946, all in 1102.29.1, Birmingham World Office Files, Department of Archives and Manuscripts, Birmingham Public Library, Birmingham, Ala.; and Alabama State Teachers Association, "Report of Committee on Resolutions and Legislation," 28 March 1947, box 1, Emory O. Jackson Papers, A423, Birmingham Civil Rights Institute, Birmingham, Ala.

36. J. Earle Hensley to Emory O. Jackson, 26 August 1946, 1102.29.1, and "Are These Your Customers?," 1102.38.2, both in Birmingham World Office Files, Department of Archives and Manuscripts, Birmingham Public Library, Birmingham, Ala.

37. Memorandum: SAC, Birmingham, to Director, FBI, 17 July 1946, FBI Headquarters file 100-HQ-345671, Federal Bureau of Investigation, Washington, D.C., Freedom of Information Act.

38. *Atlanta Daily World*, 29 April 1940, 1.

39. *Atlanta Daily World*, 29 April 1940, 1, 8 May 1940, 2.

40. *Atlanta Daily World*, 15 March 1941, 1.

41. *Atlanta Daily World*, 17 March 1941, 1, 18 March 1941, 2, 19 August 1941, 2.

42. *Atlanta Daily World*, 22 May 1941, 6, 10 June 1941, 2.

43. *Atlanta Daily World*, 10 July 1941, 1.

44. *Atlanta Daily World*, 10 August 1942, 3.

45. *Atlanta Daily World*, 13 October 1942, 6.

46. McGuire, *At the Dark End*, 13, 25–38, 55–56, quote 26.

47. There were, unfortunately, plenty of chances for Jackson to work for justice against sexual violence. He also used his paper to demand action in the rape cases of Viola White in 1946 and Gertrude Perkins in 1949. McGuire, "It Was Like All," 911. He continued his activism in the next decade, using his paper to urge action during the Montgomery bus boycott. Thornton, *Dividing Lines*, 602.

48. McGuire, *At the Dark End*, 6–39, quote 39; and *Atlanta Daily World*, 19 September 1945, 6.

49. Memorandum: SAC, Birmingham, to Director, FBI, 17 July 1946, FBI Headquarters file 100-HQ-345671, Federal Bureau of Investigation, Washington, D.C., Freedom of Information Act. Jackson subscribed to the *Worker* in 1945, according to "an informant whose reliability is unquestioned." He was executive secretary of the Birmingham NAACP as of 1946.

50. "The wisest among my race understand that the agitation of questions of social equality is the extremest folly," said Washington (Aiello, *Battle for the Souls*, 39). Washington advised Black people to avoid politics, but he ignored his own advice. In 1896, he endorsed William McKinley over the populist Democrat William Jennings Bryan. He was close to McKinley's Republican successor, Theodore Roosevelt, even though Roosevelt subscribed to the theories of social Darwinism. Washington even had dinner at the White House in 1901, infuriating the white South. He tried to use his influence to convince Roosevelt to appoint Black nominees to political positions. He also tried to persuade railroad executives to improve conditions on segregated coaches, but this kind of action, like his work to eliminate grandfather clauses, he kept secret. For more on Washington's role as a self-proclaimed pragmatist, see Aiello, *Battle for the Souls*. For the *World*'s lack of Taylor coverage, see any *Birmingham World* edition from 5 September 1944 through 30 October 1944.

51. Lambert, *Battle of Ole Miss*, 51–52; and *Atlanta Daily World*, 30 January 1946, 1.

52. *Atlanta Daily World*, 29 September 1946, 1.

53. *Atlanta Daily World*, 3 January 1947, 1. A 1945 study made the case that the Black press's penchant to persuade was essentially a function of adult education, and almost all of the editors polled in the study agreed that one of the principal roles of the press was to educate readers. Lawson, "Adult Education Aspects."

54. *Atlanta Daily World*, 3 July 1947, 5, 25 September 1947, 4, 2 October 1947, 2, 6 January 1948, 4, 27 January 1948, 2, 4 February 1948, 2, 28 December 1948, 1; Foster, "Boswellianism"; Kirkland, "Mobile and the Boswell Amendment"; and Barnard, *Dixiecrats and Democrats*.

55. *Atlanta Daily World*, 5 August 1947, 4.

56. *Shelley v. Kraemer*, 334 U.S. 1 (1948); Henkin, "*Shelley v. Kraemer*"; *Tropical Dispatch*, 8 May 1948, 1; and Higginbotham, "Race, Sex, Education."

57. *Atlanta Daily World*, 5 May 1948, 6; and *Alabama Tribune*, 14 May 1948, 8; Brown-Nagin, *Courage to Dissent*, 69; and Gordon, *Georgia Negro*, 356. For the fight to apply the Supreme Court decisions to housing policy in Atlanta, see Brown-Nagin, *Courage to Dissent*, 69–82.

58. Weaver and Page, "Black Press and the Drive," 23; *Atlanta Daily World*, 21 January 1948, 6; and *Alabama Tribune*, 23 January 1948, 1, 8.

59. For an example of portraying the decision as a cop-out, see *Los Angeles Sentinel*, 26 February 1948, 7. For an example of the Democratic Party theory, see *Indianapolis Recorder*, 28 February 1948, 10.

60. *Atlanta Daily World*, 22 January 1948, 4, 24 February 1948, 2; and *Alabama Tribune*, 20 February 1948, 8, 27 February 1948, 1.

61. *Alabama Tribune*, 20 February 1948, 8, 27 February 1948, 1.

62. Sitkoff, "Harry Truman and the Election"; Busch, *Truman's Triumphs*; Donaldson, *Truman Defeats Dewey*; Divine, "Cold War and the Election"; Maze and White,

Henry A. Wallace; Culver and Hyde, *American Dreamer*; and Devine, *Henry Wallace's 1948 Presidential Campaign*.

63. Executive Order 9981: Establishing the President's Committee on Equality of Treatment and Opportunity in the Armed Services (1948); and Jon E. Taylor, *Freedom to Serve*, 87–119.

64. *Alabama Tribune*, 30 July 1948, 8.

65. Frederickson, *Dixiecrat Revolt*; Cohodas, *Strom Thurmond and the Politics*; and Buchanan, "Dixiecrat Rebellion."

66. *Atlanta Daily World*, 8 April 1948, 3, 19 October 1948, 1, 6 May 1949, 1; *Alabama Tribune*, 23 July 1948, 8, 13 August 1948, 8, 13 May 1948, 1; and Van Auken, "Negro Press," 431.

67. *Atlanta Daily World*, 14 May 1949, 6, 8 November 1949, 6.

68. *Atlanta Daily World*, 19 January 1950, 2; and Grafton and Permaloff, *Big Mules and Branchheads*, 161–176.

69. *Atlanta Daily World*, 2 August 1951, 1, 12 August 1951, 1, 17 September 1952, 4, 2 December 1952, 6.

70. *Atlanta Daily World*, 7 May 1954, 1, 14 September 1954, 1.

71. *Birmingham News*, 16 June 1946, A10; *Birmingham World*, 4 June 1946, 1; and Memorandum: SAC, Birmingham, to Director, FBI, 17 July 1946, FBI Headquarters file 100-HQ-345671, Federal Bureau of Investigation, Washington, D.C., Freedom of Information Act.

72. Memorandum: SAC, Birmingham, to Director, FBI, 17 July 1946, FBI Headquarters file 100-HQ-345671. Federal Bureau of Investigation, Washington, D.C., Freedom of Information Act. Communist-baiting the Southern Conference for Human Welfare was a common tactic and ultimately derailed the group in 1948. Goldfield, *Black, White, and Southern*, 70.

73. Memorandum: SAC, Birmingham, to Director, FBI, 17 July 1946, FBI Headquarters file 100-HQ-345671, Federal Bureau of Investigation, Washington, D.C., Freedom of Information Act.

74. Ibid. When Jackson wrote to the bureau in March 1954 asking for a copy of a J. Edgar Hoover article, an internal memorandum noted that a *Birmingham World* article by Cliff MacKay from 27 March 1942 had implied that there was racial discrimination in the FBI. (Hoover, "head of our esteemed G-Men," thus far "has refused to see the value of employing Negro agents." If that weren't bad enough, "by denying employment to one group of loyal Americans solely on the grounds of color, he lends himself a party to the unity-wrecking campaign of our enemies.") The memo also repeated the earlier claim that Jackson had been a member of the Communist Party in 1941. Leadership decided as a remedy to the conundrum to send Jackson a copy of the article, but to do so without a cover letter. Memorandum: M. A. Jones to Mr. Nichols, 25 March 1954, FBI Headquarters file 100-HQ-345671, Federal Bureau of Investigation, Washington, D.C., Freedom of Information Act; and *Birmingham World*, 27 March 1942, 7.

75. Emory O. Jackson to C. A. Scott, 4 October 1946, 6 December 1946, both in 1102.1.5.1, Birmingham World Office Files, Department of Archives and Manuscripts, Birmingham Public Library, Birmingham, Ala. Also in October 1946, Jackson complained to his brother Bernard E. Jackson—in his capacity as circulation director for the paper—that carrier routes had yet to be improved or systematized and no efforts

had been made to get new subscribers. Not only did Jackson have to deal with nepotism in the Scott enterprise, he had to deal with the consequences of his own nepotism. Emory O. Jackson to Bernard E. Jackson, 4 October 1946, 1102.1.5.4, ibid.

76. Emory O. Jackson to C. A. Scott, 1 July 1947, 12 September 1947, 3 December 1948, 13 May 1949, all in 1102.1.5.1, Birmingham World Office Files, Department of Archives and Manuscripts, Birmingham Public Library, Birmingham, Ala.

77. Thurgood Marshall to Emory O. Jackson, 30 September 1947, 1102.1.1.2, Birmingham World Office Files, Department of Archives and Manuscripts, Birmingham Public Library, Birmingham, Ala. See also Foster, "Boswellianism"; and Kirkland, "Mobile and the Boswell Amendment."

78. Conference of Alabama Branches of the NAACP, Minutes, "Here Is the Boswell Amendment (No. 4)," 1102.1.1.2, Birmingham World Office Files, Department of Archives and Manuscripts, Birmingham Public Library, Birmingham, Ala.; and *Tropical Dispatch*, 1 January 1949, 1.

79. *Birmingham World*, 17 September 1946, 1, 6, 27 September 1946, 1, 1 October 1946, 1, 29 October 1946, 1, 8, 1 November 1946, 1, 5 November 1946, 1, 8, 8 November 1946, 1.

80. Daniel E. Byrd to Emory O. Jackson, 20 February and 6 March 1947, Gloster B. Current to Emory O. Jackson, 12 and 21 March 1947, James Herndon to Emory O. Jackson, 24 February 1947, John H. Davis to Emory O. Jackson, 14 March 1947, Tommie Lucile Johnson to Emory O. Jackson, 22 March and 2 April 1947, W. W. Law to Emory O. Jackson, 27 March 1947, Emory O. Jackson to Frank, 28 April 1947, J. E. Pierce, circular letter, 30 April 1947, Walter White to Emory O. Jackson, 9 June 1947, Emory O. Jackson to Gloster B. Current, 10 April 1947, Gloster B. Current to Emory O. Jackson, 10 June 1947, L. C. Jamar to Emory O. Jackson, n.d., all in 1102.1.1.2, Birmingham World Office Files, Department of Archives and Manuscripts, Birmingham Public Library, Birmingham, Ala. Jackson was in constant contact with other rights leaders in the city. Robert Durr, who worked with Jackson on NAACP matters, was also the editor of the *Birmingham Weekly Review*, a direct competitor of the *Birmingham World*. This demonstrates that the competition between papers was not as important as racial progress. Robert Durr, Memorandum, Joint Committee Investigating Housing Shortage, 29 October 1947, 1102.1.1.15, Birmingham World Office Files, Department of Archives and Manuscripts, Birmingham Public Library, Birmingham, Ala.

81. Emory O. Jackson to Gloster Current, 10 April 1947, "5th Regional Headquarters, 3002 Danneel Street, New Orleans 15, Louisiana," both in 1102.1.1.2, Birmingham World Office Files, Department of Archives and Manuscripts, Birmingham Public Library, Birmingham, Ala.

82. Oliver Harrington to Emory O. Jackson, 8 May 1947, 1102.1.1.2, Birmingham World Office Files, Department of Archives and Manuscripts, Birmingham Public Library, Birmingham, Ala.

83. "The NAACP: Operation Suffrage," Annual Report, Secretary, Birmingham Branch, NAACP, 4 December 1947, 1102.1.1.2, Birmingham World Office Files, Department of Archives and Manuscripts, Birmingham Public Library, Birmingham, Ala.

84. Emory O. Jackson to James W. Morgan, 21 July 1947, 1102.1.4.4, Birmingham World Office Files, Department of Archives and Manuscripts, Birmingham Public Library, Birmingham, Ala.; and *Pittsburgh Courier*, 19 July 1947, 4. See also *Birmingham World* editions throughout July 1947.

85. The *Memphis World*, for its part, reported the Syndicate coverage from Birmingham. There were also problems in Montgomery, and the *Memphis World* ran the Syndicate's story from that city, written by correspondent Rosa Parks. Other than that, the *World* gave no editorial space to the controversy. Emory O. Jackson to Walter White, 9, 25, and 31 December 1947, Emory O. Jackson to John Lewis, n.d., Emory O. Jackson to Winthrop W. Aldrich, 22 December 1947, Walker C. Blount to Emory O. Jackson, 12 January 1948, all in 1102.1.1.15, Birmingham World Office Files, Department of Archives and Manuscripts, Birmingham Public Library, Birmingham, Ala.; and "Honor B'ham Editor for Civil Rights Fight," box 148, folder 10, Claude A. Barnett Papers: The Associated Negro Press, 1918–1967, pt. 2, Associated Negro Press Organizational Files, 1920–1966, Chicago Historical Society, Chicago, Ill. See also Laurie B. Green, *Battling the Plantation Mentality*, 118–129; John White, "Civil Rights in Conflict"; and Little, "Freedom Train."

86. *Birmingham World*, 19 December 1947, 1, 23 December 1947, 1, 8; and *Memphis World*, 16 December 1947, 1, 2, 4, 26 December 1947, 1, 8.

87. *Birmingham Age-Herald*, 30 January 1948, 1, 2; and Emory O. Jackson to Charles V. Hendley, 30 January 1948, 1102.1.1.13, Birmingham World Office Files, Department of Archives and Manuscripts, Birmingham Public Library, Birmingham, Ala. When Dothan, Alabama, hired its first Black policeman in May 1948, Jackson wrote to the town's police chief and asked for a statement "so that this very favorable publicity can rebound to the credit of our state." Emory O. Jackson to Eddie Kelley, 25 May 1948, ibid.

88. Emory O. Jackson to Louis A. Eckl, 24 February 1948, 1102.1.1.3, Birmingham World Office Files, Department of Archives and Manuscripts, Birmingham Public Library, Birmingham, Ala.; and Ottley, *"New World A-Coming,"* 279–280. The national push to capitalize the *N* in "Negro" began in the late 1920s, led by the Black press.

89. Emory O. Jackson to Editor of the Post, 27 February 1948, 1102.1.1.3, Birmingham World Office Files, Department of Archives and Manuscripts, Birmingham Public Library, Birmingham, Ala.

90. Emory O. Jackson, circular letter, April 1948, 1102.1.1.3, and "Law Enforcement Officers: Negro Homicides," box 9 (1940s), both in Birmingham World Office Files, Department of Archives and Manuscripts, Birmingham Public Library, Birmingham, Ala.

91. Emory O. Jackson to Walter White, 21 February 1948, Emory O. Jackson to Thurgood Marshall, 21 February 1948, both in 1102.1.1.3, Birmingham World Office Files, Department of Archives and Manuscripts, Birmingham Public Library, Birmingham, Ala.

92. Emory O. Jackson to John L. LeFlore, 9 July 1948, Thurgood Marshall to Emory O. Jackson, 13 July 1948 (quote 1), Thurgood Marshall to John L. LeFlore, 13 July 1948 (quote 2), George N. Leighton to Emory O. Jackson, 12 August 1948, all in 1102.1.1.3, Birmingham World Office Files, Department of Archives and Manuscripts, Birmingham Public Library, Birmingham, Ala.

93. Emory O. Jackson to Walter White, 22 May 1948, Emory O. Jackson to the Members of the Program Committee, Jefferson County Progressive Democratic Council, n.d., both in 1102.1.1.3, J. E. Pierce to Emory O. Jackson, 26 July 1948, 1102.1.1.21, all in Birmingham World Office Files, Department of Archives and Manuscripts, Birmingham Public Library, Birmingham, Ala.; and Roberts and Klibanoff, *Race Beat*, 51–52.

94. "Call and Challenge to Political Action," 9 September 1948, box 9 (1940s), Birmingham World Office Files, Department of Archives and Manuscripts, Birmingham Public Library, Birmingham, Ala.

95. Emory O. Jackson to L. A. Scott, 19 January and 2 February 1949, both in 1102.1.5.2, Birmingham World Office Files, Department of Archives and Manuscripts, Birmingham Public Library, Birmingham, Ala.

96. Emory O. Jackson to Gloster B. Current, 28 December 1949, 1102.1.1.3, Birmingham World Office Files, Department of Archives and Manuscripts, Birmingham Public Library, Birmingham, Ala. Jackson was a serial complainer and a serial resigner. In July 1949, for example, he stunned local NAACP members by resigning as secretary of the Birmingham branch. The executive committee, however, refused to accept his resignation, asking him to stay on for the rest of the calendar year. J. J. Green to Emory O. Jackson, 29 July 1949, ibid.

97. Advertisers, unnumbered box, Emory O. Jackson Papers, A423, Birmingham Civil Rights Institute, Birmingham, Ala.; Biow Company, Inc., to the Birmingham World, 6 April 1949, 20 June 1949, 2 May 1949, "Insertion Order: Interstate United Newspapers, Inc.," 18 April 1949, William G. Black to Emory O. Jackson, 10 March 1949, Biow Company, Inc., to the Birmingham World, 8 March 1949, 20 April 1949, all in 1102.28.9, Birmingham World Office Files, Department of Archives and Manuscripts, Birmingham Public Library, Birmingham, Ala. Advertising ran the gamut in the *Birmingham World*. In 1949, the Alabama Power Company advertised in the *World* for fish farming through the Extension Service of Auburn Polytechnic Institute. "6000 Places to Fish," 1102.28.14, ibid.

98. Louisville and Nashville Railroad Company, Alabama Intrastate Newspaper Advertising Contract, "Order for Advertising, 18 August 1949," Emory O. Jackson to Passenger Agent, L&N Ticket Office, 28 August 1948, both in 1102.28.10, Birmingham World Office Files, Department of Archives and Manuscripts, Birmingham Public Library, Birmingham, Ala.

99. Emory O. Jackson to Wallace Brothers & Company, 31 March 1949, 1102.28.15, and "Are These Your Customers?," 1102.38.2, both in Birmingham World Office Files, Department of Archives and Manuscripts, Birmingham Public Library, Birmingham, Ala. The paper charged five cents for Tuesday's edition and six cents for Friday's edition. Newsboys paid two and a half cents each on Tuesdays and three and a half cents on Fridays for the papers, then sold them for a profit. Emory O. Jackson to Samuel L. Reeve, 25 February 1949, 1102.28.15, ibid.

100. Emory O. Jackson to Sarah Simmons, 8 March 1949, Emory O. Jackson to Juan Lucianna, 24 June 1949, Emory O. Jackson to Ralph Hammond, 10 January 1949, all in 1102.28.15, Birmingham World Office Files, Department of Archives and Manuscripts, Birmingham Public Library, Birmingham, Ala.; Arthur Johnson to Emory O. Jackson, 15 January 1949, Paul R. Jones to Emory O. Jackson, 23 January 1949, Emory O. Jackson to W. C. Patton, 24 February 1949, all in 1102.1.1.3, ibid.; and Emory O. Jackson to Peggie Faulks Jones, 18 September 1952, 1102.29.14, ibid.

101. Alexander M. Campbell to Emory O. Jackson, 12 April 1949, 23 May 1949, 1102.1.4.1; Emory O. Jackson, A. C. Maclin, and J. J. Green to C. Floyd Eddins, 20 July 1949, Emory O. Jackson to Howard H. Sullinger, n.d., both in 1102.1.1.3, all in Birmingham World Office Files, Department of Archives and Manuscripts, Birmingham Public Library, Birmingham, Ala.

102. Emory O. Jackson to Roy Wilkins, 7 December 1949, 1102.1.1.3, Birmingham World Office Files, Department of Archives and Manuscripts, Birmingham Public Library, Birmingham, Ala.

103. Emory O. Jackson, circular letter to local pastors, n.d., Emory O. Jackson to John Temple Graves, 24 September 1949, both in 1102.1.1.3, Birmingham World Office Files, Department of Archives and Manuscripts, Birmingham Public Library, Birmingham, Ala.

104. *Birmingham World*, 16 August 1949, 1. This was perhaps the most sensational example of the paper's coverage, but the *World* covered the zoning fight throughout. See, for example, *Birmingham World*, 18 August 1949, 1, 8, 23 August 1949, 1, 6, 26 August 1949, 1, 8.

105. Emory O. Jackson, circular letter to local pastors, n.d., Emory O. Jackson to [unnamed], 9 August 1949, both in 1102.1.1.3, Birmingham World Office Files, Department of Archives and Manuscripts, Birmingham Public Library, Birmingham, Ala.

106. J. J. Green to Tom Clark, 13 August 1949, J. J. Green to Eugene (Bull) Connor, 15 August 1949, both in 1102.1.1.3, Birmingham World Office Files, Department of Archives and Manuscripts, Birmingham Public Library, Birmingham, Ala.; and *Birmingham World*, 16 August 1949, 1.

107. Emory O. Jackson to Anne Rutledge, 27 August 1949, 1460.1.1, Birmingham World Office Files, Department of Archives and Manuscripts, Birmingham Public Library, Birmingham, Ala.

108. Emory O. Jackson to Editor, *Birmingham News Age-Herald*, 13 February 1950, 1102.1.1.17, Birmingham World Office Files, Department of Archives and Manuscripts, Birmingham Public Library, Birmingham, Ala.

109. Emory O. Jackson to C. A. Scott, 6 July 1950, Emory O. Jackson to L. A. Scott, 8 August 1950, both in 1102.1.5.1, Birmingham World Office Files, Department of Archives and Manuscripts, Birmingham Public Library, Birmingham, Ala.; and 1951 Circulation Sheet, box 9, folder 33, Emory O. Jackson Papers, A423, Birmingham Civil Rights Institute, Birmingham, Ala. In September he forwarded a letter from a concerned national advertising agency to demonstrate that it wasn't just sibling rivalry or paranoia that drove his frustration. Emory O. Jackson to C. A. Scott, 11 September 1950, 1102.1.5.1, Birmingham World Office Files, Department of Archives and Manuscripts, Birmingham Public Library, Birmingham, Ala.

110. Numbers derived from "Birmingham World Financial Report," 17 August 1950, "Birmingham World Circulation Report, Week Ending Aug. 17, 1950, Delivery," "Birmingham World Circulation Report for Week Ending Thursday, August 17, 1950," all in 1102.28.11, Birmingham World Office Files, Department of Archives and Manuscripts, Birmingham Public Library, Birmingham, Ala. Additional autumn weekly circulation reports are in the same folder.

111. Emory O. Jackson to C. A. Scott, 21 November 1950, 1102.1.5.1, Birmingham World Office Files, Department of Archives and Manuscripts, Birmingham Public Library, Birmingham, Ala.

112. Emory O. Jackson to C. A. Scott, 7 February 1951, 1102.1.5.1, Emory O. Jackson to L. A. Scott, 12 February 1951, 1102.1.5.2, both in Birmingham World Office Files, Department of Archives and Manuscripts, Birmingham Public Library, Birmingham, Ala. Inquiries for advertising rates coming from outside the local area were run through the central office in Atlanta. Emory O. Jackson to C. A. Scott, 31 August 1951, 1102.1.5.1, ibid.

113. The ANP assigned numbers to each correspondent and included those numbers at the end of stories in releases. Jackson's number was 48. Claude A. Barnett to Naomi Rowe, 15 May 1946, Claude A. Barnett to Emory O. Jackson, 11 February 1947, Robert M. Ratcliffe to Emory O. Jackson, 15 January 1948, Emory O. Jackson to William G. Nunn, 12 July 1953, C. W. MacKay to Emory O. Jackson, 18 January 1952, all in 1102.1.3.9, Birmingham World Office Files, Department of Archives and Manuscripts, Birmingham Public Library, Birmingham, Ala.; John H. Sengstacke to Emory O. Jackson, 21 July 1944, 1102.1.3.12, ibid.; and John H. McCray to Emory O. Jackson, 9 December 1946, 1102.1.4.1, ibid.

114. Frank L. Stanley to All Members of the Association, 30 August 1945, 1102.1.3.12, Birmingham World Office Files, Department of Archives and Manuscripts, Birmingham Public Library, Birmingham, Ala.

115. Dowdal H. Davis to Emory O. Jackson, 28 May 1947, Thomas W. Young, National Negro Publishers Association, circular letter, 25 July 1947, both in 1102.1.3.12, Birmingham World Office Files, Department of Archives and Manuscripts, Birmingham Public Library, Birmingham, Ala.

116. Thomas W. Young to Members of NNPA, 23 October 1947, Thurgood Marshall, "Statement of Policy Concerning the NAACP Education Cases," September 1947, both in 1102.1.3.12, Birmingham World Office Files, Department of Archives and Manuscripts, Birmingham Public Library, Birmingham, Ala.

117. Carl Murphy to Thomas Young, 8 October 1947, 1102.1.3.12, Birmingham World Office Files, Department of Archives and Manuscripts, Birmingham Public Library, Birmingham, Ala.

118. President, Negro Newspaper Publishers Assoc. to Editor, *Norfolk Ledger-Dispatch*, 5 September 1948, Thomas W. Young to Emory O. Jackson, 1 October 1948, both in 1102.1.3.12, Birmingham World Office Files, Department of Archives and Manuscripts, Birmingham Public Library, Birmingham, Ala. For more on Davis Lee, see Aiello, *Grapevine of the Black South*, 140–159.

119. "Birmingham World Financial Report for Week Ending Thursday, August 14, 1952," 1102.28.12, Birmingham World Office Files, Department of Archives and Manuscripts, Birmingham Public Library, Birmingham, Ala. Additional weekly circulation reports for 1952 are in the same folder.

120. Emory O. Jackson to J. Howard McGrath, n.d., 1102.1.1.4, Emory O. Jackson to William Partlow Jr., 13 January 1950, 1102.1.1.17, both in Birmingham World Office Files, Department of Archives and Manuscripts, Birmingham Public Library, Birmingham, Ala.

121. Emory O. Jackson to Thurgood Marshall, n.d., "Statement of Mr. Zack L. Gunn," 17 July 1950, both in 1102.1.1.4, Birmingham World Office Files, Department of Archives and Manuscripts, Birmingham Public Library, Birmingham, Ala.

122. Emory O. Jackson to Carolyn Mardis, 15 October 1951, 1102.1.1.4, Birmingham World Office Files, Department of Archives and Manuscripts, Birmingham Public Library, Birmingham, Ala.

123. Emory O. Jackson and R. L. Alford to Laurie C. Battle, 12 January 1952, 1102.1.1.4, Birmingham World Office Files, Department of Archives and Manuscripts, Birmingham Public Library, Birmingham, Ala. Because of such problems, Jackson worked tirelessly for a new branch of the NAACP in Phenix City. Emory O. Jackson to Zack Warren, 2 April 1951, box 6, Correspondence-NAACP, Emory O. Jackson Papers, A423, Birmingham Civil Rights Institute, Birmingham, Ala.

124. Roberts and Klibanoff, *Race Beat*, 52, 128–130, 131. For more on the integration of the University of Alabama, see Clark, *Schoolhouse Door*.

125. C. A. Scott to Emory O. Jackson, 7 January 1953, Emory O. Jackson to C. A. Scott, 1 August 1953, both in 1102.1.5.1, Birmingham World Office Files, Department of Archives and Manuscripts, Birmingham Public Library, Birmingham, Ala.

126. William G. Nunn to Emory O. Jackson, 24 June 1953, C. G. Gomillion to Emory O. Jackson, 6 July 1953, and C. G. Gomillion, "Racial Differentials in Public Education in Alabama," all in 1102.1.1.16, Birmingham World Office Files, Department of Archives and Manuscripts, Birmingham Public Library, Birmingham, Ala.

127. "Birmingham World Financial Report for Week Ending Thursday, 8 April 1954," "Birmingham World Financial Report for Week Ending Thursday, 15 April 1954," "Birmingham World Financial Report for Week Ending Thursday, 6 May 1954," all in 1102.28.13, Birmingham World Office Files, Department of Archives and Manuscripts, Birmingham Public Library, Birmingham, Ala. Additional weekly circulation reports for 1954 are in the same folder.

128. Emory O. Jackson to C. A. Scott, 13 July 1953, 1 August 1953, C. A. Scott to Emory O. Jackson, 20 August 1953, all in 1102.1.5.1, Birmingham World Office Files, Department of Archives and Manuscripts, Birmingham Public Library, Birmingham, Ala.

129. C. A. Scott to Emory O. Jackson, 12 October 1953, 1102.1.5.1, Birmingham World Office Files, Department of Archives and Manuscripts, Birmingham Public Library, Birmingham, Ala.

130. Carl Murphy to Emory O. Jackson, 1 July 1953, 1102.1.1.5, Birmingham World Office Files, Department of Archives and Manuscripts, Birmingham Public Library, Birmingham, Ala.

131. Roy Wilkins to Emory O. Jackson, 14 August 1953, 1102.1.1.5, Birmingham World Office Files, Department of Archives and Manuscripts, Birmingham Public Library, Birmingham, Ala.

Chapter 5. Tennessee

1. *Nashville Independent*, 13 June 1931, 1, 11 July 1931, 1, 27 February 1932, 1 (available from the Tennessee State Library and Archives, Nashville). In the same month as the *World*'s founding and the *Independent*'s participation in the Syndicate, papers in Chattanooga, Tennessee, and Greenville, South Carolina, joined as well. The *Chattanooga Tribune* was a project of John E. Oakes, who moved the following year to Memphis to manage the *Memphis World*, another Syndicate paper. The *Carolina Enterprise* was the inheritor of the *Southern Enterprise*, a Black Greenville weekly published by C. C. Clarkson, which had begun in 1914. "Be Just and Fear Not: Let All the Ends Thou Aimest at Be Thy People," read the masthead. The *Southern Enterprise* was a six-page text-heavy weekly with no photographs; it emphasized church and civic news, supplemented by local advertising and nationally syndicated material. Though it is not the same paper as the later *Carolina Enterprise*, the similar names within a relatively close time frame clearly demonstrate at least some connection. There is also a legacy of Greenville *Enterprise*s going back to the 1870s. *Chattanooga City Directory, 1929* (Chattanooga, Tenn.: Connelly Directory Co., 1929), 1388; *Chattanooga City Directory, 1930* (Chattanooga, Tenn.: Rothberger Directory Co., 1930), 1428; *Memphis City Directory, 1932* (Memphis, Tenn.: R. L. Polk & Co., 1932), 795;

Memphis City Directory, 1934 (Memphis, Tenn.: R. L. Polk & Co., 1934), 730; *Memphis City Directory, 1935* (Memphis, Tenn.: R. L. Polk & Co., 1935), 745; "About the Southern Enterprise," Chronicling America, Historic American Newspapers, Library of Congress, http://chroniclingamerica.loc.gov/lccn/sn93067720/, accessed 24 October 2014; and *Southern Enterprise*, 6 March 1926, 1, 5 (available from South Caroliniana Library, University of South Carolina, Columbia).

2. Among that competition was the *Nashville Clarion*, which published for much of the early century, edited by E. W. D. Isaac. The market remained crowded throughout the 1930s, as rival syndicates also attempted to move into the city with short-lived papers. The *Nashville Defender*, for example, first appeared in May 1938, published by D. J. Fabree and "dedicated to economic equality and social justice for the Negro." *Nashville Clarion*, 18 April 1931, 1, 2; *Nashville Defender*, 5 May 1938; and Shannon, "Tennessee," 335.

3. *Atlanta Daily World*, 8 July 1932, A1, 18 March 1934, A1. The paper was listed in Syndicate records as the Nashville edition of the *Southern World* in 1935, managed by Jasper C. Horne. Born in North Carolina in 1897, Horne worked by 1930 as a line operator for a publishing plant in Nashville. He graduated by 1935 to managing the Nashville edition of the *Southern World*. *Pittsburgh Courier*, 5 August 1967, 2; Fifteenth Census of the United States, 1930: Nashville City, Tenn., sheet 82A; *Nashville City Directory, 1949* (St. Louis, Mo.: R. L. Polk & Co., 1949), 442; and "Scott Newspaper Service [syndicating service], 1935," OBV136, Atlanta Daily World Records, 1931–1996, Manuscript Collection no. 1092, Manuscript, Archives, and Rare Book Library, Emory University, Atlanta, Ga. (hereinafter "Scott Newspaper Service, 1935"). John R. Patterson grew up in Washington, D.C., before attending the University of Cincinnati and Prairie View College. After graduation, he worked at Tuskegee—where his brother Frederick Patterson soon became the school's president—before entering the newspaper business. In August 1934, Scott recalled Patterson to Atlanta to become assistant general manager and director of circulation for the *Atlanta Daily World*. He replaced W. C. Kelley. At the same time, C. A. appointed his brother L. A., a former principal, as general circulation manager for the Syndicate and general manager of the *Memphis World*. L. A. Scott, who attended Tennessee A&I in Nashville, was the general manager of the *Birmingham World* before moving into education. Patterson was replaced by Lloyd E. Heath (though Heath was gone by December). *Atlanta Daily World*, 19 August 1934, 1, 4 October 1934, 3, 12 December 1934, 3, 5 May 1935, 9; *Nashville City Directory, 1933* (St. Louis, Mo.: R. L. Polk & Co., 1933), 677; *N. W. Ayer & Son's Directory, 1934*, 863; "Scott Newspaper Service [syndicating service], 1936," OBV137, Atlanta Daily World Records, 1931–1996, Manuscript Collection no. 1092, Manuscript, Archives, and Rare Book Library, Emory University, Atlanta, Ga. (hereinafter"Scott Newspaper Service, 1936"); "Scott Newspaper Service [syndicating service], 1937," OBV138, ibid. (hereinafter "Scott Newspaper Service, 1937").

4. *Nashville World*, 1 September 1933, 1, 8, 14 June 1935, 1, 6 (available from the Tennessee State Library and Archives, Nashville).

5. *Atlanta Daily World*, 9 June 1936, 3, 19 June 1936, 4, 23 June 1936, 3, 15 July 1936, 3; *Indianapolis City Directory, 1918* (Indianapolis, Ind.: R. L. Polk & Co., 1918), 272; *Nashville City Directory, 1920* (Nashville, Tenn.: Marshall-Bruce-Polk Company, 1920), 94; *Nashville City Directory, 1926* (Nashville, Tenn.: Marshall-Bruce-Polk Company, 1926), 165; *Nashville City Directory, 1929* (St. Louis, Mo.: R. L. Polk & Co.,

1929), 212; *Nashville City Directory, 1930* (St. Louis, Mo.: R. L. Polk & Co., 1930), 225; *Nashville City Directory, 1931* (St. Louis, Mo.: R. L. Polk & Co., 1931), 209; and *Nashville City Directory, 1937* (St. Louis, Mo.: R. L. Polk & Co., 1937), 97.

    6. *Atlanta Daily World*, 10 May 1936, 1, 20 June 1936, 1, 26 June 1936, 1, 4 July 1936, 1, 16 July 1936, 1, 25 July 1936, 4, 14 October 1936, 2, 31 December 1936, 2, 28 January 1937, 1, 9 February 1937, 6.

    7. *Atlanta Daily World*, 30 November 1934, 6, 7 December 1934, 6, 8 May 1936, 6, 23 May 1936, 4, 28 August 1936, 6, 15 January 1937, 6.

    8. Goldfield, *Black, White, and Southern*, 27.

    9. *Memphis World*, 28 June 1931, 1, 3, 16 September 1931, 8, 9 February 1932, 1. During the Depression, financial problems forced the paper to move from three editions per week to two. Shannon, "Tennessee," 339–340. Though Swingler was a native Arkansan, he had spent much of his time in Lincoln, Nebraska, where he attended college. *Lincoln City Directory, 1927* (Detroit, Mich.: R. L. Polk & Co., 1927), 466; *Lincoln City Directory, 1931* (Kansas City, Mo.: R. L. Polk & Co., 1931), 453; *Polk's Memphis City Directory, 1932* (Memphis, Tenn.: R. L. Polk & Co., 1932), 997; *Polk's Memphis City Directory, 1935* (Memphis, Tenn.: R. L. Polk & Co., 1935), 947; *Polk's Memphis City Directory, 1938* (Memphis, Tenn.: R. L. Polk & Co., 1938), 986; *Polk's Memphis City Directory, 1939* (Memphis, Tenn.: R. L. Polk & Co., 1939), 926; *Polk's Memphis City Directory, 1940* (Memphis, Tenn.: R. L. Polk & Co., 1940), 876; and Sixteenth Census of the United States, 1940: Memphis, Tenn., sheet 1B.

    10. Shannon, "Tennessee," 340–341.

    11. *Memphis World*, 26 July 1931, 1, 8, 16 September 1931, 1, 22 March 1932, 8.

    12. *Memphis World*, 18 September 1931, 8.

    13. *Memphis World*, 15 April 1932, 1.

    14. Shannon, "Tennessee," 340.

    15. Ibid., 340–341.

    16. The *Recorder* was published by John Henderson. In August 1937, some of his students played at the junior program of the annual NAACP meeting in St. Louis. "Scott Newspaper Service, 1935"; "Scott Newspaper Service, 1936"; "Scott Newspaper Service, 1937"; *City Directory of Knoxville, Tenn. and Suburbs, 1909* (Knoxville, Tenn.: Knoxville Directory Co., 1909), 717; *Knoxville, Tenn. Directory, 1915* (Knoxville, Tenn.: Knoxville Directory Co., 1915), 244; *City Directory of Knoxville, 1921* (Knoxville, Tenn.: City Directory Company of Knoxville, 1921), 575; *Knoxville City Directory, 1927* (Knoxville, Tenn.: City Directory Co. of Knoxville, 1927), 834; *Knoxville City Directory, 1933* (Knoxville, Tenn.: City Directory Co. of Knoxville, 1933), 914; *Knoxville City Directory, 1938* (Knoxville, Tenn.: City Directory Co. of Knoxville, 1938), 978; Fifteenth Census of the United States, 1930: Knoxville City, Tenn., sheet 18A; and Sixteenth Census of the United States, 1940: Knoxville City, Tenn., sheet 61A.

    17. *Atlanta Daily World*, 29 December 1934, 4, 17 July 1935, 6, 19 August 1937, 2.

    18. *Atlanta Daily World*, 21 December 1935, 2.

    19. The paper was referring to the Costigan-Wagner Bill, an antilynching law submitted in 1934 by Senators Robert F. Wagner and Edward P. Costigan. *Atlanta Daily World*, 29 May 1936, 6, 16 October 1936, 6.

    20. Robinson began his career by working as a laborer for the Vesta Gas Range and Manufacturing Company in 1918, before becoming a janitor at Chattanooga City Hall and then a truant officer at the local board of education. This was not the typical

route to a career in journalism. *Atlanta Daily World*, 19 September 1936, 4, 8 October 1936, 6; "Interview with Clarence B. Robinson"; "Scott Newspaper Service, 1935"; "Scott Newspaper Service, 1936"; *Chattanooga City Directory, 1919* (Chattanooga, Tenn.: Connelly Directory Co., 1919), 653; *Chattanooga City Directory, 1927* (Chattanooga, Tenn.: Connelly Directory Co., 1927), 1658; *Chattanooga City Directory, 1931* (Chattanooga, Tenn.: Rothberger Directory Co., 1931), 1436; and *Chattanooga City Directory, 1942* (Chattanooga, Tenn.: Rothberger Directory Co., 1942), 1768.

21. *Atlanta Daily World*, 19 March 1935, 2; and Shannon, "Tennessee," 336–338. The article framed his defeat by titling its coverage "Walter Robinson Still Recognized as a Political Power in Chattanooga Despite Vote Loss." Robinson remained no stranger to self-aggrandizement in his newspaper reporting.

22. Shannon, "Tennessee," 338.

23. Ibid., 339; and *Atlanta Daily World*, 21 September 1936, 2, 14 November 1936, 2, 5 December 1936, 2.

24. *Atlanta Daily World*, 5 October 1936, 2.

25. *Atlanta Daily World*, 3 July 1937, 1, 28 August 1937, 8.

26. *Atlanta Daily World*, 1 February 1935, 6.

27. *Atlanta Daily World*, 13 April 1936, 1, 14 April 1936, 1, 26 June 1937, 8, 28 January 1938, 2.

28. *Atlanta Daily World*, 4 April 1938, 1; C. Alvin Hughes, "We Demand Our Rights"; and Richards, "Southern Negro Youth Congress."

29. *Atlanta Daily World*, 19 December 1938, 2.

30. *Atlanta Daily World*, 9 March 1935, 6, 21 April 1935, 6, 18 May 1935, 1, 7 July 1935, 1; *Jackson Tennessee Consurvey Directory, 1937* (Springfield, Ill.: Baldwin Consurvey Co., 1937), 402; *Jackson Tennessee Consurvey Directory, 1942* (Hebron, Nebr.: Mullin-Kille Co., 1942), 443; and "Scott Newspaper Service, 1935."

31. Wilson's partner in the endeavor was Curtis Wood, his classmate at Knoxville College. Its first issue appeared on Friday, May 27.

32. *Atlanta Daily World*, 26 May 1938, 2, 3 August 1938, 1, 12 August 1938, 2, 19 August 1938, 1, 20 August 1938, 4, 22 August 1938, 1, 23 August 1938, 1, 31 August 1938, 1.

33. Shannon, "Tennessee," 342–343.

34. Egerton, *Speak Now against the Day*, 363–365; Shannon, "Tennessee," 343; Beeler, "Race Riot in Columbia, Tennessee"; and O'Brien, *Color of the Law*, 78–88.

35. Shannon, "Tennessee," 344; and Egerton, *Speak Now against the Day*, 213–216. The *World* got its way. Randolph called off the march in return for Roosevelt's creation of the Fair Employment Practices Committee. Garfinkel, *When Negroes March*; Pfeffer, *A. Philip Randolph, Pioneer*; and Lucander, *Winning the War for Democracy*.

36. *Atlanta Daily World*, 2 September 1939, 6.

37. *Atlanta Daily World*, 29 April 1939, 1, 23 June 1939, 6, 27 May 1940, 1. The Young Men's Progressive Business Club was formed in the summer of 1939, and one of its founders declared that "too long have we been blind-folded here in Chattanooga, not knowing what we should do about the idea[l] type of manhood. Therefore, I can say that one of our objectives will be to fight the great prevailing ignorance among our people here in regard to real manhood." *Atlanta Daily World*, 7 July 1939, 2.

38. Egerton, *Speak Now against the Day*, 185–197; Aldon D. Morris, *Origins*, 167; and *Atlanta Daily World*, 17 April 1940, 1. See also Krueger, *And Promises to Keep*.

39. *Atlanta Daily World*, 15 April 1940, 1, 17 April 1940, 1.
40. *Atlanta Daily World*, 29 January 1941, 1.
41. *Atlanta Daily World*, 1 March 1941, 1.
42. *Atlanta Daily World*, 21 March 1942, 1.
43. *Atlanta Daily World*, 10 February 1943, 6, 8 May 1943, 6, 25 March 1944, 4.
44. *Smith v. Allwright*, 321 U.S. 649 (1944); *Plessy v. Ferguson*, 163 U.S. 537 (1896); *Williams v. Mississippi*, 170 U.S. 213 (1898); Klarman, "White Primary Rulings"; and Hine, *Black Victory*.
45. *Atlanta Daily World*, 14 April 1944, 4.
46. Shannon, "Tennessee," 335–336.
47. In 1913, Porter became the secretary of the National Negro Press Association. In 1920, he married community activist Drusilla Tandy Nixon. She was from Ohio, but met Porter while working in Atlanta. The pair had a child, Dorothy M. L. Porter, in February 1922 but divorced later that year, with Drusilla accusing Porter of beating and abusing her during her pregnancy. In the 1930s, he studied law at New York University (while still publishing the paper), and he established a law practice in Knoxville in 1938. For the next twelve years, he used his position to work for Black rights in Knoxville and beyond. He died in 1950. Booker, *History of Mechanicsville*, 23; and "Nixon, Drusilla Elizabeth Tandy," Texas State Historical Association, http://www.tshaonline.org/handbook/online/articles/fni18, accessed 2 March 2014.
48. There are several editions of the *East Tennessee News* that survive, most of them prior to Syndicate contact. My analysis is based on a comparison of the available editions. *East Tennessee News*, 26 March 1936, 31 March 1938, 5 May 1938, 14 October 1943 (available from the Tennessee State Library and Archives, Nashville).
49. *Atlanta Daily World*, 27 April 1939, 6.
50. *Atlanta Daily World*, 28 February 1940, 1, 9 April 1941, 1.
51. *Atlanta Daily World*, 25 July 1941, 6.
52. *Atlanta Daily World*, 15 June 1942, 6. Of course, the *Journal* editorialized in the same week that the state's reduction of the cost of the poll tax was a mistake. *Knoxville Journal*, 7 June 1942, 2, 9 June 1942, 4.
53. *Atlanta Daily World*, 20 February 1942, 1.
54. *Atlanta Daily World*, 17 June 1943, 6.
55. *Atlanta Daily World*, 21 September 1943, 6.
56. *Atlanta Daily World*, 27 September 1944, 6, 6 December 1944, 5.
57. *Atlanta Daily World*, 1 October 1943, 6.
58. *Atlanta Daily World*, 5 June 1946, 6.
59. *Memphis World*, 29 February 1944, 6, 31 August 1945, 6.
60. *Memphis World*, 1 March 1946, 1, 5 March 1946, 1, 5, 6, 8 March 1946, 8, 12 March 1946, 1.
61. *Memphis World*, 19 August 1947, 1, 6.
62. *Memphis World*, 6 August 1948, 8, 8 August 1948, 8, 2 August 1949, 6. None of the paper's records survive. There is a collection of photographs from the paper beginning in the early 1950s, but those photographs were taken by *World* photographers. The *World* was the author, not the subject, of the photos, and thus they provide little edification for a study of the newspaper itself. See Memphis World Photographs, MS.3181, Special Collections, University of Tennessee Libraries, Knoxville.
63. *N. W. Ayer & Son's Directory, 1932*, 902; *N. W. Ayer & Son's Directory, 1949*, 927; and *N. W. Ayer & Son's Directory, 1952*, 928.

64. *Memphis World*, 21 April 1950, 8, 15 August 1950, 8, 16 October 1951, 6.
65. Burma, "Analysis," 180; and Washburn, *African American Newspaper*, 182–186.
66. *Memphis World*, 26 June 1951, 1; Roberts and Klibanoff, *Race Beat*, 94–95; and Michaeli, *Defender*, 305–307. Swingler was replaced as editor by Chester M. Hampton. The *World*'s new manager was A. G. Shields, who formerly ran the *Arkansas World* in nearby Little Rock. Shannon, "Tennessee," 344–345. At the same time, Sengstacke bought the *New York Age*, a bastion of Black journalism.
67. *Tri-State Defender*, 3 November 1951, 6, 6 November 1951, 4.
68. Memorandum: SAC, Memphis to Director, FBI, 6 July 1953, FBI Headquarters file 100-HQ-404266, Federal Bureau of Investigation, Washington, D.C., Freedom of Information Act.
69. Ibid. See also "Negro Editors on Communism," 17, 119.
70. Memorandum: SAC, Atlanta to Director, FBI, 16 July 1953, FBI Headquarters file 100-HQ-404266, Federal Bureau of Investigation, Washington, D.C., Freedom of Information Act; and Goldfield, *Black, White, and Southern*, 50–51. For more on the Southern Conference for Human Welfare, see chapter 6.
71. Director, FBI to SAC, Memphis, 22 July 1953, FBI Headquarters file 100-HQ-404266, Federal Bureau of Investigation, Washington, D.C., Freedom of Information Act.
72. Shannon, "Tennessee," 346.
73. *Tri-State Defender*, 2 February 1952, 1, 4, 22 March 1952, 4, 21 June 1952, 1, 2, 5, 6, 23 August 1952, 4.
74. Shannon, "Tennessee," 336–338.
75. *Chattanooga Observer*, 4 July 1947, 8 (available from the Tennessee State Library and Archives, Nashville).
76. *Chattanooga Observer*, 25 July 1947, 1.
77. *Chattanooga Observer*, 1 August 1947, 1.
78. *Atlanta Daily World*, 20 July 1945, 2, 2 March 1946, 1, 31 July 1946, 1, 21 August 1946, 2, 4 February 1947, 6.
79. *Atlanta Daily World*, 20 November 1948, 3.
80. *Chattanooga Observer*, 16 April 1948, 1, 7 May 1948, 1; and *Shelley v. Kraemer*, 334 U.S. 1 (1948).
81. *Chattanooga Observer*, 30 July 1948, 1, 6 August 1948, 1, 20 August 1948, 1 (quote), 8 (quote), 31 December 1948, 1.
82. *Chattanooga Observer*, 3 December 1948, 1.
83. *Atlanta Daily World*, 14 August 1948, 1, 14 December 1948, 2.
84. *Chattanooga Observer*, 21 January 1949, 1, 4 February 1949, 1, 4 March 1949, 1, 11 March 1949, 8 (quote), 18 March 1949, 1.
85. Zangrando, *NAACP Crusade against Lynching*; Pinar, "NAACP and the Struggle"; Hixson, "Moorfield Storey and the Defense"; Harvey, "Constitutional Law"; and Wolters, *Negroes and the Great Depression*, 337–340.
86. *Atlanta Daily World*, 2 June 1951, 5, 10 December 1952, 1.
87. *Chattanooga Observer*, 20 April 1951, 8, 28 September 1952, 8.
88. *Atlanta Daily World*, 25 December 1952, A1, 29 January 1953, 2.
89. *Atlanta Daily World*, 10 April 1953, 4.
90. *Atlanta Daily World*, 12 August 1954, 6.
91. *Atlanta Daily World*, 21 October 1950, 6, 12 November 1950, 7, 16 December 1950, 3, 18 July 1951, 4, 4 October 1951, 4; and *Nashville Sun*, 7 October 1950 (avail-

able from the Tennessee State Library and Archives, Nashville). The *Nashville Sun* was occasionally published in Clarksville, Tennessee, about forty-five miles from Nashville, and was also sometimes listed as the *Clarksville Sun* in SNS records. The paper survived until May 1952.

92. *Nashville Sun*, 21 October 1950, 1, 8, 28 October 1950, 4.

93. *Atlanta Daily World*, 28 September 1950, 1, 4 October 1950, 1, 22 June 1951, 4.

94. *Atlanta Daily World*, 19 April 1951, 1, 23 November 1951, 1, 30 November 1951, 1; and *Nashville Sun*, 21 August 1951, 1.

95. *Atlanta Daily World*, 6 July 1951, 1, 7 December 1951, 2, 13 December 1951, 6.

96. Rosenthal, "Southern Black Student Activism," 114; Stuckert, "Negro College—A Pawn," 1; Jencks and Reisman, "American Negro College," 29; and Miles, *Radical Probe*, 194–197.

97. Rosenthal, "Southern Black Student Activism," 115–118; Fidler, "Academic Freedom," 415; Johnson, "Student Protest at Fisk University"; Du Bois, "Hampton Strike"; Logan, *Howard University*, 120–122; and Gates, "Negro Students Challenge Social Forces."

98. *Atlanta Daily World*, 6 February 1952, 2.

99. *Atlanta Daily World*, 17 January 1953, 1, 20 March 1953, 5, 15 April 1953, 1, 22 April 1953, 6, 29 April 1953, 8, 14 May 1953, 2, 20 January 1954, 4.

100. *Atlanta Daily World*, 8 April 1953, 1, 29 April 1953, 1.

101. *Atlanta Daily World*, 22 April 1953, 1.

Chapter 6. Mississippi and Louisiana

1. *Atlanta Daily World*, 22 July 1932, A1, 23 July 1932, 1.

2. Of those thirty-three Black periodicals in the state, fifteen were commercial, six religious, two fraternal, and ten educational. Julius Eric Thompson, *Black Press in Mississippi*, 16. See also *N. W. Ayer & Son's Directory*, 1933–1939.

3. Julius Eric Thompson also mentions the focus on social pages, lurid headlines of sex and murder, sports, and entertainment news, similar to the kinds of material being published by other Scott papers throughout the region. Thompson, *Black Press in Mississippi*, 17.

4. Painter, "Black Journalism," 32; and Julius Eric Thompson, *Black Press in Mississippi*, 17. Slightly more engaged was the *Greenville Leader*, published from 1930 to 1939 in Greenville, Mississippi, which was part of the Syndicate between 1932 and 1934. *Greenville Leader*, 11 April 1936, 18 March 1936, 1, 26 February 1938, 1 (available from the Mississippi Department of Archives and History, Jackson).

5. Fourteenth Census of the United States, 1920: Natchez, Miss., sheet 3A; "Scott Newspaper Service [syndicating service], 1935," OBV136, Atlanta Daily World Records, 1931–1996, Manuscript Collection no. 1092, Manuscript, Archives, and Rare Book Library, Emory University, Atlanta, Ga. (hereinafter "Scott Newspaper Service, 1935"); "Scott Newspaper Service [syndicating service], 1936," OBV137, ibid. (hereinafter "Scott Newspaper Service, 1936"); and *Atlanta Daily World*, 4 January 1934, 4, 15 February 1934, 5, 24 February 1934, 6, 3 March 1934, 1, 3 April 1934, 1, 7 April 1934, 1, 10 April 1934, 1, 21 April 1934, 1, 5, 22 April 1934, A3, 24 April 1934, 3, 28 April 1934, 1, 6, 4 May 1934, 6, 24 June 1934, A2, 3 January 1935, 6. See also Moody, *Coming of Age in Mississippi*.

6. *Weekly Echo*, 29 July 1932, 1 (available from the Mississippi Department of Archives and History, Jackson). The *Echo* was a publication of the Holbrook Benevolent Association, which emphasized getting medical care and decent burials for Black residents in and around Meridian. Announcements for the association, which encouraged readers to buy HBA policies and attend meetings of HBA boards, dominated the paper's advertising. See, for example, *Weekly Echo*, 5 August 1932, 4; "Oral History with Charles Lemuel Young, Sr."; and Holbrook Benevolent Association, "Constitution and By-Laws."

7. *Weekly Echo*, 29 July 1932, 2, 5 August 1932, 2, 19 August 1932, 2; and *Atlanta Daily World*, 27 August 1932, 4, 28 August 1932, 2.

8. *Weekly Echo*, 26 August 1932, 1, 9 September 1932, 1, 16 September 1932, 2, 23 September 1932, 1, 4 November 1932, 1. A substantial advertisement in the *Echo* trumpeted the Good-Will Printing Company. "No job too large, no job too small," it claimed. "We print 'em all." That advertisement, combined with the simple linear columnar structure of the paper, a brief four pages devoid of pictures or creative design, makes it seem as though the paper was largely paying the Syndicate for the gravure weekly, which it would first showcase in its 14 October edition. The *Echo*'s editorial masthead noted its membership in the NNPA, but listed no other affiliations. Still, fortunes for the *Echo* were looking up; there were advertisements for a new salesman and for newsboys. *Weekly Echo*, 29 July 1932, 3–4, 12 August 1932, 2. The Syndicate's gravure weekly provided the first pictures the paper featured, dramatically adding to the straight-column news. *Weekly Echo*, 14 October 1932, 5–8.

9. "Scott Newspaper Service, 1935"; and *Atlanta Daily World*, 30 May 1935, 6, 12 June 1935, 5.

10. No editions of the Syndicate's *Meridian Progress* survive. There was in the 1930s a paper called the *American Progress* published in Meridian, but it was actually a southern Louisiana vehicle devoted to Huey Long's political machine. It was at various times published in Meridian, New Orleans, and Hammond, depending on the strength of the anti-Long faction. See *American Progress* (New Orleans), 24 August 1933, 1; and *American Progress* (Meridian), 2 August 1935, 1 (both available from Manuscript, Archives, and Rare Book Library, Emory University, Atlanta, Ga.); and the *Progress* (Hammond), 3 September 1939, 1 (available from Hill Memorial Library, Louisiana State University, Baton Rouge).

11. Julius Eric Thompson, "Mississippi," 182–183, 186–187.

12. *Atlanta Daily World*, 5 June 1941, 2, 19 June 1941, 4. For more on Greene, see Aiello, *Grapevine of the Black South*, 124–139.

13. *Jackson Advocate*, 2 August 1941, 8.

14. *Jackson Advocate*, 15 November 1941, 8; and *Atlanta Daily World*, 16 November 1941, 4.

15. *Jackson Advocate*, 1 November, 1941, 8.

16. *Jackson Advocate*, 21 March 1942, 1; and *Atlanta Daily World*, 21 March 1942, 6. For more on the Commission on Interracial Cooperation, which was founded in Georgia, see Gordon, *Georgia Negro*, 335–339.

17. *Jackson Advocate*, 17 October 1942, 8; and *Atlanta Daily World*, 20 October 1942, 6.

18. *Atlanta Daily World*, 22 October 1942, 1; and *Jackson Advocate*, 17 October 1942, 1, 8.

19. *Atlanta Daily World*, 14 January 1943, 1.
20. *Atlanta Daily World*, 12 April 1943, 1; and *Daily Worker*, 25 April 1943, 1.
21. *Atlanta Daily World*, 19 January 1943, 6.
22. *Atlanta Daily World*, 22 February 1943, 6.
23. *Atlanta Daily World*, 1 July 1943, 6.
24. *Atlanta Daily World*, 2 July 1943, 5; and *Parker et al. v. State*, 194 Miss. 895 (1943).
25. *Atlanta Daily World*, 14 July 1944, 2, 28 July 1944, 4.
26. *Jackson Advocate*, 30 December 1944, 8; and *Atlanta Daily World*, 28 December 1944, 6.
27. *Atlanta Daily World*, 30 June 1945, 5.
28. *Jackson Advocate*, 24 February 1945, 8.
29. Dulles, "Thoughts on Soviet Foreign Policy"; and *Atlanta Daily World*, 22 June 1946, 6.
30. *Jackson Advocate*, 6 April 1946, 8, 6 July 1946, 1, 4; and *Atlanta Daily World*, 3 July 1946, 1, 10 July 1946, 6. Bilbo, who was on the ballot for reelection that year, was still able to win despite the Black votes against him. *Atlanta Daily World*, 4 July 1946, 1.
31. Lambert, *Battle of Ole Miss*, 14, 18–19, 21–23, 24–25; and Bilbo, *Take Your Choice*.
32. McMillen, *Dark Journey*, 257–281; and Lambert, *Battle of Ole Miss*, 26–27, 28–29, 52.
33. *Atlanta Daily World*, 26 July 1950, 4, 6 May 1951, 1, 8 May 1951, 1.
34. The Library of Congress lists a *Banner County Outlook* serving Jackson and Hinds County, which started in 1949. It was published by Walter D. Davis in Flora, Mississippi, from December 1949 to January 1951, when it moved to Jackson. Though its dates align with those of the *Jackson Banner*, the *Banner County Outlook* was a white paper. *Banner County Outlook*, 18 May 1951, 1 (available from the Mississippi Department of Archives and History, Jackson).
35. *Atlanta Daily World*, 8 April 1951, 1, 24 June 1951, 1.
36. Lambert, *Battle of Ole Miss*, 71, 74–79.
37. *Louisiana Weekly*, 16 September 1967, 1, 5. When Taylor left the paper in 1927, Dejoie replaced him with Peter Crutchfield, who also worked for United Life Insurance Company. Beginning in 1929, Dejoie became president of United Life. DeCuir, "Attacking Jim Crow," 156–159; and Thomas J. Davis, "Louisiana," 167–168.
38. Moran, "Public Relief in Louisiana," 369–370; and Tobin, "Early New Deal," 313.
39. *Atlanta Daily World*, 22 July 1932, A1. The *Weekly*'s advertising was predominantly local, but there were national ads for hair straighteners, skin bleaches, and patent medicines. The staff of the *Weekly* sent its news and pictures to Atlanta via air mail, the final copy arriving around 7:30 on Wednesday night. Syndicate staff placed the copy and added its own to fill any remaining spaces, and the *Weekly* went to press around 3:00 a.m. on Thursday. That put the *Weekly* in the middle of the Syndicate's production schedule. It first printed the *Jackson World* and *Memphis World* before the *Weekly*. The plant then printed the *Atlanta Daily World*'s national and city editions before printing its *World* papers from Jacksonville, Nashville, and Birmingham. Blackwell, "Black-Controlled Media in Atlanta," 13; *Atlanta Daily World*, 1 September 1932, A1; and DeCuir, "Attacking Jim Crow," 159–160.

40. *Atlanta Daily World*, 4 August 1932, A5.

41. *Louisiana Weekly*, 10 May 1930, 4, 11 June 1927, 6; and DeCuir, "Attacking Jim Crow," 160–161.

42. DeCuir, "Attacking Jim Crow," 170–172.

43. *Atlanta Daily World*, 4 August 1932, A6, 11 August 1932, A1, 15 September 1932, A1, 28 October 1932, 1, 6 January 1934, 3.

44. *Atlanta Daily World*, 13 August 1932, 4, 19 August 1932, 6.

45. *Atlanta Daily World*, 8 September 1932, A6, 9 September 1932, A6. "Mr. Hoover may not be responsible for the depression," the *Weekly* wrote in another syndicated editorial, "but as for the exclusion of colored labor at Las Vegas, the exploitation of labor in the spillway region, and other instances too numerous to mention, we ask whether or not if the president who is commander-in-chief of the army and the work under its immediate supervision is not to a very large extent, partly responsible for those morbid conditions." *Atlanta Daily World*, 15 September 1932, A6.

46. *Atlanta Daily World*, 23 September 1932, A6, 7 October 1932, A6, 28 October 1932, 6, 11 November 1932, 6, 13 November 1932, A8, 16 November 1932, A6, 26 November 1932, 4.

47. In 1947, LaFourche was writing for the *Tropical Dispatch* in Miami. "Scott Newspaper Service, 1936"; "Scott Newspaper Service [syndicating service], 1937," OBV138, Atlanta Daily World Records, 1931–1996, Manuscript Collection no. 1092, Manuscript, Archives, and Rare Book Library, Emory University, Atlanta, Ga.; and *Atlanta Daily World*, 15 May 1947, 4.

48. *Atlanta Daily World*, 7 July 1934, 2, 14 July 1934, 2, 4, 13 August 1934, 1.

49. *Atlanta Daily World*, 21 July 1934, 4.

50. *Atlanta Daily World*, 4 September 1934, 2.

51. Aiello, *Kings of Casino Park*, 138, 211–212; *Baltimore Afro-American*, 3 November 1979, 13; *1933 Monroe City Directory, 1933* (Monroe, La.: Interstate City Directory, 1933), 123; *Atlanta Daily World*, 7 August 1937, 2, 12 August 1937, 5, 13 August 1937, 2, 6, 15 September 1937, 6; and *Carolina Times*, 26 July 1941, 1.

52. *Atlanta Daily World*, 1 February 1937, 1; *Monroe News Star*, 22 January 1937, 2, 3; *Monroe Morning World*, 29 January 1937, 4; and Criminal Index, Fourth Judicial District Court, Ouachita Parish, Monroe, La.

53. Though its front-page emphasis was national in scope, its advertisements were almost uniformly for Monroe businesses. *Southern Broadcast*, 11 July 1936, 1–10. Surviving issues of the *Southern Broadcast*, including those cited below, are available at the New York Public Library.

54. *Southern Broadcast*, 18 July 1936, 4. Other editions continued in this fashion. The principal international stories in the summer of 1936 were the Italian assault on Ethiopia, Haile Selassie's attempt to save it, and the success of Jesse Owens at the 1936 Olympics in Germany. *Southern Broadcast*, 26 July 1936, 1 August 1936, 8 August 1936, 15 August 1936, 22 August 1936, 29 August 1936. Editorials covered the plight of tenant farmers, the problem of unequal education and the dilapidated state of Black schools in the South, the benefits of Rooseveltian democracy, and Joe Louis—always Joe Louis. *Southern Broadcast*, 5 September 1936, 4, 17 October 1936, 4, 14 November 1936, 4. In 1937, the *Broadcast* began publishing in a tabloid format and added a page of comic strips. With that exception, the content remained static under the watchful eye of Briscoe. *Southern Broadcast*, 1 May 1937, 8 May 1937, 15 May 1937, 22 May 1937, 29 May 1937, 5 June 1937, 12 June 1937, 26 June 1937; and *Mon-*

roe, Louisiana and West Monroe, Louisiana City Directory, 1938–1939 (Parsons, Kans.: Interstate Directory Co., 1938), 367. I have found nothing, however, on the paper in the parish's incorporation or conveyance books. *General Index to Incorporation Recordings, L–Z*, Ouachita Parish Clerk of Court, Monroe, La.; and *Vendor Index to Conveyances, MNOP, from the Beginning through 1980*, Ouachita Parish Clerk of Court, Monroe, La.

55. *Atlanta Daily World*, 28 August 1940, 2, 24 May 1941, 2, 8 September 1941, 6; Oliver, "History and Development of the *Atlanta Daily World*," 406; *Monroe, Louisiana and West Monroe, Louisiana City Directory, 1940–1941* (Parsons, Kans.: C. B. Page Directory Co., 1940), 395. The paper did not officially incorporate in Monroe. *General Index to Incorporation Recordings, L–Z*, Ouachita Parish Clerk of Court, Monroe, La.; and *Vendor Index to Conveyances, TUV, from the Beginning through 1980*, Ouachita Parish Clerk of Court, Monroe, La.

56. *Atlanta Daily World*, 10 November 1937, 2, 17 December 1937, 5; *Baton Rouge City Directory, 1929* (Springfield, Mo.: Interstate Directory Co., 1929), 339; *Baton Rouge City Directory, 1934* (New Orleans, La.: R. L. Polk & Co., 1934), 287; and Sixteenth Census of the United States, 1940: New Orleans City, La., sheet 13A.

57. *Baton Rouge Post*, 25 December 1937, 1–8, 8 January 1938, 8, 15 January 1938, 1, 8, 22 January 1938, 1, 8, 29 January 1938, 1, 8 (quote).

58. Quote from Sartain, *Invisible Activists*, 120. Johnson was a devoted Methodist who argued for the redemptive power of suffering, much as civil rights activists like Martin Luther King Jr. would argue in the following generation. Sixteenth Census of the United States, 1940: Alexandria, La., sheet 14B; and Sartain, *Invisible Activists*, 120–127.

59. *Atlanta Daily World*, 12 January 1942, 1, 14 January 1942, 1; and Sartain, *Invisible Activists*, 129–130.

60. *Atlanta Daily World*, 22 January 1942, 1.

61. *Atlanta Daily World*, 22 January 1942, 1, 25 January 1942, 1, 27 January 1942, 1.

Chapter 7. The Syndicate Moves West

1. The one article syndicated by the SNS reported on Forrest City's annual Peach Festival. "For the first time in the history of the Peach Festival," the paper explained, "the colored citizens of Forrest City took an active and distinctive part in the celebration. Negro residents of the city joined in the festivities with lawn parties, dances, and choral singing, on the invitation of the Festival promoters." *Atlanta Daily World*, 27 July 1936, 1; "Flash-Flash-Flash" and "Strike-Join Unemployed-Which," *Southern Liberator*, April 1936, Southern Tenant Farmers Union in the News, Southern Tenant Farmers Union Papers, 1934–1970, microfilm S3–S64, University of Arkansas, Fayetteville; and Junne, *Blacks in the American West*, 191.

2. The group described itself as "the largest colored ass'n in the South." Most of the news in the paper's one surviving edition—prior to its time with the SNS—was local, featuring crime stories and civic news supplemented by Associated Negro Press content. *Sunlight*, 1 March 1938, 1–4 (available at the Arkansas Collection, F419.P5 S8 Mr 1 1938, Special Collections, University of Arkansas Libraries, Fayetteville).

3. There was another paper, seemingly unrelated, known as the *Eastern Arkansas World*, edited by Thomas J. Brown in Earle, Arkansas, as of 1941. The Little Rock ver-

sion was listed as the *Arkansas Mediator and World* as of March 1943. *N. W. Ayer & Son's Directory, 1932*, 62; and *Atlanta Daily World*, 8 July 1941, 6.

4. *Atlanta Daily World*, 24 October 1941, 1, 8 June 1942, 1, 9 June 1942, 1.

5. The history of the Black press in Little Rock was long. The *Survey-Journal*, founded in the early 1930s, was a vestige of the *Arkansas Survey*, published in the 1920s. Before that, there was the *American Guide* in the 1890s, the *Arkansas Weekly Mansion* in the 1880s, and the *Arkansas Freeman* in the 1860s following the Civil War. *Arkansas Survey-Journal*, 28 September 1940, 1, 2; *Arkansas Survey*, 20 September 1924, 1, *American Guide*, 28 March 1896, 1, 2; *Arkansas Weekly Mansion*, 4 August 1883, 1, 2; and *Arkansas Freeman*, 28 September 1869, 1, 2.

6. *Arkansas World*, 21 September 1940, 1, 2, 3, 4, 8. At the same time, there were also the requisite advertisements for skin whiteners.

7. *Atlanta Daily World*, 16 April 1942, 7, 12 September 1942, 2.

8. *Atlanta Daily World*, 6 May 1940, 6, 29 May 1943, 5; and Aiello, *Grapevine of the Black South*, 103.

9. *Atlanta Daily World*, 3 October 1945, 2.

10. *Atlanta Daily World*, 26 September 1946, 4.

11. *Atlanta Daily World*, 22 January 1947, 2.

12. *Atlanta Daily World*, 7 May 1947, 6, 14 June 1947, 4.

13. *Atlanta Daily World*, 15 October 1947, 6.

14. *Atlanta Daily World*, 22 March 1951, 3. The synergistic urge to support businesses remained, however. In November 1951, for example, the paper devoted almost as much page space as it had to the Curry ejection to plans for a new restaurant and nightclub in Crittenden County, largely because *World* editor A. G. Shields was one of the lead investors and the general manager of the enterprise. *Atlanta Daily World*, 4 February 1948, 2, 14 April 1948, 2, 11 May 1949, 6, 8 November 1951, 2; and *Oklahoman*, 1 December 1996, 22.

15. *Atlanta Daily World*, 16 January 1952, 6, 23 January 1952, 6.

16. *Atlanta Daily World*, 20 February 1952, 6, 24 February 1952, 4.

17. *Atlanta Daily World*, 15 February 1934, 6. The paper lasted until 1945, though its relationship with the Syndicate ended in 1938. Diana J. Kleiner, "Fort Worth Mind," Handbook of Texas Online, http://www.tshaonline.org/handbook/online/articles/ eef08, accessed 10 October 2013; "The Afro-Texas Press: The Early Years," http://afrotexan.com/AfroPress/year_ book_1938.htm, accessed 10 October 2013; *Fort Worth City Directory, 1933–1934* (Dallas, Tex.: Morrison & Fourmy Directory Co., 1933), 791; and *Fort Worth City Directory, 1936* (Dallas, Tex.: Morrison & Fourmy Directory Co., 1936), 582.

18. *Atlanta Daily World*, 1 June 1934, 8.

19. *Atlanta Daily World*, 29 June 1934, 6.

20. *Atlanta Daily World*, 5 October 1936, 2, 7 November 1936, 4, 21 November 1936, 7; and Marquart, Ekland-Olson, and Sorensen, *Rope, the Chair, and the Needle*, 49.

21. *Atlanta Daily World*, 1 June 1934, 8, 22 June 1934, 6, 15 April 1937, 4, 18 September 1937, 4. Melton and Wise remained the paper's editors long after its contact with the Syndicate ended. Surviving issues from the 1940s demonstrate that the paper remained much the same. It encouraged readers to pay the poll tax. It covered meetings of the NAACP and the 1943 speech of A. Philip Randolph in the city. *Fort Worth Mind*, 13 November 1943, 1, 18 January 1947, 5.

22. *Atlanta Daily World*, 11 March 1934, 1.

23. Smallwood, "Texas," 360–361, 364; and *Dallas Express*, 18 January 1941, 1. See also Cox, *First Texas News Barons*; and Margot, *"Dallas Express."*

24. *Galveston Voice*, 3 October 1931, 1–4.

25. *Atlanta Daily World*, 5 February 1936, 2, 28 April 1936, 2, 14 May 1936, 6, 19 June 1936, 5. The paper's editor was Charles Williams. For more on the Lindbergh kidnapping, see chapter 2.

26. *Atlanta Daily World*, 20 August 1936, 6. The *Enterprise* reported on two Black citizens of West Texas who were called for jury duty, only to be sent home after officials realized that they were not white. Both were told to "just forget it" upon arrival. The paper included no commentary on the event, no screed on the injustice of being denied a place in the jury box, because that would have threatened both the paper and the insurance company attached to it. Still, the paper did provide a detailed account of the rejection, and the information itself was the most important indictment. Black readers wouldn't need additional commentary to be frustrated by the actions of San Angelo officials. *Atlanta Daily World*, 20 August 1936, 6, 26 October 1936, 2, 10 December 1936, 5, 11 December 1936, 6; "Scott Newspaper Service [syndicating service], 1935," OBV136, Atlanta Daily World Records, 1931–1996, Manuscript Collection no. 1092, Manuscript, Archives, and Rare Book Library, Emory University, Atlanta, Ga. (hereinafter "Scott Newspaper Service, 1935"); and "Scott Newspaper Service [syndicating service], 1936," OBV137, ibid., (hereinafter "Scott Newspaper Service, 1936").

27. *Amarillo City Directory, 1934* (El Paso, Tex.: Hudspeth Directory Co., 1934), 193; *Amarillo City Directory, 1936–37* (El Paso, Tex.: Hudspeth Directory Co., 1936), 201; and *Atlanta Daily World*, 18 August 1937, A1, A7. There is one issue of an *East Texas Times* that survives, but it is a white weekly. *East Texas Times*, 3 July 1936, 1 (available at the Dolph Briscoe Center for American History, University of Texas, Austin).

28. *Galveston Guide*, 17 April 1937, 1–8 (available at the Dolph Briscoe Center for American History, University of Texas, Austin).

29. The paper later became known as the *Good Neighbor Interpreter* under the leadership of Leona Washington. Glasrud and Wintz, "Black Renaissance," 176.

30. *Atlanta Daily World*, 3 September 1940, 6.

31. *Atlanta Daily World*, 30 October 1940, 6.

32. *Atlanta Daily World*, 14 March 1935, 6.

33. Several editions of the *Muskogee Lantern* survive, but those are from a period before SNS affiliation. Like other papers whose previous editions exist, they demonstrate the dramatic improvement the Syndicate made. The *Lantern*'s surviving editions from 1930 show a simple six-column, four-page weekly without pictures or creative layout. *Muskogee Lantern*, 11 January 1930, 18 January 1930, 25 January 1930.

34. *Atlanta Daily World*, 7 January 1939, 4.

35. James B. Morris Papers, 1926–1972, R21, Special Collections, State Historical Society of Iowa, Iowa City; *Des Moines Register*, 18 February 2007, 12; "Scott Newspaper Service, 1935"; and Tom Longden, "J. B. Morris Pursued Equal Opportunities," *Des Moines Register*, 8 February 2009, 12. The original *Bystander* ownership group was led by local businessman William Coalson, and the editorial portion of the paper was headed by Charles and Thadius Ruff, brothers who relinquished the paper's operations two years later to law student John Lay Thompson. Thompson made the pa-

per into a juggernaut, pressing for subscriptions across the state and even initiating "black economic boycotts" against white businesses that did not advertise in his newspaper. It was a bold move, a reversal of the typical Black southern policy of moderating coverage to curry favor with white advertisers. Ultimately, the demands of publishing took their toll, and Thompson sold to Morris in 1922. He continued to publish the paper until his death in 1972.

36. Pride, "Register and History," 88–89.

37. Longden, "J. B. Morris Pursued Equal Opportunities"; and Robert V. Morris, "The Iowa Bystander."

38. *Atlanta Daily World*, 12 April 1934, 1, 17 September 1934, 4. That said, there were plenty of stories that Black southerners did recognize, as when the Christ Sanctified Holy Church of Des Moines filed suit to keep the Reverend Arthur Brewer from preaching. *Atlanta Daily World*, 21 September 1935, 2; and Aiello, "Calumny in the House."

39. John Hammond Moore, "Angelo Herndon Case"; Herndon, *Let Me Live*; Charles H. Martin, *Angelo Herndon Case*; and *Herndon v. Lowry*, 301 U.S. 242 (1937).

40. *Atlanta Daily World*, 6 August 1939, 1, 16 October 1939, 6, 22 January 1940, 3.

41. *Atlanta Daily World*, 22 January 1940, 3, 25 July 1940, 6, 31 May 1941, 4, 18 July 1941, 6; Garfinkel, *When Negroes March*; Pfeffer, *A. Philip Randolph, Pioneer*; and Lucander, *Winning the War for Democracy*.

42. *Atlanta Daily World*, 26 February 1943, 2.

43. *Atlanta Daily World*, 21 July 1942, 1, 22 July 1942, 1, 22 December 1942, 3, 5 February 1943, 3, 26 February 1943, 2, 22 June 1943, 3, 7 July 1943, 2, 8 August 1943, 1, 10 April 1945, 6. The paper also covered more sensational crime stories, like an August 1936 domestic dispute where a wife stabbed her husband in the chest, or a December 1936 robbery case in which nine different conspirators pled guilty, or a death that same month at the hands of a "fit of epilepsy" of a local "dashing and splashing connoisseur of questionable intoxicants." *Atlanta Daily World*, 5 August 1936, 2, 20 August 1936, 2, 14 December 1936, 3, 24 December 1936, 1, 1 January 1937, 2.

44. "Economic and Social Development," Works Progress Administration Records, box 6, folder 95, Dr. C. C. and Mabel L. Criss Library Special Collections, University of Nebraska, Omaha.

45. The Syndicate's *Phoenix Index* lasted until 1942. It was followed by the *Arizona Sun*, edited by Doc Benson, which was published from 1942 to 1962. *Arizona Republic*, 20 November 1912, 11, 28 May 1951, 10; Fifteenth Census of the United States, 1930: Phoenix, Ariz., sheet 5A; *Phoenix City Directory, 1941* (Phoenix: Arizona Directory Company, 1941), 193; Matthew C. Whitaker, "Rise of Black Phoenix"; Pride, "Register and History," 53; and Crudup, "African Americans in Arizona," 97–100.

46. For example, *Phoenix Index*, 12 August 1939, 8 (available at Archives and Public Records, Arizona State Library, Phoenix, as are all editions of this paper cited below).

47. *Phoenix Index*, 23 December 1939, 8, 14 September 1940, 4, 28 September 1940, 4, 21 December 1940, 4, 28 December 1940, 2, 18 January 1941, 2, 21 February 1942, 7.

48. *Phoenix Index*, 19 August 1939, 1, 8, 7 October 1939, 8, 18 November 1939, 8, 9 December 1939, 8, 16 December 1939, 8, 23 December 1939, 4.

49. Parks quoted in Wolseley, *Black Press, USA*, 60; *Twin City Herald*, 19 February 1938, 2; and *Atlanta Daily World*, 1 May 1934, 3.

50. *Twin City Herald*, 14 January 1939, 4, 22 April 1939, 2.

51. *Twin City Herald*, 13 January 1940, 1, 2 (quotes), 20 January 1940, 1. The paper also, like many of its Syndicate peers, pushed voting as the fundamental right of citizenship, but with voting rights secured in Minnesota, the *Herald* instead made an effort to convince readers to vote for the candidate most qualified and with the best interests of Black people in mind. "Some of us think that no democratic candidate would consider a Negro as anything but a slave," but such relied on the same prejudice used by white southerners. The Democratic Party looked different in the North, and there were plenty of qualified candidates that concerned themselves with racial issues and did not call themselves Republicans. "As a minority group we, of course, cannot allow ourselves to become so divided as to defeat any proposition of racial value." *Twin City Herald*, 20 January 1940, 2.

52. Next door in Wisconsin, there was a self-described "semi-monthly" published in Milwaukee titled the *Bay View Observer*, "devoted to the welfare of Bay View, Tippecanoe and St. Francis" neighborhoods and published by E. F. Zillman. It survives while the *Milwaukee Observer* does not, but they were not the same paper. Zillman's was a white neighborhood paper. See, for example, *Bay View Observer*, 28 January 1937, 2.

Chapter 8. From the Upper South to the Midwest

1. Wright, "Black Political Insurgency in Louisville," 9, 13–15; and *Atlanta Daily World*, 4 September 1932, 1. Isaac Willis Cole was born on 22 January 1887 in Memphis. In 1928, Cole served as recording secretary of the National Negro Publishers Association. *Western Outlook*, 28 April 1928, 1; and "I. Willis Cole," Department of Health, Certificate of Death, state file no. 2852, Bureau of Vital Statistics, Commonwealth of Kentucky.

2. *Atlanta Daily World*, 21 July 1932, A1, 30 July 1932, A1, 6 August 1932, A1, A2, 4 September 1932, 1, 14 September 1932, A2, 7 October 1932, A10; and *Louisville Leader*, 2 April 1932, 2, 18 June 1932, 7. The *Leader* was an established entity. It had no need for printing services like most of the Syndicate papers. The I. Willis Cole Publishing Company, in fact, supplemented the paper's income with printing "for weddings, parties, banquets, dinners and all society and church affairs." Cole also maintained the Leader News Shoppe at 422–424 South Sixth Street, and he advertised in the *Leader*'s pages that the store sold the latest editions of the *Crisis* and *Opportunity*.

3. Also in 1933, the *Louisville Independent News* commented on the successful candidacy of Rufus Atwood for the presidency of the Kentucky Negro Education Association. So the paper's activism was clearly known as early as 1933. Gerald L. Smith, *Black Educator*, 89–90.

4. *Indianapolis Recorder*, 27 May 1933, 1; and Wright, "Black Political Insurgency in Louisville," 9, 13–15. In 1917, Warley had been party to a lawsuit that ultimately ended the city's residential segregation ordinance. Charles Buchanan, a white man, had sold a piece of property to Warley, who couldn't complete the sale because, he argued, the city's new residential segregation ordinance wouldn't allow him to. The case eventually made its way to the U.S. Supreme Court, where the justices invalidated the segregation law on Fourteenth Amendment grounds, thus stopping similar ordinances from developing throughout the South. *Buchanan v. Warley*, 245 U.S. 60 (1917); and Sullivan, *Lift Every Voice*, 72–73.

5. *Atlanta Daily World*, 19 November 1937, 6; and Sixteenth Census of the United States, 1940: Louisville City, Ky., sheet 1A.

6. *Atlanta Daily World*, 28 March 1938, 2, 29 April 1938, 2. Interestingly, there was a white man in Kentucky named William W. Worley, who published the *Kentucky Observer and Reporter* in Lexington in the first half of the nineteenth century. Lowell Hayes Harrison, *New History of Kentucky*, 159; and Staples, *History of Pioneer Lexington*, 7.

7. Pride, "Register and History," 256; and Syrjamaki, "Negro Press in 1938," 47–48.

8. *Atlanta Daily World*, 1 December 1939, 6, 21 October 1941, 1, 29 December 1942, 1; Hardin, "Kentucky Is More or Less Civilized"; and Luther Adams, *Way Up North in Louisville*, 99–104.

9. Among the quoted was I. Willis Cole, editor of the rival *Louisville Leader*. *Atlanta Daily World*, 7 November 1939, 6, 5 April 1940, 2.

10. *Atlanta Daily World*, 29 June 1940, 2, 12 July 1940, 2.

11. *Atlanta Daily World*, 22 July 1941, 5, 10 September 1941, 6.

12. *Atlanta Daily World*, 3 April 1942, 6.

13. *Atlanta Daily World*, 30 September 1942, 2, 5 November 1942, 6, 10 November 1942, 6. The Black waiters' support for white waitresses was a story in the white press as well, providing the union with almost universally positive press in the city. *Louisville Courier Journal*, 5 September 1942, 6, 6 September 1942, 6, 10 September 1942, 13, 28 September 1942, 6.

14. *Atlanta Daily World*, 3 June 1943, 1, 15 June 1943, 1, 25 June 1943, 2; and *World Telegram*, 18 November 1939, 8, 10 August 1940, 8.

15. *Atlanta Daily World*, 31 May 1935, 6, 15 July 1935, 6, 28 October 1935, 4. Cochran began at the *Lexington Herald* before starting her own paper. "Scott Newspaper Service [syndicating service], 1935," OBV136, Atlanta Daily World Records, 1931–1996, Manuscript Collection no. 1092, Manuscript, Archives, and Rare Book Library, Emory University, Atlanta, Ga. (hereinafter "Scott Newspaper Service, 1935"); "Scott Newspaper Service [syndicating service], 1936," OBV137, ibid. (hereinafter "Scott Newspaper Service, 1936"); *Lexington City Directory, 1928* (Columbus, Ohio: R. L. Polk & Co., 1928), 153; *Lexington City Directory, 1931–1932* (Columbus, Ohio: R. L. Polk & Co., 1931), 151; *Lexington City Directory, 1937* (Columbus, Ohio: R. L. Polk & Co., 1937), 113; *Lexington City Directory, 1939* (Cincinnati, Ohio: R. L. Polk & Co., 1939), 131; and *Lexington City Directory, 1940* (Cincinnati, Ohio: R. L. Polk & Co., 1940), 138. Women had an important history in Black southern journalism dating to the nineteenth century, feeding particularly from the boom in Black newspapers in the 1890s. See Aiello, *Grapevine of the Black South*, ch. 4.

16. *Atlanta Daily World*, 12 July 1935, 6, 3 August 1935, 2, 28 October 1935, 4.

17. *Kentucky New Era*, 2 April 1964, 8, 21 June 1966, 1, 2, 13 February 1989, 15; *Willis v. Walker*, 136 F.Supp. 177 (1955); Glazier, *Been Coming Through*, 168, 190–191; Ellis, *History of Education in Kentucky*, 278–279; and *Atlanta Daily World*, 28 November 1935, 4, 4 December 1935, 5, 5 December 1935, 5.

18. Wilkinson, "Big-Band Jazz," 51–52; and *West Virginia Weekly*, 28 October 1933, 1 (available at the Archives Library, West Virginia Division of Culture and History, Charleston). Wilkinson's article is what led to the discovery of the paper's surviving editions. Christopher Wilkinson, Department of Music, College of Creative Arts, West

Virginia University, Morgantown, correspondence with the author; "Scott Newspaper Service, 1935"; "Scott Newspaper Service, 1936"; *N. W. Ayer & Son's Directory, 1936*, 665, 930; and *Statesville Record and Landmark*, 3 September 1959, 7.

19. While the gravure weekly did include advertising, there was none in the eight-page SNS feature section included with the *Weekly*. Though that section dominated the paper, SNS news was also included in the first section of the paper, along with that of the ANP and others. That syndicated material provided the bulk of the paper's heavy coverage of Scottsboro and its continued aftermath, for example. Like so many other struggling enterprises, the *Weekly* used guilt as an advertising mechanism. "Help West Virginians!!" the paper exclaimed in one ad. "We have had too many news failures in our state. Let's do our part by keeping the *West Virginia Weekly* supported and alive. Buy a copy each week." *West Virginia Weekly*, 28 October 1933, 6, 7–14, 4 November 1933, 6, 7, 18 November 1933, 5, 7–14, 25 November 1933, 1, 3.

20. *West Virginia Weekly*, 28 October 1933, 2, 18 November 1933, 2. By 1935, the *Weekly* was no longer with the SNS, and the difference in quality was stark. It had become a simple four-page, columnar weekly with few photos, no layout design innovations, and little of the fearlessness promised two years earlier. The masthead asked readers, "Help Us to Build in Our Midst the Greatest Negro Weekly Newspaper in West Virginia," but the paper's greatness had clearly passed. A paper that had originally sold for ten cents under the Syndicate now sold for three. *West Virginia Weekly*, 13 September 1935, 1–4, 22 November 1935, 1–4.

21. *Atlanta Daily World*, 16 November 1938, 1, 3 April 1939, 3, 27 July 1942, 5, 19 August 1942, 2. Mitchell would later serve as an alternate delegate from Huntington at the 1948 Republican National Convention. *Pittsburgh Courier*, 26 August 1933, 20; and "West Virginia Delegation to the 1948 Republication National Convention," Political Graveyard, http://politicalgraveyard.com/bio/mitchell5.html#958.91.65, accessed 2 March 2014.

22. *Atlanta Daily World*, 23 July 1932, 1.

23. The *Gary American*, an already established entity founded in the 1920s, became part of the Syndicate after the same trip, beginning in the same month of August 1932. Pride, "Register and History," 238; and Wolseley, *Black Press, USA*, 73–74.

24. *Atlanta Daily World*, 17 October 1932, 6, 24 October 1932, 4.

25. *Atlanta Daily World*, 17 October 1932, 6.

26. *Evansville Argus*, 15 October 1938, 1.

27. The *Nashville World*'s Ric Roberts was also close to *World Telegram* illustrator Willard Mullin. *Atlanta Daily World*, 9 July 1939, 8, 25 August 1940, 4. There was an earlier *Indianapolis World* in the city from the 1880s to the early 1900s. It was a weekly Black paper published by A. E. Manning, but it was unrelated to any later version associated with the SNS. Ratzlaff, "Illustrated African American Journalism," 131–132; and *Indianapolis World*, 27 January 1900.

28. Still, in the spirit of fairness, Porter wrote about the "parts played by Negroes" on the staff of Indiana native Willkie. *Atlanta Daily World*, 27 June 1940, 6, 7 August 1940, 6, 25 August 1940, 4; and *World Telegram*, 18 November 1939, 1, 8, 10 August 1940, 8.

29. *World Telegram*, 2 September 1939, 6, 25 November 1939, 8, 20 January 1940, 8.

30. *Atlanta Daily World*, 7 November 1939, 2, 6 August 1940, 5; and *World Telegram* 3 August 1940, 1.

31. *World Telegram*, 25 November 1939, 1, 9 December 1939, 1, 8 (quote), 30 December 1939, 1.
32. *South Bend Forum*, 26 May 1923.
33. *Atlanta Daily World*, 11 January 1936, 4.
34. *Atlanta Daily World*, 31 January 1936, 6.
35. *Atlanta Daily World*, 8 February 1935, A6, 18 April 1936, 1.
36. *Atlanta Daily World*, 27 January 1940, 1, 14 March 1940, 2, 25 April 1940, 5, 3 August 1940, 5, 30 August 1940, 6, 8 December 1941, 2, 2 January 1943, 2.
37. *Atlanta Daily World*, 3 August 1940, 5, 7 October 1940, 1 (quote); *Chicago Defender*, 28 September 1940, 1, 14. Though no editions of the *Times* survive from the Syndicate period, a selection of editions beginning in 1949 do survive and emphasize news of the Baha'i Church and its adherents. *Illinois Times*, 14 October 1949, 1, 4, 3 February 1950, 1, 24 February 1950, 1 (available at the University of Illinois, Champaign-Urbana); Melinda Roundtree, "The Other *Illinois Times*," Illinois Times Vertical File, Local History Ephemera Series, Champaign County Historical Archives, Urbana Free Library, Urbana, Ill.; *News-Gazette* (Champaign-Urbana), 11 January 1988, C1; Pride, "Register and History," 230; and Belles, "Black Press in Illinois," 346.
38. *Atlanta Daily World*, 3 August 1940, 3, 5, 12 September 1941, 8, 25 January 1943, 2. By 1949, after the paper's time with the Syndicate, it had shrunk to a four-page weekly with two pages of local advertisements. But Edgar Harris was still willing to make political stands in the small amount of page space available to him. He pushed for a permanent FEPC and for an end to southern segregation. *Illinois Times*, 3 February 1950, 4, 17 February 1950, 4, 24 February 1950, 1, 14 March 1950, 5.
39. William Wayne Griffin, *African Americans*, 98.
40. *Atlanta Daily World*, 28 September 1932, A1, 13 January 1934, 2, 19 January 1934, 1, 20 January 1934, 1, 27 January 1934, 1.
41. *Atlanta Daily World*, 12 January 1934, 2.
42. The *Voice* lasted at least until 1941. Claude A. Barnett Papers: The Associated Negro Press, 1918–1967, pt. 2, Associated Negro Press Organizational Files, 1920–1966, Chicago Historical Society, Chicago, Ill., edited by August Meier and Elliott Rudwick, University Publications of America microfilm, reel 21, "Member Newspapers cont," 0021; Pride, "Register and History," 221, 328; *Columbus Advocate*, 6 April 1940 (available at the Ohio Historical Society, Columbus); and *Atlanta Daily World*, 24 February 1934, 2, 10 March 1934, 3, 31 July 1934, 3, 7 August 1934, 2. The *Advocate* studied Ohio relief programs that "affect the Negro," but the results of its investigations did not make it into syndication. *Atlanta Daily World*, 27 April 1934, 2, 28 August 1934, 1.
43. *Atlanta Daily World*, 23 August 1934, 6, 13 September 1934, 6, 21 September 1934, 8.
44. *Atlanta Daily World*, 8 March 1934, 1, 22 March 1934, 1. The *Cleveland Advocate* existed from World War I to 1922, competing with Harry C. Smith's *Cleveland Gazette* and Garrett A. Morgan's *Cleveland Call*. In 1924, Ormond Forte, a native of Barbados, entered the city's Black newspaper competition by founding the *Cleveland Herald*, which existed through the 1920s. (Meanwhile, the *Call* and the *Cleveland Post* merged in 1926 to create the *Cleveland Call and Post*, which lasted through the 1930s.) After the *Herald*, Forte published the *Eagle*. *Cleveland City Directory, 1922*

(Cleveland, Ohio: Cleveland Directory Co., 1922), 1089; *Cleveland City Directory, 1923* (Cleveland, Ohio: Cleveland Directory Co., 1923), 1108; *Cleveland City Directory, 1937* (Cleveland, Ohio: Cleveland Directory Co., 1937), 374; Fifteenth Census of the United States, 1930: Cleveland, Ohio, sheet 22A; "Forte, Ormond Adolphus"; and William Wayne Griffin, *African Americans*, 98.

45. *Atlanta Daily World*, 19 January 1934, 1, 27 January 1934, 2, 2 March 1934, 4, 29 April 1935, 2.

46. *Atlanta Daily World*, 19 July 1934, 6. Vaughn was an Alabama native who served several terms on the Youngstown City Council. Work, *Annual Encyclopedia of the Negro*, 86; *Atlanta Daily World*, 7 November 1937, 4, 25 December 1937, A2; Sixteenth Census of the United States, 1940: Toledo, Ohio, sheet 10A; and "Scott Newspaper Service, 1936." Jackson published another paper, the *Toledo Tribune*, from 1937 to 1938, and again affiliated with the Syndicate.

47. *Atlanta Daily World*, 15 July 1938, 1, 12 September 1938, 6, 17 October 1938, 1, 28 October 1938, 4.

48. *Atlanta Daily World*, 21 April 1939, 2.

49. *New York Age*, 4 June 1932, 1; *Pittsburgh Courier*, 4 September 1937, 8; *California Eagle*, 25 September 1936, 1; and Sixteenth Census of the United States, 1940: Cleveland, Ohio, sheet 9A.

50. According to a June 1949 article in the *Baltimore Afro-American*, Cheeks held a valid press credential that entitled him to inspect criminal records for the previous eighteen years. *California Eagle*, 25 September 1936, 1; *Indianapolis Recorder*, 7 July 1949, 1; and *Baltimore Afro-American*, 28 June 1949, 3.

51. *Atlanta Daily World*, 31 March 1941, 2, 12 September 1941, 1, 15 September 1941, 1, 13 January 1943, 2, 15 February 1943, 6, 1 April 1943, 6, 16 June 1943, 2, 15 October 1943, 5, 7 December 1943, 3.

52. *Atlanta Daily World*, 17 January 1943, 1, 27 August 1943, 2.

53. *Atlanta Daily World*, 23 June 1939, 1, 28 November 1942, 3.

54. *Atlanta Daily World*, 12 January 1940, 3, 14 August 1940, 2, 4 December 1941, 5.

55. *Atlanta Daily World*, 23 October 1942, 6.

56. Duncan, *Survey of Cincinnati's Black Press*, 51–53 (Andrews quote 53); and *Cincinnati Enquirer*, 18 July 1954, 16. The *Independent*'s offices were at 653 West Court Street in Cincinnati. Andrews provided jobs for young West End residents hoping to break into the business. She finally sold the paper in 1954 and then spent the rest of her career running the M. M. Andrews Funeral Chapel in Avondale. Duncan, *Survey of Cincinnati's Black Press*, 53, 55. Sadie Mae Oliver in "The History and Development of the *Atlanta Daily World*" lists a *Cincinnati Observer* as being published by the Syndicate at this time, though she almost surely means the *Independent*.

57. *Atlanta Daily World*, 25 June 1943, 1, 26 June 1943, 1, 1 July 1943, 1.

58. *Atlanta Daily World*, 11 September 1943, 1.

59. *Atlanta Daily World*, 29 October 1944, 4, 9 August 1945, 5, 28 August 1945, 6.

60. *Atlanta Daily World*, 24 June 1947, 5, 14 June 1949, 3. There are several editions of the paper that survive following the paper's time with the Syndicate, which came to a close in March 1950. A May 1951 edition, for example, included an editorial advocating for proportional representation in city voting because it would make Black representation more possible. Its lead story described the city's League of

Playground Mothers Clubs finally agreeing to include five Negro Playground Mothers Clubs in its membership in a contentious 25–18 vote. It was another move toward integration in the city. Two years later, the bulk of the news content was national, though there was a page devoted to the West End. Andrews sold the paper in 1954. *Cincinnati Independent*, 19 May 1951, 1, 2, 23 May 1951, 1. While there is no mention of the *Independent* in the Library of Congress records, Andrews provided several editions of the paper to Mae Najiyyah Duncan prior to her death in 1991, and Duncan then donated those to the Moorland-Spingarn Research Center at Howard University, Washington, D.C.

Chapter 9. The North

1. Fred Carroll, *Race News*, 4–6.
2. Gooden, "Visual Representations of Feminine Beauty," 85; Mack, "Dissent and Authenticity," 135; and Solomon, *Cry Was Unity*, 4–9.
3. *Atlanta Daily World*, 23 November 1932, A1, 5 October 1932, 1, 23 November 1932, A1; and Crusader News Agency, Press Releases, 1933–1934, Schomburg Center for Research in Black Culture, New York Public Library. For more on Euel Lee, alias Orphan Jones, see Joseph E. Moore, *Murder on Maryland's Eastern Shore*.
4. *Memphis World*, 15 April 1932, 6.
5. The *Buffalo Star* lasted until 1948, when it became the *Empire Star*, which survived into the 1950s. Magliulo, "Andrew J. Smitherman"; *Western Star*, 21 July 1834, 1 (available from the New York Heritage Digital Collections, https://nyheritage.org/); and Wolseley, *Black Press, USA*, 50. For more on the Tulsa race massacre and Red Summer, see Ellsworth, *Death in a Promised Land*; Brophy, *Reconstructing the Dreamland*; McWhirter, *Red Summer*; Robert Whitaker, *On the Laps of Gods*; and Kerlin, *Voice of the Negro*.
6. *Buffalo Star*, 4 January 1946, 1, 4, 11 January 1946, 1, 4, 18 January 1946, 1, 4, 25 January 1946, 1, 4, 1 February 1946, 1, 13, 8 February 1946, 4, 15 February 1946, 1, 4 (available at the Buffalo and Erie County Public Library, Buffalo, N.Y.).
7. *Atlanta Daily World*, 8 January 1940, 2, 24 January 1940, 2, 15 February 1941, 4, 28 June 1941, 1.
8. The Progress News Service of Newark had the slogan "A Negro newspaper in every home in America," and though it doesn't seem to have had a long life, its presence did seem to contribute to ending the relationship between the Syndicate and the *Newark Herald*. *New York Amsterdam News*, 13 April 1932, 10; and *Atlanta Daily World*, 6 August 1932, 4, 20 August 1932, 1, 2 October 1932, 2, 11 October 1932, 2.
9. Pride, "Register and History," 302; *Newark Herald*, 11 June 1938, 1, 6, 18 June 1938, 1, 6, 2 July 1938, 1, 6, 9 July 1938, 1, 6, 16 July 1938, 1, 6, 23 July 1938, 1, 2, 6, 30 July 1938, 1, 6, 6 August 1938, 1, 6, 3 September 1938, 1, 4, 8; and *New Jersey Herald News*, 11 April 1942, 1, 7, 18 September 1943, 1, 7, 10 March 1945, 1, 6, 13 April 1946, 1, 8, 16 (available at the James Brown African American Room, Newark Public Library, Newark, N.J.).
10. *Bridgeton City Directory, 1937–38* (New York: R. L. Polk & Co., 1937), 204; *Atlantic City Directory, 1938–39* (Philadelphia, Pa.: R. L. Polk & Co., 1938), 788.
11. *Atlanta Daily World*, 1 February 1936, 2, 19 August 1936, 5, 26 September 1936, 5.
12. *Atlanta Daily World*, 13 June 1935, 2.

13. *Atlanta Daily World*, 12 September 1935, 6.

14. *Atlanta Daily World*, 25 June 1936, 2. Actual segregation was still a problem in Atlantic City, however. Though New Jersey had a state civil rights law that outlawed segregation, the *Eagle* reported on a local bar that refused to serve beer to Black customers, noting that patrons who were refused had the right to sue the establishment for up to $500 and almost pushing one of the victims of the bar's rejection to take that action. Another publication, the *Atlantic City Tribune* run by Clay Claiborne, maintained the Syndicate's presence in the northeastern home of the vice trade in the 1940s. *Atlanta Daily World*, 30 January 1942, 6, 23 February 1942, 2, 24 April 1942, 1, 1 November 1945, 1, 19 January 1946, 1.

15. *The Greater Hartford Directory, 1935* (Hartford, Conn.: Price & Lee, 1935), 770; *The Greater Hartford Directory, 1937* (Hartford, Conn.: Price & Lee, 1937), 932; *The Greater Hartford Directory, 1940* (Hartford, Conn.: Price & Lee, 1940), 934; and *Atlanta Daily World*, 22 June 1936, 1, 8 August 1936, 7, 1 November 1936, 4, 5 December 1936, 2, 1 January 1937, 2, 6. The paper's editor was Alver W. Napper, who also served as state supervisor for the Black Works Progress Administration of Connecticut. While attending a WPA supervisors conference in Atlanta in August 1936, he visited the Syndicate plant and executive offices and met with C. A. Scott "regarding plans for the future expansion of the *Advocate*."

16. *Atlanta Daily World*, 3 May 1936, 1. In July 1937, the Syndicate replaced the *Advocate* in Hartford with the *Connecticut Labor News*, published by William Stevens. Scott Newspaper Service [syndicating service], 1936," OBV137, Atlanta Daily World Records, 1931–1996, Manuscript Collection no. 1092, Manuscript, Archives, and Rare Book Library, Emory University, Atlanta, Ga. (hereinafter "Scott Newspaper Service, 1936"); and *Atlanta Daily World*, 31 July 1937, 2, 4 September 1937, 6, 7 September 1937, 6. Another paper called the *Connecticut Labor News* was published in New Haven in the early 1920s. There are several surviving editions, but that paper was a white union weekly. *Connecticut Labor News*, 21 January 1921, 1, 22 September 1923, 1, 28 February 1925, 1 (available at the Connecticut State Library, Hartford).

17. *Atlanta Daily World*, 10 August 1932, A1, 11 August 1932, A6, 17 August 1932, A5, 18 August 1932, 5, 23 August 1932, A5. The paper ran from 1922 to 24 March 1935 as the *Independent*. From 1935 to 1938 it was the *Tribune-Independent*. Pride, "Register and History," 274.

18. *Detroit Independent*, 13 January 1923, 1–6. Syndicated stories were from the Preston News Service. The paper's managing editor was William J. Robinson; its advertising and circulation manager was Walter A. Ellis.

19. That ideal could also work the other way. In 1925, for example, a residential segregation clash in Detroit, which ultimately led to violence, spread by way of the Associated Negro Press across the country. Black newspapers everywhere took up the cause of an embattled Detroit family defending itself from a white onslaught after attempting to move into a white neighborhood, but that coverage was particularly pronounced in the South. It was a case of race violence and segregation, but it was in the North, which, fitting the model of practical radicalism, gave southern papers far more willingness to demonstrate a virulent militancy. It lessened the consequences for them from the defensive white South, but at the same time gave them an opportunity to ardently criticize segregation. Boyle, *Arc of Justice*, 219, 245.

20. The Congress of Youth was supported by DePriest, who occasionally spoke to

meetings of the group. *Atlanta Daily World*, 8 April 1934, A1, 25 May 1934, 1; and *Indianapolis Recorder*, 9 May 1931, 1.

21. *Atlanta Daily World*, 2 February 1934, 2, 5 February 1934, 2.

22. Despite Black participation in the sheriff's office, there were no Black members of the police force. *Atlanta Daily World*, 17 August 1937, 1. There was a Peter Fisher who worked as a printer at 548 Sherman I Geo Center in the teens and from 1920 to 1921 at Reardon-Parsall Company. Despite the name and job similarities, however, this Fisher seems to be someone separate. Fourteenth Census of the United States, 1920: Detroit, Mich., sheet 18B; and "Petry Fisher and Sadie E. Overton," Marriage License, Wayne County, Michigan, no. 512255, 193208, 1937, Michigan Department of Community Health, Division for Vital Records and Health Statistics.

23. *Atlanta Daily World*, 5 July 1935, 6, 14 October 1935, 6, 29 May 1937, 5.

24. Astor, "... *And a Credit*," 47; and Fenderson, "Negro Press," 184.

25. Margolick, *Beyond Glory*; Sklaroff, *Black Culture*, 123–157; Erenberg, *Greatest Fight*; Robert Drake, "Joe Louis, the Southern Press"; and Roberts, *Joe Louis*.

26. *Atlanta Daily World*, 14 August 1936, 3, 6 September 1936, 4, 1 July 1937, 1.

27. *Atlanta Daily World*, 28 May 1936, 1, 13 July 1937, 1. For more on the Black Legion, see Dillard, *Faith in the City*, 89–92; Newton, *FBI and the KKK*; Norwood, *Strikebreaking and Intimidation*, 130, 196–197; Fox, *Everyday Klansfolk*, 199–212; and Black Legion Collection, Clark Historical Library, Central Michigan University, Mt. Pleasant.

28. *Atlanta Daily World*, 24 July 1937, 4; Fourteenth Census of the United States, 1920: Detroit, Mich., sheet 4B; Fifteenth Census of the United States, 1930: Detroit, Mich., sheet 24A; "About Us," *Michigan Chronicle*, http://michronicleonline.com/about-us/, accessed 31 October 2014; and folders 1 and 2, box 124, and folder 14, box 127, ser. 10: Other Sengstacke Newspapers, 1936–1997, Abbot-Sengstacke Family Papers, 1847–1997, Carter G. Woodson Regional Library, Vivian G. Harsh Research Collection of Afro-American History and Literature, Chicago Public Library, Chicago, Ill. Though there are some gaps in available issues, the bulk of the *Chronicle*'s coverage from 1939 to the present remains extant (available at the Library of Michigan, Lansing). See, for example, *Michigan Chronicle*, 14 January 1939.

29. The consumers association was also known as the Paradise Valley Better Business Council. *Atlanta Daily World*, 17 August 1937, 1; *Pittsburgh Courier*, 5 February 1938, 22, 3 July 1937, 2; *Afro-American*, 23 January 1937, 2, 30 September 1939, 21; *New York Age*, 27 March 1954, 22; Wilson and Cohassey, *Toast of the Town*, 46; Bjorn, *Before Motown*, 21, 41–42; and Borden, *Detroit's Paradise Valley*, 9.

30. *Atlanta Daily World*, 7 August 1937, 5, 21 August 1937, 8, 27 August 1937, 3, 4 September 1937, 5.

31. *Atlanta Daily World*, 27 September 1937, 2. For more on the Black Hand Squad, see Buccellato, *Early Organized Crime in Detroit*, 26–38.

32. The two cities on the lowest end of that spectrum were Birmingham and Mobile, Alabama. *Atlanta Daily World*, 5 November 1937, 1, 10 May 1938, 6; and *Consumption Habits of the American People*, 1–14.

33. Michaeli, *Defender*, 216–217. See also *Louisville Defender*, 6 January 1951. The paper was still published into the twenty-first century.

34. *Atlanta Daily World*, 28 March 1938, 2, 7 April 1938, 6, 15 April 1938, 5, 23 May 1938, 6, 17 June 1938, 3, 22 July 1938, 2, 3, 5 August 1938, 5. The Library of

Congress lists one edition of the *Michigan State Echo* as surviving, but it has not been located.

35. *Atlanta Daily World*, 25 July 1938, 2, 14 November 1938, 6, 20 December 1938, 6, 16 January 1939, 2, 26 May 1939, 2.

36. The group was originally known as the Michigan Newspaper Syndicate in the summer of 1938, as White was creating his phalanx of papers, but by the end of that year, he had given it his name, an evolution mirroring its parent company to the south. *Atlanta Daily World*, 29 October 1938, 6, 20 December 1938, 6.

37. *Atlanta Daily World*, 8 July 1938, 6, 16 September 1938, 1, 9 December 1938, 1, 1 January 1939, 6.

38. The dean of Hamtramck historians is Greg Kowalski. For more on the city, see his *Wicked Hamtramck: Lust, Liquor, and Lead*; *Hamtramck: The Driven City*; and *Hamtramck: Then and Now*.

39. *Atlanta Daily World*, 29 July 1938, 2, 30 July 1938, 4, 1 September 1938, 2, 27 July 1939, 2. The paper was also known as the *Hamtramck and Detroit Echo* and the *Hamtramck and North Detroit Echo*.

40. *Atlanta Daily World*, 29 August 1939, 2, 29 November 1941, 1.

41. *Atlanta Daily World*, 29 October 1938, 6, 4 November 1939, 6, 6 June 1940, 6, 4 March 1941, 2 (quote), 5 September 1941, 2, 5 December 1941, 5, 22 June 1943, 3, 2 November 1943, 2. White and his newspaper colleague Rollo S. Vest had a radio program called the *Negro Sunday Evening Hour* from 5:30 to 6:00 on Detroit's WJBK. One of the interviewees on that program in 1941 was Petry Fisher, the Detroit newspaperman and former member of the SNS. White was married to Hazel L. White who, as of November 1939, began teaching French and Spanish at Samuel Huston College in Austin, Texas. She returned to Hamtramck, White's home base, in June 1940.

42. *Atlanta Daily World*, 2 May 1939, 2.

43. *Atlanta Daily World*, 6 July 1939, 5, 18 August 1939, 6.

44. *Brownsville Weekly News*, 15 January 1939, 4, 19 March 1939, 4, 14 October 1939, 4 (available at the Library of Michigan, Lansing); *Flint-Brownsville News*, 18 November 1939, 1 (available at the Library of Michigan, Lansing); "About Brownsville Weekly News," Library of Congress Historic American Newspapers, http://chroniclingamerica.loc.gov/lccn/sn96076907/, accessed 9 March 2014; and "About Flint Brownsville News," Library of Congress Historic American Newspapers, http://chroniclingamerica.loc.gov/lccn/sn96076908/, accessed 22 October 2014.

45. *Atlanta Daily World*, 19 October 1938, 2, 5 December 1941, 2, 11 February 1942, 6.

46. *Brownsville Weekly News*, 15 January 1939, 1, 11 November 1939, 1.

47. *Flint-Brownsville News*, 9 December 1939, 1; and *Atlanta Daily World*, 5 May 1941, 1, 5 February 1941, 6 (quote). For more on Randolph and the March on Washington, see chapters 6 and 7.

48. *Flint-Brownsville News*, 20 January 1940, 1–4, 8, 3 February 1940, 1; and *Atlanta Daily World*, 29 January 1940, 6.

49. *Flint-Brownsville News*, 8 March 1941, 8, 5 April 1941, 1–4, 8, 15 September 1941, 1, 8, 21 November 1941, 1, 8. There were other papers in Michigan that allied with the Scott Syndicate without participating with Leroy White, such as the *Kalamazoo Guide* and *Battle Creek Tribune*. Both were short-lived efforts published briefly in 1939. There had been a *Battle Creek Tribune* published in the 1880s, a continuation of the *Michigan Tribune* published in the 1870s. It was a white weekly, however, that had

no relation to the later twentieth-century Black weekly. *Michigan Tribune*, 17 June 1882 (available at the Library of Michigan, Lansing).

50. *Atlanta Daily World*, 1 April 1941, 1. There was a *Detroit Echo* published in the late 1870s in the city. It was, however, a white paper with no relation to the twentieth-century Black incarnation. *Detroit Echo*, 20 November 1879 (available at the Library of Michigan, Lansing).

51. *Atlanta Daily World*, 15 April 1941, 1, 23 November 1941, 5.

52. *Atlanta Daily World*, 10 February 1942, 1, 2 March 1942, 1. Detroit's racialized housing problems stemmed from the early role of Black workers in the auto industry. Henry Ford had hired Black nonunion workers in the 1920s for his factories, but those opportunities evolved into stagnant jobs that kept Black workers at or below the poverty line. They turned ultimately to unionism as a method of organizing against workplace problems, housing problems, and problems with racist groups in the city. Meier and Rudwick, *Black Detroit and the Rise*; and Bates, *Making of Black Detroit*.

53. *Atlanta Daily World*, 17 April 1942, 1, 18 April 1942, 1, 1 May 1942, 1. In May 1942, the paper reported on a letter sent to Michigan congressmen by the Civil Rights Federation, which described "subversive activity in Detroit" involving Nazi sympathizers and charged the House Un-American Activities Committee, chaired by Texas Democrat Martin Dies, with "failure to take action against the Fifth Column." *Atlanta Daily World*, 4 May 1942, 6. Walter Goodman, *Committee*; and O'Reilly, *Hoover and the Unamericans*.

54. *Atlanta Daily World*, 9 March 1943, 1, 15 June 1943, 2; and Peterson, *Planning the Home Front*.

55. Sitkoff, "Detroit Race Riot"; Capeci and Wilkerson, *Layered Violence*; Sugrue, *Origins of the Urban Crisis*; and Shogan and Craig, *Detroit Race Riot*. For representative syndicated coverage, see *Atlanta Daily World*, 22 June 1943, 1, 6, 23 June 1943, 1, 6, 24 June 1943, 1.

56. *Atlanta Daily World*, 23 June 1943, 1, 24 June 1943, 1, 29 June 1943, 1; and Aiello, *Grapevine of the Black South*, 107–123.

57. *Atlanta Daily World*, 22 June 1943, 3.

58. *Atlanta Daily World*, 25 May 1943, 1, 3 June 1943, 1, 4 June 1943, 1, 7 June 1943, 1 (quote).

59. *Atlanta Daily World*, 10 July 1943, 5, 12 July 1943, 6, 13 July 1943, 1, 14 July 1943, 2, 29 July 1943, 5, 3 August 1943, 1.

60. *Atlanta Daily World*, 15 August 1943, 4, 9 November 1943, 1.

61. Pride, "Register and History," 276; and *Atlanta Daily World*, 26 January 1940, 2, 9 May 1940, 2, 4 March 1941, 2.

Conclusion. The Twilight of the Scott Syndicate

1. Emory O. Jackson to Anne Rutledge, 26 March 1955, 1460.1.4, Birmingham World Office Files, Department of Archives and Manuscripts, Birmingham Public Library, Birmingham, Ala.

2. Roberts and Klibanoff, *Race Beat*, 120; and Mangun, *Editor Emory O. Jackson*, 139–240.

3. Lambert, *Battle of Ole Miss*, 37–38; and Hodding Carter, *Their Words Were Bullets*, 50. Much of this and the next eight paragraphs appears in substantially similar form in the conclusion of Aiello, *Grapevine of the Black South*. That is intentional.

4. Cruse, *Crisis of the Negro Intellectual*, 65.

5. Doxey A. Wilkerson, "Negro Press," 511; and Singer, "Mass Society, Mass Media," 140–141.

6. Ottley, *"New World A-Coming,"* 268; Mims, *Advancing South*, 268; and Gordon, *Georgia Negro*, 265. See also Ottley, *Lonely Warrior*.

7. Roberts and Klibanoff, *Race Beat*, 76.

8. Thomas Sancton explained in the 1940s: "When a white man first reads a Negro newspaper, it is like getting a bucket of cold water in the face." Sancton, "Negro Press," 558. See also Jordan, *Black Newspapers and America's War*, 3; and Kreiling, "Making of Racial Identities."

9. In the 1960s, SERS was rechristened the Race Relations Information Center; it lasted until 1972. Gilpin, "Charles S. Johnson," 197.

10. Odum-Hinmon, "Cautious Crusader," 7–8. Peter Kellogg identifies an "atrocity orientation," in which people or groups notice racism at the onset of atrocities—riots, lynchings, assassinations, and so on—but are unable or unwilling to acknowledge the institutional causes of such violent acts, the subtle racism and discrimination that are foundational for the more overt behaviors. That atrocity orientation might help to explain, at least in part, the Black southern press's reaction to some civil rights activities.

11. Kellogg, "Northern Liberals and Black America," 109–113.

12. Thornbrough, "American Negro Newspapers," 467–468.

Bibliography

Newspapers

This book discusses the content of many newspapers that no longer survive through using syndicated stories printed in larger Black newspapers, like the *Atlanta Daily World*. What follows is a list of the main newspapers I viewed or cited in the notes. When these papers are only available in archives, the location is listed in the first citation in the notes.

Afro-American
Alabama Tribune
American Guide
American Progress (Meridian)
American Progress (New Orleans)
Arizona Republic
Arkansas Freeman
Arkansas Survey
Arkansas Survey-Journal
Arkansas Weekly Mansion
Arkansas World
Atlanta Constitution
Atlanta Daily World
Atlanta Independent
Atlanta World
Banner County Outlook
Baton Rouge Post
Bay View Observer
Birmingham Age-Herald
Birmingham News
Birmingham Post
Birmingham World
Brownsville Weekly News
Buffalo Star
California Eagle
Cape Fear Journal
Carolina Lighthouse
Carolina Times
Charleston Messenger
Chattanooga Observer
Chicago Defender
Chicago Daily Tribune
Cincinnati Independent
Cleveland Gazette
Colored Citizen
Columbus Advocate
Connecticut Labor News
Daily Worker
Dallas Express
Des Moines Register
Detroit Echo
Detroit Independent
East Tennessee News
East Texas Times
Evansville Argus
Flint Brownsville News
Florida Sun
Fort Worth Mind
Galveston Examiner
Galveston Guide
Galveston Voice
Greenville Leader
Houston Informer
Illinois Times
Indianapolis Recorder
Indianapolis World
Jackson Advocate
Jacksonville Tribune
Kentucky New Era
Lighthouse and Informer
Los Angeles Sentinel
Louisiana Weekly
Louisville Defender
Louisville Leader
Memphis World
Miami Times
Michigan Chronicle
Michigan Tribune
Mississippi Tribune
Mississippi Weekly
Mobile Press Forum Sun
Monroe Morning World
Monroe News Star
Montgomery Advertiser
Muskogee Lantern
Nashville Clarion
Nashville Defender
Nashville Independent
Nashville Sun
Nashville World
Negro World
Newark Herald
New Jersey Herald News
News-Gazette (Champaign-Urbana)
New York Age
New York Amsterdam News
New York Times

Nite-Life	Southern Enterprise	Tropical Dispatch
Oklahoma Black Dispatch	Southern Liberator	Tuscaloosa Gazette
Oklahoman	Southern Worker	Tuscaloosa News
Pee Dee Advocate	Southwest Georgian	Twin City Herald
Philadelphia Tribune	Spartanburg Herald	Weekly Echo
Phoenix Index	St. Louis Argus	Weekly Progress
Pittsburgh Courier	State	Western Outlook
Progress	Statesville Record and Landmark	Western Star
Savannah Journal		West Virginia Weekly
South Bend Forum	Sunlight	Wilmington Journal
Southern Broadcast	Tri-State Defender	World Telegram

Archival Collections

Abbot-Sengstacke Family Papers, 1847–1997, Carter G. Woodson Regional Library, Vivian G. Harsh Research Collection of Afro-American History and Literature, Chicago Public Library, Chicago, Ill.

Afro-American Newspapers Archives and Research Center, Baltimore, Md.

Alabama Department of Archives and History, Montgomery.

Archives Library, West Virginia Division of Culture and History, Charleston.

Archives and Public Records, Arizona State Library, Phoenix.

Arkansas Collection, F419.P5 S8 Mr 1 1938, Special Collections, University of Arkansas Libraries, Fayetteville.

Atlanta Daily World Records, 1931–1996, Manuscript Collection no. 1092, Manuscript, Archives, and Rare Book Library, Emory University, Atlanta, Ga.

Birmingham World Office Files, Department of Archives and Manuscripts, Birmingham Public Library, Birmingham, Ala.

Black Archives History and Research Foundation of South Florida, Miami.

Black Legion Collection, Clark Historical Library, Central Michigan University, Mt. Pleasant.

Buffalo and Erie County Public Library, Buffalo, N.Y.

C. C. [Charles Clinton] Spaulding Papers, 1905–1985, Rare Book, Manuscript, and Special Collections Library, Duke University, Durham, N.C.

Claude A. Barnett Papers: The Associated Negro Press, 1918–1967, pt. 2, Associated Negro Press Organizational Files, 1920–1966, Chicago Historical Society, Chicago, Ill.

Connecticut State Library, Hartford.

Crusader News Agency, Press Releases, 1933–1934, Schomburg Center for Research in Black Culture, New York Public Library.

Dolph Briscoe Center for American History, University of Texas, Austin.

Emory O. Jackson Papers, A423, Birmingham Civil Rights Institute, Birmingham, Ala.

George Washington Carver Correspondence, 1932–1939, unprocessed collection, Amistad Research Center, Tulane University, New Orleans, La.

Hill Memorial Library, Louisiana State University, Baton Rouge.

Illinois Times Vertical File, Local History Ephemera Series, Champaign County Historical Archives, Urbana Free Library, Urbana, Ill.

James Brown African American Room, Newark Public Library, Newark, N.J.

James B. Morris Papers, 1926–1972, R21, Special Collections, State Historical Society of Iowa, Iowa City.
John H. McCray Papers, South Caroliniana Library, University of South Carolina, Columbia.
Library of Michigan, Lansing.
Memphis World Photographs, MS.3181, Special Collections, University of Tennessee Libraries, Knoxville.
Mississippi Department of Archives and History, Jackson.
National Archives and Records Administration, Atlanta, Ga.
New York Heritage Digital Collections, https://nyheritage.org/.
Office of Archives and History, State Archives of North Carolina, Raleigh.
Ohio Historical Society, Columbus.
Papers of Governor Fuller Warren, ser. 253, State Archives of Florida, Tallahassee.
Southern Tenant Farmers Union Papers, 1934–1970, microfilm S3–S64, University of Arkansas, Fayetteville.
Special and Area Studies Collections, George A. Smathers Libraries, University of Florida, Gainesville.
Tennessee State Library and Archives, Nashville.
U.S. Works Progress Administration, Federal Writers' Project, Folklore Project, Life Histories, 1936–1939, Manuscript Division, Library of Congress, Washington, D.C.
Works Progress Administration Records, Dr. C. C. and Mabel L. Criss Library Special Collections, University of Nebraska, Omaha.

Legal Decisions

Benton v. Commonwealth, 89 Va. 570 (1893).
Brown v. Lee, 331 F.2d 142 (1964).
Buchanan v. Warley, 245 U.S. 60 (1917).
Chambers v. Florida, 309 U.S. 227 (1940).
Chaney v. Saunders, 3 Munf. 51 (Va. 1811).
Chapman v. King, 154 F.2d 460 (1946).
Davis v. Commonwealth, 99 Va. 868 (1901).
Dean v. Commonwealth, 45 Va. (4 Gratt.) 210 (1847).
Gainer v. School Board of Jefferson County, Alabama, 135 F.Supp 559 (1955).
Henderson v. U.S., 339 U.S. 816 (1950).
Herndon v. Lowry, 301 U.S. 242 (1937).
Hey v. Commonwealth, 73 Va. (32 Gratt.) 946 (1879).
Lee v. Peek, 240 S.C. 203 (1962).
Lee v. Peek, 371 U.S. 184 (1962).
McLaurin v. Oklahoma State Regents, 339 U.S. 637 (1950).
Mills v. Board of Education of Anne Arundel County, 30 F.Supp. 245 (1939).
Missouri ex rel. Gaines v. Canada, 305 U.S. 337 (1938).
Mosley v. State, 211 Ga. 611 (1955).
Norris v. Alabama, 294 U.S. 587 (1935).
Parker et al. v. State, 194 Miss. 895 (1943).
People v. Hall, 4 Cal. 399 (1854).
Plessy v. Ferguson, 163 U.S. 537 (1896).

Rogers v. Alabama, 192 U.S. 226 (1904).
Shelley v. Kraemer, 334 U.S. 1 (1948).
Sipuel v. Board of Regents of the University of Oklahoma, 332 U.S. 631 (1948).
Smith v. Allwright, 321 U.S. 649 (1944).
State v. Fisher, 1 H. & J. 750 (Md. 1805).
Sweatt v. Painter, 339 U.S. 629 (1950).
Tademy v. Scott, 68 F.Supp. 556 (1945).
Tademy v. Scott, 157 F.2d 826 (1946).
Thomas v. Pile, 3 H. & McH. 241 (Md. 1794).
U.S. v. Classic, 313 U.S. 299 (1941).
U.S. v. Fisher, 25 F.Cas. 1086 (D.C. 1805).
U.S. v. Mullany, 27 F.Cas. 20 (D.C. 1808).
Williams v. Mississippi, 170 U.S. 213 (1898).
Willis v. Walker, 136 F.Supp. 177 (1955).

Government Documents

"Daniel Joseph Jenkins." Standard Certificate of Death, file no. 10220, State of South Carolina, Bureau of Vital Statistics, Columbia.

Department of Commerce. "Negro Newspapers and Periodicals in the United States: 1937." *Statistical Bulletin*, no. 1 (May 1938).

Department of Commerce. "Negro Newspapers and Periodicals in the United States: 1938." *Statistical Bulletin*, no. 1 (May 1939).

"Eugene Jack Smith." Serial no. 2156, order no. 1963, North Carolina World War II Draft Registration Cards, RG 147, box 339, Records of the Selective Service System, 1926–1975, National Archives Southeast Region, Atlanta, Ga.

Florida Passenger Lists, 1898–1951, U.S. Citizen Passenger Lists of Vessels Arriving at Key West, Florida, Records of the Immigration and Naturalization Service, 1787–2004.

General Index to Incorporation Recordings, L–Z, Ouachita Parish Clerk of Court, Monroe, La.

"Houston, Henry." Certificate of Death, 11 August 1952, 17297, North Carolina State Board of Health, Bureau of Vital Statistics, Charlotte.

"I. Willis Cole." Department of Health, Certificate of Death, state file no. 2852, Bureau of Vital Statistics, Commonwealth of Kentucky.

"Joseph L. Alexander." Certificate of Death, 21037, North Carolina State Board of Health, Bureau of Vital Statistics, North Carolina Death Certificates, 1909–1975, microfilm S.123, rolls 19–242, 280, 313–682, 1040–1297, North Carolina State Archives, Raleigh.

List or Manifest of Alien Passengers for the United States, SS Captain Roberts, list 18, 29 April 1946, Records of the Immigration and Naturalization Service, no. 85, Passenger Lists of Vessels Arriving at Miami, Florida, National Archives and Records Administration, Washington, D.C.

"Petry Fisher and Sadie E. Overton." Marriage License, Wayne County, Michigan, no. 512255, 193208, 1937, Michigan Department of Community Health, Division for Vital Records and Health Statistics.

Vendor Index to Conveyances, MNOP, from the Beginning through 1980. Ouachita Parish Clerk of Court, Monroe, La.

Vendor Index to Conveyances, TUV, from the Beginning through 1980. Ouachita Parish Clerk of Court, Monroe, La.

Other Sources

Adams, James Eli. *A History of Victorian Literature.* New York: Wiley, 2012.
Adams, Luther. *Way Up North in Louisville: African American Migration in the Urban South, 1930–1970.* Chapel Hill: University of North Carolina Press, 2010.
Agee, James, and Walker Evans. *Let Us Now Praise Famous Men.* New York: Houghton Mifflin, 1941.
Aiello, Thomas. *The Battle for the Souls of Black Folk: W. E. B. DuBois, Booker T. Washington, and the Debate That Shaped the Course of Civil Rights.* Westport, Conn.: Praeger, 2016.
Aiello, Thomas. "Calumny in the House of the Lord: The 1932 Zion Traveler Church Shooting." In *Louisiana beyond Black and White: Recent Interpretations on Race and Race Relations,* ed. Michael Martin, 17–34. Lafayette: University of Louisiana Press, 2011.
Aiello, Thomas. *The Grapevine of the Black South: The Scott Newspaper Syndicate in the Generation before the Civil Rights Movement.* Athens: University of Georgia Press, 2018.
Aiello, Thomas. *The Kings of Casino Park: Black Baseball in the Lost Season of 1932.* Tuscaloosa: University of Alabama, 2011.
Alexander, Michelle. *The New Jim Crow: Mass Incarceration in the Age of Colorblindness.* New York: New Press, 2010.
American Civil Liberties Union. *The Bill of Rights in War.* New York: ACLU, 1942.
Anderson, Karen. *Changing Woman: A History of Racial Ethnic Women in Modern America.* New York: Oxford University Press, 1996.
Anderson, William. *The Wild Man from Sugar Creek: The Political Career of Eugene Talmadge.* Baton Rouge: Louisiana State University Press, 1975.
Aptheker, Herbert. *A Documentary History of the Negro People in the United States.* Vol. 7. New York: Citadel, 1969.
Astor, Gerald. *". . . And a Credit to His Race": The Hard Life and Times of Joseph Louis Barrow, a.k.a. Joe Louis.* New York: Saturday Review Press, 1974.
Atlanta—You Ought to Know Your Own! 1937 Directory and Souvenir Program of the National Negro Business League Convention. Atlanta, Ga.: Arnett G. Lindsay, 1937.
Avins, Alfred. "Right to Be a Witness and the Fourteenth Amendment." *Missouri Law Review* 31 (Fall 1966): 471–504.
Bacote, C. A. "The Negro in Atlanta Politics." *Phylon* 16 (Fourth Quarter 1955): 333–350.
Bacote, Clarence. "The Negro in Georgia Politics, 1880–1908." PhD diss., University of Chicago, 1955.
Bailey, Amy Kate, and Stewart E. Tolnay. *Lynched: The Victims of Southern Mob Violence.* Chapel Hill: University of North Carolina Press, 2015.
Bailey, Frankie Y., and Alice P. Green. *"Law Never Here": A Social History of African American Responses to Issues of Crime and Justice.* Westport, Conn.: Praeger, 1999.
Baker, R. Scott. *Paradoxes of Desegregation: African American Struggles for Educational Equity in Charleston, South Carolina, 1926–1972.* Columbia: University of South Carolina Press, 2006.

Baker, Scott. "Pedagogies of Protest: African American Teachers and the Civil Rights Movement." *Teachers College Record* 113 (December 2011): 2777–2803.

Baker, Scott. "Testing Equality: The National Teacher Examination and the NAACP's Legal Campaign to Equalize Teachers' Salaries in the South, 1936-1963." *History of Education Quarterly* 35 (Spring 1995): 49–64.

Baker, Thomas Harrison. *The "Memphis Commercial Appeal": A History of a Southern Newspaper*. Baton Rouge: Louisiana State University Press, 1971.

Baker, William J. *Jesse Owens: An American Life*. New York: Macmillan, 1986.

Baldwin, James. *The Evidence of Things Not Seen*. New York: Henry Holt, 1985.

Barnard, William D. *Dixiecrats and Democrats: Alabama Politics, 1942-1950*. Tuscaloosa: University of Alabama Press, 1974.

Barnett, Albert G. "Why Can't We Have Negro Dailies?" *Afro-American Youth* 1 (December 1937): 4–7.

Bates, Beth Tompkins. *The Making of Black Detroit in the Age of Henry Ford*. Chapel Hill: University of North Carolina Press, 2014.

Bedingfield, Sid. "The Dixiecrat Summer of 1948: Two South Carolina Editors—a Liberal and a Conservative—Foreshadow Modern Political Debate in the South." *American Journalism* 27 (Summer 2010): 91–114.

Bedingfield, Sid. "John H. McCray, Accom[m]odationism, and the Framing of the Civil Rights Struggle in South Carolina, 1940-48." *Journalism History* 37 (Summer 2011): 91–101.

Bedingfield, Sid. *Newspaper Wars: Civil Rights and White Resistance in South Carolina, 1935-1965*. Urbana: University of Illinois Press, 2017.

Beecher, John. "The Sharecroppers Union in Alabama." *Social Forces* 13 (October 1934–May 1935): 124–132.

Beeler, Dorothy. "Race Riot in Columbia, Tennessee, February 25-27, 1946." *Tennessee Historical Quarterly* 39 (Spring 1980): 49–61.

Beezer, Bruce. "Black Teachers' Salaries and the Federal Courts before *Brown v. Board of Education*: One Beginning for Equality." *Journal of Negro Education* 55 (Spring 1986): 200–213.

Behling, Charles F. "South Carolina Negro Newspapers: Their History, Content, and Reception." MA thesis, University of South Carolina, 1964.

Belles, A. Gilbert. "The Black Press in Illinois." *Journal of the Illinois State Historical Society* 68 (September 1975): 344–352.

Berg, A. Scott. *Lindbergh*. New York: G. P. Putnam's Sons, 1998.

Bernstein, Matthew. "Nostalgia, Ambivalence, Irony: 'Song of the South' and Race Relations in 1946 Atlanta." *Film History* 8, no. 2 (1996): 219–236.

Biagi, Shirley, and Marilyn Kern-Foxworth. *Facing Difference: Race, Gender, and Mass Media*. Thousand Oaks, Calif.: Pine Forge, 1997.

Bilbo, Theodore G. *Take Your Choice: Separation or Mongrelization*. Poplarville, Miss.: Dream House, 1947.

Bjorn, Lars. *Before Motown: A History of Jazz in Detroit, 1920-60*. Ann Arbor: University of Michigan Press, 2001.

Black, Dan A., et al. "The Impact of the Great Migration on Mortality of African Americans: Evidence from the Deep South." *American Economic Review* 105 (February 2015): 477–503.

Blackmon, Douglas. *Slavery by Another Name: The Re-Enslavement of Black Americans from the Civil War to World War II*. New York: Random House, 2008.

Blackwell, Gloria. "Black-Controlled Media in Atlanta, 1960–1970: The Burden of the Message and the Struggle for Survival." PhD diss., Emory University, 1973.

Blakeney, Lincoln Anderson. "A Sociological Analysis of a Negro Newspaper: The Atlanta Daily World." MA thesis, Atlanta University, 1949.

Booker, Robert J. *A History of Mechanicsville, 1875-2008: A Glimpse of People, Places, and Events of Knoxville's Elite Black Community and Their Contributions to Society.* Knoxville, Tenn.: Knoxville's Community Development Corporation, 2008. http://www.kcdc.org/Libraries/Exec_Mngmnt_Documents/theStoryofMechanicsville.sflb.ashx, accessed 2 March 2014.

Borden, Ernest H. *Detroit's Paradise Valley.* Mt. Pleasant, S.C.: Arcadia, 2003.

Boston, Michael B. *The Business Strategy of Booker T. Washington: Its Development and Implementation.* Gainesville: University Press of Florida, 2010.

Boyd, Bill. *Blind Obedience: A True Story of Family Loyalty and Murder in South Georgia.* Macon, Ga.: Mercer University Press, 2000.

Boyle, Kevin. *Arc of Justice: A Saga of Race, Civil Rights, and Murder in the Jazz Age.* New York: Henry Holt, 2004.

Brooks, Maxwell. "Content Analysis of Leading Negro Newspapers." PhD diss., Ohio State University, 1953.

Brooks, Maxwell. "A Sociological Interpretation of the Negro Newspaper." MA thesis, Ohio State University, 1937.

Brophy, Alfred L. *Reconstructing the Dreamland: The Tulsa Race Riot of 1921, Race Reparations, and Reconciliation.* New York: Oxford University Press, 2002.

Brown, James Seay, Jr., ed. *Up before Daylight: Life Histories from the Alabama Writers' Project, 1938-1939.* Tuscaloosa: University of Alabama Press, 1982.

Brown, M. Christopher, II. "Collegiate Desegregation as Progenitor and Progeny of *Brown v. Board of Education*: The Forgotten Role of Postsecondary Litigation, 1908-1990." *Journal of Negro Education* 73 (Summer 2004): 341–349.

Brown-Nagin, Tomiko. *Courage to Dissent: Atlanta and the Long History of the Civil Rights Movement.* New York: Oxford University Press, 2011.

Brundage, W. Fitzhugh. *Lynching in the New South: Georgia and Virginia, 1880-1930.* Urbana: University of Illinois Press, 1993.

Buccellato, James. *Early Organized Crime in Detroit: Vice, Corruption, and the Rise of the Mafia.* Charleston, S.C.: History Press, 2015.

Buchanan, Scott. "The Dixiecrat Rebellion: Long-Term Partisan Implications in the Deep South." *Politics and Policy* 33 (November 2005):754–769.

Bullock, Penelope L. "Profile of a Periodical: The 'Voice of the Negro.'" *Atlanta Historical Bulletin* 21 (Spring 1977): 95–114.

Burma, John H. "An Analysis of the Present Negro Press." *Social Forces* 26 (December 1947): 172–180.

Burma, John H. "The Future of the Negro Press." *Negro Digest* 6 (February 1948): 67–70.

Busch, Andrew E. *Truman's Triumphs: The 1948 Election and the Making of Postwar America.* Lawrence: University Press of Kansas, 2012.

Butler, Paul. "Racially Based Jury Nullification: Black Power in the Criminal Justice System." *Yale Law Journal* 105 (December 1995): 677–725.

Campbell, James. *Crime and Punishment in African American History.* New York: Palgrave Macmillan, 2013.

Capeci, Dominic J., and Martha Wilkerson. *Layered Violence: The Detroit Rioters of 1943*. Jackson: University Press of Mississippi, 1991.

Carlin, Amanda. "The Courtroom as White Space: Racial Performance as Noncredibility." *UCLA Law Review* 63 (2016): 450–484.

Carlton, David L., and Peter A. Coclanis, eds. *Confronting Southern Poverty in the Great Depression: The Report on Economic Conditions of the South with Related Documents*. Boston, Mass.: St. Martin's, 1996.

Carroll, Brian. *When to Stop the Cheering? The Black Press, the Black Community, and the Integration of Professional Baseball*. New York: Routledge, 2006.

Carroll, Fred. *Race News: Black Journalists and the Fight for Racial Justice in the Twentieth Century*. Urbana: University of Illinois Press, 2017.

Carter, Dan T. *Scottsboro: A Tragedy of the American South*. New York: Oxford University Press, 1969.

Carter, Hodding. *Their Words Were Bullets: The Southern Press in War, Reconstruction, and Peace*. Athens: University of Georgia Press, 1969.

Chafe, William H. *Civilities and Civil Rights: Greensboro, North Carolina, and the Black Struggle for Freedom*. New York: Oxford University Press, 1980.

Chambliss, Rollin. *What Negro Newspapers of Georgia Say about Some Social Problems*. Athens: University of Georgia Press, 1934.

Chang, Derek. *Citizens of a Christian Nation: Evangelical Missions and the Problem of Race in the Nineteenth Century*. Philadelphia: University of Pennsylvania Press, 2010.

Chappell, David L. *A Stone of Hope: Prophetic Religion and the Death of Jim Crow*. Chapel Hill: University of North Carolina Press, 2004.

Christian, Charles M. *Black Saga: The African American Experience: A Chronology*. New York: Civitas, 1999.

Clark, E. Culpepper. *The Schoolhouse Door: Segregation's Last Stand at the University of Alabama*. New York: Oxford University Press, 1993.

Clayton, Bruce, and John A. Salmond. *Southern History: Ideas and Actions in the Twentieth Century*. New York: Rowman and Littlefield, 1999.

Cohen, William. *At Freedom's Edge: Black Mobility and the Southern White Quest for Racial Control, 1861–1915*. Baton Rouge: Louisiana State University Press, 1991.

Cohodas, Nadine. *Strom Thurmond and the Politics of Southern Change*. Macon, Ga.: Mercer University Press, 1995.

Coleman, Ada F. "The Salary Equalization Movement." *Journal of Negro Education* 16 (Spring 1947): 235–241.

Collins, Ernest M. "Cincinnati Negroes and Presidential Politics." In *The Negro in Depression and War: Prelude to Revolution, 1930–1945*, ed. Bernard Sternsher, 258–263. Chicago, Ill.: Quadrangle, 1969.

Connolly, N. D. B. *A World More Concrete: Real Estate and the Remaking of Jim Crow South Florida*. Chicago, Ill.: University of Chicago Press, 2014.

Consumption Habits of the American People. Washington, D.C.: U.S. Bureau of Labor Statistics, 1938.

Cooper, Caryl A. "Percy Greene and the *Jackson Advocate*." In *The Press and Race: Mississippi Journalists Confront the Movement*, ed. David R. Davies, 55–84. Jackson: University Press of Mississippi, 2001.

Covington, Howard E., and Marion A. Ellis, eds. *The North Carolina Century: Tar Heels Who Made a Difference, 1900–2000*. Chapel Hill: University of North Carolina Press, 2002.

Cox, Patrick. *The First Texas News Barons*. Austin: University of Texas Press, 2009.
Crespino, Joseph. *Strom Thurmond's America*. New York: Macmillan, 2012.
Crudup, Keith. "African Americans in Arizona: A Twentieth Century History." PhD diss., Arizona State University, 1998.
Cruse, Harold. *The Crisis of the Negro Intellectual*. 1967; rpt., New York: New York Review of Books, 2005.
Culver, John C., and John Hyde. *American Dreamer: The Life and Times of Henry A. Wallace*. New York: Norton, 2002.
Dalfiume, Richard M. "The 'Forgotten Years' of the Negro Revolution." In *The Negro in Depression and War: Prelude to Revolution, 1930-1945*, ed. Bernard Sternsher, 298-316. Chicago, Ill.: Quadrangle, 1969.
Dann, Martin E., ed. *The Black Press, 1827-1890: The Quest for National Identity*. New York: Capricorn, 1971.
Davis, Benjamin, Jr. *Communist Councilman from Harlem*. New York: International Publishers, 1969.
Davis, Christopher Brian. "Emory O. Jackson: A Traditionalist in the Early Civil Rights Fight in Birmingham, Alabama." MA thesis, University of Alabama at Birmingham, 2006.
Davis, Frank Marshall. "Negro America's First Daily." *Negro Digest* 5 (1946): 86-88.
Davis, Thomas J. "Louisiana." In *The Black Press in the South, 1865-1979*, ed. Henry Lewis Suggs, 151-176. Westport, Conn.: Greenwood, 1983.
DeCuir, Sharlene Sinegal. "Attacking Jim Crow: Black Activism in New Orleans, 1925-1941." PhD diss., Louisiana State University, 2009.
De Hart, Jane Sherron. "Second Wave Feminism(s) and the South: The Difference That Differences Make." In *Women of the American South: A Multicultural Reader*, ed. Christie Anne Farnham, 273-301. New York: New York University Press, 1997.
Delombard, Jeannine Marie. "Representing the Slave: White Advocacy and Black Testimony in Harriet Beecher Stowe's *Dred*." *New England Quarterly* 75 (March 2002): 80-106.
deShazo, Richard D., and Lucius Lampton. "The Educational Struggles of African American Physicians in Mississippi: Finding a Path toward Reconciliation." *Journal of the Mississippi State Medical Association* 54 (July 2013): 189-198.
Detweiler, Frederick. *The Negro Press in the United States*. Chicago, Ill.: University of Chicago Press, 1922.
Detweiler, Frederick G. "The Negro Press Today." *American Journal of Sociology* 44 (November 1938): 391-400.
Devine, Thomas W. *Henry Wallace's 1948 Presidential Campaign and the Future of Postwar Liberalism*. Chapel Hill: University of North Carolina Press, 2013.
Dillard, Angela D. *Faith in the City: Preaching Radical Social Change in Detroit*. Ann Arbor: University of Michigan Press, 2007.
Dittmer, John. *Black Georgia in the Progressive Era, 1900-1920*. Urbana: University of Illinois Press, 1977.
Divine, Robert A. "The Cold War and the Election of 1948." *Journal of American History* 59 (June 1972): 90-110.
Dolan, Mark K. "Extra! *Chicago Defender* Race Records Ads Show South from Afar." *Southern Cultures* 13 (Fall 2007): 106-124.
Donaldson, Gary A. *Truman Defeats Dewey*. Lexington: University Press of Kentucky, 1999.

Doreski, C. K. *Writing America Black: Race Rhetoric in the Public Sphere*. New York: Cambridge University Press, 1998.

Dorsey, Allison. *To Build Our Lives Together: Community Formation in Black Atlanta, 1875-1906*. Athens: University of Georgia Press, 2004.

Douglass, Frederick. *The Life and Times of Frederick Douglass*. Boston: De Wolfe, Fiske, 1881.

Drago, Edmund L. *Black Politicians and Reconstruction in Georgia: A Splendid Failure*. Baton Rouge: Louisiana State University Press, 1982.

Drake, Robert. "Joe Louis, the Southern Press, and the 'Fight of the Century.'" *Sport History Review* 43 (May 2012): 1–17.

Drake, St. Clair, and Horace R. Cayton. *Black Metropolis: A Study of Negro Life in a Northern City*. Vol. 1. New York: Harper and Row, 1962.

Dray, Philip. *At the Hands of Persons Unknown: The Lynching of Black America*. New York: Modern Library, 2002.

Du Bois, W. E. B. "The Hampton Strike." *Nation*, 2 November 1927, 471–472.

Dulles, John Foster. "Thoughts on Soviet Foreign Policy and What to Do about It." *Life* 26 (3 June 1946): 113–125.

Duncan, Mae Najiyyah. *A Survey of Cincinnati's Black Press and Its Editors, 1844–2010*. Bloomington, Ind.: Xlibris, 2011.

Duncombe, Stephen. *Notes from Underground: Zines and the Politics of Alternative Culture*. London: Verso, 1997.

Durr, Robert. *The Negro Press: Its Character, Development, and Function*. Jackson: Mississippi Division, Southern Regional Council, 1947.

Dyreson, Mark. "American Ideas about Race and Racism in the Era of Jesse Owens: Shattering Myths or Reinforcing Scientific Racism." *International Journal of the History of Sport* 25, no. 2 (2008): 247–267.

Dyreson, Mark. "Jesse Owens: Leading Man in Modern American Tales of Racial Progress and Limits." In *Out of the Shadows: A Biographical History of the African American Athlete*, ed. David W. Wiggins, 111–131. Fayetteville: University of Arkansas Press, 2006.

Dyreson, Mark. "Marketing National Identity: The Olympic Games of 1932 and American Culture." *OLYMPIKA: The International Journal of Olympic Studies* 4 (1995): 23–48.

Egerton, John. *Speak Now against the Day: The Generation before the Civil Rights Movement in the South*. Chapel Hill: University of North Carolina Press, 1995.

Eig, Jonathan. *Opening Day: The Story of Jackie Robinson's First Season*. New York: Simon and Schuster, 2007.

Ellis, William E. *A History of Education in Kentucky*. Lexington: University of Kentucky Press, 2011.

Ellsworth, Scott. *Death in a Promised Land: The Tulsa Race Riot of 1921*. Baton Rouge: Louisiana State University Press, 1992.

Elson, Charles Meyer. "The Georgia Three-Governor Controversy of 1947." *Atlanta Historical Bulletin* 20 (Fall 1976): 72–95.

Erenberg, Lewis A. *The Greatest Fight of Our Generation: Louis v. Schmeling*. New York: Oxford University Press, 2005.

Eskew, Glenn T. *But for Birmingham: The Local and National Movements in the Civil Rights Struggle*. Chapel Hill: University of North Carolina Press, 1997.

Evans, Elizabeth Sandidge. "Atlanta Negro Chamber of Commerce." In *Encyclopedia of African American Business*, vol. 1, ed. Jessie Carney Smith, 152–153. Westport, Conn.: Greenwood, 2006.

Evans, Sara. *Personal Politics: The Roots of Women's Liberation in the Civil Rights Movement and the New Left*. New York: Knopf, 1979.

Fagan, Benjamin. *The Black Newspaper and the Chosen Nation*. Athens: University of Georgia Press, 2016.

Farrar, Hayward. *The "Baltimore Afro-American," 1892–1950*. Westport, Conn.: Greenwood, 1998.

Fassin, Didier. *Enforcing Order: An Ethnography of Urban Policing*. Cambridge: Polity, 2013.

Fassin, Didier, and Richard Rechtman. *The Empire of Trauma: An Inquiry into the Condition of Victimhood*. Princeton, N.J.: Princeton University Press, 2009.

"Federal Court Orders Equal Teachers' Salaries in Maryland County." *Crisis* 46 (December 1939): 372.

Feldman, Ruth Elaine. "A Checklist of Atlanta Newspapers, 1846–1948." MA thesis, Emory University, 1949.

Fenderson, Lewis H. "The Negro Press as a Social Instrument." *Journal of Negro Education* 20 (Spring 1951): 181–188.

Ferguson, Karen. *Black Politics in New Deal Atlanta*. Chapel Hill: University of North Carolina Press, 2002.

Fidler, William P. "Academic Freedom in the South Today." *AAUP Bulletin* 51 (Winter 1965): 413–421.

Field, Marshall. *The Negro Press and the Issues of Democracy*. Chicago, Ill.: American Council on Race Relations, 1944.

Finkle, Lee. *Forum for Protest: The Black Press during World War II*. Rutherford, N.J.: Fairleigh Dickinson University Press, 1975.

Fisher, Jim. *The Lindbergh Case*. New Brunswick, N.J.: Rutgers University Press, 1987.

Flynt, Wayne. *Poor but Proud: Alabama's Poor Whites*. Tuscaloosa: University of Alabama Press, 1989.

"Forte, Ormond Adolphus." In *Encyclopedia of Cleveland History*, Case Western Reserve University, http://ech.case.edu/cgi/article.pl?id=FOA, accessed 30 October 2014.

"Fortune Press Analysis: Negro Press." *Fortune* 31 (May 1945): 233–238.

Foster, Vera Chandler. "Boswellianism: A Technique in the Restriction of Negro Voting." *Phylon* 10 (First Quarter 1949): 26–37.

Fox, Craig. *Everyday Klansfolk: White Protestant Life and the KKK in 1920s Michigan*. East Lansing: Michigan State University Press, 2011.

Frazier, E. Franklin. *Black Bourgeoisie*. New York: Free Press, 1957.

Frederickson, Kari. *The Dixiecrat Revolt and the End of the Solid South, 1932–1968*. Chapel Hill: University of North Carolina Press, 2001.

Friedman, Lawrence J. "Life in the Lion's Mouth: Another Look at Booker T. Washington." *Journal of Negro History* 59 (October 1974): 337–351.

Fultz, Michael. "'The Morning Cometh': African-American Periodicals, Education, and the Black Middle Class, 1900–1930." *Journal of Negro History* 80 (Summer 1995): 97–112.

Gamson, William A., and Gadi Wolfsfeld. "Movements and Media as Interacting Systems." *Annals of the American Academy of Political and Social Science* 528 (July 1993): 114-125.

Garfinkel, Herbert. *When Negroes March: The March on Washington Movement in the Organizational Politics for FEPC.* New York: Atheneum, 1969.

Garland, Phyl. "The Black Press: Down but Not Out." *Columbia Journalism Review* 21 (September-October 1982): 43-50.

Garrett, Franklin M. *Atlanta and Environs: A Chronicle of Its People and Events.* Vol. 2. Athens: University of Georgia Press, 1954.

Garrett, Marie. "Charles Clinton Spaulding (1874-1952)." In *Encyclopedia of African-American Business*, ed. Jessie Carney Smith, 741-745. Westport, Conn.: Greenwood, 2006.

Gates, Maurice. "Negro Students Challenge Social Forces." *Crisis* 42 (August 1935): 233.

Gatson, Paul M. *The New South Creed: A Study in Southern Mythmaking.* New York: Knopf, 1970.

Gershenhorn, Jerry. *Louis Austin and the Carolina Times: A Life in the Long Black Freedom Struggle.* Chapel Hill: University of North Carolina Press, 2018.

Giddings, Paula. *When and Where I Enter: The Impact of Black Women on Race and Sex in America.* New York: Morrow, 1984.

Gilmore, Glenda Elizabeth. *Defying Dixie: The Radical Roots of Civil Rights, 1919-1950.* New York: Norton, 2008.

Gilmore, Glenda Elizabeth. *Gender and Jim Crow: Women and the Politics of White Supremacy in North Carolina, 1896-1920.* Chapel Hill: University of North Carolina Press, 1996.

Gilpin, Patrick J. "Charles S. Johnson and the Southern Educational Reporting Service." *Journal of Negro History* 63 (July 1978): 197-208.

Glasrud, Bruce A., and Cary D. Wintz. "The Black Renaissance in the Desert Southwest." In *The Harlem Renaissance in the American West: The New Negro's Western Experience*, ed. Bruce A. Glasrud and Cary D. Wintz, 170-182. New York: Routledge, 2012.

Glazier, Jack. *Been Coming Through Some Hard Times: Race, History, and Memory in Western Kentucky.* Knoxville: University of Tennessee Press, 2013.

Godshalk, David Fort. *Veiled Visions: The 1906 Atlanta Race Riot and the Reshaping of American Race Relations.* Chapel Hill: University of North Carolina Press, 2005.

Goings, Kenneth G., and Gerald L. Smith. "'Unhidden' Transcripts: Memphis and African American Agency, 1862-1920." *Journal of Urban History* 21 (March 1995): 372-394.

Goldfield, David R. *Black, White, and Southern: Race Relations and Southern Culture.* Baton Rouge: Louisiana State University Press, 1990.

Gooden, Amoaba. "Visual Representations of Feminine Beauty in the Black Press: 1915-1950." *Journal of Pan African Studies* 4 (June 2011): 81-96.

Goodman, James. *Stories of Scottsboro.* New York: Random House, 1994.

Goodman, Walter. *The Committee: The Extraordinary Career of the House Committee on Un-American Activities.* New York: Farrar Straus and Giroux, 1968.

Gordon, Asa. *The Georgia Negro.* Ann Arbor: University of Michigan Press, 1937.

Gore, George W. *Negro Journalism: An Essay on the History and Present Conditions of the Negro Press.* Greencastle, Ind.: DePauw University, 1922.

Grafton, Carl, and Anne Permaloff. *Big Mules and Branchheads: James E. Folsom and Political Power in Alabama.* Athens: University of Georgia Press, 1985.

Gray-Ray, Phyllis, et al. "African Americans and the Criminal Justice System." *Humboldt Journal of Social Relations* 21, no. 2 (1995): 105–117.

"The Great Migration, 1910 to 1970." U.S. Census Bureau, https://www.census.gov/dataviz/visualizations/020/508.php, accessed 13 September 2012.

Green, Ben. *Before His Time: The Untold Story of Harry T. Moore, America's First Civil Rights Martyr.* New York: Free Press, 1999.

Green, Laurie B. *Battling the Plantation Mentality: Memphis and the Black Freedom Struggle.* Chapel Hill: University of North Carolina Press, 2007.

Greene, Melissa Fay. *The Temple Bombing.* 1996; rpt., Cambridge, Mass.: Da Capo, 2006.

Griffin, William Wayne. *African Americans and the Color Line in Ohio, 1915–1930.* Columbus: Ohio State University Press, 2005.

Griffin, Willie J. "An Indigenous Civil Rights Movement: Charlotte, North Carolina, 1940–1963." MA thesis, Morgan State University, 2006.

Grillo, Evelio. *Black Cuban, Black American: A Memoir.* Houston, Tex.: Arte Publico, 2000.

Grose, Charles. "Black Newspapers in Texas, 1868–1970." PhD diss., University of Texas, 1972.

Grossman, James. *Land of Hope: Chicago, Black Southerners, and the Great Migration.* Chicago, Ill.: University of Chicago Press, 1989.

Hahn, Steven. *A Nation under Our Feet: Black Political Struggles in the Rural South from Slavery to the Great Migration.* Cambridge, Mass.: Harvard University Press, 2003.

Hardin, John A. *Fifty Years of Segregation: Black Higher Education in Kentucky, 1904–1954.* Lexington: University Press of Kentucky, 1997.

Hardin, John A. "'Kentucky Is More or Less Civilized': Alfred Carroll, Charles Eubanks, Lyman Johnson, and the Desegregation of Kentucky Higher Education, 1939–1949." *Register of the Kentucky Historical Society* 109 (Summer–Autumn 2011): 327–350.

Harlan, Louis R. *Booker T. Washington: The Making of a Black Leader, 1856–1901.* New York: Oxford University Press, 1972.

Harlan, Louis R. *Booker T. Washington: The Wizard of Tuskegee, 1901–1915.* New York: Oxford University Press, 1983.

Harlan, Louis R. "The Secret Life of Booker T. Washington." *Journal of Southern History* 37 (August 1971): 393–416.

Harrison, Cynthia. *On Account of Sex: The Politics of Women's Issues, 1945–1968.* Berkeley: University of California Press, 1988.

Harrison, Lowell Hayes. *A New History of Kentucky.* Lexington: University Press of Kentucky, 1997.

Harvey, William B. "Constitutional Law: Anti-Lynching Legislation." *Michigan Law Review* 47 (January 1949): 369–377.

Hauke, Kathleen A. *Ted Poston: Pioneer American Journalist.* Athens: University of Georgia Press, 1998.

Heitzeg, Nancy A. "'Whiteness,' Criminality, and the Double-Standards of Deviance/ Social Control." *Contemporary Justice Review* 18, no. 2 (2015): 197–214.

Hemmingway, Theodore. "South Carolina." In *The Black Press in the South, 1865– 1979*, ed. Henry Lewis Suggs, 289–312. Westport, Conn.: Greenwood, 1983.

Henderson, Alexa Benson. *Atlanta Life Insurance Company: Guardian of Black Economic Dignity*. Tuscaloosa: University of Alabama Press, 1990.

Henderson, Alexa Benson. "Heman E. Perry and Black Enterprise in Atlanta, 1908– 1925." *Business History Review* 61 (Summer 1987): 216–242.

Henkin, Louis. "*Shelley v. Kraemer*: Notes for a Revised Opinion." *University of Pennsylvania Law Review* 110 (February 1962): 473–505.

Henri, Florette. *Black Migration: Movement North, 1900–1920*. Garden City, N.Y.: Anchor Press/Doubleday, 1975.

Herndon, Angelo. *Let Me Live*. 1937; rpt., Ann Arbor: University of Michigan Press, 2007.

Higginbotham, A. Leon, Jr. "Race, Sex, Education and Missouri Jurisprudence: *Shelley v. Kraemer* in a Historical Perspective." *Washington University Law Review* 67, no. 3 (1989): 673–708.

Higginbotham, A. Leon, Jr. *Shades of Freedom: Racial Politics and Presumptions of the American Legal Process*. New York: Oxford University Press, 1996.

Hine, Darlene Clark. *Black Victory: The Rise and Fall of the White Primary in Texas*. Millwood, N.Y.: KTO, 1979.

Hixson, Jr., William B. "Moorfield Storey and the Defense of the Dyer Anti-Lynching Bill." *New England Quarterly* 42 (March 1969): 65–81.

Hogan, Lawrence D. *A Black National News Service: The Associated Negro Press and Claude Barnett*. Hackensack, N.J.: Fairleigh Dickinson University Press, 1984.

Hogan, Lawrence D. *Shades of Glory: The Negro Leagues and the Story of African-American Baseball*. Washington, D.C.: National Geographic, 2006.

Holbrook Benevolent Association. "Constitution and By-Laws of the Holbrook Benevolent Association of the State of Mississippi." E185.93 M6 H569 1900Z, Department of Archives and Special Collections, University of Mississippi, Oxford.

Horne, Gerald. *Black Liberation/Red Scare: Ben Davis and the Communist Party*. Newark: University of Delaware Press, 1994.

Horne, Gerald. *The Rise and Fall of the Associated Negro Press: Claude Barnett's Pan-African News and the Jim Crow Paradox*. Urbana: University of Illinois Press, 2017.

Horne, Jackie C. *History and Construction of the Child in Early British Children's Literature*. Farnham, England: Ashgate, 2013.

Hornsby, Alton, Jr. "Georgia." In *The Black Press in the South, 1865–1979*, ed. Henry Lewis Suggs, 119–150. Westport, Conn.: Greenwood, 1983.

Hornsby, Alton, Jr. "The Negro in Atlanta Politics, 1961–1973." *Atlanta Historical Bulletin* 21 (Spring 1977): 7–33.

Howard, Victor B. *Black Liberation in Kentucky: Emancipation and Freedom, 1862– 1884*. Lexington: University Press of Kentucky, 1983.

Howard, Victor B. "The Black Testimony Controversy in Kentucky, 1866–1872." *Journal of Negro History* 58 (April 1973): 140–165.

"Howard, William Schley." In *Biographical Directory of the United States Congress, 1774–Present*. http://bioguide.congress.gov/scripts/biodisplay.pl?index=H000849, accessed 13 May 2014.

Hughes, C. Alvin. "We Demand Our Rights: The Southern Negro Youth Congress, 1937–1949." *Phylon* (First Quarter 1987): 38–50.

Hughes, Langston. "Battle of the Ballot." In *The Collected Works of Langston Hughes*, vol. 10: *"Fight for Freedom" and Other Writings on Civil Rights*, ed. Christopher C. De Santis, 117–122. Columbia: University of Missouri Press, 2001.

Hunter, Gary Jerome. "Don't Buy from Where You Can't Work: Black Urban Boycott Movements during the Depression, 1929–1941." PhD diss., University of Michigan, 1977.

Hurd, Michael. *"Collie J": Grambling's Man with the Golden Pen*. Haworth, N.J.: St. Johann Press, 2007.

Ingham, John N., and Lynne B. Feldman, *African American Business Leaders: A Biographical Dictionary*. Westport, Conn.: Greenwood, 1994.

"An Interview with Clarence B. Robinson." Tennessee State University, April 1983, http://ww2.tnstate.edu/library/digital/interview2.htm, accessed 13 October 2013.

Interview with John McCray by Worth Long and Randall Williams. Emory University, Atlanta, Ga., http://beck.library.emory.edu/southernchanges/articlephp?id=sc19-1_003, accessed 4 January 2014.

James, Rawn, Jr. *Root and Branch: Charles Hamilton Houston, Thurgood Marshall, and the Struggle to End Segregation*. New York: Bloomsbury, 2010.

Janken, Kenneth Robert. *White: The Biography of Walter White, Mr. NAACP*. New York: Free Press, 2003.

Jencks, Christopher, and David Reisman. "The American Negro College." *Harvard Educational Review* 37 (Winter 1967): 3–60.

"Jervay, T. C." NewStories: An Oral History of North Carolina News Workers and News Makers, University of North Carolina School of Journalism and Mass Communication, http://hallsoffame.jomc.unc.edu/jervay-t-c/, accessed 4 January 2014.

Johnson, Charles S. *Growing Up in the Black Belt: Negro Youth in the Rural South*. Washington, D.C.: American Council on Education, 1941.

Johnson, Guy. "Some Factors in the Development of Negro Social Institutions in the United States." *American Journal of Sociology* 40 (November 1934): 329–337.

Johnson, Marcia Lynn. "Student Protest at Fisk University in the 1920s." *Negro History Bulletin* 33 (October 1970): 137–140.

Jones, Allen W. "The Black Press in the 'New South': Jesse C. Duke's Struggle for Justice and Equality." *Journal of Negro History* 64 (Summer 1979): 215–228.

Jones, Allen Woodrow. "Alabama." In *The Black Press in the South, 1865–1979*, ed. Henry Lewis Suggs, 23–64. Westport, Conn.: Greenwood, 1983.

Jones, Edward A. "Morehouse College in Business Ninety Years—Building Men." *Phylon* 18 (Third Quarter 1957): 237.

Jones, Jacqueline. *Labor of Love, Labor of Sorrow: Black Women, Work, and the Family from Slavery to the Present*. New York: Basic, 1985.

Jones-Brown, Delores D. "Race as a Legal Construct: The Implications for American Justice." In *The System in Black and White: Exploring the Connections between Race, Crime, and Justice*, ed. Michael W. Markowitz and Delores D. Jones-Brown, 137–152. Westport, Conn.: Praeger, 2000.

Jones Ross, Felicia G. "Mobilizing the Masses: The *Cleveland Call and Post* and the Scottsboro Incident." *Journal of Negro History* 84 (Winter 1999): 48–60.

Jopling, Hannah. *Life in a Black Community: Striving for Equal Citizenship in Annapolis, Maryland, 1902-1952*. Lanham, Md.: Lexington, 2015.

Jordan, William G. *Black Newspapers and America's War for Democracy, 1914-1920*. Chapel Hill: University of North Carolina Press, 2001.

Junne, George H., Jr. *Blacks in the American West and Beyond–America, Canada, and Mexico: A Selectively Annotated Bibliography*. Westport, Conn.: Greenwood, 2000.

Kelleher, Daniel T. "The Case of Lloyd Lionel Gaines: The Demise of the Separate but Equal Doctrine." *Journal of Negro History* 56 (October 1971): 262-271.

Kellogg, Peter J. "Northern Liberals and Black America: A History of White Attitudes, 1936-1952." PhD diss., Northwestern University, 1971.

Kelly, Robin D. G. *Hammer and Hoe: Alabama Communists during the Great Depression*. Chapel Hill: University of North Carolina Press, 1990.

Kennedy, William Jesse, Jr. *The North Carolina Mutual Story: A Symbol of Progress, 1898-1970*. Durham, N.C.: North Carolina Mutual Life Insurance Company, 1970.

Kerber, Linda K. *No Constitutional Right to Be Ladies: Women and the Obligations of Citizenship*. New York: Hill and Wang, 1998.

Kerlin, Robert T. *The Voice of the Negro (1919)*, ed. Thomas Aiello. Lewiston, N.Y.: Edwin Mellen Press, 2013.

Kessler, Lauren. *The Dissident Press: Alternative Journalism in American History*. New York: SAGE, 1984.

King, Gilbert. *Devil in the Grove: Thurgood Marshall, the Groveland Boys, and the Dawn of a New America*. New York: Harper, 2012.

Kirby, John B. *Black Americans in the Roosevelt Era: Liberalism and Race*. Knoxville: University of Tennessee Press, 1980.

Kirk, John A. "The NAACP Campaign for Teachers' Salary Equalization: African American Women Educators and the Early Civil Rights Struggle." *Journal of African American History* 94 (Fall 2009): 529-552.

Kirkland, Scotty E. "Mobile and the Boswell Amendment." *Alabama Review* 65 (July 2012): 205-249.

Klarman, Michael J. "*Brown*, Racial Change, and the Civil Rights Movement." *Virginia Law Review* 80 (January 1994): 7-150.

Klarman, Michael J. "The Racial Origins of Modern Criminal Procedure." *Michigan Law Review* 99 (October 2000): 48-97.

Klarman, Michael J. "The White Primary Rulings: A Case Study in the Consequences of Supreme Court Decisionmaking." *Florida State University Law Review* 29 (October 2001): 55-107.

Klinkner, Philip A., and Rogers M. Smith. *The Unsteady March: The Rise and Decline of Racial Equality in America*. Chicago, Ill.: University of Chicago Press, 1999.

Knowlton, Christopher. *Bubble in the Sun: The Florida Boom of the 1920s and How It Brought on the Great Depression*. New York: Simon and Schuster, 2021.

Kowalski, Greg. *Hamtramck: The Driven City*. Charleston, S.C.: Arcadia, 2002.

Kowalski, Greg. *Hamtramck: Then and Now*. Charleston, S.C.: Arcadia, 2010.

Kowalski, Greg. *Wicked Hamtramck: Lust, Liquor, and Lead*. Charleston, S.C.: History Press, 2010.

Kreiling, Albert Lee. "The Making of Racial Identities in the Black Press: A Cultural Analysis of Race Journalism in Chicago, 1878-1929." PhD diss., University of Illinois, 1973.

Krueger, Thomas A. *And Promises to Keep: The Southern Conference for Human Welfare, 1938–1948*. Nashville, Tenn.: Vanderbilt University Press, 1967.

Kuhn, Clifford M., Harlon E. Joy, and E. Bernard West. *Living Atlanta: An Oral History of the City, 1914–1948*. Athens: University of Georgia Press, 1990.

Lamb, Chris. *Blackout: The Untold Story of Jackie Robinson's First Spring Training*. Lincoln: University of Nebraska Press, 2006.

Lambert, Frank. *The Battle of Ole Miss: Civil Rights v. States' Rights*. New York: Oxford University Press, 2010.

Lanctot, Neil. *Negro League Baseball: The Rise and Ruin of a Black Institution*. Philadelphia: University of Pennsylvania Press, 2004.

Lau, Peter F. *Democracy Rising: South Carolina and the Fight for Black Equality since 1865*. Lexington: University Press of Kentucky, 2006.

Lawson, Marjorie MacKenzie. "The Adult Education Aspects of the Negro Press." *Journal of Negro Education* 14 (Summer 1945): 431–436.

LeCour, Joseph B. "The Negro Press as a Business." *Crisis* 48 (April 1941): 108, 141.

Lee, Alfred McClung. *The Daily Newspaper in America: The Evolution of a Social Instrument*. 1937; rpt., New York: Macmillan, 1947.

Lee, Davis. "The Future of the Negro." Manuscript, Archives, and Rare Book Library, Emory University, Atlanta, Ga.

LeFlouria, Talitha L. *Chained in Silence: Black Women and Convict Labor in the New South*. Chapel Hill: University of North Carolina Press, 2015.

Leonard, Kevin Allen. "Is That What We Fought For? Japanese Americans and Racism in California: The Impact of World War II." *Western Historical Quarterly* 21 (November 1990): 463–482.

Lerner, Gerda, and Linda K. Kerber. *The Majority Finds Its Past: Placing Women in History*. Chapel Hill: University of North Carolina Press, 2005.

Lewis, Freda Darlene. "The *Jackson Advocate*: The Rise and Eclipse of a Leading Black Newspaper in Mississippi, 1939–1964." MS thesis, Iowa State University, 1984.

Lewis, Willard "Chuck." *Citizens Trust Bank History*. Atlanta, Ga.: Citizens Trust Bank, 2001.

Lisio, Donald. *Hoover, Blacks, and Lily-Whites: A Study of Southern Strategies*. Chapel Hill: University of North Carolina Press, 1985.

Little, Stuart J. "The Freedom Train: Citizenship and Postwar Political Culture, 1946–1949." *American Studies* 34 (Spring 1993): 35–67.

Loeb, Charles. Introduction to *The Negro Newspaper*, ed. Vishnu V. Oak. 1948; rpt., Westport, Conn.: Negro Universities Press, 1976.

Logan, Rayford W. *Howard University: The First Hundred Years, 1867–1967*. New York: New York University Press, 1968.

Lomax, Louis E. *The Negro Revolt*. New York: Harper, 1962.

Long, Michael G., ed. *First Class Citizenship: The Civil Rights Letters of Jackie Robinson*. New York: Henry Holt, 2007.

Lopez, Antonio M. *Unbecoming Blackness: The Diaspora Cultures of Afro-Cuban America*. New York: New York University Press, 2012.

Lorence, James J. *A Hard Journey: The Life of Don West*. Urbana: University of Illinois Press, 2007.

Lorence, James J. *The Unemployed People's Movement: Leftists, Liberals, and Labor in Georgia, 1929–1941*. Athens: University of Georgia Press, 2009.

Lucander, David. *Winning the War for Democracy: The March on Washington Movement, 1941-1946*. Urbana: University of Illinois Press, 2014.

Lynchings by States and Race, 1882-1959. Tuskegee, Ala.: Department of Records and Research, Tuskegee Institute, 1959.

Mack, Kenneth W. "Dissent and Authenticity in the History of American Radical Politics." In *Dissenting Voices in American Society: The Role of Judges, Lawyers, and Citizens*, ed. Austin Sarat, 105-143. New York: Cambridge University Press, 2012.

Magliulo, Myrna Colette. "Andrew J. Smitherman: A Pioneer of the African American Press, 1909-1961." *Afro-Americans in New York Life and History* 34 (July 2010): 76-118.

Mancini, Matthew J. *One Dies, Get Another: Convict Leasing in the American South, 1866-1928*. Columbia: University of South Carolina Press, 1996.

Mangum, Charles S., Jr. *The Legal Status of the Negro*. Chapel Hill: University of North Carolina Press, 1940.

Mangun, Kimberley. *Editor Emory O. Jackson, the "Birmingham World," and the Fight for Civil Rights in Alabama, 1940-1975*. New York: Peter Lang, 2019.

Margo, Robert A. *Race and Schooling in the South, 1880-1950: An Economic History*. Chicago, Ill.: University of Chicago Press, 1990.

Margolick, David. *Beyond Glory: Joe Louis vs. Max Schmeling, and a World on the Brink*. New York: Vintage, 2005.

Margot, Louis. "The *Dallas Express*: A Negro Newspaper—Its History, 1892-1971, and Its Point of View." MA thesis, East Texas State University, 1971.

Marquart, James W., Sheldon Ekland-Olson, and Jonathan R. Sorensen. *The Rope, the Chair, and the Needle: Capital Punishment in Texas, 1923-1990*. Austin: University of Texas Press, 1994.

Martin, Charles H. *The Angelo Herndon Case and Southern Justice*. Baton Rouge: Louisiana State University Press, 1976.

Martin, Charles H. "Race, Gender, and Southern Justice: The Rosa Lee Ingram Case." *American Journal of Legal History* 29 (July 1985): 251-268.

Martin, Tony. *The Pan-African Connection: From Slavery to Garvey and Beyond*. Dover, Mass.: Majority Press, 1983.

Martindale, Carolyn. *The White Press and Black America*. Westport, Conn.: Greenwood, 1986.

Mason, Herman "Skip," Jr. *Black Atlanta in the Roaring Twenties*. Charleston, S.C.: Arcadia, 1997.

"The Masquerade Is Over." *Crisis* 46 (June 1939): 179.

Matthews, Glenna. *The Rise of Public Woman: Woman's Power and Woman's Place in the United States, 1630-1970*. New York: Oxford University Press, 1992.

Maze, John, and Graham White. *Henry A. Wallace: His Search for a New World Order*. Chapel Hill: University of North Carolina Press, 1995.

McCray, John H. "The Arraignment of Student Inertia." *Mule's Ear* 11 (February 1935): 1, 4.

McCray, John H. "In Defense of Student Education." *Mule's Ear* 8 (March 1932): 2-3.

McCray, John H. "Talladega Beauties." *Mule's Ear* 8 (March 1932): 3-4.

McCray, John H. "World Peace." *Mule's Ear* 8 (March 1932): 1.

McDaniel, Karen Cotton. "Elizabeth 'Lizzie' Fouse (1875-1952): Challenging Stereotypes and Building Community." In *Kentucky Women: Their Lives and Times*, ed. Melissa A. McEuen and Thomas H. Appleton Jr., 274–293. Athens: University of Georgia Press, 2015.

McDowell, A. "The Young Men's Progressive Club." *Academy Herald* 1 (May 1909): 25–26.

McDowell, Deborah E. *Leaving Pipe Shop: Memories of Kin.* New York: Scribner's, 1997.

McDowell, Winston. "Race and Ethnicity during the Harlem Jobs Campaign, 1932–35." *Journal of Negro History* 69 (Summer-Fall 1984): 134–143.

McGuire, Danielle L. *At the Dark End of the Street: Black Women, Rape, and Resistance.* New York: Knopf, 2010.

McGuire, Danielle L. "'It Was Like All of Us Had Been Raped': Sexual Violence, Community Mobilization, and the African American Freedom Struggle." *Journal of American History* 91 (December 2004): 906–931.

McKenzie, Andre, et al. "Transmission Network Analysis to Complement Routine Tuberculosis Contact Investigations." *American Journal of Public Health* 97 (March 2007): 470–477.

McMillen, Neil. *Dark Journey: Black Mississippians in the Age of Jim Crow.* Urbana: University of Illinois Press, 1989.

McNair, Glenn. *Criminal Injustice: Slaves and Free Blacks in Georgia's Criminal Justice System.* Charlottesville: University of Virginia Press, 2009.

McNeil, Genna Rae. *Groundwork: Charles Hamilton Houston and the Struggle for Civil Rights.* Philadelphia: University of Pennsylvania Press, 1983.

McPheeters, Annie L. *Negro Progress in Atlanta, Georgia, 1950–1960: A Selected Bibliography on Human Relations from Four Atlanta Newspapers.* Atlanta, Ga.: West Hunter Branch, Atlanta Public Library, 1964.

McWhirter, Cameron. *Red Summer: The Summer of 1919 and the Awakening of Black America.* New York: Henry Holt, 2011.

McWhorter, Diane. *Carry Me Home: Birmingham, Alabama, the Climactic Battle of the Civil Rights Revolution.* New York: Simon and Schuster, 2001.

Meier, August, and Elliott Rudwick. *Black Detroit and the Rise of the UAW.* 1979; rpt., Ann Arbor: University of Michigan Press, 2007.

Merritt, Carole. *The Herndons: An Atlanta Family.* Athens: University of Georgia Press, 2002.

Michaeli, Ethan. *The Defender: How the Legendary Black Newspaper Changed America.* Boston, Mass.: Houghton Mifflin Harcourt, 2016.

Miles, Michael. *The Radical Probe: The Logic of Student Rebellion.* New York: Atheneum, 1971.

Milton, Joyce. *Loss of Eden: A Biography of Charles and Anne Morrow Lindbergh.* New York: HarperCollins, 1993.

Mims, Edwin. *The Advancing South: Stories of Progress and Reaction.* New York: Doubleday, 1926.

Mixon, Gregory. *The Atlanta Riot: Race, Class, and Violence in a New South City.* Gainesville: University Press of Florida, 2005.

Montgomery, David, Louis Schmier, and David Williams. "The Other Depression: A Farm Security Administration Family in Carroll County, 1941." *Georgia Historical Quarterly* 77 (Winter 1993): 811–822.

Moody, Anne. *Coming of Age in Mississippi.* New York: Bantam Dell, 1968.

Moore, John Hammond. "The Angelo Herndon Case, 1932–1937." *Phylon* 32 (Spring 1971): 60–71.

Moore, Joseph E. *Murder on Maryland's Eastern Shore: Race, Politics, and the Case of Orphan Jones.* Mt. Pleasant, S.C.: History Press, 2011.

Moran, Robert E., Sr. "Public Relief in Louisiana from 1928 to 1960." *Louisiana History* 14 (Fall 1973): 369–385.

Morris, Aldon D. *The Origins of the Civil Rights Movement: Black Communities Organizing for Change.* New York: Free Press, 1984.

Morris, James McGrath. *Eye on the Struggle: Ethel Payne, the First Lady of the Black Press.* New York: HarperCollins, 2015.

Morris, Robert V. "The Iowa Bystander." *Iowa Pathways*, Iowa Public Television, http://www.iptv.org/IowaPathways/mypath.cfm?ounid=ob_000289, accessed 4 January 2014.

Morris, Thomas D. "Slaves and the Rules of Evidence in Criminal Trials." *Chicago-Kent Law Review* 68 (June 1993): 1209–1240.

Muhammad, Khalil Gibran. *The Condemnation of Blackness: Race, Crime, and the Making of Modern Urban America.* Cambridge, Mass.: Harvard University Press, 2011.

Mullen, Bill. "Popular Fronts: *Negro Story* Magazine and the African American Literary Response to World War II." *African American Review* 30 (Spring 1996): 5–15.

Murphy, James Bradford. "A Study of the Editorial Policies of the *Atlanta Daily World*: 1952–1955." MA thesis, Emory University, 1961.

Murray, Hugh T., Jr. "The NAACP versus the Communist Party: The Scottsboro Rape Cases, 1931–1932." In *The Negro in Depression and War: Prelude to Revolution, 1930–1945*, ed. Bernard Sternsher, 267–281. Chicago, Ill.: Quadrangle, 1969.

"The Negro Daily: An Analysis of Twenty-Three Issues of the *Atlanta Daily World* during the Period July 4 to August 5, 1945." *Monthly Summary of Events and Trends in Race Relations* (August–September 1945): 59–62.

"Negro Editors on Communism." *Crisis* 41 (April 1932): 17, 119.

"Negro Publishers." *Time*, 15 June 1942, 70–72.

Nelson Chesman & Co.'s Newspaper Rate Book. New York: Nelson Chesman, 1921.

Nelson, David J. *How the New Deal Built Florida Tourism: The Civilian Conservation Corps and State Parks.* Gainesville: University Press of Florida, 2019.

Newkirk, Vann Roeshard. "The Development of the National Association for the Advancement of Colored People in Metropolitan Charlotte, North Carolina, 1919–1965." PhD diss., Howard University, 2002.

Newton, Michael. *The FBI and the KKK: A Critical History.* Jefferson, N.C.: McFarland, 2005.

Norrell, Robert J. *Up from History: The Life of Booker T. Washington.* Cambridge, Mass.: Belknap, 2009.

Norris, Clarence, and Sybil D. Washington. *The Last of the Scottsboro Boys.* New York: G. P. Putnam's Sons, 1979.

Norwood, Stephen H. *Strikebreaking and Intimidation: Mercenaries and Masculinity in Twentieth Century America.* Chapel Hill: University of North Carolina Press, 2002.

N. W. Ayer & Son's Directory of Newspapers and Periodicals, 1928–1955. Philadelphia, Pa.: N. W. Ayer & Son, 1928–1955.

Oak, Vishnu V. *The Negro Newspaper.* Yellow Springs, Ohio: Antioch, 1948.

O'Brien, Gail Williams. *The Color of the Law: Race, Violence, and Justice in the Post-World War II South*. Chapel Hill: University of North Carolina Press, 1999.

Odum-Hinmon, Maria E. "The Cautious Crusader: How the *Atlanta Daily World* Covered the Struggle for African American Rights from 1945 to 1985." PhD diss., University of Maryland, 2005.

O'Kelly, Charlotte G. "Black Newspapers and the Black Protest Movement: Their Historical Relationship, 1827–1945." *Phylon* 43 (First Quarter 1982): 1–14.

Oliver, Sadie Mae. "The History and Development of the *Atlanta Daily World*." MA thesis, Hampton Institute, 1942.

"An Oral History with Charles Lemuel Young, Sr." Civil Rights Documentation Project, University of Southern Mississippi, http://www.usm.edu/crdp/html/transcripts/young_charles-i.shtml, accessed 30 October 2014.

"Oral History with Mr. Percy Greene." University of Southern Mississippi Center for Oral History and Cultural Heritage, http://digilib.usm.edu/cdm/ref/collection/coh/id/2796, accessed 6 August 2014.

O'Reilly, Kenneth. *Hoover and the Unamericans: The FBI, HUAC, and the Red Menace*. Philadelphia, Pa.: Temple University Press, 1983.

Oshinsky, David M. *Worse than Slavery: Parchman Farm and the Ordeal of Jim Crow Justice*. New York: Free Press, 1997.

Ottley, Roi. *The Lonely Warrior: The Life and Times of Robert S. Abbott*. Chicago, Ill.: Henry Regnery, 1955.

Ottley, Roi. *"New World A-Coming": Inside Black America*. New York: Arno Press and the New York Times, 1969.

Pacifico, Michele F. "Don't Buy Where You Can't Work: The New Negro Alliance of Washington." *Washington History* 61 (Spring–Summer 1994): 66–88.

Painter, Nell Irvin. "Black Journalism: The First Hundred Years." *Harvard Journal of Afro-American Affairs* 2, no. 2 (1971): 30–32.

Perry, Samuel. "In Defense of the Negro Press." *Harvard Guardian* 7 (December 1942): 15–19.

Peterson, Sarah Jo. *Planning the Home Front: Building Bombers and Communities at Willow Run*. Chicago, Ill.: University of Chicago Press, 2013.

Pfaff, Daniel W. "The Press and the Scottsboro Rape Cases, 1931–1932." *Journalism History* 1 (Autumn 1974): 72–76.

Pfeffer, Paula. *A. Philip Randolph, Pioneer of the Civil Rights Movement*. Baton Rouge: Louisiana State University Press, 1990.

Phillips, Osborne. "A Sociological Study of Editorials of the *Atlanta Independent*." MA thesis, Atlanta University, 1948.

Pierce, Richard B. *Polite Protest: The Political Economy of Race in Indianapolis, 1920–1970*. Bloomington: Indiana University Press, 2005.

Pilat, Oliver. *Pegler: Angry Man of the Press*. Boston, Mass.: Beacon, 1963.

Pinar, William F. "The NAACP and the Struggle for Anti-Lynching Federal Legislation, 1917–1950." *Counterpoints* 163 (2001): 683–752.

Pincus, Samuel R. *The Virginia Supreme Court, Blacks, and the Law, 1870–1902*. New York: Garland, 1990.

Pitch, Anthony S. *The Last Lynching: How a Gruesome Mass Murder Rocked a Small Georgia Town*. New York: Skyhorse, 2016.

Pleasants, Julian M. *Buncombe Bob: The Life and Times of Robert Rice Reynolds*. Chapel Hill: University of North Carolina Press, 2000.

Pleij, Herman. "The Late Middle Ages and the Rhetoricians, 1400–1560." In *A Literary History of the Low Countries*, ed. Theo Hermans, 81–83. Rochester, N.Y.: Camden House, 2009.

Pomerantz, Gary M. *Where Peachtree Meets Sweet Auburn: The Saga of Two Families and the Making of Atlanta*. New York: Scribner's, 1996.

Poston, Ted. "The Negro Press." *Reporter*, December 6, 1949, 14–16.

Prattis, Percival L. "Racial Segregation and Negro Journalism." *Phylon* 8 (Fourth Quarter 1947): 305–313.

Prattis, Percival L. "The Role of the Negro Press in Race Relations." *Phylon* 7 (Third Quarter 1946): 273–283.

Pride, Armistead Scott. "A Register and History of Negro Newspapers in the United States, 1827–1950." PhD diss., Northwestern University, 1950.

Printing the Dream: 75 Years of Atlanta Daily World. Atlanta Interfaith Broadcasters, 2003.

"Publishers: Owners of Negro Newspapers Are Hard-Headed, Farsighted, Race Conscious Businessmen." *Ebony*, November 1949, 47–51.

Rampersad, Arnold. *Jackie Robinson: A Biography*. New York: Knopf, 1997.

Ratzlaff, Aleen J. "Illustrated African American Journalism: Political Cartooning in the *Indianapolis Freedom*." In *Seeking a Voice: Images of Race and Gender in the 19th Century Press*, ed. David B. Sachsman, S. Kittrell Rushing, and Roy Morris Jr., 131–140. West Lafayette, Ind.: Purdue University Press, 2009.

Rhodes, Jane. *Mary Ann Shadd Cary: The Black Press and Protest in the Nineteenth Century*. Bloomington: Indiana University Press, 1998.

Rice, Mitchell F., and Woodrow Jones Jr. *Public Policy and the Black Hospital: From Slavery to Segregation to Integration*. Westport, Conn.: Greenwood, 1994.

Richards, Johnetta Gladys. "The Southern Negro Youth Congress: A History, 1937–1949." PhD diss., University of Cincinnati, 1987.

Roberts, Gene, and Hank Klibanoff. *The Race Beat: The Press, the Civil Rights Struggle, and the Awakening of a Nation*. New York: Vintage, 2007.

Roberts, Randy. *Joe Louis: Hard Times Man*. New Haven, Conn.: Yale University Press, 2010.

Robinson, Stephen Robert. "The Black New South: A Study of Local Black Leadership in Virginia and Alabama, 1874–1897." PhD diss., University of Southampton, 2010.

Rose, Chanelle Nyree. *The Struggle for Black Freedom in Miami: Civil Rights and America's Tourist Paradise, 1896–1968*. Baton Rouge: Louisiana State University Press, 2015.

Rosenberg, Gerald. *The Hollow Hope: Can Courts Bring about Social Change?* Chicago, Ill.: University of Chicago Press, 1991.

Rosenthal, Joel. "Southern Black Student Activism: Assimilation vs. Nationalism." *Journal of Negro Education* 44 (Spring 1975): 113–129.

Rosich, Katherine J. *Race, Ethnicity, and the Criminal Justice System*. Washington, D.C.: American Sociological Association, 2007.

Rothman, Joshua D. *Notorious in the Neighborhood: Sex and Families across the Color Line in Virginia, 1787–1861*. Chapel Hill: University of North Carolina Press, 2003.

Rozier, John Wiley. "A History of the Negro Press in Atlanta." MA thesis, Emory University, 1949.

Rutledge, Anne G. *Emory O. Jackson: Warrior.* N.p.: CreateSpace, 2014.
Sancton, Thomas. "The Negro Press." *New Republic*, 26 April 1943, 558–560.
Sarratt, Reed. *The Ordeal of Desegregation: The First Decade.* New York: Harper and Row, 1966.
Sartain, Lee. *Invisible Activists: Women of the Louisiana NAACP and the Struggle for Civil Rights, 1915–1945.* Baton Rouge: Louisiana State University Press, 2007.
Scott, Alexis. Interview, Family Business Radio, 12 January 2012. In possession of author.
Scott, Ruth Emmeline. "The Problem of Studying Certain Accounting Features of Negro and Foreign Language Weekly Newspapers in the United States, 1938." MA thesis, Atlanta University, 1939.Secrest, Andrew. "In Black and White: Press Opinion and Race Relations in South Carolina, 1954–1964." PhD diss., Duke University, 1971.
Shannon, Samuel. "Tennessee." In *The Black Press in the South, 1865–1979*, ed. Henry Lewis Suggs, 313–356. Westport, Conn.: Greenwood, 1983.
Shofner, Jerrell H. "Florida." In *The Black Press in the South, 1865–1979*, ed. Henry Lewis Suggs, 91–118. Westport, Conn.: Greenwood, 1983.
Shogan, Robert, and Tom Craig. *The Detroit Race Riot: A Study in Violence.* Philadelphia, Pa.: Chilton, 1964.
Simmons, Charles A. *The African American Press: A History of News Coverage during National Crises, with Special Reference to Four Black Newspapers, 1827–1965.* Jefferson, N.C.: McFarland, 1998.
Simons, William. "Jackie Robinson and the American Mind: Journalistic Perceptions of the Reintegration of Baseball." *Journal of Sport History* 12 (Spring 1985): 39–64.
Singer, Benjamin D. "Mass Society, Mass Media and the Transformation of Minority Identity." *British Journal of Sociology* 24 (June 1973): 140–150.
Sitkoff, Harvard. "The Detroit Race Riot, 1943." *Michigan History* 53 (May 1969): 183–206.
Sitkoff, Harvard. "Harry Truman and the Election of 1948: The Coming of Age of Civil Rights in American Politics." *Journal of Southern History* 37 (November 1971): 597–616.
Sitkoff, Harvard. *A New Deal for Blacks: The Emergence of Civil Rights as a National Issue*, vol. 1: *The Depression Decade.* New York: Oxford University Press, 1978.
Sklaroff, Lauren. *Black Culture and the New Deal: The Quest for Civil Rights in the Roosevelt Era.* Chapel Hill: University of North Carolina Press, 2009.
Skotnes, Andor. "Buy Where You Can Work: Boycotting for Jobs in African-American Baltimore, 1933–1934." *Journal of Social History* 27 (Summer 1994): 735–761.
Skotnes, Andor. *A New Deal for All? Race and Class Struggles in Depression-Era Baltimore.* Durham, N.C.: Duke University Press, 2013.
Slate, Nico. *Colored Cosmopolitanism: The Shared Struggle for Freedom in the United States and India.* Cambridge, Mass.: Harvard University Press, 2012.
Slavens, George Everett. "Missouri." In *The Black Press in the South, 1865–1979*, ed. Henry Lewis Suggs, 211–256. Westport, Conn.: Greenwood, 1983.
Smallwood, James. "Texas." In *The Black Press in the South, 1865–1979*, ed. Henry Lewis Suggs, 357–378. Westport, Conn.: Greenwood, 1983.
Smith, Gerald L. *A Black Educator in the Segregated South: Kentucky's Rufus B. Atwood.* Lexington: University Press of Kentucky, 1994.

Smith, J. Douglas. *Managing White Supremacy: Race, Politics, and Citizenship in Jim Crow Virginia*. Chapel Hill: University of North Carolina Press, 2002.

Smock, Raymond. *Booker T. Washington: Black Leadership in the Age of Jim Crow*. Chicago, Ill.: Ivan R. Dee, 2009.

Solomon, Mark. *The Cry Was Unity: Communists and African Americans, 1917–36*. Jackson: University Press of Mississippi, 1998.

"The South's Greatest Negro Newspaper." *Negro Digest* 7 (July 1949): 39.

Standing, Theodore. "A Study of Negro Nationalism." PhD diss., State University of Iowa, 1932.

Staples, Charles R. *The History of Pioneer Lexington, 1779–1806*. 1939; rpt., Lexington: University of Kentucky Press, 1996.

Sterner, Richard. *The Negro's Share: A Study of Income, Consumption, Housing, and Public Assistance*. New York: Harper and Brothers, 1943.

Strain, Christopher B. *Pure Fire: Self-Defense as Activism in the Civil Rights Era*. Athens: University of Georgia Press, 2005.

Strickland, Arvarh E. "Booker T. Washington: The Myth and the Man." *Reviews in American History* (December 1973): 559–564.

Strother, T. Ella. "The Race-Advocacy Function of the Black Press." *Black American Literature Forum* 12 (Autumn 1978): 92–99.

Stuckert, Robert P. "The Negro College–A Pawn of White Domination." *Wisconsin Sociologist* 3 (January 1964): 1–8.

Suggs, Henry Lewis. "Black Strategy and Ideology in the Segregation Era: P. B. Young and the *Norfolk Journal and Guide*, 1910–1954." *Virginia Magazine of History and Biography* 91 (April 1983): 161–190.

Suggs, Henry Lewis. "Conclusion." In *The Black Press in the South, 1865–1979*, ed. Henry Lewis Suggs, 423–430. Westport, Conn.: Greenwood, 1983.

Suggs, Henry Lewis. "Origins of the Black Press in the South." In *The Black Press in the South, 1865–1979*, ed. Henry Lewis Suggs, 3–22. Westport, Conn.: Greenwood, 1983.

Suggs, Henry Lewis. "P. B. Young of the *Norfolk Journal and Guide*: A Booker T. Washington Militant, 1904–1928." *Journal of Negro History* 64 (Autumn 1979): 365–376.

Suggs, Henry Lewis, and Bernadine Moses Duncan. "North Carolina." In *The Black Press in the South, 1865–1979*, ed. Henry Lewis Suggs, 257–288. Westport, Conn.: Greenwood, 1983.

Sugrue, Thomas J. *The Origins of the Urban Crisis*. Princeton, N.J.: Princeton University Press, 1996.

Sullivan, Patricia. *Lift Every Voice: The NAACP and the Making of the Civil Rights Movement*. New York: New Press, 2009.

Sutton, Willis A., Jr. "The Talmadge Campaigns: A Sociological Analysis of Political Power." PhD diss., University of North Carolina, 1952.

Sweet, Frank W. *Legal History of the Color Line: The Rise and Triumph of the One Drop Rule*. Palm Coast, Fla.: Backintyme, 2005.

Syrjamaki, John. "The Negro Press in 1938." *Sociology and Social Research* 24 (September–October 1939): 43–52.

Talley, Robert. *One Hundred Years of the "Commercial Appeal": The Story of the Greatest Romance in American Journalism, 1840–1940*. Memphis, Tenn.: Memphis Publishing, 1940.

Taylor, George C. L. "The Modern Negro Press." *Southern Workman* 61 (August 1932): 341–346.

Taylor, Jon E. *Freedom to Serve: Truman, Civil Rights, and Executive Order 9981.* New York: Routledge, 2013.

Teel, Leonard Ray. "W. A. Scott and the Atlanta World." *American Journalism* 6, no. 3 (1989): 158–178.

Terkel, Studs. *Hard Times: An Oral History of the Great Depression.* 1970; rpt., New York: New Press, 2005.

Teske, Steven. *Unvarnished Arkansas: The Naked Truth about Nine Famous Arkansans.* Little Rock, Ark.: Butler Center Books, 2012.

Thomas, Norman. *Human Exploitation in the United States.* New York: Frederick A. Stokes, 1934.Thompson, Charles H. "Progress in the Elimination of Discrimination in White and Negro Teachers' Salaries." *Journal of Negro Education* 9 (January 1940): 1–4.

Thompson, Julius Eric. *Black Life in Mississippi: Essays on Political, Social, and Cultural Studies in a Deep South State.* Lanham, Md.: University Press of America, 2001.

Thompson, Julius Eric. *The Black Press in Mississippi, 1865–1985.* Gainesville: University Press of Florida, 1993.

Thompson, Julius Eric. "Mississippi." In *The Black Press in the South, 1865–1979*, ed. Henry Lewis Suggs, 177–210. Westport, Conn.: Greenwood, 1983.

Thompson, Julius Eric. *Percy Greene and the "Jackson Advocate": The Life and Times of a Radical Conservative Black Newspaperman, 1897–1977.* Jefferson, N.C.: McFarland, 1994.

Thornbrough, Emma Lou. "American Negro Newspapers, 1880–1914." *Business History Review* 40 (Winter 1966): 467–490.

Thornton, J. Mills. *Dividing Lines: Municipal Politics and the Struggle for Civil Rights in Montgomery, Birmingham, and Selma.* Tuscaloosa: University of Alabama Press, 2002.

Tindall, George Brown. *South Carolina Negroes, 1877–1900.* Columbia: University of South Carolina Press, 1952.

Tischauser, Leslie V. *The Changing Nature of Racial and Ethnic Conflict in United States History.* Lanham, Md.: University Press of America, 2002.

Tobin, Sidney. "The Early New Deal in Baton Rouge as Viewed by the Daily Press." *Louisiana History* 10 (Fall 1969): 307–337.

Toppin, Edgar A. *A Biographical History of Blacks in America since 1528.* New York: David McKay, 1971.

Tushnet, Mark V. *Making Civil Rights Law: Thurgood Marshall and the Supreme Court, 1936–1961.* New York: Oxford University Press, 1994.

Tygiel, Jules. *Baseball's Great Experiment: Jackie Robinson and His Legacy.* New York: Oxford University Press, 1983.

Van Auken, Cecilia. "The Negro Press in the 1948 Presidential Election." *Journalism Quarterly* 26 (December 1949): 431–435.

Vogel, Todd, ed. *The Black Press: New Literary and Historical Essays.* New Brunswick, N.J.: Rutgers University Press, 2001.

Vowels, Robert C. "Atlanta Negro Business and the New Black Bourgeoisie." *Atlanta Historical Bulletin* 21 (Spring 1977): 48–63.

Wade-Gayles, Gloria. "Black Women Journalists in the South, 1880–1905: An Approach to the Study of Black Women's History." *Callaloo* 11–13 (February–October 1981): 138–152.

Waller, George. *Kidnap: The Story of the Lindbergh Case*. New York: Dial, 1961.

Wardlaw, Harold Clinton. "A Gatekeeper Analysis of Minority and Majority Newspapers: *Atlanta Inquirer*, *Atlanta World*, and *Atlanta Constitution*." MA thesis, University of Georgia, 1969.

Ware, Susan. *Holding Their Own: American Women in the 1930s*. New York: Twayne, 1982.

Warren, Harris Gaylord. *Herbert Hoover and the Great Depression*. New York: Norton, 1967.

"W. Ashbie Hawkins (1861–1941)." MSA SC 3520-12415. Archives of Maryland (Biographical Series). http://msa.maryland.gov/megafile/msa/speccol/sc3500/sc3520/012400/012415/html/12415bio.html, accessed 15 October 2013.

Washburn, Patrick S. *The African American Newspaper: Voice of Freedom*. Evanston, Ill.: Northwestern University Press, 2006.

Washburn, Patrick S. *A Question of Sedition: The Federal Government's Investigation of the Black Press during World War II*. New York: Oxford University Press, 1986.

Washington, Booker T., and W. E. B. Du Bois. *The Negro in the South: His Economic Progress in Relation to His Moral and Religious Development*. Philadelphia, Pa.: George W. Jacobs, 1907.

Wattley, Cheryl Elizabeth Brown. *A Step toward Brown v. Board of Education: Ada Lois Sipuel Fisher and Her Fight to End Segregation*. Norman: University of Oklahoma Press, 2014.

Weare, Walter. *Black Business in the New South: A Social History of the North Carolina Mutual Insurance Company*. Durham, N.C.: Duke University Press, 1993.

Weare, Walter. "Charles Clinton Spaulding: Middle Class Leadership in the Age of Segregation." In *Black Leaders of the Twentieth Century*, ed. John Hope Franklin and August Meier, 167–189. Urbana: University of Illinois Press, 1982.

Weaver, Bill, and Oscar C. Page. "The Black Press and the Drive for Integrated Graduate and Professional Schools." *Phylon* 43 (First Quarter 1982): 15–28.

Weill, Susan M. "Mississippi's Daily Press in Three Crises." In *The Press and Race: Mississippi Journalists Confront the Movement*, ed. David R. Davies, 17–54. Jackson: University Press of Mississippi, 2001.

Weiner, Leo. *Africa and the Discovery of America*. Vols. 1–3. Philadelphia, Pa.: Innes & Sons, 1920–1922.

Welky, David B. "Viking Girls, Mermaids, and Little Brown Men: U.S. Journalism and the 1932 Olympics." *Journal of Sport History* 24 (Spring 1997): 24–49.

Wexler, Laura. *Fire in a Canebrake: The Last Mass Lynching in America*. New York: Scribner's, 2003.

Whitaker, Matthew C. "The Rise of Black Phoenix: African-American Migration, Settlement and Community Development in Maricopa County, Arizona 1868–1930." *Journal of Negro History* 85 (Summer 2000): 197–209.

Whitaker, Robert. *On the Laps of Gods: The Red Summer of 1919 and the Struggle for Justice That Remade a Nation*. New York: Crown, 2008.

White, Colleen R. "The *Jackson Advocate*, 1938–1995: A Historical Overview." MA thesis, University of Mississippi, 1996.

White, John. "Civil Rights in Conflict: The 'Birmingham Plan' and the Freedom Train, 1947." *Alabama Review* 52 (April 1999): 128–136.

White, John. "Edgar Daniel Nixon: A Founding Father of the Civil Rights Movement." In *Portraits of African American Life since 1865*, ed. Nina Mjagkij, 199–217. Wilmington, Del.: Scholarly Resources, 2003.

White, Walter. *A Man Called White*. Bloomington: University of Indiana Press, 1948.

White, Walter. "Portrait of a Communist." *Negro Digest* 9 (February 1951): 84–85.

Wilkerson, Doxey A. "The Negro Press." *Journal of Negro Education* 16 (Autumn 1947): 511–521.

Wilkerson, Isabel. *The Warmth of Other Suns: The Epic Story of America's Great Migration*. New York: Vintage, 2010.

Wilkinson, Christopher. "Big-Band Jazz in Black West Virginia, 1930–1942." *West Virginia History: A Journal of Regional Studies* 1 (Spring 2007): 23–53.

Wilson, Clint C., II. *Black Journalists in Paradox: Historical Perspectives and Current Dilemmas*. Westport, Conn.: Greenwood, 1991.

Wilson, Sunnie, and John Cohassey. *Toast of the Town: The Life and Times of Sunnie Wilson*. Detroit, Mich.: Wayne State University Press, 2005.

Winner, Lauren F. "Doubtless Sincere: New Characters in the Civil Rights Cast." In *The Role of Ideas in the Civil Rights South*, ed. Ted Ownby, 157–169. Jackson: University Press of Mississippi.

Wolseley, Roland E. *The Black Press, USA*. Ames: Iowa State University Press, 1971.

Wolters, Raymond. *Negroes and the Great Depression: The Problem of Economic Recovery*. Westport, Conn.: Greenwood, 1970.

Work, Monroe M., ed. *Annual Encyclopedia of the Negro*. Tuskegee, Ala.: Tuskegee Institute Press, 1937.

Wright, George C. "Black Political Insurgency in Louisville, Kentucky: The Lincoln Independent Party of 1921." *Journal of Negro History* 68 (Winter 1983): 8–23.

Wye, Christopher G. "Merchants of Tomorrow: The Other Side of the 'Don't Spend Your Money Where You Can't Work' Movement." *Ohio History* 93 (Winter–Spring 1985): 40–67.

Wynne, Lewis N. "Brownsville: The Reaction of the Negro Press." *Phylon* 33 (Second Quarter 1972): 153–160.

Young, Consuelo. "A Study of Reader Attitudes toward the Negro Press." *Journalism Quarterly* 21 (Summer 1944): 148–152.

Young, P. B., Jr. "The Negro Press—Today and Tomorrow." *Opportunity* 17 (July 1939): 204–205.

Zangrando, Robert L. *The NAACP Crusade against Lynching, 1909–1950*. Philadelphia, Pa.: Temple University Press, 1980.

Ziff, W. B. *The Negro Market: Published in the Interest of the Negro Press*. Atlanta, Ga.: W. B. Ziff, 1932.

"Ziff's List of Negro Papers." In *Nelson Chesman & Co.'s Newspaper Rate Book*, 392–393. New York: Nelson Chesman, 1921.

Zimmerman, Andrew. *Alabama in Africa: Booker T. Washington, the German Empire, and the Globalization of the New South*. Princeton, N.J.: Princeton University Press, 2012.

Index

Africa and the Discovery of America (Weiner), 83
African Blood Brotherhood for African Liberation and Redemption, 225
Afro American Insurance Company, 38
Agar, Herbert, 168
Agee, James, 82
Agricultural Adjustment Act, 182
Agricultural Adjustment Administration, 168
Alabama Committee for Equal Justice, 100
Alabama Negro Baptist, 98
Alabama Negro Press Association, 111
Alabama Polytechnic Institute, 104
Alabama Power Company, 299n97
Alabama Progressive Democratic Association, 116
Alabama Science Association, 93
Alabama State Teachers Association, 93
Alabama State Teachers College, 292n10
Alabama State University, 47
Alabama Supreme Court, 86, 89, 90, 101
Alabama Tribune, 14, 17, 84, 89, 95, 101, 103–104, 106, 154
Albany State University, 25
Alcorn A&M College, 149–150, 175
Aldrich, Winthrop, 113
Alexander, Joseph L., 78–79
Alexandria Observer, 184–185
Alexandria Riot, 184–185
Allen, C. W., 292n8
Allen, William, 280n7
Amarillo Herald, 195
American Association of University Professors, 162
American Baptist College, 130
American Civil Liberties Union, 245
American Federation of Labor, 42, 98, 141, 241–242, 243; Hod Carriers Union, 141

American Heritage Foundation Freedom Train, 113–114
American Legion, 45, 46–47, 167
American Progress, 309n10
Ames, Jessie Daniel, 32–33, 169
Anderson, Marian, 145
Anderson, S. E., 58
Anderson, W. D., 27
Anderson Messenger, 59
Andrews, Mary M. Norris, 222, 320n56
Anti-Boswell Amendment Committee, 111
Arizona Gleam, 202
Arizona Sun, 315n45
Arkansas Mediator and World, 313n3
Arkansas Survey-Journal, 188, 313n5
Arkansas World, 17, 187–189, 307n66
Army Nurse Corps, 201
Arnall, Ellis, 32
Arnold, Luke, 134
Asheville World, 77
Associated Correspondents of Race Newspapers, 275n9
Associated Negro Press, 122, 187, 213, 226; international coverage, 49; syndication, 5–6, 58, 312n2, 322n19; use by SNS, 58, 72, 144, 149, 250
Astor, Gerald, 234
Atlanta College of Mortuary Science, 202
Atlanta Daily World, 39, 131, 160, 199; advertising, 74; advocacy of, 13–14, 25, 103, 138, 251; conservatism of, 24; editorial policy, 18, 34, 152, 206; role in Atlanta, 20, 37, 54; SNS flagship, 5–6, 36, 211, 212, 310n39; southern advocacy, 3
Atlanta Independent, 1, 37, 226
Atlanta Life Insurance, 202, 211
Atlanta Police Department, 235
Atlanta Political and Civic League, 138

Index

Atlanta University, 22, 39, 138, 204
Atlanta World, 1, 36, 88, 278n22
Atlantic City Eagle, 229
Atlantic City Tribune, 322n14
Austin, Louis E., 74, 290n61, 290n62
Austin Messenger, 194
Austin Negro Citizens Council, 194

Baer, Max, 234
Bailey, Thomas L., 173
Baker, Cora, 283n45
Baker, Nathaniel N., 49, 283n45
Baker, Robert, 57
Ballin, Caroline Collier, 100
Baltimore Afro-American, 1, 4, 5, 53, 60, 122
Banks, E. W., 164
Banner County Outlook, 310n34
Baptist Ministers Alliance of Alexandria, 185
Barnett, Claude, 6, 49
Barnett, Fred L., 201
Bartlesville Voice, 197, 267
Basie, Count, 95
Bates, Ruby, 85, 293n14
Baton Rouge Post, 183
Battle, Laurie, 125
Battle Creek Tribune, 324n49
Bayou State Register, 17
Bay View Observer, 316n52
Bedingfield, Sid, 60, 65, 288n32
Beeler, Roy, 160
Behling, Charles F., 65
Bell, William, 104
Benedict, Ruth, 196
Benson, Doc, 315n45
Beshears, Helen Dameron, 199
Bethune, Mary McLeod, 52, 200, 284n49
Beveridge, William, 171
Biddings, Emanuel, 75
Biddle, Merrill, 229
Biggins, Wittie Anna, 131–132, 213
Bilbo, Theodore, 122, 143, 148–149, 169, 310n30; *Take Your Choice*, 174
Biow Company, 117
Birmingham Age-Herald, 94, 114
Birmingham News, 98, 108, 120
Birmingham Police Department, 115, 118
Birmingham Post, 114, 119
Birmingham Post-Herald, 127
Birmingham World, 130; activism of, 95, 100, 113–114, 119, 125, 129; advertising in, 117; Emory Jackson frustration with, 94, 110, 121, 247; Emory Jackson work with, 90–91, 108, 116; FBI and, 296n74; Scotts and, 303n3
Black Legion, 46, 235
Black Star Line, 226
Blakeney, Lincoln, 1
Bomar, A. O., 278n22
Bomar, Lynn, 149
Booker T. Washington Trade Association, 232
Boston, Beulah, 163
Boston Guardian, 213
Boston University, 22
Boswell Amendment, 102, 110–111, 115
Bowden, Jasper Lawrence, 48
Boyle, Joy, 140
Bozeman, James, 84
Bracy, Rosa Brown, 152
Braddock, Jim, 233, 234
Brady, St. Elmo, 93
Branch, Lewis Linden, 59, 286n11
Brewer, Arthur, 315n38
Bricker, John, 222
Briggs, Cyril, 225–226
Briscoe, Sherman, 182, 311n54
Brooklyn Dodgers, 69
Brown, Gladys, 237
Brown, Richard, 37
Brown, Robert Glen, 78
Brown, Thomas J., 312n3
Brown, Will, 188–189
Browning, Gordon, 160
Brown-Nagin, Tomiko, 14, 50, 284n46
Brownsville Weekly News, 241
Brown v. Board of Education, 17, 30, 59, 91, 126–127; activism and, 162, 176, 218, 284n46; elections and, 159; journalism and, 55, 91, 250–251
Bryan, William Jennings, 295n50
Bryant, Golee B., 232
Bryant, Ira, 131–132
Bryant, Mansfield Edward, 82
Buchanan, Charles, 316n4
Buffalo Star, 227, 321n5
Bunche, Ralph, 47
Bureau of Labor Statistics, 237
Burke, Clifford, 7
Burke, Thomas, 220

Burma, John, 151
Burton, Harold H., 220
Byrd, Richard, 30
Byrnes, James, 60

Cannon, Poppy, 17
Canty, Frank W., 229
Cape Fear Journal, 72, 73
Carolina Enterprise, 302n1
Carolina Lighthouse, 59
Carolina Times, 73, 74, 289n61
Carolina Tribune, 73
Carolina World, 58
Carolinian, 289nn57–58
Carr, Johnnie, 99
Carroll, Brian, 69
Carroll, Fred, 18, 225
Carver, George Washington, 145, 277n2
Catholic Review, 183
Chambers v. Florida, 51
Chamlee, George W., 142
Champaign Times, 217
Chandler, A. K., 197
Chandler, Happy, 207–208
Chandler, Ralph, 146–147
Charleston City Council, 56
Charleston Messenger, 56, 59
Charleston Telegram, 58
Charlotte Post, 71
Chase, Homer Bates, 153
Chattanooga City Council, 142
Chattanooga Observer, 17, 136–138, 141–144, 154–159
Chattanooga Tribune, 302n1
Cheeks, Eugene Francis, 220, 320n50
Chicago Defender, 216; activism of, 13, 15, 16, 178, 213; conflict with SNS, 135, 155, 235–236; differences with southern journalism, 230, 249; as employer, 73; journalism of, 1, 4, 5, 6, 24, 34; work with SNS journalists, 99
Christian Star, 73
Cincinnati Independent, 222–223
Cincinnati News, 219
Cincinnati Reds, 224
Cincinnati Union, 217
Civic and Political League of Atlanta, 23
Civilian Conservation Corps, 47, 78, 229
Civil War, 2, 72, 135, 313n5

Civil Works Administration, 38
Claflin University, 73
Claiborne, Clay, 322n14
Clark, Magnus, 241
Clark, Tom, 119
Clark College, 22, 152–153
Clarke, Joseph A., 228
Clarkson, C. C., 302n1
Clarksville Sun, 308n91
Clawson, Don M., 15
Clayton, T. M., 75
Clement, A. J., 63
Clement, Frank, 159
Cleveland Advocate, 319n44
Cleveland Call, 319n44
Cleveland Call and Post, 221, 319n44
Cleveland Eagle, 218
Cleveland Gazette, 24, 319n44
Cleveland Guide, 220
Cleveland Indians, 70, 288n43
Cleveland Plaindealer, 221
Cleveland Post, 319n44
Coalson, William, 314n35
Cochran, Lucy J., 209–210, 317n15
Cocking, Walter, 32
Cold War, 30, 105
Cole, I. Willis, 205–206, 316n1, 316n2, 317n9
Coleman, F. D., 159
Colored Citizen (Pensacola), 284n49
Colored Democratic Party, 63
Colored Masonic Temple, 114
Colored Women's Work Committee of Miami, 38
Columbus Advocate, 21, 218
Columbus Voice, 3, 217
Columbus Weekly News, 217
Columbus World, 28, 30, 278nn22–23
Comiskey Park, 233
Commission on Interracial Cooperation, 74, 169, 193, 290n68
Committee on Civil Rights, 70, 122, 160
Communist Party, USA, 75, 89, 152–153, 226, 296n74; Alabama State Committee, 109
Congress of Industrial Organizations, 115, 187, 243
Congress of Youth, 232, 322n20
Connecticut Labor News, 322n16
Connor, Eugene, 90, 113, 116, 120, 122
Corinthian Gazette, 166

Costigan, Edward P., 304n19
Council on Race Relations, 43
Crooms, Hattie, 193
Crum, Francis P., 56
Crump, Edward "Boss," 140
Crusader, 225–226
Crusader News Agency, 225–226
Cruse, Harold, 248
Crutchfield, Peter, 310n37
Cunningham, L. D., 83
Cunningham, Leroy, 206
Current, Gloster, 111, 116
Curry, Morris Alexander, 190, 313n14
Cuttings, 79

Dabney, Wendell P., 217
Dadeville Riot, 91
Daily Worker, 99, 100
Dallas Express, 194
Dallas Post, 291n1
Darcy, Robert, 51
Daughters of the American Revolution, 145
Davis, Ben, 37, 226
Davis, Ben, Jr., 226
Davis, Cecil A., 231
Davis, Harry E., 217
Davis, Water D., 310n34
Dayton Forum, 217
Dayton Progress, 219–220
Dejoie, Constant Charles, 176–177, 310n37
Delta Phi Delta Journalistic Society, 27
Democratic National Committee, 194
DePriest, Oscar, 232, 322n20
Des Moines Register, 198
Detroit Independent, 3, 231
Detroit riots of 1943, 140, 244
Detroit World, 232–233, 237
Detroit World Echo, 242–243
Detweiler, Frederick, 4
DeVaughn, George G., 282–283n40
Dewey, Thomas, 105
Dickson, Joe, 90, 91
Dickson, M. D., 215–216
Dies, Martin, 325n53
Dirst, Viola, 220
Dixon, Dean, 117
Dixon, Frank, 98
Dobbs, John Wesley, 23
Dobbs, Pauline T., 109

Doby, Larry, 70, 288n43
Doreski, C. K., 12, 55
Dothan Eagle, 98
Double-V campaign, 223
Douglass, Frederick, 6, 196
Dowdell, John D., 84
Drewry, Prince, 240–241
Duke, Jesse Chisholm, 85
Dulles, John Foster, 173
Duncan, Mae Najiyyah, 321n60
Dunjee, Roscoe, 197
Durham Dispatch, 75, 77
Dyer, Leonidas C., 157

Eamans, Frank, 243
Earle, Willie, 67
Earnest McCarty Defense Fund Committee, 193
East Carolina News, 80
Eastern Arkansas World, 312n3
East Tennessee Hospital Association, 146
East Tennessee News, 43, 144–149, 306n48
East Texas Times, 194, 195
Eddins, C. Floyd, 118
Edison, Thomas, 145
Egerton, John, 3, 11
Eisenhower, Dwight D., 152, 158
Ellis, Walter A., 322n18
Empire Star, 321n5
Eubanks, Charles, 207–208
Evans, Aroy R., 228
Evans, Van Pell, 195
Evans, Walker, 82
Evans, William H., 215
Evansville Argus, 213

Fabree, D. J., 303n2
Fair Employment Practices Commission, 45, 95, 105, 227–228, 305n35, 319n38
Falls City News, 207
Farley, James T., 194
Farm Security Administration, 171
Federal Bureau of Investigation, 189, 216, 246; coverage of, in Black press, 67; investigating Black press, 26, 95, 108, 152–153, 296n74; investigating communism, 100, 109; investigating threats to Black press, 53
Federal Emergency Relief Administration, 177

Federal Public Housing Authority, 244
Fess, Simeon D., 290n68
Fidler, William P., 162
Fifteenth Amendment, 120, 143
First African Baptist Church, 33
Fisher, Peter, 323n22
Fisher, Petry, 233, 235, 324n41
Fisher-Lightfoot Publishing Company, 235
Fisk University, 93, 130, 137, 160–161
Flint-Brownsville News, 241, 242
Florida American, 49
Florida A&M University, 43, 47, 284n49
Florida Crusade, 49
Florida East Coast Dispatch, 40
Florida East Coast Railroad, 42, 48
Florida Guardian, 49
Florida Record Dispatch, 53
Florida Spur, 54
Florida State Negro Civic Council, 42
Florida State Newspaper League, 47
Florida Supreme Court, 283n40
Florida Tattler, 52
Folsom, James, 45, 102, 106–107, 109
Folsom Vote Probe Committee, 124
Fontillo-Nanton, H. E., 73
Ford, Henry, 325n52
Ford Motor Company, 167, 243
Forte, Ormond Adolphus, 218, 319n44
Fortune, 34
Fort Valley Normal and Industrial College, 22
Fort Worth Mind, 191
Fourteenth Amendment, 12, 24, 102, 143, 156, 316n4
Francis, Daniel R., 41, 46, 47, 282n28, 282n31
Francis, Willie, 189
Frazier, E. Franklin, 5
Ft. Myers World, 49

Gainer, Ruby Jackson, 109
Gaines, Lloyd, 15–16, 23–24
Galloway, C. C., 201
Galveston Guide, 195
Galveston Voice, 194–195
Gandhi, Mohandas, 247
Garvey, Marcus, 226
Gary American, 3, 318n23
Gayle, James, 178
Georgia Baptist College, 27–28
Georgia Normal College, 22, 33

Georgia State College, 32
Gibson, Alberta, 199, 201–202
Gibson, H. B., 95
Gilmore, Glenda, 11–12, 290n61
Glover, Beatrice, 77
Goebel Brewing, 236
Goldfield, David, 132
Gomillion, C. G., 126
Good Neighbor Interpreter, 314n29
Good-Will Printing Company, 309n8
Gordon, Asa, 28, 31–32, 249
Gordon, B. F., 215
Gordon, Eugene, 99
Gore, Edward T., 297n1
Grady, Henry, 85
Graham, Clarence Houston, 135
Grand Rapids Echo, 238
Granmer, E. H., 78
Grapevine of the Black South, The (Aiello), 19
Graves, Bibb, 86, 90
Graves, John Temple, 119, 128
Graves, T. M., 39
Gray, Rev. W., 201, 202
Great Depression: economics of, 18–21, 54, 57, 135, 179; effects on activism, 23, 161, 283n40; effects on Black business, 76, 195–196, 211; effects on Black population, 7–8, 37, 77; effects on newspapers, 38, 84, 164–166, 178, 198, 289n56, 292n6, 304n9
Great Migration: demographics of, 6; effects on Black population, 10–12, 34; effects on individuals, 53, 79, 220; effects on North, 178, 198, 219, 229, 233; effects on South, 7, 147, 171, 196; effects on West, 200, 201; SNS follows, 3, 9, 18–19, 224, 226, 246, 250
Great Protective Association, 187
Greene, Percy, 167–168
Greensboro Tribune, 79
Greenville Leader, 167, 308n4
Greenville World, 58, 286n6
Greer, John P., 137
Griffin, Marvin, 34, 279n38
Grillo, Evelio, 49
Groveland murders, 55
Gunn, Zack I., 124

Hahn, Steven, 2, 11
Hall, Robert, 25

Index

Hamilton, Mary, 142–143
Hamitic League of the World, 225
Hampton, Chester M., 307n66
Hampton, Wade, 61
Hampton Institute, 73, 161, 198
Hamtramck Echo, 238, 239, 240
Hamtramck Housing Commission, 239, 240, 245
Handy, W. C., 153
Hannon, Alberta, 284n49
Harden, P. L., 139
Harper, Lucius, 235
Harrington, Oliver, 112
Harris, Blanche, 216
Harris, Edgar G., 216, 319n38
Hart, Sylvanus H., 283n40
Hartford Advocate, 231
Harvard University, 83, 284n49
Haughton, L. M., 293n18
Hawkins, James, 88
Hawkins, Laura, 37
Hearst, William Randolph, 133
Heath, Lloyd E., 303n3
Heflin, J. Thomas, 89–90, 293n20
Hemmingway, Theodore, 56
Henderson, John, 304n16
Henderson v. United States, 15, 16
Hendley, Charles V., 114
Hensley, J. Earle, 95
Henson, Matthew, 117
Herald (Yazoo City), 176
Herndon, Angelo, 199, 231
Hill, Charles L., 68
Hines, Kathryn Olive, 29
Hitler, Adolf, 51, 79, 188, 197, 216, 195, 287n29
Hocutt, Thomas R., 74
Hodges, V. W., 22, 25
Hoey, Clyde R., 290n68
Hoffman, Harold G., 228, 230
Holbrook Benevolent Association, 309n6
Holder, Oscar E., 80
Holder, William D., 139
Holley, J. W., 22–23, 33
Home Owners Loan Corporation, 203
Hoover, Herbert, 212, 290n68, 311n45
Hoover, J. Edgar, 246, 296n74
Horne, Gerald, 49
Horne, Jasper C., 303n3
Horton, John Benjamin, 201

House Un-American Activities Committee, 152, 325n53
Houston, Charles Hamilton, 139, 208
Houston, Henry, 71
Houston Guide, 194
Houston Informer, 194, 213, 280n7, 281n11
Howard, Charles P., 199–200
Howard University, 142, 145, 161
Hubert, B. F., 32
Hubert, R. H., 278n22
Hunter Street Baptist Church, 141
Hyatt, C. L., 162

Ideal Review (Bridgeton, N.J.), 229
Illinois Central Railroad, 166
Illinois Times, 216
Imperial Mutual Benefit Association, 48
Independent Call, 162, 163
Indianapolis Recorder, 3, 16, 24, 212
Indianapolis World, 318n27
Ingram, Harvey, 198
Ingram, Rosa Lee, 26–27
International Association of Chiefs of Police, 245
International Labor Defense, 75, 86, 199, 226
Iowa Bystander, 198
Iowa Observer, 198, 199
Irvin, C. A., 46
Isaac, E. W. D., 303n2
I. Willis Cole Publishing Company, 316n2

Jackson, Alberta Kertz, 219
Jackson, A. T., 21
Jackson, Bernard E., 296n75
Jackson, E. G., 99, 102, 107, 293n18
Jackson, Emory O., 90–93, 95, 99–100, 108, 125, 126, 244, 247, 293n26
Jackson, James Edward, 152
Jackson, Perry B., 220
Jackson Advocate, 167–174
Jackson Banner, 17, 175, 310n34
Jackson College, 64
Jackson Daily News, 176
Jackson Echo, 238
Jackson State Times, 176
Jackson Times, 139
Jacksonville Mirror, 216
Jacksonville Progressive News, 48, 51
Jacksonville Tribune, 280n7, 282n40
Jacksonville World, 36–38, 279n1

Jackson World, 164, 310n39
Jackson World Publishing Company, 164
Jefferson County Board of Registrars, 108, 118, 124
Jeffries, Bertrand, 213
Jenkins, Daniel, 56, 285n1
Jennings, C. W., 39
Jervay, Paul Reginald, 73, 289n57
Jervay, Robert Smith, 72–73
Jervay, Thomas Clarence, 73
Jervay, William, 72
Johnson, A. N., 292n6
Johnson, Arthur, 32
Johnson, George, M., 13
Johnson, Georgia M., 184–185, 312n58
Johnson, Henry, 77
Johnson, Jack, 234
Johnson, James Weldon, 235
Johnson, Mordecai W., 142
Johnson, Paul, 168
Johnson, Robert, 39
Johnson, Wes, 90
Johnson, Willie, 240
Johnston, Olin, 61
Jones, C. H., 187–188
Jones, S. L., 287n29
Jones, Thomas E., 161
Jordan, Louis, 224
Julius Rosenwald Fund, 49

Kalamazoo Guide, 324n49
Kansas City Call, 213
Kansas City Monarchs, 68
Kansas City Southern Railway, 190
Keelin, James, 26
Kefauver, Estes, 142, 159
Keller, Eloise, 85
Kellogg, Peter, 326n10
Kennedy, John F., 153
Kentucky Observer and Reporter, 317n6
Kentucky State College, 208
Kessler, Lauren, 9
Key, James L., 134
Kilby Prison, 85–89, 101
King, J. Franklin, 228
King, Martin Luther, Jr., 51, 99, 127, 247, 294n31, 312n58
King, Martin Luther, Sr., 281n14
King, William E., 194
Kinship networks, 2, 9, 11, 21, 247

Klibanoff, Hank, 125, 151
Knight, Thomas, 87
Knights of Pythias, 176
Knoxville College, 139, 305n31
Knoxville Journal, 146
Knoxville Progress Post, 139
Knoxville Recorder, 135
Korean War, 105
Kreiling, Albert Lee, 250
Ku Klux Klan: coverage of, 43–44, 45, 52, 58, 71, 74, 148, 214, 239–240, 242; integration and, 250–251; other white supremacist organizations and, 235, 294n33; terrorism of, 28, 40–41, 46, 93, 139, 163, 169, 243

Labat, George, 178
LaFourche, James B., 46, 180–181, 311n47
Landon, Alf, 136, 234
Langston University, 12, 104
Lansing Echo, 246
Law, H. L., 196
Lee, Davis, 53, 59, 123
Lee, Euel, 226
Lee, Henry, 107
Leggett, Gilbert, 49
Leibowitz, Samuel L., 89
LeMoyne Junior College, 205
Let Us Now Praise Famous Men (Agee and Evans), 82–83
Lewis, J. J., 21, 277n2
Lewis, Morris, 232
Lewis, Rufus, 99
Lexington Herald, 317n15
Lexington Record, 209
Life magazine, 173
Lightfoot, Roy, 235–236
Lighthouse and Informer, 59–70, 122, 148
Lincoln University, 13, 24
Lindbergh, Charles A., 38, 195, 280n7
Logan, Rayford, 138
Long, Augustine V., 50
Long, Huey P., 32, 181, 309n10
Los Angeles Sentinel, 16
Lost Cause, 174
Louis, Joe, 64–65, 69, 196, 233–234, 288n29, 311n54
Louisiana State University, 32, 237
Louisiana Weekly, 176–180, 212
Louisville Defender, 237

362 Index

Louisville Herald Tribune, 207
Louisville Independent News, 206, 316n3
Louisville Leader, 205–206, 212, 317n9
Louisville News, 207, 213
Lucas, Clarence, 214
Lucy, Autherine, 125

MacArthur, Douglas, 209
Mackay, Cliff, 25, 199, 296n74
Macon Broadcast, 27
Macon Telegraph and Evening News, 28
Macon Water Commission, 27
Magic Printing Company, 280n8
Mahammitt, T. P., 201
Manning, A. E., 318n27
March on Washington for Jobs and Freedom, 140, 170, 200
Marion County Citizen, 54
Maroon Tiger, 91
Marshall, Thurgood, 67, 102, 110, 115–116, 123, 124, 139, 143, 208, 245
Marshall Tribune, 194
Martin, Louis, 235
Martinez, Daniel F., 77–78, 290n68, 291n70
Maryland Court of Appeals, 23
Mason, Sanders, 39–40, 281n11
Mays, Benjamin, 16
Mays, Edward, 155
McCarty, Earnest, 193
McComb County Echo, 240
McCord, Jim Nance, 149
McCoy, Cullen E., 53–54
McCray, John Henry, 59–71, 122
McDade, George, 163
McDaniel, Vernon, 50
McGee, Willie, 175
McGill, Samuel, 51
McGuire, Danielle, 99–100
McHenry, Louis, 210
McKaine, Osceola, 60
McKeever, Albert, 52–53
McKibben, Sam, 131
McKinley, William, 295n50
McLaurin, George, 15
McLaurin v. Oklahoma State Regents, 15, 16, 17
McLendon, J. A., 188–189
Mechanics and Farmers Bank, 74
Meharry Medical College, 14–15, 54, 104, 130, 160

Melton, Raymond L., 191, 193, 313n21
Memphis World, 121, 132–135, 140, 148–153, 159, 226, 290n68, 298n85, 302n1, 303n3, 310n39
Meridian Progress, 167, 309n10
Metcalf, C. M., 239–240
Metcalfe, Ralph, 79
Metropolitan Detroit Youth Council, 245
Metropolitan Life Insurance Company, 230
Miami Herald, 43, 47
Miami Negro Business Men's Association, 46
Miami Times, 38, 40, 282n28
Michaeli, Ethan, 4
Michigan Chronicle, 13, 16, 235–237, 242, 246
Michigan Newspaper Syndicate, 324n36
Michigan State Echo, 237, 324n34
Michigan Tribune, 324n49
Michigan World, 233–235
Miller, B. M., 88
Miller, Kelly, 212–213
Miller, Loren, 226
Miller, P. K., 187
Mims, Edwin, 249
Mink Slide Riot, 112, 140, 149
Mississippi Negro Defense Council, 168
Mississippi World, 165
Missouri ex rel. Gaines, 12, 23–24, 59, 64, 92, 95, 160, 208
Missouri Medical School, 13
Missouri Supreme Court, 24
Mitchell, Arthur W., 97
Mitchell, J. Carl, 211–212, 318n21
Mitchell, William H., 183
Mixon, W. H., 291n1
Mizell, Von D., 54
Mobile Forum, 83
Mobile Press, 83, 146
Mobile Press Forum, 83
Mobile Press Forum Sum, 84
Mobile Register, 146
Mobile Sun, 83
Mobile Weekly Press, 292n6
Montgomery, Olin, 86, 292n12
Montgomery, Robert H., 141
Montgomery Advertiser, 96, 98
Montgomery Bus Boycott, 100, 247, 250, 294n47
Montgomery Civic League, 292n10
Montgomery Herald, 85
Montgomery Improvement Association, 247

Montgomery Progressive Democratic Association, 108
Montgomery State Teachers College, 104
Montgomery World, 84–85, 87–89
Monthly Summary, 94
Monuments Baptist Church, 142
Moody, Anne, 165
Moore, A. M., 290n64
Moore, Harry T., 55
Moran, C. Nelson, 198
Morehouse College, 16, 27, 54, 91, 211
Morgan, Garrett A., 319n44
Morris, Clyde, 198
Morris, James B., 198–199, 315n35
Morris College, 63
Mozique, Douglas W., 165
Mule's Ear, 59
Mullin, Willard, 318n27
Mundt-Nixon communist registration bill, 153
Murphy, Carl, 53, 123, 128
Murray, Donald, 23
Muscogee Cimiter, 227
Muscogee Star, 227
Muskogee Lantern, 197, 314n33
Mutual Benefit, Health and Accident Association, 278n15
Myers, Pollie Anne, 125

Napper, Alver W., 322n15
Nashville Clarion, 303n2
Nashville Defender, 303n2
Nashville Globe, 130
Nashville Independent, 130
Nashville Sun, 159, 163, 308n91
Nashville World, 130–131, 213
National Association for the Advancement of Colored People (NAACP), 162, 232; in Alabama, 118–119, 124–125; antilynching effort, 101, 157, 183; criticized by white southerners, 248; in Detroit, 234–235, 242–245; Emory Jackson and, 91, 93, 99, 108–116, 295n49, 297n80, 299n96, 301n123; in Florida, 283n40; in Georgia, 16, 22; integration and, 123, 175–176, 251; in Iowa, 198; in Kentucky, 210; Legal Defense Fund, 23–24, 102, 103, 126, 128; in Louisiana, 184–185, 189; in North Carolina, 77; in Ohio, 217; press criticism, 145; press support, 55, 66, 67, 118, 145–146, 150, 153, 178, 193; protest/advocacy, 139, 142, 166, 179; Scottsboro and, 86, 88–89; teacher salaries and, 50; in Texas, 313n21; voting rights and, 14, 41; in West Virginia, 211–212; Youth Council, 237
National Baptist Convention, 200
National Conference of Colored Railroad Firemen, 111
National Fire Insurance, 231
National Labor Relations Act, 154
National Mediation Board, 42
National Negro Business Progressive Association, 228
National Negro Press Association, 123, 306n47
National Negro Publishers Association, 13, 25, 63, 67, 122, 123, 188, 209, 221, 316n1; Advertising Society, 122; Washington bureau, 182
National Recovery Administration, 82
National Student League, 161
National Sunday School and Baptist Training Union Congress, 222–223
National Urban League, 82, 238–239
Negro Bar Association, 198
Negro Citizens Service League, 41
Negro History Week, 85, 135
Negro National League, 70
Negro Steering Committee for Better Housing, 239–240
Negro Teachers League, 145
Negro Voters League, 136, 210
Negro Waiters Union, 209
Negro Watchman, 85
Negro Welfare Federation, 40
Negro Womanhood Defense Committee, 175
Newark Evening News, 178
Newark Herald, 3, 228, 321n8
New Bern World, 77–78
New Deal, 27, 139, 203, 214, 290n68
New Journalism, 232
Newman, Cecil E., 203
New Orleans Broadcast, 46, 180
New Orleans Herald, 176
News World (Detroit), 235–237
New York Age, 212, 307n66
New York Amsterdam News, 14, 24, 213, 225
New York Journal, 133
New York University, 306n47
New York World, 133
Nixon, Drusilla Tandy, 306n47

Nixon, E. D., 99, 100, 108, 247
Nixon, Richard, 153
Norfolk Journal and Guide, 4, 73, 123, 213, 249
Norris, Clarence, 86, 89, 101, 292n12
North Carolina A&T, 77
North Carolina College for Negroes, 74
North Carolina Commission on Interracial Cooperation, 290n68
North Carolina Mutual Life Insurance, 62, 63, 74, 75–76, 202, 211, 290n64
Northwestern University, 59
Nunn, William G., 126, 128

Oakes, J. E., 132, 302n1
O'Daniel, W. Lee, 228
Ohio Recorder, 217
Ohio State Highway Patrol, 221–222
Ohio State University, 79
Ohio Torch, 217
Oklahoma Black Dispatch, 197–198
Oklahoma Defender, 197
Oklahoma Supreme Court, 13
Olympic Games, 79, 179, 311n54
Omaha Chronicle, 201
Omaha Enterprise, 201
Omaha Guide, 201
Omaha Monitor, 201
Operation Suffrage, 112
Orlando Sun, 48–49
Orleans Parish School Board, 179
Orphans Aid Society, 285n1
Ottley, Roi, 249
Ovington, Mary White, 232
Owens, Jesse, 79, 311n54
Owensboro Eagle, 210

Page, Oscar, 16
Paige, Satchel, 70
Painter, Nell Irvin, 165, 275n9
Palm Beach Record, 281n16
Palm Beach Tribune, 48, 283n40
Palmetto Leader, 60
Palmetto State Teachers' Association, 63, 66
Panama City World, 49
Paradise Valley Consumers Association, 235–236
Paradise Valley News, 235
Parker, Elijah, 171–172
Parker, George Wells, 225

Parks, Gordon, 203
Parks, Raymond, 99
Parks, Rosa, 99, 100, 247, 298n85
Patrick, Luther, 109
Patterson, E. L., 281n14
Patterson, Frederick Douglass, 136, 142, 303n3
Patterson, Heywood, 86, 89, 91, 292n12
Patterson, John R., 130–132, 136, 303n3
Patterson, Pat, 136
Patterson, Thomas, 156
Pee Dee Advocate, 285n3
Pee Dee Weekly, 57, 285n3
Pensacola Brotherhood, 284n49
Pensacola Courier, 49–50, 283n45
Pensacola Enterprise, 291n1
People's Informer, 59
People's Insurance Company, 279n6, 280n6
Peoria Informer, 215–216
Pepsi, 117
Perkins, Gertrude, 294n47
Perry, J. E., 203
Peterson, Willie, 87–88
Philadelphia Tribune, 13, 19, 213
Philip-Morris, 117
Phoenix Index, 201–202, 315n45
Phoenix Tribune, 201
Phyllis Wheatley House, 204
Pickens, William, 183
Pittsburgh Courier, 212, 230; activism, 15, 148; civil rights coverage, 24, 52, 112; cooperation with SNS publishers, 282n40; Great Migration and, 147; in South, 34, 122, 135; syndicate, 1, 5
Plessy v. Ferguson, 16, 23, 102, 144
Pontiac Echo, 238
Porter, Dorothy M. L., 306n47
Porter, G. L., 213, 318n28
Porter, James H., 27
Porter, Webster L., 144–145, 306n47
Portier, O. T., 48
Poston, Ted, 17–18
Powell, A. C., 222
Powell, Adam Clayton, 52, 172
Powell, Ozie, 89, 292n12
Prairie View A&M University, 202, 303n3
Price, Victoria, 85, 293n14
Pridgett, Roddie, 171
Progressive Democratic Party, 60, 64
Progress News Service, 228, 321n8

Psychiana Corporation, 188
Public Guide, 135–136, 139
Pulitzer, Joseph, 133
Purdy, James H., 152

Queen, Robert, 228
Quizz Club, 27

Race Relations Information Center, 326n9
Randolph, A. Philip, 105, 140, 170, 200, 213n21, 225, 242, 305n35
Rankin, John, 169
Reconstruction, 2, 11, 61, 64, 72, 83, 85, 174, 248
Redmond, Pauline, 138
Red Summer, 226, 227
Reeves, Henry E. Sigismund, 38, 280n8, 282n28
Republican National Convention, 318n21
Republican Sentinel, 85
Reynolds, Henry G., 241–242
Reynolds, Robert Rice, 80
Rickey, Branch, 68–69
Rives, John, 217
Roberson, William, 292n12
Roberts, Gene, 125, 151
Roberts, Ric, 39, 318n27
Robertson, J. B. A., 227
Robinson, Jackie, 68–70, 288n43
Robinson, Walter C., 136–137, 138, 141, 154, 158–159, 304n20
Robinson, William H., 210
Robinson, William J., 322n18
Roddy, Stephen, 86
Roger Williams College, 77
Rolla School of Mines, 13
Roman, Al, 221
Roosevelt, Eleanor, 111, 132, 141, 200
Roosevelt, Franklin D., 132, 154; appeals to, 142, 185; Black Cabinet of, 30, 76; criticism by Black leaders, 37, 215–216, 244; election of, 4, 136, 180; NAACP and, 245; negotiations of, 194, 202, 305n35; quoted in Syndicate papers, 41; Scottsboro and, 91; support in non-Syndicate papers, 213; support in Syndicate papers, 145, 188, 212, 234–235, 290n68; Truman and, 105, 106; white criticism of, 27
Roosevelt, Theodore, 37, 295n50
Rosenthal, Joel, 161

Rowland, Thomas, 199
Roxborough, John, 233
Ruff, Charles, 314n35
Ruff, Thadius, 314n35

Salvation Army, 219
Samms, Ted, 48
Samuel Huston College, 324
Samuels, Viola, 77
San Angelo Enterprise, 195
Sancton, Thomas, 326n8
Sanford, S. V., 32
Saunders, Robert H., 49
Savannah Journal, 31
Schmeling, Max, 234
Schultz, John W., 138–139
Schuyler, George, 148
Scott, Cornelius, 5, 10, 21, 25, 46, 62, 63, 94, 120, 123, 125, 152, 153, 303n3, 322n15
Scott, L. A., 116, 120, 303n3
Scott, William Alexander, 1, 10, 36, 39, 131, 164, 177, 186, 208, 212, 237
Scott Newspaper Syndicate, 3, 5–11, 14, 16, 19, 249, 250, 318n27; in Alabama, 84–85, 87–88, 94, 100, 103, 110, 247; in Arizona, 202; in Florida, 36, 37, 39–40, 47–49; founding and evolution, 1, 186, 247–248, 250, 251; in Georgia, 20, 24, 33, 34; gravure, 318n19; in Indiana, 212–213, 215; in Kentucky, 205–210; in Louisiana, 177, 180, 182, 185; in Michigan, 232–238, 242, 246, 324n41; in Minnesota, 204; in Mississippi, 167; in New Jersey, 228–229; in New York, 226–228; in North Carolina, 71, 75, 80; in Ohio, 219–220, 223–224; in Oklahoma, 198, 314n33; in South Carolina, 58; in Tennessee, 130–131, 138–139, 142, 144, 154, 155, 159, 163; in Texas, 191, 194, 195, 196; in West Virginia, 211, 318n20
Scottsboro Boys, 26, 84–91, 101, 139, 161, 193, 318n19
Scottsboro Defense Committee, 89
Screws, M. Claude, 278n15
Screws, William Preston, 97
Searles, A. C., 25–26, 209, 278n15
Secrest, Andrew, 65
Selassie, Haile, 311n54
Selby, E. A., 131
Selma Post, 82, 291n1

366 Index

Sengstacke, Robert, 122, 151, 235, 236, 237, 307n66
Shankland, Frank S., 199
Shannon, Samuel, 141
Shaw University, 137
Shelley v. Kramer, 102, 103, 155
Sheppard, J. E., 283
Sheppard, William, 84
Shields, A. G., 188, 307n66, 313n14
Shofner, Jerrell H., 284n49
Shores, Arthur, 95, 110
Shorter College, 187
Shreveport Afro-American, 177
Shreveport World, 287n29
Simons, William, 69
Singer, Benjamin, 249
Singleton, Minnie D., 28
Sipuel, Ada Lois, 12–15, 104
Sipuel v. Board of Regents of the University of Oklahoma, 13–15
Smith, Eugene Jack, 286n6
Smith, Guy, 146
Smith, Harry C., 319n44
Smith, Johnnie B., 101
Smith, Lonnie, 143
Smith, Thomas S., 197
Smitherman, Andrew J., 227–228
Smith v. Allwright, 67, 102, 110, 143–144, 155
Sojourner Truth Citizens Committee, 243
Solomon, Samuel B., 41
South Bend Citizen, 215
South Bend Forum, 215
South Carolina College for Negroes, 161
South Carolina State A&M College, 32
Southern Advocate, 165
Southern Broadcast, 183
Southern Christian Leadership Conference, 294n31
Southern Conference for Human Welfare, 108, 109, 141, 153, 296n72; Advisory Council of the Committee for Alabama, 109; Southern Conference Educational Fund, 153
Southern Education Reporting Service, 250
Southern Enterprise, 302n1
Southern Independent, 94
Southern Liberal Organization, 187
Southern Liberator, 187

Southern Negro Youth Congress, 100, 108–109, 115, 138, 152
Southern Newspaper Syndicate, 1, 3, 36, 76, 130, 177
Southern Newspaper Union, 71
Southern Patriot, 153
Southern Regional Council, 63, 68, 160, 288n41
Southern School News, 250–251
Southern Tenant Farmers Union, 187
Southern University, 176, 182
Southern World, 303n3
Southwestern Torch, 196
Southwest Georgian, 17, 22, 25, 26, 34, 278n15
Spann, J. T., 284n49
Sparks, Chauncey, 98–99
Spaulding, Charles Clinton, 74, 75, 76, 290n64
Spelman College, 222
Spencer, William H., 28, 278n22
Spencer, William H., Jr., 28
Spokesman (Minneapolis), 203, 266
Standard Advertiser, 74
States' Rights Democratic Party, 106
State Teachers College for Negroes, 22
State Training and Agricultural School for Negro Boys, 147
Stevens, William, 322n16
Stewart, Lawrence, 238
Stimson, Henry, 185
St. Louis Argus, 3, 13, 15, 16, 212
St. Louis Call, 281n11
St. Paul Recorder, 203
St. Petersburg World, 49
Stratford, John Ed, 26
Stroh's Brewing Company, 235–236
Strother, T. Ella, 4
Struggle (Evansville, Ind.), 213
Sullinger, Howard, 118
Sunday School Union, 131
Sunlight, 187
Sweatt, Herman Marion, 15–16, 112
Sweatt v. Painter, 16, 17, 112, 123
Swift Memorial College, 145
Swingler, Lewis Ossie, 132, 140, 151, 304n9, 307n66

Taft-Hartley Act, 101–102, 154–155
Taggart, E. W., 110

Take Your Choice (Bilbo), 174
Talladega College, 59
Talmadge, Eugene, 22, 32, 33, 98, 155, 208
Talmadge, Herman, 16, 34
Tammany Hall, 227, 228
Tampa Journal, 49
Tampa World, 39, 281n11
Taylor, Delphine W., 177
Taylor, O. C. W., 176, 310n37
Taylor, Percy, 29–30, 278n23
Taylor, Porcher, 52
Taylor, Recy, 99–101
Tennessee A&I State College, 160, 303n3
Tennessee State University, 85, 130, 149, 150
Tennessee Valley Authority, 135, 137, 139, 141, 214
Texas Civil Court of Appeals, 112
Texas Commission on Interracial Cooperation, 193
Texas Examiner, 195
Texas Freeman, 194
Thomas, Ike, 32
Thomas, Jesse O., 280n7
Thomas, Lawson E., 42
Thompson, Howard, 166
Thompson, John B., 142
Thompson, John Lay, 314–315n35
Thompson, Julius Eric, 308n3
Thompson, Melvin, 34
Thornbrough, Emma Lou, 251
Thurmond, J. Strom, 67, 106
Till, Emmett, 151, 157
Tillman, Ben, 37
Tilly, M. E., 160
Time magazine, 123
Tobias, Channing H., 43
Tolan, Eddie, 79
Tolbert, Willie, 60
Toledo Press, 219
Toledo Voice, 221
Tolson, Melvin, 54
Trenton Record, 228
Trenton World, 228
Tri-City Observer, 199
Tri-State Defender, 151
Tri-State News, 211, 212
Tropical Dispatch, 15, 39–41, 44, 46, 282n31, 311n47
Troutman, Leonard, 232

Truman, Harry S.: Black correspondence with, 68, 70; military desegregation, 105; NAACP and, 101; 1948 election, 106, 116, 150, 157; SNS coverage of, 46, 122, 154, 158, 190
Truth, Sojourner, 196, 243, 244
Tubbs, V. Trenton, 27–28, 278n18
Tucker, Charles Eubank, 206–207
Tulsa race massacre, 227
Turner, Mary, 215
Tuskegee Institute, 136, 137, 142; advertising, 202; conservatism, 21, 30, 31, 167; correspondence with SNS, 126, 277n2; employment, 303n3
Twin City Herald, 203, 204
Twin City Tribune, 183
Twine, W. H., 227
Tyler Tribune, 195

Unemployment Compensation Commission, 228
United Auto Workers, 243
United Life Insurance Company, 310n37
United Nations, 140
United Registration Committee, 108
United Sons of Dixie, 94, 294n33
United States Department of Commerce, 9
United States Department of Justice, 17, 94, 118, 119
United States Department of War, 185, 200, 209
United States Railway Mail Service, 176
United States Supreme Court: Angelo Herndon case, 199; Black jury service, 78, 139; *Brown v. Board of Education*, 108, 126–128, 160; *Chambers v. Florida*, 51; due process claims, 172; executions, 55, 189; *McLaurin v. Oklahoma*, 15, 17; *Missouri ex rel. Gaines*, 12, 23–24, 95, 96; race murders, 278n15; railroad segregation, 97; residential segregation, 316n4; Scottsboro, 86, 89; *Shelley v. Kraemer*, 102, 155; *Sipuel v. Oklahoma*, 12–13, 15, 104; *Smith v. Allwright*, 143–144; *Sweatt v. Painter*, 17; teacher salaries, 97; white primaries, 37, 41, 63, 172–174
United States v. Classic, 41
United Transport Service Employees of America, 42

Index

Universal Negro Improvement Association, 226, 233
Universal Relief Insurance Company, 195
University of Alabama, 96, 118, 125
University of California, Los Angeles, 68
University of Cincinnati, 222
University of Georgia, 22, 32, 208
University of Kentucky, 207–208
University of Louisville, 207
University of Maryland, 23
University of Mississippi, 149
University of Missouri, 24
University of North Carolina, 74, 290n61
University of Oklahoma, 12, 15, 104, 142
University of Tennessee, 160, 163
University of Texas, 15–16, 141

Vandenberg, Arthur, 242
Vardaman, James, 37
Vaughn, C. E., 292n8
Vaughn, William S., 219, 320n46
Vest, Rollo S., 324n41
Vesta Gas Range and Manufacturing Company, 304n20
Veterans Administration, 173
Vicksburg Tribune, 167
Vinson, Fred, 102
Virginia State University, 73, 161
Voting Rights Act, 102

W. A. Biggins Commercial College, 131
Waco Post-Dispatch, 195
Wagner, Robert F., 304n19
Walden, Austin, 103
Walker, William O., 221
Wallace, Henry, 105
Ward, Govan, 78
Ward, Morris M., 229
Warley, Bill, 206–207, 316n4
Warlick, William, 72
Washington, Booker T., 56, 84, 100, 295n50
Washington, F. E., 284n49
Washington, Leona, 314n29
Washington Tribune, 54
Waterloo Observer, 199
Watson, Avery D., 219
Wayne State University, 237
Weaver, Bill, 16
Weaver, Robert, 30

Weekly Echo, 165
Weems, Charlie, 89, 292n12
Weiner, Leo, 83
Welky, David, 79
Wells, Ida B., 157
Wesley, Carter, 123, 194
Western Dispatch, 202
Western Star (Buffalo), 227
West Tennessee Teachers Association, 133
West Virginia Weekly, 210, 266, 318n19
What's News (Danville, Ill.), 217
White, Albert, 177, 195
White, Hazel L., 324n41
White, Leroy G., 11, 232, 237, 239, 243, 245, 246, 324n49
White, Viola, 294n47
White, Walter, 14, 17, 30, 111, 115, 128, 146, 150, 243, 245
White Citizens Councils, 176
White Newspaper Syndicate, 238, 240–242, 245–246, 267
White Supremacy League, 94, 294n33
Whitley, Robert, 37
Whittaker, M. F., 32
Wilburn, William Howard, 195
Wilkerson, Doxey, 249
Wilkins, Roy, 118, 128
Williams, Augusta, 87
Williams, Charles, 314n25
Williams, Dent, 88
Williams, Eugene, 292n12
Williams, H. R., 292n8
Williams, John Albert, 201
Williams, L. D., 159
Williams, Marvin E., 196
Williams, Nat D., 140
Williams, Nell, 87, 88
Williams v. Mississippi, 102
Willkie, Wendell, 213–214, 318n28
Wilmington Journal, 73, 289n58
Wilmington Star, 73
Wilson, Edwin A., 139, 305n31
Wilson, Sunnie, 236
Wise, C. R., 191, 313n21
Wolfe, Tom, 232
Women's Army Auxiliary Corps, 200
Wood, Curtis, 305n31
Wood, Jennie, 87
Woodson, Carter G., 135

Woodson, George, 198
Works Progress Administration, 17, 322n15
World Telegram (Indianapolis), 213–214
World War I: Black press after, 2, 225, 319n44; demographic change and, 178, 217; race advocacy after 223, 251, 294n33; veterans, 60, 88, 167, 198, 235
World War II: Black press during, 6, 9, 54, 188; demographic change and, 200, 223; race advocacy during, 30, 34, 61, 91, 101, 140; racism during, 148; SNS during, 8, 28, 48, 65, 146, 154, 289n52; veterans, 104, 234; victory, 105
Worley, William W., 317n6
Wright, Andy, 89, 292n12

Wright, Fielding, 175
Wright, Netrel, 131
Wright, Roy, 292n12
Wynne, Lewis, 37

Xavier University, 202

Young, Francis, 162
Young, Roy L., 166
Young, Thomas, 123
Young Men's Progressive Business Club, 305n37
Youngstown Challenger, 219

Zillman, E. F., 316n52

www.ingramcontent.com/pod-product-compliance
Lightning Source LLC
Chambersburg PA
CBHW011713290426
44113CB00019B/2656